Competition for Land
in the American South

The Conservation Foundation is a nonprofit research and communications organization dedicated to encouraging human conduct to sustain and enrich life on earth. Since its founding in 1948, it has attempted to provide intellectual leadership in the cause of wise management of the earth's resources. The Conservation Foundation is affiliated with World Wildlife Fund.

Competition for Land in the American South

Agriculture, Human Settlement, and the Environment

Robert G. Healy

The Conservation Foundation
Washington, D.C.

Competition for Land in the American South:
Agriculture, Human Settlement, and the Environment

Cover design by Sally A. Janin
Typography by Rings-Leighton, Ltd., Washington, D.C.
Printed by Victor Graphics, Inc., Baltimore, Maryland

The Conservation Foundation
1255 23rd Street, N.W.
Washington, D.C. 20037

Library of Congress Cataloging in Publication Data
Healy, Robert G.
   Competition for land in the American South.
   Includes index.

   1. Land use, Rural—Southern States. 2. Agriculture—Economic Aspects—Southern States. 3. Forests and forestry—Economic aspects—Southern States. 4. Real estate development—Southern States. 5. Soil conservation—Southern States. 6. Conservation of natural resources—Southern States. I. Title.

HD266.A13H43 1985   333.76'13'0975   85-25459
ISBN 8-89164-094-0

Contents

Foreword

— Wm. K Reilly

Today there appears to be very little public concern about the ability of the United States to continue to produce vast quantities of grain, meat, wood fiber, and other products at the relatively low prices that domestic and foreign consumers have historically enjoyed. Indeed, policy makers and the press are preoccupied with quite the opposite problem—how to rein in and "downsize" an agricultural system that is so productive that it threatens farmers with bankruptcy. Wood supplies, too, seem plentiful, and cattle prices are so low as to be unprofitable for many producers.

Already forgotten, it seems, are the anxieties of the 1970s, when high export demand for grain and booming lumber and paper consumption caused rapid price increases and led many observers to conclude that a permanent state of increased scarcity was in the offing. This sort of shift, from deep pessimism about resource adequacy to buoyant optimism (and consequent neglect of the subject) has occurred several times during the last century. In the past, worries about resources tended to surface when a sudden upsurge in demand for food or wood, often associated with a wartime economy, drove prices upward. Later, when demand slackened somewhat, the concern evaporated.

The cyclical public concern about resource adequacy, motivated by short-term considerations, contrasts with what I believe to be the real public need—for periodic long-term assessment of the condition of resources and of trends in their development and use. American society has become industrialized and urbanized over time, but much of its prosperity still rests on the productive power of its rural land. This book tries to add to our understanding of long-term land adequacy at the national level by taking a comprehensive look at land-use conditions and trends in a single section of the country, the South.

As its author, land economist Robert G. Healy, points out, there are several reasons why the land-use situation in the South should be of national interest. First, the South is important in its own right

as a commodity producer. It is now the nation's largest producer
of forest products, a major source of soybeans, poultry, and
aquaculture production, an increasing factor in the cattle industry,
and home to a quarter of the national population. Second, the South
has a disproportionate share of the national supply of land on which
crop agriculture, forestry, and grazing might expand. The South
may thus be even more important to the agricultural future of the
United States than it is at present.

Third, the South is notable for the flexibility of its land base.
Unlike the Midwest or the Pacific Northwest, where large areas
of land are uniquely suited to a particular use (growing grains and
trees respectively), the South has tens of millions of acres that can,
if demand warrants, be devoted to crops, or to grazing, or to
forestry. It is also the site of sprawling industrial and residential
settlement, as well as of growing pressure to preserve environmental and recreational values. The South therefore offers a sort
of laboratory for examining the competition among alternative uses
of land. It is a competition that will be ever more relevant to the
nation as a whole as total demand for all the products of land expands in the future.

Healy's book is notable for taking a long-term and comprehensive view of the alternative competing uses of southern land. In
this, it quite closely reflects what I believe is one of The Conservation Foundation's greatest institutional strengths. We take considerable pride in having a staff that spans many disciplines, that
seeks to understand society's economic and social goals as well
as its environmental ones, and that tries to identify important issues
rather than merely fashionable ones.

The Foundation's first annual report, for the year 1949, described
its founders' plans for a research program for the new organization, "It was planned," the report asserted, "that the Foundation's
research program should begin with 'casing studies' to determine
what is now known and what more needs to be found out about
the distribution, renewal and consumption of various resources
in different places, about their relationship to the environment and
to each other and about appropriate techniques for their conservation, growth and use." Healy's book is in essence such a 'casing
study' of land use in the South.

One of the strengths of this study, I believe, is that the author
makes a very careful assessment of the present land-use situation

in the South before trying to peer into the future. The book offers a view of the present southern landscape and of how it developed that highlights features very different from those generally focused on in discussions of the South. It discusses the South's newly modernized agriculture and its changing crop mix, the problems and potentials of its timber growers, the fascinating evolution of its beef-cattle industry, and the changes in its settlement patterns and its natural ecosystems.

After recounting the truly revolutionary land-use changes of years past, Healy sees the likelihood of still further ones in the future. Some of these stem from possible future demands: for expanded exports of soybeans and wood products, for low-fat, grass-fed beef, for additional housing and industrial sites. In many cases, the South will be disproportionately affected by marginal increases in national or international demands because other regions of the country have relatively less capacity to expand production. In crop production, for example, he likens the South to the "ready reserve" in a nation's armed services—somewhat neglected in ordinary times, but very necessary in extreme circumstances.

Other changes in the South are likely to come from changing technology. In crop production, there are exciting possibilities in irrigation, in multiple cropping, and in the introduction of new crops, including biomass-for-energy crops. In forestry, there may be new ways to make use of the region's abundant hardwood resource. In animal production, there may be new grazing systems and new types of forages. All of these developments have the potential for either positive or negative impacts on the environment and on other of the region's "unpriced values."

After taking a careful look at various long-term projections for the region—and pointing out some of their limitations—Healy concludes that the South is unlikely to face a land shortage, in the sense of being unable to raise production of any given commodity in the face of increased demand. But it will, because of the high degree of adaptability of its land base, face continuing land competition, in the sense of several uses competing for the same land. Even without significant growth in total land requirements for crop production, forestry, grazing, or human settlement, there are likely to be continuing shifts of land from one use to another. And many of these shifts, Healy argues, will have significant impacts on the natural environment and the South's overall quality of life.

The key to resource planning in the South, Healy maintains, is to realize that uncertainty is inevitable and to take an approach to land use sufficiently conservative so that important long-term opportunities are not unnecessarily foreclosed. Because of the length of the necessary planning horizon and the multiplicity of forces affecting supply and demand, some reasonable assumptions lead to projections of massive expansions in land use; other reasonable assumptions to projections of very small changes. Healy therefore suggests a "foresight and insurance" strategy that would recognize the existence of continuing competition for land and that would focus policy interventions on carefully exploiting the South's special resource endowment in a manner that can be sustained indefinitely and with minimum impact on unpriced values.

The book's final chapter contains many specific ideas about how a reasonable level of insurance for the future might be obtained at relatively modest cost. It contains suggestions for improving farm and forest productivity, for conserving productive resources, and for protecting the natural and human environment. Nearly all the policy suggestions, Healy observes, have precedent someplace within the South. The abundance of solid, implementable ideas shows that some southerners have already taken important steps down the path that is traced in great detail in this book.

William K. Reilly
President
The Conservation Foundation

Preface

This book is an analysis of the contemporary land-use situation and of trends in the American South, the section of the nation stretching along the Atlantic and Gulf coasts from Virginia into East Texas and extending northward to Kentucky and Arkansas. But it is also meant to be a contribution to the national literature on the long-run adequacy of the productive land base.

In undertaking this study, I have tried to do two things that have tended to be slighted in earlier land-use literature. First, I have attempted to analyze simultaneously all of the alternative uses of rural land as they exist now and as they might develop in the future. In general, people who look at land supply tend to do so from the standpoint of an academic discipline associated with only one of the major uses of rural land. Agricultural economists worry about the supply of cropland; foresters worry about the forest land base. People who work in animal husbandry study the supply of land suitable for grazing, and regional planners consider the implications of suburban expansion and rural settlement. Environmentalists and persons concerned with natural systems and with wildlife habitats delve deeply into the effects of land-use change but rarely analyze economic and social causes. This disciplinary bias is not only true of university research but also affects government agencies, whose interests are also fragmented by subject area.

The single-use focus has led all but a handful of researchers to ignore the growing competition among several alternative uses of land, a phenomenon that may lead to the problem of "double-counted land." Agricultural economists believe that the long-term national land supply for their use will be adequate, because there are approximately 150 million acres of so-called "potential cropland," that is, land not now in crops but with the physical and economic potential for crop use. Foresters believe that there are well over 100 million acres of forestland owned neither by industry nor government on which intensive forestry can be newly practiced. Grazing experts enthuse about the possibilities for expanding cattle production by bringing now ungrazed land into production. And demographers and others studying rural settlement point out that there is plenty of unused or lightly used land for the expansion of cities and for urban-to-rural migrants to buy and subdivide.

Almost never is it recognized that the land considered available to each use is subject to a very high degree of overlap. Nearly all of the "potential cropland" is already in forest or grazing use. Says a U.S. Forest Service researcher, in one of the few extant comments on this subject in the land-use literature, "While [potential croplands] are technically convertible to crop production, they are already producing red meat, dairy products, and wood products. Shifting them to crop production would directly affect production of these other agricultural products."* Each rural productive use of land seems poised to expand onto lands coveted by others for some other use or in many cases already used for something else. And much of the potential supply of land is subject to environmental constraints—high erodibility, too much water or too little, or significant scenic or habitat values.

A second distinctive feature of this study is its concentration on a single section of the country. This is in contrast to most of the land-adequacy literature, which tends to be national rather than regional in focus. That focus is appropriate in that so many products of land are traded in national markets, but it leads to a tendency to treat all land as interchangeable, one acre for another, and ignores the pronounced regional differences in land suitability and in the likelihood of environmental impacts. Potential cropland, for example, is not evenly distributed around the country but is concentrated in certain regions and subregions. The distribution of future agricultural and forestry investment opportunities differs from the current distribution of those activities. And the environmental impact of creating new farmland by irrigating an acre of Arizona desert is not at all the same as the impact of achieving the same end by filling an acre of wetland in North Dakota's prairie pothole country or clearing an acre of forest in Arkansas.

---

*Thomas Schenarts, *Agricultural Land Use Shifts and Cropland Potentials,* Technical Paper 5 (Washington, D.C.: National Agricultural Lands Study, 1981).

Recognizing these shortcomings of the existing land-use literature
led me to undertake a study that would simultaneously consider
all of the major economic uses of land—crops, wood production,
grazing, and human settlement—as well as the many environmental
values provided by land in its natural and developed states. It also
impelled me to study a single section of the country, one large
enough to be of national significance and sufficiently diverse to
contain regional diversity and allow detailed consideration of
spatial differences in production advantages and enviromental
constraints.

Several factors made it almost inevitable that I would write a book
about land use in the South. By "the South," I mean all or part of
the 13 states lying in the nation's southeast quadrant, particularly
the great stretch of pine-growing territory stretching from Virginia
into Texas. In this region, all of the major alternative uses of rural
land have been growing rapidly—crop agriculture, grazing, wood
production, and human settlement. And long-term projections
show all of these uses have the potential for significant additional
growth. The South's natural environments are very diverse, are
frequently of great regional and even national significance, and are
rapidly being degraded by the expansion of other land uses.

Of particular importance is the fact that, more than in any other
large area of the country, rural land in the South tends to be close
to the economic margin of conversion from one use to another.
Indeed, during this century, tens of millions of acres of southern
land have gone from crops to grazing to forest and back again.
Unlike the Corn Belt or the Pacific Northwest, where a large proportion of the land is particularly suited for one use over another—
grains and trees, respectively—much of the South's rural land tends
to be capable of several uses without being uniquely specialized
to any single use. The region is therefore an ideal laboratory for
studying the competition among alternative land uses and the
response of those uses to changes in demand and in technologies.

In this study, I have tried to look at the South as it is rather than
as it was. The history of the South, including the history of how
its rural land has been used, is indeed fascinating. But more recent
developments in southern land use, those that have occurred since
the end of the Great Depression, have not been given the attention they deserve. As a result, the popular image of the rural South
is curiously out of step with the reality. I have tried to remedy this

situation by describing how land is now used in the South and, more important, what economic and noneconomic motivations lie behind the decisions of the landowners.

Organization of the Book

The organization of this book is quite simple. Chapter 1 presents an overview of the several uses now competing for land within the South, defines the geographic limits of the area studied, and presents some summary data on present land uses. The four succeeding chapters examine, in turn, the demand prospects and technology trends for the major economic uses of southern land: crop agriculture (chapter 2), wood production (chapter 3), animal agriculture (chapter 4), and human settlement (chapter 5). In each case, the chapter briefly discusses the historical development in the South of a given use; analyzes its relationship to the land base, both quantitatively and qualitatively; and explores the economic and technological forces that are likely to determine its future demands for land. Each chapter concludes with a review of available projections of the future demands that, under various assumptions, a given use will make on the South's rural land base. As is typical of nearly all of the existing literature on rural land use, these projections take little or no account of the expansion of competing uses as a possible constraint.

Chapter 6 analyzes the impacts of competing land uses on some important "unpriced values," including soil erosion, water, wildlife habitat, and esthetics. These are commodities that have either a positive (water) or a negative (erosion) value to society but that are not produced in response to the price signals generated by market demands.

Chapter 7 considers explicitly the competition among alternative uses, market and nonmarket, for the South's land. It looks at how the degree of competition is affected by alternative demand and productivity assumptions and identifies particular uses and particular geographic areas that will be most affected when overall levels of demand are high.

The final chapter (chapter 8) deals with land policy. It argues that land policies will be implemented in the South only if they provide solutions to clearly identifiable problems. The chapter then presents a number of specific policy proposals. Many of them are

ideas that have originated within the South, often policies successfully being pursued in one or more states or localities but potentially applicable to problems found in a broad range of areas.

Because of the sheer scope of my chosen subject, and the large
volume of material that must be covered, certain important, but
peripheral, topics are not addressed. Chief among them is pollution caused by industry, by point discharges of sewage effluent,
or by disposal of toxic chemicals other than those used in agriculture. Also, mining and oil and gas development are treated in terms
of land consumption and land alteration but only incidentally as
sources of air and water pollution.

Information Sources

This book is based on extensive travels in the rural South and on
interviews with hundreds of southerners with expertise in the
various uses of southern land. I visited most of the principal agricultural and wood-producing areas of the South and talked with
foresters, agronomists, soil scientists, farmers, wildlife managers,
extension agents, forage experts, regional planners, agricultural
economists, and environmental activists. I visited, and discussed
my ideas in seminars, at most of the South's land-grant universities.
I also drove down many southern highways and back roads, often
stopping to inquire why a particular field was being irrigated or
where timber from a roadside clearcut was going to be sold. I visited
a number of industrial forestry operations in the South, from
woodlot to pulp mill, and walked through wildlands with
preservation-minded biologists. Employees of many government
agencies, from the U.S. Department of Agriculture to state wildlife
and forestry departments, shared their expertise and frequently
drove me around the countryside. A big timber company flew me
in a helicopter over its North Carolina pine plantations, and two
University of Tennessee graduate students showed me how to date
old farm structures in East Tennessee.

However, personal observation, though important, had to be
secondary to the vast lode of information provided by the many
researchers who have conducted studies on one aspect or another
of land use in the South. Although, as I have mentioned, existing
land-use studies are constrained by disciplinary limits, there ex-
ists within each of several disciplines a rich literature on the indi-

vidual uses of southern land—on their history, their current condition, policy issues, and future prospects. My research colleagues, particularly at the land-grant colleges and at various public and private research institutes, were extremely generous in making available both published and unpublished work.

Unless otherwise specified, land-use and commodity-production data are from the following standard sources: U.S. Department of Agriculture, *Agricultural Statistics* (various years); U.S. Bureau of the Census, *Census of Agriculture* (various years); U.S. Bureau of the Census, *Census of Population* (various years); U.S. Bureau of the Census, *State and Metropolitan Area Data Book;* U.S. Forest Service, *An Analysis of the Timber Situation in the United States, 1952-2000* (Washington, D.C.: U.S. Government Printing Office, 1982); and unpublished computer printouts from the U.S. Soil Conservation Service, National Resources Inventory, 1982 (released in 1984).

Where statistics on land use or agricultural production are presented, an effort was made where possible to use the year 1982. This was done for two reasons. First, it is the year covered by the latest available *Census of Agriculture* as well as by the U.S. Soil Conservation Service's National Resources Inventory. Those surveys are the most complete single sources on how land in the United States is used. Second, 1982 was a year of relatively normal agricultural output, unlike the two succeeding years, in which cropland use was significantly affected by the Payment in Kind (PIK) and other temporary land retirement programs. In 1982, the amount of cropland used for crops nationally was 383 million acres, just short of the record 387 million set in 1981 and in line with the average of 376 million for the 1978-80 period. (In 1983, cropland used for crops fell to only 333 million; in 1984, it was 370 million.) In a few cases, 1982 data are simply unavailable, and the latest obtainable figures are used. For example, most regionwide forestry data are for the year 1977.

Sprinkled through the book are brief quotations, some from other studies and published reports, some the words of individual southerners. Unless otherwise indicated, the quotations are taken from my own interviews.

Acknowledgments

Considerations of space make it impossible to thank the hundreds
of people who helped me with this project, though they have my
deepest gratitude. However, there are some individuals and institutions whose special role deserves particular acknowledgment. First,
I would like to thank the members of a project advisory committee, who in individual consultations and in a meeting convened
in Atlanta early in the project contributed greatly to my approach
to the subject. They are: Charles S. Aiken, Department of
Geography, University of Tennessee; Robert F. Barnes, Agricultural
Research Service, U.S. Department of Agriculture, New Orleans,
Louisiana; Evert K. Byington, Winrock International Livestock
Research and Training Center, Morrilton, Arkansas; Leon
Danielson, Department of Economics and Business, North Carolina
State University, Raleigh, North Carolina; W.N. Haynes, School of
Forest Resources, University of Georgia, Athens, Georgia; Herbert
A. Knight, Southeastern Forest Experiment Station, U.S. Forest Ser-
vice, Asheville, North Carolina; Gary D. Lynne, Department of
Food and Resource Economics, University of Florida, Gainesville,
Florida; Douglas T. McGinty, Department of Biology, Huntingdon
College, Montgomery, Alabama; and Hans Neuhauser, The Georgia
Conservancy, Savannah, Georgia.

Second, I would like to thank some fellow researchers who were
particularly helpful in providing information or advice during the
course of the study. Ralph J. Alig, of the U.S. Forest Service, and
Burton C. English, of the Center for Agricultural and Rural Development, Iowa State University, shared their published and
unpublished projections of future land use in the South. H. Thomas
Frey, a geographer with the Economic Research Service, U.S.
Department of Agriculture, was an unfailing source of land-use data
and of advice on its reliability. He also contributed the dot maps
reproduced in chapter 2. Evert K. Byington made it possible for
me to spend two weeks at Winrock International in Morrilton,
Arkansas, where he and his colleagues helped me understand the
southern beef-cattle industry. Robert E. Sojka, a soil scientist at the
Coastal Plains Soil and Water Conservation Research Center, U.S.

Department of Agriculture, Florence, South Carolina, contributed many insights to the discussion of the future of crop agriculture in the South. Norman A. Berg, former chief of the Soil Conservation Service, U.S. Department of Agriculture, and Hal Heimstra and Nancy Bushwick, of the National Association of State Departments of Agriculture, were very helpful in providing information on several aspects of agricultural land conservation. Roger Anderson served as a very able research assistant during the early months of the study, as did Steve Gold during the study's second summer.

A third group that made a major contribution to the study are persons who reviewed and commented on the entire manuscript or on individual chapters. They include several members of the advisory committee and fellow researchers already mentioned, as well as Pierre Crosson, Resources for the Future, Washington, D.C.; John Fraser Hart, University of Minnesota; George Johnson, U.S. Department of Agriculture; and W.W. McPherson, University of Florida, each of whom read the entire manuscript, and Robert Slocum, National Forest Products Association; Joe McClure and Dwight Hair, U.S. Forest Service; Stephen G. Boyce and William C. Davis, Duke University; and Henry Gilliam, North Carolina State University. Also commenting on all or part of the manuscript were John H. Noble, Robert Peters, Edwin H. Clark, William E. Shands, and Philip C. Metzger, of The Conservation Foundation. None of the reviewers, of course, should be held responsible for the final product.

A fourth group of people to whom thanks are due are those who helped with the production of the manuscript and of the book. They include editors Robert J. McCoy and Bradley B. Rymph and secretaries Debbie Johnson, Annette Webb, and Joy Patterson.

Finally, special thanks are due to the W. Alton Jones Foundation, Charlottesville, Virginia, and to the Winthrop Rockefeller Foundation, Little Rock, Arkansas, which provided major financial support for this undertaking.

Executive Summary

A traveler returning to almost anywhere in the American South after an absence of 50 years would hardly recognize the landscape. Some of the changes—the modernization of southern industry, the growth of southern cities, and the recent acquisition over much of the South's territory of a "'Sunbelt" aura of modernity and expansiveness—are quite familiar to people both within the region and outside it. But the equally dramatic changes in southern agriculture, forestry, and rural settlement are far less widely appreciated.

These changes have literally revolutionized how land in the South is used. And they have had major impacts, both positive and negative, on the quality of the environment.

Perhaps the most dramatic change has been in the extent and location of cotton production. Although cotton is still a profitable crop in the South, its total acreage has fallen from 23 million acres on the eve of the Great Depression to fewer than 3 million acres today. Most of the South's present cotton growing is concentrated in a narrow band within 100 miles of the Mississippi River, and cultivation of cotton has been all but abandoned in hundreds of counties, stretching across the Piedmont and Coastal Plain from Virginia to East Texas. In many places where cotton was once king, it has been replaced by a crop that as recently as the 1930s was regarded as an agricultural curiosity, used mainly as a forage crop for grazing. This is the soybean, now the South's most widely grown crop, planted on more acres than cotton at its height and frequently destined for the export market.

Another notable change has been the massive shift of farm people out of the rural South, many of them to southern cities and northern factories. Particularly since about 1970, many of the South's rural areas have been resettled, usually by different people, in somewhat different locations, and certainly in a different relationship to the land. Today, only 1 out of every 39 southerners lives on a farm, and even within *rural* areas the proportion is 1 in 15. The pattern of settlement has also changed, with scattered farmhouses and sharecropper cabins replaced by sprawling "developments" and by individual houses strung out along the roadsides.

Yet another change to the southern landscape is the total cessation of farming on millions of acres of hilly and broken farmland in the Upland South and in the Piedmont and its replacement by other millions of acres of flatter land in the Delta and the Coastal Plain. Most of this was associated with the exodus of the sharecropper labor force and with the exhaustion of the soil. It was also favored by the soil requirements of the South's changing crop mix and the replacement of mule-powered agriculture by machines, which cannot operate as effectively on small, sloping fields.

Much of the former cropland is now grown up in trees and has become an important supplier to the South's lumber and paper industry—many, many times larger than that of the 1930s—and the pine plywood industry, which 50 years ago did not even exist. Indeed, one of the most striking changes in the rural southern landscape over the past 50 years, rivaling the decline of cotton and the departure of the sharecropper, has been the introduction of the intensively managed forest. One has only to drive from Richmond to Norfolk, or Charleston to Savannah, or anywhere in Northern Florida, to see this new phenomenon—ranks of planted loblolly or other pines, most of them owned by big wood-processing firms, growing at rates far faster than in unmanaged forests.

The viewer returning to the southern landscape would be greatly struck by the environmental changes as well. The reforestation of former cropland in the South, whether by planted pines or natural regeneration, has covered up many of the scars of the severe soil erosion that had long plagued the region. Gullies big enough to swallow a tractor are hardly noticeable in today's woods, and abundant ground cover conceals, in many places, a total absence of topsoil.

But there has been a drastic diminution of other woodlands, the great bottomland hardwood forest that extended for miles on both sides of the Mississippi and its many tributaries. Rich in wildlife, and not heavily logged until the early 20th century, the bottomland forest fell victim to high soybean demand and new mechanized land-clearing technologies. Of an original 24 million acres, only an estimated 5.2 million remain. Most of these former woodlands are now in rice and soybeans, huge flat fields with a Midwestern appearance belying the fact that not long ago they were densely forested.

It is difficult to believe that future landscape change in the South will be nearly as radical as what the region has experienced since the 1930s. Additional changes, however, are likely to occur, some beneficial, others less so. Some appear fairly easy to predict; others cannot be foreseen. What can southern policy makers do now to better cope with uncertainty about the South's land-use future? And how can they best prepare the South to seize the opportunities that may arise and to avoid some of the possible problems?

Projecting Future Land Use

Because two of the major uses of land, forestry and urbanization, represent very long-lived commitments of capital, the appropriate time horizon for planning is necessarily quite long. The need to plan far ahead is further underlined by the sobering fact that a child born in the South today, with a life expectancy of 75 years, will spend more than half of his or her lifetime in the world as it will be after the year 2020. A very long-range view is therefore necessary not just to protect the interests of hypothetical "future generations" but to ensure an adequate provision for many persons alive today.

Taking such a long-range view, it becomes apparent that **there is a very broad range of potential levels of demand on the South's land base. Most depend on factors that cannot be predicted with exactness, and many of these factors lie beyond the control of southern policy makers**:

- the value of the dollar relative to other currencies, a key deter- minant of the level of foreign demand for U.S. agricultural products;
- the performance of the forestry sectors in Canada and Latin America, and U.S. government policy on cutting old-growth timber in national forests;
- the degree of consumer preference for beef relative to other foods;
- the extent to which water shortages in irrigated regions of the West cause some crops and feedlots to shift toward the South;
- the worldwide redistribution of industrial employment, which

could directly affect the competitiveness of many manufacturing plants in the rural South and the livelihoods of their
workers;
- scientific developments, such as the application to crops, farm
  animals, and trees of new techniques of genetic engineering.

All of the above factors, as well as others not mentioned, will
help determine long-run patterns of land use in the South. **Perhaps
the single key variable affecting future land use in the South
will be the demand for cropland**. The South is unusually well
endowed with "potential cropland," that is, land not now used
for crops but considered by the U.S. Department of Agriculture
to have good potential for conversion. For each acre presently used
for crops, the South has an additional seven-tenths of an acre of
potential cropland. The Corn Belt, by contrast, has much less scope
for such expansion, with only two-tenths of an acre of potential
cropland for each acre now in production.

**Barring major climate change, or technological
developments greatly affecting the competitiveness of agriculture elsewhere in the United States, the amount of
southern cropland is likely to increase significantly only if
there is continued growth in foreign demand for U.S. agricultural products**. The current consensus outlook is that this will
not occur soon, but the long-term outlook does not preclude the
possibility.

In the long run, there are some intriguing possibilities for raising agricultural productivity in the South, now rather low on a per-
acre basis, and making the region more competitive with other sections of the country. These include irrigation, to compensate for
the South's erratic summer rainfall; double or even triple cropping,
to take advantage of the long growing season; and more effective
or less expensive methods for dealing with the South's many agricultural pests. There is also scope for development of new crops,
including biomass energy crops, as well as new cropping systems.
These possibilities are less likely to increase the total acreage of
cropland in the South than to shift its location.

**If there is a future overall expansion in cropland in the
South, the impacts on grazing land are likely to be more
severe than impacts on forestland**. In some "high demand"
scenarios, nearly 50 percent of current grazing land would be
converted to crops. The demand for southern forage will increase

if consumer preferences change in the direction of greater acceptance of low-fat, pasture-raised beef. But much of the South's cattle industry is based on the availability of cheap land and cheap labor, and it is very vulnerable to competing demands for those factors of production.

Another important influence on the future southern landscape is the path taken to increase future wood output. Forecasters look for a continued expansion of demand for the South's lumber and paper; demand could be particularly high if wood-product exports can be further promoted. The forest-products industry, which owns 19 percent of the South's forestland, is aggressively trying to raise output per acre on its land and to convert hardwood stands to more commercially valuable softwoods. Often this means replanting harvested land in pine plantations.

But the "nonindustrial private landowners" (mostly farmers, heirs, or investors), who own 71 percent of the South's forestland, tend to be much less interested in spending large amounts of money to raise productivity. Much of their land, neglected after harvest, is regenerating in low-value hardwoods. The future forest landscape of the South will be greatly influenced by the relative emphasis given by the nonindustrial owners to their three major production alternatives: to emulate the pine plantations of industry; to continue to practice relative neglect; or to use low-investment, but information-intensive, methods of management, sometimes called "soft silviculture," that raise productivity, though rarely to plantation levels.

The extension of urban and built-up areas in the South represents a significant demand for land, but one that will in the foreseeable future continue to be small relative to the total land base. As the U.S. population rises to 300 million, a prospect that may not occur until about 2030, the South will require between 8 and 21 million additional acres of urban and built-up land. Although this is small relative to the region's total land base (it is 3 to 7 percent of the South's total nonfederal, nonurban land), its impact could be somewhat magnified by the tendency of land of better than average quality to be urbanized and by management problems connected with the interspersing of built-up land and land devoted to agriculture and wood production.

Even if total demands on land do not rise greatly, future

land-use changes are likely to have major impacts on the South's "unpriced values." These are things, including wildlife, water, topsoil, and esthetics, that are of significant value to society but that do not enter the economic decision making of land users because their value is not represented by market prices. Among the foreseeable negative impacts on unpriced values are continued draining and clearing of wetlands, pollution of groundwater by agricultural chemicals, soil erosion and sedimentation, and reduction in wildlife habitats. Higher-than-current levels of demand for agricultural and forest products would greatly increase these damages, both by putting more sensitive lands into production and by encouraging more intensive management of lands already in use.

Preparing for the Future

If one takes a long-term view of land use, it is easy to be discouraged by the many uncertainties that arise: uncertainties as to future demands, particularly the difficult-to-forecast international demands; uncertainties about technologies; uncertainties about the application or effectiveness of current public policies that create or foreclose future land-use options. There are so many variables affecting southern land in the long run that even the most carefully laid quantitative plans would very likely be far wide of their intended mark.

But leaving land-use decisions solely to the market would probably result in foreclosing important long-term options because of short-term gains. Certainly it would result in neglect of many important unpriced values.

The best approach to land-use uncertainty is to know enough about the economic and technological forces driving the use of land to get an early warning of changes when they occur and to keep options open when this can be done at a relatively low cost. This might be termed a "foresight and insurance" strategy.

The analysis presented in this study is intended to be a contribution toward better foresight by describing present patterns of land use in the South, outlining how those patterns developed, and identifying the factors most likely to influence future patterns. The analysis indicates that the best way for the South to take advantage of its land resource, while prudently "insuring" against future land-use problems would involve action along three fronts:

- further developing agriculture and forestry by increasing pro-

duction and efficiency;
- conserving economically valuable land and resources;
- protecting and enhancing the natural and human environment.

There are a number of specific ways in which these objectives can be promoted by public policy or by organized private action. The majority of these involve actions by state governments within the South.

Developing Southern Agriculture and Forestry

Although crop agriculture in the South has improved greatly since the 1930s, there is a very wide scope for further development, particularly in raising yields. **A portion of the resources going into agricultural research should be redirected toward "reinventing" southern agriculture, developing new cropping systems based on the South's fundamental resource endowments, including its long growing seasons and available water.** This may include development of low-cost irrigation systems, greater multiple cropping, and introduction of new crops, including crops created or improved by genetic engineering.

In animal agriculture, there are exciting possibilities in aquaculture, in improving forages and forage management, and in breeding better cattle. The greatest development opportunities for the South's cattle industry may not be in production but in marketing—**southern beef producers should move aggressively to promote consumer acceptance of leaner cuts of grass-fed beef.**

Although forestry based on intensively managed pine plantations has a major place in the future landscape of the South, more attention should be paid to other forms of wood production, particularly those that better fit the objectives of the nonindustrial private owners who control more than two-thirds of the South's timberland. **A new area of emphasis should be finding and diffusing new methods of "soft silviculture" that involve low initial investment and are compatible with nontimber objectives, including wildlife and esthetics.**

New ways should also be found to substitute hardwoods for softwoods in making timber products. This would reduce the current demand imbalance between softwood and hardwood trees and would provide a market for hardwood thinnings that could encourage owners to upgrade timber stands.

A great deal of information about the South's land base will be required if agricultural and forestry research is to fully realize its potential. **Government and private researchers should mine the rich lode of land-use data newly released by the Soil Conservation Service, while new subregional data collection efforts should concentrate on geographic problem areas: rural-urban fringes, areas of wetland drainage, places with substantial recreational development or a changing structure of landownership, and "hot spots" of changing land use.**

State and federal governments are already making substantial efforts to raise wood production in the South. Rather than spend more money on traditional subsidies to a relatively small number of landowners, resources should be redirected within the timber sector so as to better promote long-term investment by the majority of owners. **The present system of cost-sharing on a first-come, first-served basis should be replaced by a universally available reforestation tax credit directly financed by a state severance tax on harvested timber.**

To improve stumpage markets and encourage owners to improve forest management, **state governments should create "timber development districts" (TDDs) in promising but underproductive forest areas, usually several counties in extent**. Within a TDD there would be special incentives for both improved forest management and for siting new forest-products plants. The costs would be financed by state revenue bonds, amortized by the proceeds from an additional timber severance tax, levied only within the TDD.

Other ways of further developing the South's wood production potential include greater state attention to export promotion, better information on prices of land and timber, and modification of present systems of preferential assessment of timberland to ensure that land enrolled in the programs is soundly managed. **To deal with the important problem of small tract size, new ways should be found to encourage cooperation in management and marketing among owners of nearby or adjacent tracts.** One possible option would be to create a "public interest forestry consulting firm," either at the state level or regionwide, modeled after the successful New England Forestry Foundation.

Conserving Productive Land and Resources

In developing the South's natural resources, care must be taken to ensure that development options are sustainable in the long run. Even now, some uses of land in the South are permanently damaging the renewable resource base.

One problem is the loss of farm- and forestland to various "built-up" uses. Although some land conversions are surely necessary to accommodate growing population and industry, it seems wise to guide development so that impacts on other land users are minimized. **Both the goals and the mechanics of agricultural land retention appear to favor identifying fairly large aggregates of land or "districts" where agriculture or forestry uses are given clear priority.** The entire range of policy tools should be concentrated in these districts, including preferential assessment, right-to-farm protections, and exemptions from fees for urban infrastructure.

Other steps that should be taken to limit unnecessary conversions of resource lands are the timely publication of prime farmland maps for each of the South's counties and adoption of state policies that try to steer state-funded development away from important agricultural and forest properties.

A major threat to agricultural sustainability is soil erosion. **Erosion control efforts should be "targeted" on the most erodible land, not spread out evenly over all agricultural lands or made available on a first-come, first-served basis.** Targeting is particularly relevant to the South because of the drastic differences in erosion rates from one physiographic region to another. **There should also be a major effort to take certain of the most erodible, and difficult to treat, lands out of crop production entirely.** Recently released government data show that there are 5 million acres of cropland in the South where erosion is currently severe and where potential erodibility is so high that it could be reduced to a tolerable level only by conversion to grass or trees. **Farmers should be paid to take this land out of crop use, just as was done in the Soil Bank program of the 1950s and 1960s.**

Although the South has ample water for most uses, in most places, most of the time, it has a tendency to periodic drought, as well as growing competition for water within some local areas. After inventorying water use and identifying and protecting the needs of instream uses, **state governments should move deliberately to set up a system that codifies the right to use water and specifies how the burden of drought will be apportioned among users.** For long-term water management, the best approach may be to create a system based primarily on freely transferable private property rights.

Protecting the Natural and Human Environment

Even if the South moves toward sustainable development of its rural resources, many of its "unpriced values" would still be threatened. Specific steps should be taken to protect natural systems as well as some of the cultural and esthetic values so much prized by southern residents.

Among the most valued—and most threatened—natural lands in the southern states are the wetlands. Coastal wetlands are now fairly well protected but inland or freshwater wetlands are not. **Certain public subsidies, including tax subsidies, that promote the draining and clearing of freshwater wetlands should be removed. There should be an accelerated program to monitor wetland status and trends in the South. And the U.S. Army Corps of Engineers should be instructed by Congress to extend its Section 404 program to cover a wider range of wetland types and a larger number of agricultural and forestry activities.**

Several southern states have been among the pioneers in setting up "natural heritage programs" to identify environmentally critical lands and set preservation priorities. **These important programs should be given sufficient monies to complete the inventory work and to initiate needed land-preservation projects.** Nonprofit organizations, timber companies and individual landowners should be encouraged to undertake such projects as well.

The South could benefit greatly if ties between wildlife policies and natural areas protection were made more explicit. The trend toward establishing state programs for nongame wildlife is encouraging, but it would be unfortunate if the single-species model so dominant in game management is tranferred into the nongame area. **Nongame programs should be used to move wildlife management away from individual species and toward the**

management of multi-species systems. Greater involvement of environmental groups in the nongame programs and closer ties to state natural heritage programs may be one way to ensure that this opportunity will not slip away.

Although public lands occupy less than 10 percent of the South's land area, their size, their scenic qualities, and their management objectives give them a special role. **The overarching principle guiding the management of public lands should be to provide market and nonmarket goods that are not adequately provided on the South's private lands.** This management principle suggests that public land managers should pay more attention to how nearby private lands are being managed and should manage the public lands to complement, rather than to imitate, the actions of the private owners.

The visual environment of the rural South may be even more in need of attention than is the natural environment. Among the obvious threats are urban sprawl, neglect of desirable features of the historic landscape, and lack of regional identity in new development. **A major public education and consciousness-raising effort is needed to get ordinary people across the South interested in their "built environment," both at the scale of individual buildings and at the scale of entire landscapes.** This effort should enlist state and local governments, philanthropic organizations, schools and colleges, environmental organizations, and museums. There should also be more inventories of valued features of the man-made environment, including human-modified landscapes. And there is a great deal of scope for creating a new southern architectural tradition that would borrow themes from the South's past in building new institutional, commercial, and residential structures.

Greater policy attention ought also to be paid to the pervasive visual clutter along southern roads and highways. This requires attention by all levels of government, including county and city governments.

The quality of the South's drinking water is threatened from a variety of sources, including residential and agricultural land uses. **Important aquifer recharge areas should be protected from the impacts of unplanned human settlement and from pollution with agricultural chemicals.** Better information should be secured about what chemicals are infiltrating into water supplies, and prevention strategies should be initiated. Although these steps may be costly, the costs are low compared with those of living with permanently polluted water supplies.

The visitor returning to the South after an absence of 50 years would indeed find many changes in the landscape, many for the better, some for the worse. The rather modest policy suggestions made here will, with luck, go a long way toward ensuring that future visitors will have reason to admire what today's southerners did with the land within their care.

Competition for Land in the American South

Chapter 1

Introduction: The New Competition for Southern Land

In the summer of 1982, several hundred employees of Georgia-Pacific, a giant forest-products corporation, moved into a new 52-story building in downtown Atlanta. Georgia-Pacific had relocated its corporate headquarters from Portland, Oregon, a change widely regarded as a symbolic affirmation of the rise of the South over the past three decades to its present position as the nation's most important wood-producing region.

This shift has coincided with, and to a great degree has depended on, a fundamental change in the nature of forest management in the United States—from a sort of hunter-gatherer economy based on harvesting naturally provided "old growth" timber, to a more agricultural economy based on planting, intensive management, and harvesting of trees over repeated cycles. In recent years, the stock of old-growth timber, most of which is found in the Pacific Northwest, has been depleted. The attention of the forest-products industry, therefore, has focused increasingly on finding new, highly productive lands on which trees can be grown like crops.[1]

Large quantities of this type of land exist in the southeastern quadrant of the United States, particularly in the broad Coastal Plain and Piedmont area stretching from Virginia to East Texas and eastern Oklahoma and extending inland to the ridges and valleys of the Appalachians. In this section of the country, abun-

1

dant solar energy and plentiful water allow very rapid tree growth, particularly of Southern Pine species which are valuable for lumber, plywood, and pulp. Since 1950, virtually all of the nation's large timber and paper concerns have purchased extensive tracts of land in the South. And within the last decade, the intensification of forest management on these and other southern lands has been dramatic.

Wood, Crops, and Livestock

The importance of the South as a wood producer, both in absolute and in relative terms, is expected to continue to rise. In 1976, 45 percent of the nation's softwood timber came from the South, compared to 41 percent from the Pacific states. By 2030, according to U.S. Forest Service projections, 51 percent will come from the South and only 31 percent from the Pacific states.[2] In 1980, when a forest industry committee identified profitable opportunities nationwide for future timber management, nearly 70 percent were in the South, 117 million acres in all.[3]

The South, acknowledged to be the major timber growing region of the future, is where the greatest opportunity for increasing the timber supply lies.

U.S. FOREST SERVICE, Renewable Resources Planning Act, Environmental Impact Statement, 1980

Even these prospects could understate the future of southern wood production if, as some experts believe, the international trade in wood products grows. The huge paper industries in such countries as Japan and West Germany are increasingly looking to the southeastern United States for new pulp supplies. With fast-growing trees, high-technology mills, and abundant water and energy, the South is becoming recognized as the world's lowest-cost producer of market pulp. A large Finnish paper company, in partnership with an American firm, recently built a $540 million pulp mill near Hattiesburg, Mississippi. The Finnish firm will export its share of the pulp to Europe. According to the president of one of Florida's largest banks; "The [South] is capable of doubling its timber production in the next 20 years and assuming a leadership role in the world timber market comparable to the one the South once held with cotton and tobacco.''

Expansion of the southern forest-products industry over the last three decades has been made possible by the availability of land at low prices, much of it land abandoned by marginal farmers. But agriculture is no longer declining in the South, and this could produce a major problem for both the forest industry and the farmer. The same land, water, and solar energy that make very productive timber stands are also in many cases conducive to raising soybeans or providing forage for cattle. As U.S. food exports have increased (particularly since 1973) and land in other parts of the country has been lost to urban expansion, farmers have turned south in search of a new frontier of cheap, fertile land.

The National Agricultural Lands Study projected that, to meet domestic and foreign demand for grains in the year 2000, between 77 and 113 million additional acres would need to be planted.[4] Another agricultural projection, done in 1980 for Resources for the Future, estimated that 68 to 73 million additional acres would be needed by the year 2005.[5] This land would have to be selected from a nationwide stock of 153 million acres of ''potential cropland,'' land that has physical characteristics suitable for crop growing but is not now put to that use. Almost one-third of this potential cropland lies in the South, the greatest concentration anywhere in the country.[6] Most of it is now devoted to forest, pasture, or range.

If expansion of agriculture onto forestland could present problems for an expanding forest products industry, might not conversion of the South's extensive grazing land offer the most likely alternative? Perhaps not easily, for grazing experts point out that the high cost of feeding beef cattle on grain and the public's increased acceptance of lower-fat, grass-fed beef have led to increased demands on the nation's range and pasture lands. Some of the most productive of these lands are in the southern states. Until fairly recently, disease and parasite problems had restrained the southern livestock industry. But new drugs and better livestock breeding have greatly reduced these problems and, according to livestock experts, may have set the stage for a major expansion. One government projection placed southern grazing in the year 2000 at 70 percent over the 1976 level.[7]

Perhaps the most interesting attribute of the southern states is that they are potentially affected by *so many* alternative agricultural demands. In the words of Dr. Thomas N. Shiflet, director of Ecological Sciences for the Soil Conservation Service: "The combination of climate and growing season makes the South an extremely versatile area. It's our best tree-growing area, it's good for growing many crops, and it's good for pasture. That just about guarantees a future competition for land."

The South has a bigger biomass going for it—there are so many more ways of increasing production than there are in the West. If we have increases in cattle numbers it will be in the South, not in the West.

RICHARD WHEELER, Winrock International
Livestock Research and Training Center,
Morrilton, Arkansas

Human Settlement and the Environment

All of the demands on the productive abilities of southern land are occurring in a section of the United States that has been experiencing great economic and demographic change. These changes, including major industrial and residential growth and dispersal, have placed their own demands on southern land. The South's population grew by 20.5 percent during the 1970s; only the West grew faster. Southerners also tend to favor low-density patterns of settlement. This is partly due to their greater-than-average propensity to live in rural areas; partly due to the fact that southern cities tend to be sprawling. In the South, the average amount of land consumed per resident is greater than it is in other sections of the country.

Population and industrial growth have also had other, more subtle impacts on southern land. In many areas, rural land has increasingly gone out of the hands of farmers and into the hands of nonresident, often urban, owners. The latter, who have inherited their property from relatives or purchased it for recreation or investment, are often unwilling or unable to manage the land to its full potential. The management behavior of "nonindustrial private forest owners," for example, has frequently been identified as one of the most important uncertainties for long-term forest management in the South. The ownership problem is compounded by widespread division of land into smaller parcels (which creates diseconomies of scale for almost any productive use) and by the interspersion of urban and rural land uses, to the detriment of both.

Shifts in land uses in the South have produced significant environmental changes as well. Clearing of bottomland hardwood forests to make way for soybeans has eliminated vast areas of wildlife habitat in several southern river systems. Of the 24 million acres of forested wetlands originally lying in the alluvial floodplain of the Mississippi River, only 5.2 million remain.[8] Nearly all of the land cleared has become cropland; in recent years, 80 percent has gone into soybeans. Some clearing has continued even in years when millions of acres of southern cropland have been withheld from cultivation because of overproduction of grain and cotton. Nor are crops the only consumers of wetlands. In eastern North Carolina, peat bogs and "pocosin" wetlands covering hundreds of thousands of acres have been drained and cleared for high-yield pine plantations.[9]

Some 35 million Coastal Plain acres that are now in forest are capable of sustained cropping and another five million on the Outer Coastal Plain can be converted to cropland through drainage. Obviously our greatest national reserves of agricultural land are there.

MERLE C. PRUNTY, *Southeastern Geographer,* May 1977

Expansion of crop production onto former pasture- or forestland is generally accompanied by an increase in soil erosion, a particularly intense problem in the South, which already has some of the highest average erosion rates in the nation. The most recent national erosion inventory found that nearly 40 percent of southern cropland is losing more than five tons of soil per acre each year to water-induced erosion. (Erosion of five tons per acre or less is generally considered "tolerable" on cropland.) Assuming a high projected level of future cropland demand, which would cause even more marginal land to be brought into production, erosion of southern cropland could easily double in the next 30 years. Erosion not only threatens future soil productivity but contributes to water pollution and to silt buildup in watercourses and reservoirs.

Competition for southern land has also produced an incipient competition for southern water.[10] Average rainfall is relatively high in the South compared to the West and parts of the Midwest. Indeed, water constraints are among the factors restricting agricultural expansion in other parts of the country and increasing pressure on southern cropland. Yet the seasonal distribution of rainfall in the South is not optimal for crop production, and southern farmers have increasingly learned that they can increase yields by irrigating. Within the last decade, for example, about one million acres in southern Georgia and northern Florida alone were brought under irrigation, mainly using spray equipment of the sort common in Nebraska and California. Some of the water used is drawn from surface sources, but much is groundwater.

In the South, particularly on the Coastal Plain, we have a real coincidence of a "Water Belt" with the so-called Sunshine Belt, and it is here that I believe the developmental potential embodied in the "Sunshine" concept is greatest.

MERLE C. PRUNTY, *Southeastern Geographer*,
May 1977

More intensive use of water in the South has thus far had two side effects. First, in several local areas, pumping of groundwater by agricultural irrigators has lowered the water pressure within underground aquifers. This has dried up wells and, in some coastal locations, has allowed saltwater to infiltrate into wellfields, poisoning the water supply of a number of communities. Second, there is growing interest in the ownership of water rights. In the South, where historically there has been ample water for all users, legal rights to water have not been firmly established. Southern water users are increasingly aware that they must establish firm property rights in that resource if they are to protect themselves in future competition for it.

The Policy Issues

The prospective competition for land and water poses important issues for southern policy makers. First, it raises questions about some of their fondest hopes for the South's long-term economic growth. The South has a bright future as a producer, and possibly as an exporter, of forest products—provided that the forestland base can be maintained and provided that nonindustrial owners manage their holdings more productively. The South can greatly expand its agricultural output—provided that urbanization and erosion do not claim too much of its productive land. The South can make the transition from low-wage industries to high-technology ones—provided that its living environment remains sufficiently pleasant to attract a highly skilled, but highly mobile, population of technicians and entrepreneurs. If alternative uses of land come into direct competition, the ability to forecast demands and their likely outcomes would become increasingly important to policy makers.

A second issue for southern policy makers is the impact of land-use competition on various "unpriced" values, particularly environmental values. The competition among the various uses of land is resolved by a decentralized, free-market process that is driven by the profit-motivated decisions of millions of individual and corporate landowners. This process is remarkably effective in many ways, but it has some notable shortcomings. The market gives heavy weight, for example, to the present-day farmer's need for income, very little to future generations' need for fertile soil. It offers little help in managing the many conflicts arising from the juxtaposition of farms and suburbs, second homes and productive forests.

When I first got into studying land use in this area 20 years ago there was a tremendous amount of unused or unneeded rural land. There was obviously no competition for this land. That has completely changed and most land is either cropland or pasture or forest. I think we are in a new era in which there is competition for land for new uses.

JAMES S. FISHER, geographer, University of Georgia

Southern states and localities have been slow to deal with many of these market failures. In many cases, the South has taken fewer policy initiatives than have areas elsewhere with far less severe land problems. Thus, though it was said by the National Agricultural Lands Study to lead the nation in agricultural land conversion, the South contains only a handful of the more than 200 cities and counties making serious efforts to preserve productive farmland. Despite high rates of population growth, few southern jurisdictions—the exceptions are concentrated in South Florida and Northern Virginia—have shown much interest in growth management. There have been relatively few southern innovations in the regulation of forest practices, in erosion control, or in the containment of urban sprawl.

But there are some signs of change. During the last five years, nearly all of the southern states have passed "right-to-farm" laws, protecting farmers from nuisance suits brought by new, nonagricultural neighbors. Virginia and Kentucky now have agricultural district laws; more and more southern states have aggressive programs to promote better management of privately owned forests. Local groups have conducted studies of local farmland conversion problems in such areas as Fauquier County, Virginia; Orange County, North Carolina; Dade County, Florida; and the Memphis, Tennessee, metropolitan area. North Carolina is considering legislation to allow counties to establish agricultural districts and to provide cost-sharing for a pilot program to purchase development rights from farmers.

There is also increasing pressure by southern hunters and environmentalists to preserve some of the remaining bottomland hardwood forests, and there have been some important state initiatives toward that end in Louisiana and Mississippi. Florida has embarked on a major program to protect freshwater wetlands, streamcourses, and other natural areas. A number of state and local groups have successfully pushed for southern additions to the national wilderness preservation system. (There are now nearly 2.5 million acres of federal land in the South designated as wilderness. However, the South still contains only 7.6 percent of the national total of designated wilderness outside of Alaska.) And there is growing interest among southern legislators and state officials in improving water management, in protecting groundwater quality, and in raising forest productivity.

Defining the South

There are many ways to define the South. Journalist Joel Garreau, who tried to delimit the area in his book *The Nine Nations of North America*, noted that "official organizations draw boundaries enclosing anywhere from nine to seventeen states and call the place 'the South.' " Legions of geographers and political scientists have also tried to describe the boundaries of the South, using indicators that range from voting patterns to house types.

Because this book is about land, it seems logical to define the South by its physical geography, especially the combination of topography, soils, and climate suitable for growing particular types of crops and trees. But the South is also a section of the United States with a distinct history and culture, two attributes that surely must influence how land is used. It is a political region, with multistate institutions, ranging from the Southern Governors Association to the Southeastern Association of Fish and Wildlife Agencies, that can be instrumental in convening decision makers and sharing policy experiences. Finally, the South is a statistical entity, defined in one way by the U.S. Census Bureau and in another by the U.S. Department of Agriculture.[11]

All of that taken into consideration, I have defined the South for this book primarily on the basis of state boundaries (figure 1.1). It includes the following 11 states in their entirety—Virginia, Tennessee, Kentucky, North Carolina, South Carolina, Georgia, Florida, Alabama, Mississippi, Arkansas, and Louisiana. It also covers 54 counties in the eastern parts of Texas and Oklahoma.[12]

Figure 1.1
Physiographic Regions of the South

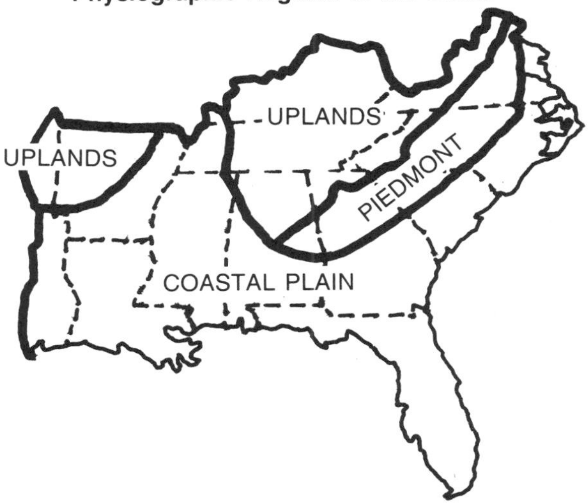

This map is drawn so that the boundaries of the physiographic regions are coterminous with the defined study area. In actuality, the regions cross over state boundaries in several places (for example, the Uplands extend into southern Missouri, and the Coastal Plain extends into parts of Maryland and Delaware).

Source: Department of Geography, University of Georgia

Unlike the remainder of Texas and Oklahoma, these counties have relatively high rainfall and are prolific producers of southern softwoods. The areas' colloquial names, "The Pineywoods," and "The Green Country," respectively, give a flavor of their predominant landscapes. Physically, historically, and culturally, they are too much like the rest of the South, as defined by state boundaries, to be excluded.

Because data are not available below the state level for a large number of aspects of land use, it is often impossible to present figures for the counties in Texas and Oklahoma or to include them in southwide totals. I have therefore consistently followed the practice of inserting the phrase "including portions of Texas and Oklahoma" wherever such substate data are included in totals; otherwise, a given total refers only to the 11 states mentioned above. All tables are explicitly labeled with respect to their geographic coverage. Because East Texas and eastern Oklahoma account for only 7.7 percent of the South's total land area, and because they are so similar in land cover and land use to much larger adjoining areas in Arkansas, Louisiana, and other states, their omission from certain totals does not significantly affect the analysis.

The South, as defined, including the aforementioned portions of Texas and Oklahoma, contains 351 million acres of land, or about 18.5 percent of the area of the United States (excluding Alaska and Hawaii). Although the South exhibits considerable variation in landforms, it is possible to divide it into three fairly distinctive physiographic regions (see figure 1.1):

- *The Coastal Plain*—a broad band of territory paralleling the seacoast from Virginia to Texas, with a deep extension up the Lower Mississippi Valley. Notable for being relatively flat, with broad, slow-moving streams and sandy or alluvial soils, the Coastal Plain is the South's dominant center for both crop and timber production. Characterized before the Civil War by plantation agriculture, it still tends to have more blacks than the rest of the South and larger landholdings. Most of the cities in the Coastal Plain are either on the seacoast or along the navigable rivers leading to the sea.
- *The Piedmont*—literally, the land "at the foot of the mountains," this area begins at the "fall line," where the coastal rivers narrow and cease to be navigable and ends at the Ap-

palachian Mountains. The land in the Piedmont is rolling to hilly, frequently dissected by streams, and with soils that are generally of red, yellow, or grayish-white clay. Historically, the region contained both small farms and large plantations, and, despite the soil's modest fertility and high erodibility, much of the land was intensively cultivated for corn and cotton. The Piedmont now contains much of the South's industry and many of its urban centers, particularly the band of cities stretching along the fall line from Washington, D.C., to Montgomery, Alabama.

- *The Uplands*—comprising generally the mountainous region of the South, the Uplands include the Appalachian Highlands in the east and the Ozark Plateau and Ouachita Mountains in the west. Although large portions of this region are too steep to cultivate and are devoted to hardwood timber and grazing, many valleys and broad plateaus in the Uplands contain some of the South's most productive farmland. Land holdings tend to be small in the valleys; often large, and in corporate hands, in the mountains.

The Coastal Plain, the largest and agriculturally most important of the three physiographic regions, contains a number of subregions.[13] In the chapters that follow, four subregions in the Coastal Plain often are singled out for separate discussion:

- *The Delta*—an area 25 to 200 miles in width on either side of the Mississippi River, beginning near the Missouri-Kentucky border and widening as it extends toward New Orleans and the Gulf. The soils of the Delta, among the most fertile in the South, have been enriched by silt carried downstream and deposited across the landscape as the river channel moved. Adjoining and interspersed with the Delta proper are deep pockets of windblown "loess" soils, which are also important areas of crop production. The Delta is the last stronghold of cotton cultivation in the South and its major soybean- and rice-producing area.

- *The Coastal Flatwoods*—the first 50 miles or so inland from the sea along the Atlantic and Gulf coasts, from Virginia to Mississippi. Lower and swampier than the rest of the Coastal Plain, the Flatwoods are heavily specialized in growing pines for pulpwood.

- *South Florida*—comprising the southern one-third of Florida, this region has a largely frost-free climate that enables it to grow tropical crops and winter vegetables that cannot be cultivated elsewhere in the South.

- *The South Atlantic Coastal Plain*—the eastern half of the Coastal Plain, excluding the Coastal Flatwoods and South Florida, and extending from Virginia southwestward into central Mississippi. An area of diversified crop production, including corn, soybeans, tobacco, and vegetables, it is also important for pine timber production.

How Southern Land Is Used

Anyone who has ever flown across the South can readily testify to the fact that a large proportion of its land is forest. Some 56.5 percent of southern land is forested, a figure considerably higher than the national average (see table 1.1). The type of forest cover varies greatly from one physiographic region to another. The Coastal Plain tends to be pine country, with great expanses of longleaf, shortleaf, and loblolly pines, the exact species mix depending on local climate and soils, as well as the varieties chosen

Table 1.1
Land Area in the South, by Use, 1982

	Percentage of total southern land	South's percentage of total U.S. land in that use	Trend 1969–82
Forest	56.5	30.5	decreasing
Cropland[1]	17.6	14.1	increasing
Used for crops	16.2	13.7	increasing
Idle	1.4	21.6	decreasing
Grazing land[2]	12.5	6.2	decreasing
Built-up[3]	6.4	25.4	increasing
Wildlife and rural parks	2.6	11.9	increasing
Other land	4.4	12.6	decreasing
Total	100.0	17.1	
Federal land	(7.0)	(5.6)	increasing

Figures are for 11 southern states and do not include Texas or Oklahoma.

[1]Cropland used for crops plus idle cropland
[2]Grassland pasture and range plus cropland used for pasture
[3]Census Bureau-defined urban land plus rural transportation area plus farmsteads, farm roads, and lanes

Source: H. Thomas Frey and Roger W. Hexem, *Major Uses of Land in the United States, 1982* (Washington, D.C.: U.S. Department of Agriculture, Economic Research Service, 1985), data adjusted to include federal forest area in forestland total; H. Thomas Frey, *Expansion of Urban Area in the United States: 1960–1980* (Washington, D.C.: U.S. Department of Agriculture, Economic Research Service, 1983).

for the extensive, often industry-owned, plantations. The Piedmont has a mixture of pines and hardwoods (oak, maple, hickory, yellow poplar). The Upland forest is predominately hardwood, with some pine and localized stands of other softwoods. Along streams in the Coastal Plain, wet soils in the root zone prevent large numbers of pines from growing and the most common trees are the "bottomland hardwoods" such as tupelo, sweetgum, cottonwood, and water oaks, sometimes with a sprinkling of softwoods such as cypress and "pond pines."

The next most widespread use of land in the South is for crops, occupying 17.6 percent of total land area. By acreage, the South's principal crops are soybeans (more than 25 million acres), wheat, corn, hay, cotton, rice, and peanuts. In terms of value of production, the ranking is rather different; tobacco, a high value crop that occupies only 827,000 acres has a value ($3.2 billion) almost as large as that of soybeans ($3.5 billion). Cropland in the South tends to be concentrated in a broad swath of the Coastal Plain extending from southern Virginia to Alabama (though there is very little in the Flatwoods area closest to the coast), in central and south Florida, in the Delta, and in the valleys that cut through the Uplands. Farming endeavors range from the part-time operator who earns a couple of thousand dollars yearly from an acre of tobacco or 20 of corn to the huge mechanized cotton and soybean operations of the Delta, which may occupy thousands of acres under one management.

Figure 1.2, which shows cropland as a percentage of total land area in the South, offers perhaps the clearest attainable overview of how agriculture and forestry divide the land. The darkest areas are those where cropland accounts for more than 30 percent of total land area; there are cropland concentrations in the Delta, South Atlantic Coastal Plain, and Upland valleys, as well as in Florida. The lighter areas, where cropland accounts for between 15 and 30 percent of total area, are concentrated in the Piedmont and scattered portions of the Uplands. The land not used for crops tends to be divided between forestry and grazing. The white areas on the map generally represent heavily forested areas; easily identifiable are the extensive pinelands stretching along the Coastal Flatwoods from southern North Carolina to northern Florida and along the Gulf, the Texas Pineywoods, and the forested regions of Arkansas and eastern Oklahoma.

Figure 1.2
Cropland as a Percent of Land Area, 1978
(All farms—county unit basis)

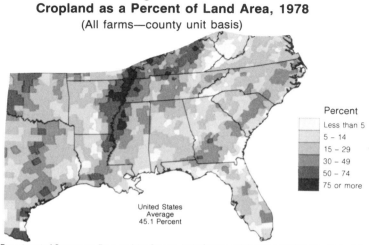

Percent
Less than 5
5 – 14
15 – 29
30 – 49
50 – 74
75 or more

United States
Average
45.1 Percent

Source: U.S. Department of Commerce, Bureau of the Census, *1978 Census of Agriculture* (Washington, D.C.: U.S. Government Printing Office, 1982). The relevant *1982 Census of Agriculture* map was not available at press time.

A third important category of land use in the South is grazing. Land used exclusively or primarily for grazing (pasture and rangeland) amounts to 41 million acres, or 12.5 percent of the land base. There is also a large, but difficult to measure, area of forestland that is grazed, often on a somewhat casual basis. Most grazing in the South is done by beef cattle, with much smaller demands by milk cows and sheep. The bulk of the region's grazing, measured by the number of animals supported, occurs on land that has been cleared but is not now used for crops. Much of this land is in the Piedmont, an area where the amount of land cultivated for crops is much smaller than it was in the past and where some abandoned cropland is now used for pasture. There is also a concentration of beef-cattle grazing in central and south Florida, on rangeland that has never been cultivated.

The "built-up" area in the South, which includes cities and suburbs, roads, airports, and farmhouses, accounts for 6.4 percent of the land base. This percentage is quite high by national standards, reflecting the great land consumption by the South's sprawling cities and towns and relatively high rural population. The South also contains "wildlife areas and rural parks," which take up 2.6 percent of the land area, and "other land," a residual classification, accounting for 4.4 percent of the land area, that includes nonforested wetlands, farm ponds, and various land uses that do not fit neatly into other categories.

One fairly important factor influencing land use in the South is federal landownership. This amounts to nearly 23 million acres, or 7.0 percent of total land area, a figure far below the proportion of federally owned land in the West, but somewhat higher than the proportion found in the Northeast or in most of the Midwest. Federal land in the South is mostly in national forests, though there are two very large national parks (Everglades and Great Smoky Mountains) and a number of smaller parks, national wildlife refuges, national seashores, and military bases. Unlike in the West, where most of the federal land is the unclaimed or reserved portion of the original public domain, much of the federal land in the South was once privately owned and was acquired by the government through purchase. For example, during the 1920s and 1930s, abandoned cropland and cutover forest was purchased by federal agencies at prices that averaged about $5.00 per acre. Replanted by the Civilian Conservation Corps and other agencies, much of this land is now productive timberland within the South's national forests. Another, smaller wave of land buying has occurred since about 1965, when the federal government began increasingly to purchase lands considered important for recreation or wildlife protection, including many coastal barrier islands and riverine wetlands.

The use of land in the South has, of course, changed over time, with particularly dramatic shifts occurring since the early 1930s. These shifts will be discussed in detail in succeeding chapters, and I will not anticipate them here. However, it may be useful to mention the most recent directions of land-use change, those taking place since 1969. For cropland, there has been a pronounced net increase, much of it due to increases in the cultivation of soybeans. Forestland and grazing land have decreased, while built-up land and land set aside for wildlife and rural parks have increased sharply. The residual category, "other land," has tended to fall in recent years, as lands previously so classified have been drained or cleared for agricultural use, urbanized, or set aside as parks or wildlife reserves.

The next several chapters look in detail at land use shifts and at some of the forces producing them. First, the South's cropland.

References

1. The forest products industry, including Georgia-Pacific, has certainly not abandoned the Pacific Northwest, which also contains large areas of land with high productivity in sustained-yield forestry. Moreover, there are still huge quantities of old growth timber in federally owned forests in the region, although it is uncertain whether it will be made available to the forest products industry, and if so, at what pace.

2. U.S. Forest Service, *An Assessment of the Forest and Range Land Situation in the United States* (Washington, D.C.: U.S. Government Printing Office, 1980).

3. Forest Industries Council, *Forest Productivity Report* (Washington, D.C.: National Forest Products Association, 1980).

4. U.S. National Agricultural Lands Study, *Final Report* (Washington, D.C.: U.S. Government Printing Office, 1981).

5. Martin E. Abel, "Growth in Demand for U.S. Crop and Animal Production by 2005," in Pierre Crosson, ed., *The Cropland Crisis: Myth or Reality?* (Baltimore: Johns Hopkins University Press for Resources for the Future, 1982), pp. 63-92.

6. Unpublished data from U.S. Soil Conservation Service, 1982 National Resources Inventory.

7. U.S. Forest Service, *An Assessment*.

8. Purificacion O. MacDonald, et al., *Documentation, Chronology and Future Projections of Bottomland Hardwood Habitat Losses in the Lower Mississippi Alluvial Plain* (Washington, D.C.: U.S. Fish and Wildlife Service, 1979).

9. Curtis J. Richardson, ed., *Pocosin Wetlands* (Stroudsburg, Pa.: Hutchinson Ross, 1981); John R. Clark and J. Benforado, eds., *Wetlands of Bottomland Hardwood Forests* (New York: Elsevier, 1981).

10. For an overview of water problems in several southern states, see *Southeast Water Resources*, vol. 1, no. 2 (Spring 1979), Chapel Hill: University of North Carolina, Water Resources Research Institute.

11. In practice, the statistical constraint proved particularly important. Many statistical series are available only at the state level. Even where county data are available, their sheer volume makes them very inconvenient to disaggregate below the state level. This consideration was overriding in my decision to exclude counties in Maryland and Missouri that are physically and culturally quite "Southern" and to include several counties in south Florida that are not.

12. Included are the 18 counties in Oklahoma for which statistics were presented in J.M. Earles, *Forest Statistics for East Oklahoma Counties* (New Orleans: U.S. Forest Service, Southern Forest Experiment Station, 1976) and the 36 counties included in the Northeast and Southeast Forest Survey regions of Texas as defined in P.A. Murphy, *East Texas Forests: Status and Trends* (New Orleans: U.S. Forest Service, Southern Forest Experiment Station, 1976). Harris County, Texas, which includes the city of Houston, was excluded.

13. The boundaries, as well as the names, of the various regions and subregions within the South are not fully standardized and vary from one source

to another. The definitions and terminology used here are based in part on the topography-based regions specified in William D. Thornbury, *Regional Geomorphology of the United States* (New York: John Wiley & Sons, 1965) and in part on the vegetation-based regions specified in U.S. Soil Conservation Service, *Major Land Resource Regions and Major Land Resource Areas of the United States* (Washington, D.C.: U.S. Government Printing Office, 1981).

Chapter 2

Crop Agriculture as a Competitor for Southern Land

On a lobby wall in the U.S. Post Office in Dardanelle, Arkansas, is a mural painted in 1939, no doubt under a Depression-era "jobs for artists" program. In the center stands a black man picking cotton, flanked by workers spinning cotton into thread and stevedores loading cotton bales onto a ship. The mural was apparently intended to depict the area's principal economic activity. In 1939, the county in which Dardanelle serves as county seat had some 2,000 farms engaged in growing cotton, on a total of over 29,000 acres.

A visitor to the Dardanelle area today would see fields of soybeans, rice, sorghum, and hay, many cattle, and a huge poultry processing plant. Cotton is nowhere in evidence. In fact, the state agricultural statistics for 1982 show not a single acre in the entire county planted to that crop. This experience, or some variant of it, has been repeated in literally hundreds of counties in a broad arc stretching from Virginia to East Texas: areas where King Cotton has been replaced by a diversified farming economy.

Southern crop agriculture has traditionally been regarded as an enterprise much out of the mainstream of U.S. farming. The region contains quite a number of farms—680,000, or 28 percent of the national total. But a disproportionate number of the South's farms are small, perhaps operated part time or on a close-to-subsistence basis. Average yields for most major crops are low by national standards. Moreover, many of the South's farms, both large and

19

small, historically specialized in crops not widely found in other regions, such as tobacco, cotton, rice, peanuts, and winter vegetables. In most other crops, the South produced barely enough to feed its own human and animal populations.

Today, much of the crop agriculture in the South is still distinctly secondary by midwestern standards. Yet the South has diversified and mechanized greatly over the last several decades, and a growing proportion of farms is thoroughly modernized. Moreover, the South has some very interesting prospects as an agricultural frontier, an area less important to the nation for its current production than for its potential contribution to future changes in production.

At present, the South contains only 14.1 percent of the nation's cropland.[1] By contrast, the nation's agricultural heartland, the Corn Belt and Northern Plains, has about the same land area as the South but contains 46 percent of total national cropland.

If one looks at land potential, rather than present land use, however, the South's possible importance to future crop production becomes apparent. The U.S. Department of Agriculture has designated as "potential cropland" land that is not now being cropped but that could be economically converted to that use. There are 153 million acres of "potential cropland" nationwide. The South contains 44 million acres, or 29 percent.[2] Of the 62 million acres nationally considered to have "high potential" for crop use, the South contains 31 percent.

Historical Development of Southern Crop Agriculture

The agricultural history of the South is long, fascinating, and impressively well documented.[3] Some of the deepest historical roots are quite relevant to explaining the present condition of southern crop agriculture.

The Kingdom of Corn and Cotton

During the 250 years between the English settlement at Jamestown and the Civil War, southern agriculture was influenced by a constantly expanding frontier. It worked its way up the river valleys of Tidewater Virginia and North Carolina, down Virginia's Shenandoah Valley, and inland from coastal settlements at Charleston, Savannah, and New Orleans. Its progress was impeded by forests, which were laboriously cleared, and by areas of wetlands, many of which resisted early attempts at drainage and were passed over. Cash crops, frequently for export, were important from the start—first indigo, rice, sugar, and tobacco; later cotton. Cotton culture was helped immeasurably by Eli Whitney's invention of the cotton gin (1793), which vastly sped the separation of seed from the cotton fiber.

A system of large, slave-operated plantations proved quite adaptable to the scale economies and high labor requirements of cotton growing, particularly in the western half of the South.[4] But the slave plantation was by no means universal. Only about 25 percent of southern whites belonged to families that owned slaves and only about 6 percent of families owned 10 or more slaves, enough to constitute a "plantation."[5] Those who did not own slaves were frequently subsistence farmers, operating on a small scale, and producing a variety of crop and animal products. Overall, corn, not cotton, was the South's most widely grown crop. In 1849, the South produced more corn than the Midwest; the acreage in corn was far higher than that in cotton, even in the four deep-South states that produced most of the nation's cotton. Corn, unlike cotton, was at that time mostly consumed on the farm—fed to hogs, chickens, and cattle, distilled into corn whiskey, or eaten by humans in the form of corn pone, johnnycake, hominy, mush, corn bread, or other foods.[6] Cotton was the principal money crop and the region's major source of wealth, but corn was vital to the survival of humans and animals alike.

The Civil War eradicated slavery but did little long-term damage to southern agriculture. Indeed, cotton production expanded greatly after the war, filling the needs of a growing world textile industry. "By the late 1920s," observes historian Gilbert Fite, "cotton was more dominant in southern agriculture than it had been a half century before."[7] In 1929, the number of acres in cotton finally equaled that in corn, though even at this near-peak each occupied less than 7 percent of the South's total land area.

The plantation system proved surprisingly adaptable to the post-Civil War loss of slave labor. The ownership of many, perhaps most, plantation units remained intact, with the needed labor supplied under a new system, called sharecropping. Although there were several variants of sharecropping, its essence was the cultivation of individual fields within a large production unit by landless agricultural laborers. Seed, mules, and virtually all the other necessary inputs were provided on a centralized basis by the landowner.[8] The small size of the units worked by the croppers—30 to 40 acres per family was typical, often divided into several "patches"—was dictated by the amount of land that could be worked with primitive equipment and by the sheer size of the available labor force. In 1930, when sharecropper numbers reached their height, there were over three-quarters of a million croppers, cultivating 32 million acres of land. An even larger total acreage was cultivated under other forms of tenancy, with the owner providing fewer inputs but often still exerting substantial control over production decisions.

Of course, even at the peak of the sharecropper era there were still large numbers of individually owned and operated family farms, particularly in the Piedmont and Uplands. Most farms were diversified, though tobacco was a particularly important cash crop. Although some of the South's family farmers were prosperous and progressive, many more were hampered by small scale, lack of education, and difficulties in obtaining capital. As successive waves of technological change swept American agriculture, beginning in the 1880s, the southern farmer clung to old ways and paid the price in low productivity and growing poverty.

A panoramic view of what southern agriculture had become by the 1920s and early 1930s would present a generally bleak picture of backwardness, poverty, and inequality. Units of operation were small, even though much of the land was in large, often absentee, ownership. According to the 1930 Census of Agriculture, the average size of farming operations in the South was only 71 acres, compared with a national average of 157. The value of machinery and implements per acre on southern farms was only two-thirds the national average.[9] Tenancy was rampant; as agricultural prices fell and boll weevil damage continued during the 1920s, many small farmers who did own land lost their property and lapsed into tenancy.

A chronic problem in the South throughout the period between the Civil War and the Depression was the high rate of rural population growth and the lack of economic opportunity outside agriculture. The pressure of population on the land, coupled with low crop prices, led farmers to try to cultivate every available acre, even if it was very erodible or otherwise unsuitable for crops. As one contemporary report put it,

> the occupancy of poor agricultural soils by poor people is greatest in the southeastern third of the United States, especially in the hilly portions of this region. . . . People continue to farm poor land either because they do not have the means to acquire better land or because they cannot get jobs that offer them more for their labor. Poor land is cheap and therefore available to poor people. It is, in fact, the only kind of land that poor people can generally get.[10]

The principal crops cultivated on this land, corn and cotton, tended to deplete soil nutrients and to promote erosion, particularly when continuously cultivated over a period of many years.[11] But the impoverished southern farmer could not afford to rest

Worn-out, severely gullied, and ultimately abandoned, this Tennessee cotton farm is shown as it appeared in 1937. Most of this eroded land has now grown up in forest, and the scars of past abuse are not readily apparent to the casual observer.

the land or rotate crops. The result was declining yields and erosion so severe that in some Piedmont and Upland counties the topsoil layer has been washed away completely.

Persistence and Change

The 1930s marked a watershed in southern agriculture, the beginning of a period of rapid and wrenching modernization that has only recently been completed. Vestiges of the past are found throughout the present-day landscape. As one historian put it,

> the rural traveler sees constant reminders of the agricultural system that once characterized the South—vacant and decaying tenant houses, sagging barns, and empty mule lots. These museum pieces stand juxtaposed with brick houses and mobile homes, bulk tobacco curers, irrigation equipment, tractors and picking machines. The revolution in southern agriculture happened so quickly that artifacts of the old days linger on; indeed the change has come in little more than a generation.[12]

Decline in Traditional Crops. Perhaps the most striking change in southern agriculture in the last generation has been the decline in acreage of some of the most important traditional crops (see table 2.1). Most dramatic has been the change in cotton, where acreage fell sharply both absolutely and relative to other crops. From a peak of more than 23 million acres in the 1920s (figure 2.1), southern cotton acreage stood at only 2.9 million in 1982. Moreover, within the South, cotton has shifted westward to the Mississippi Valley. In the old cotton region, along the Georgia-Carolina Piedmont and Coastal Plain fewer than 350,000 acres of cotton were planted in 1982. As Gilbert Fite has observed,

> Cotton is still a highly profitable and significant crop in some sections of the South, but its predominance in the region's rural economy is gone. In no major agricultural region in the United States has so fundamental a change occurred. It is as if the Great Plains had abandoned wheat or the Middle West corn, for some other crop.[13]

There are many reasons for cotton's decline, and for its shifts within the South. Among them are the loss of cotton fiber markets to synthetics; the depredations of the boll weevil (which spread through the South in the first two decades of this century); the drastic acreage reductions required as a condition of price support under the Agricultural Adjustment Act of 1933; increased labor costs due to industrialization and outmigration; and the

Table 2.1
Acreage of Principal Crops in the South
(thousand acres)

	1929	1949	1969	1982
Corn	23,940	20,417	7,896	7,446
Cotton	23,448	13,031	4,711	2,909
Hay	6,449	10,942[1]	7,340[1]	7,886[1]
Peanuts	2,207	2,348	1,076	971
Rice	598	1,011	1,194	2,190
Soybeans	1,321	2,599	13,894	25,645
Tobacco	1,667	1,454[1]	837[1]	827[1]
Wheat	1,659	2,213	1,892	9,620

Figures for 1929 represent acres harvested, while figures for 1949, 1969, and 1982 represent acres planted, unless otherwise noted. Figures are for 11 southern states and do not include Texas or Oklahoma.

[1]Area harvested

Source: U.S. Department of Commerce, Bureau of the Census, *Census of Agriculture*; U.S. Department of Agriculture, *Agricultural Statistics*.

Figure 2.1
Cotton Acreage in 1929

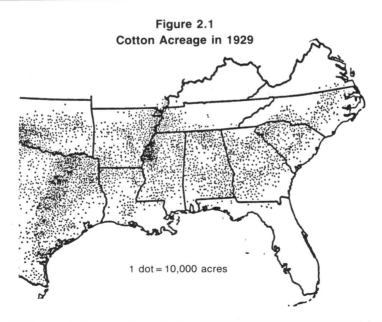

1 dot = 10,000 acres

Source: U.S. Department of Commerce, Bureau of the Census, *1930 Census of Agriculture* (Washington, D.C.: U.S. Government Printing Office).

severe depletion of continuously cropped soils by erosion. Large areas of the Piedmont and the Uplands, where cotton production had been widespread, found that their small parcels, hilly land, and uncertain rainfall were ill-adapted to the new reality of large-scale, mechanized production. Even the Delta, which was physically better suited to mechanized production, found itself in severe competition for a declining market with areas of higher productivity or lower production cost outside the South, primarily irrigated lands in California and Arizona and both irrigated and dry-land farms in West Texas. In 1980-82, these western areas produced more than two-thirds of the nation's cotton.

Corn acreage has also declined in the South, from 24 million acres in 1929, to 19 million in 1949, and only 7.4 million at its low point in 1972. Since then, acreage rose slightly in the late 1970s, but by 1982 the area planted was again only 7.4 million acres. Changing human dietary patterns and a drastic fall in the number of work animals kept on farms played a major role in reducing the demand for corn within the South. Also important was the severe competition that southern farmers faced from corn shipped in from the large, efficient farms of the Midwest. Once a common crop almost everywhere in the South, corn production is concentrated today in the South Atlantic Coastal Plain and in parts of Kentucky and Tennessee (see figure 2.2). Corn has also changed from being a subsistence crop consumed mostly on the farm where it was raised to a cash crop that enters the commercial economy.

Acreage of a third traditional southern crop, tobacco, has fallen from a high of 2.2 million acres (in 1930) to an average in recent years of fewer than a million. This modest acreage figure does not do justice to tobacco's importance in the farm economy of North Carolina and Kentucky and, to a lesser extent, several other southern states (see figure 2.2). Because of government programs that impose strict controls on planted acreage, tobacco is an extremely profitable crop for those fortunate enough to own an acreage "allotment." Net returns can top $1,000 per acre. In North Carolina, for example, tobacco is grown on only 3 percent of the farm acreage but produces 30 percent of the state's farm income. Because it is both profitable and labor intensive, tobacco is a mainstay of well over 100,000 small farms in the South—15 or 20 acres can support a family, and even a couple of acres can be a worthwhile endeavor for a part-time farmer.

Although generally not so profitable on a per-acre basis as tobacco, such crops as sugar cane, vegetables, fruits, tree nuts, and peanuts also occupy a relatively small total number of acres but make an important contribution to farm income in the South.

Mechanization. Beyond the decline in some important traditional crops, a second major change in southern agriculture has been the belated but by now substantially complete mechanization of crop production. Cotton, as traditionally cultivated in the South, was a very labor-intensive crop. As late as 1940, an acre of cotton required 98 hours of labor per season, compared with 25 for an acre of corn and about 11 for soybeans. Substantial amounts of hand labor were required at several times during the growing season—for planting, cultivating, thinning and weeding, and harvesting. Because of these requirements for labor, even large-scale southern planters were slower than their midwestern counterparts to adopt technologies (such as the farm tractor) that only mechanized part of the production process but did not enable them to retire the field hands and mules needed at other times of the season.[14] Moreover, until the beginning of World War Two, the South's huge agricultural labor force, which had virtually no alternative source of employment, kept wages extremely low.

The expansion of American industry during and after the war gave the children of southern sharecroppers and tenant farmers a new opportunity to better their lives. Millions moved to big cities in the North; others to southern centers such as Memphis, Atlanta, and Norfolk. During the same period, a number of technological innovations became available. By the mid-1950s, the southern cotton farmer finally could employ labor-saving technologies that spanned the crop cycle—tractors for plowing and cultivation, herbicides for weed control, and mechanical pickers. Debate still continues over whether mechanization forced southern farmworkers to leave agriculture, or whether their migration caused a shortage of farm labor that spurred farmers to mechanize. In any event, mechanization in cotton has been recent and rapid. Labor expended on an acre of cotton fell to 66 hours in the late 1950s, to 30 in the late 1960s, and to only 6 hours in the late 1970s.

Mechanization also affected other southern crops. Farmers found that it was cheaper to feed their pigs or chickens with corn

Figure 2.2
Location of Principal Southern Crops

Cotton Harvested, 1982
1 dot = 5,000 acres

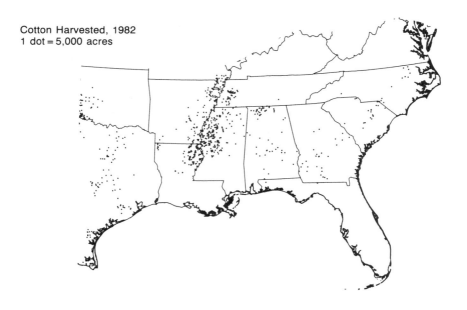

Soybeans Harvested for Beans, 1982
1 dot = 10,000 acres

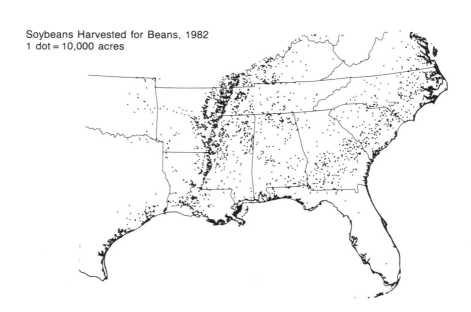

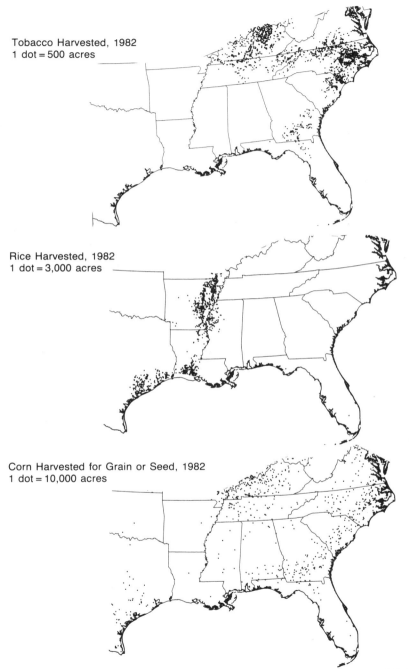

Tobacco Harvested, 1982
1 dot = 500 acres

Rice Harvested, 1982
1 dot = 3,000 acres

Corn Harvested for Grain or Seed, 1982
1 dot = 10,000 acres

Source: U.S. Department of Commerce, Bureau of the Census, *1982 Census of Agriculture* (Washington, D.C.: U.S. Government Printing Office, 1985).

produced by efficient, mechanized midwestern farms than to grow it using traditional methods. Some southern farmers, particularly those on flatter land and more fertile soils in the Coastal Plain and in western Kentucky and Tennessee, adopted the new technologies and substituted tractors for mules and chemicals for cultivators. To do this, they generally had to enlarge their scale of operations, either by buying more land or by renting it. Many more farmers, particularly in the hilly and sometimes worn-out land of the Piedmont and Uplands, could not compete. Tens of thousands left the land and moved to the cities.

The contrasts between farming systems of the 1930s and those of the 1970s in the South are perhaps the greatest, the most distinctive, that can be drawn in any American region during that time-span. With few exceptions, the region's agriculture now is wholly mechanized and capital intensive. What cannot be done with machines is rarely done.

MERLE C. PRUNTY, in James Heyl, ed., *The South: A VadeMecum* (Atlanta: Association of American Geographers, 1973)

Soybeans, which were not widespread until after the 1930s, have relied on mechanization from the start. Particularly in the Delta, they are raised in fields that are large even by midwestern standards and planted and harvested with the largest equipment available. Tobacco, the most labor intensive of southern crops, was the last to feel the impact of mechanization. Labor requirements per acre did not even begin to fall until the late 1960s.[15] The change in the last 15 years has been dramatic, though labor requirements, at over 200 hours per acre, are still many times those of other crops, and one important sector, the burley tobacco raising of Kentucky and Tennessee, is still largely unmechanized.

Mechanization had an important impact not only on labor requirements but on the whole economic structure of agriculture. Just as it had adjusted to the loss of slave labor after the Civil War, the plantation responded to mechanization by changing tenure arangements. The sharecropping system became extinct as the plantation again became cultivated as a single economic unit, with a fraction of the former croppers retained as wage laborers.[16] The high costs and significant scale economies associated with mechanization helped transform many of the sharecropper plantations into mechanized "neoplantations," where large acreages were once again cultivated as an undivided whole. They also made feasible a new kind of farm unit, dubbed the "fragmented neoplantation" by one geographer.[17] This is a group of fields, scattered within a radius of up to several miles, but operated by hired labor as a single unit. Machinery is moved from one site to another as needed. Fields might be purchased by the cultivator or rented from smaller farmers, or their heirs, who have given up farming and moved away.

The same economic rationale also motivated family farmers to expand the scale of their operations, sometimes by purchasing more land, sometimes by renting it. Today, more than half the harvested cropland in the South is part of an agricultural operation containing some owned and some rented land. As a result, tenancy has lost some of its stigma—today's tenant may have more wealth in land and machinery than the person from whom he rents the land.

Soybeans. A third major development in southern crop agriculture has been the phenomenal increase in the amount of land devoted to soybeans.[18] Over the last 50 years, the soybean has changed from a minor crop, used more for forage than as an oilseed, to an agricultural staple that is nationally second only to corn in value of production. In most recent years, soybeans have been the nation's leading agricultural export. In 1929, the South had only 1.3 million acres in soybeans; by 1964, there were 8.8 million; by 1982, there were over 25 million. Soybeans are now the leading crop in terms of acreage in every southern state except Virginia. In value of production, soybeans are the number one crop in Alabama, Mississippi, Arkansas, and Tennessee, second to tobacco in Virginia, Kentucky, and North Carolina, and second to peanuts in Georgia. In South Carolina, soybeans and tobacco have alternated as the leading crop in dollar value in recent years.

The increased popularity of soybean growing in the South was the product of changes in both demand and supply. On the demand side, U.S. entry into World War Two created a need for substitutes for animal-based fats and oils; by the war's end, many Americans had become accustomed to cooking with vegetable oil rather than lard. Also, a continuing expansion in meat consumption (first in the United States and later abroad) created a demand for the high-protein animal feed that is produced as a by-product of soybean crushing. On the supply side, many southern cotton farmers were casting about for a substitute to occupy fields removed from cotton production by acreage controls. Because farmers could choose which land they wished to idle, they tended to concentrate cotton production on the well-drained, loamy soils, abandoning the wetter, clay soil types where cotton yields were low. Soybeans are better suited to such soils and proved an excellent substitute crop on this abandoned cotton land. Moreover, soybeans require little labor, so the loss of the sharecropper force did not constrain expansion. Southern soybean acreage plateaued in the late 1960s, then rose again when agricultural exports boomed in the 1970s.

Not all of the land newly occupied by soybeans had previously been devoted to cotton. Millions of acres of low-lying land in stream valleys in Mississippi, Arkansas, and Louisiana were put into soybeans after being cleared of hardwood forest. The process was aided greatly by the development of mechanical earth-moving equipment and by federally subsidized drainage and flood control projects. Once drained and cleared of trees, the land could be "leveled" into huge flat fields ideal for mechanized cultivation. Other land brought into soybeans, particularly in the Coastal Plain, had formerly been used for growing corn—indeed, on many such sites either corn or soybeans may still be planted, depending on the farmer's estimate of which will be more profitable in the season ahead (see figure 2.2).

Although by no means as important as soybeans, rice, too, has grown in importance to the South. Its acreage has expanded greatly (mostly in Arkansas and Louisiana) in the last several decades. In 1982, 2.2 million acres of rice were planted in the South, more than two-thirds of the national total. As with soybeans, export demand is very important and production is highly mechanized. Much of the land devoted to rice has been reclaimed from wetlands.

The Shifting Cropland Base. A final change in southern crop agriculture has been a very considerable alteration in both the amount and the location of cultivated land within the South. Figure 2.3 shows that cultivated cropland ("cropland used for crops") was at levels of approximately 63 to 65 million acres

Figure 2.3
Cultivated Cropland, 1929–1983
(in million acres)

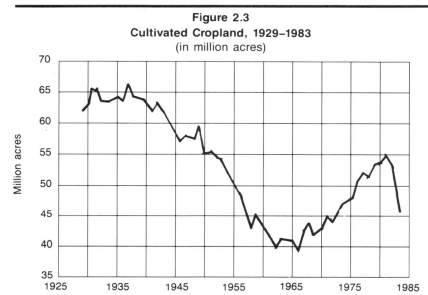

Source: Based on "cropland used for crops" series; 1929-38 data from H. Thomas Frey, U.S. Department of Agriculture, Economic Research Service; 1939-83 data from U.S. Department of Agriculture, *Economic Indicators of the Farm Sector, 1983* (Washington, D.C.: U.S. Government Printing Office, 1984). Data in both cases include West Virginia, which in census years during this period had between .7 million and 1.7 million acres of cropland used for crops. Data do not include Texas or Oklahoma.

Figure 2.4
Land Formerly Cropped

1 dot = 10,000 acres

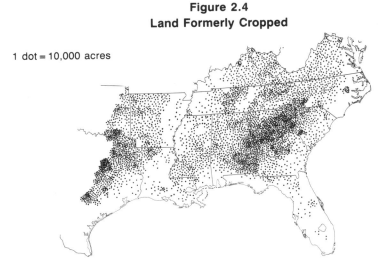

Acreage calculated as the difference between 1982 acreage harvested and the maximum acreage harvested in any year since 1880.

Source: Map drawn by H. Thomas Frey, U.S. Department of Agriculture, based on *Census of Agriculture* data.

through the 1930s. It then began a long decline, as millions of southern farmers, many of them sharecroppers, abandoned agriculture. A modern low point of fewer than 40 million acres was reached in the mid-1960s. Some of the land was taken permanently out of production and reverted to trees or was used as pasture; some was temporarily idled under government acreage reduction programs.

Subsequently, there was a modest but fairly steady increase, which picked up speed as agricultural exports boomed during the 1970s. Between 1974 and 1981, nearly all of the idle cropland and some of the pasture was put back into crop production: by 1981 cropland used for crops stood at 55.0 million acres, the highest level since 1951. It dropped slightly (to 53.6 million acres) in 1982, and then fell by 7.3 million acres in 1983, largely as a result of the federal payment-in-kind (PIK) acreage control program.

Change from agriculture to forest has been gradual rather than dramatic, ubiquitous rather than concentrated, and the map of change looks like nothing quite so much as a Rorschach test run amok. The land that has been changed from agriculture to woodland does not lie in large solid blocks, but consists of small bits and pieces that are scattered all over the county.

JOHN FRASER HART, *Annals of the Association of American Geographers,* December 1980

Although the amount of southern land used for crops in 1982 was high by the standards of the last several decades, its distribution was quite different from that prevailing in the 1930s. Most of the southern states reached their peak cropland acreage during the 1930s—for example, Georgia's 1982 cultivated cropland acreage was little more than half what it had been in 1935. Yet Florida, Arkansas, and Louisiana have had a greater acreage in crops during the last few years than ever before in their history.

Figure 2.4 provides a dramatic illustration of how crop farming has declined from its historic peak in many southern counties, particularly in the Piedmont and some of the less fertile parts of the Uplands. The figure maps, by county, the difference between acreage harvested for crops in 1982 and the acreage harvested in the year of peak crop acreage (since 1880). It thus traces the "acreage formerly cropped." During the 1920s and 1930s, much of this land had been devoted to corn or cotton.

Much of the *increase* in cropland area took place where land that had never before been cultivated was put into crop production. In many cases, the land was made arable only by drainage, forest clearing, or irrigation. In Arkansas, for example, several hundred thousand acres of bottomland hardwood forest in the Mississippi Delta were put into agriculture during the 1960s, even as long-time cropland continued to go out of cultivation in the central and western portions of the state. Likewise, in Florida and Louisiana, new lands (many of them formerly wetlands) were put into production at the same time that worn-out cotton land elsewhere in the state was going out of crops and into pasture or forest. The same thing has happened in some states where total cropland has remained below the 1930s levels. In North Carolina, for example, large areas of cleared and drained land in the portion of the state bordering the Atlantic were brought into crop production during the 1970s, despite the fact that the 1982 crop area statewide was far below levels reached in the mid-1930s.

Figures 2.5 and 2.6 show the location of cropland increase for the periods 1949-69 and 1969-82. During the earlier period, nearly all of the cropland increase took place in the Delta, mostly on cleared and drained wetlands. There was also some new land put into production in Florida. During the 1969-82 period, however, the areas of increase were more dispersed. Concentrations of new cropland are quite evident in the Delta, in coastal North Carolina, and in the winter vegetable growing area of South Florida; yet there were small areas of cropland increase throughout the Coastal Plain.

Considered together, figures 2.4, 2.5, and 2.6 illustrate the drastic shifts in the location of cultivated cropland in the South over the past 50 years, underlining the fact that simply considering net changes in area cropped would greatly understate the amount of change that has occurred. The shifts in location have two explanations. First, they are associated with a change in crops. As soybeans and rice replaced cotton and corn, farmers chose soils most suitable to the new crops. Drained wetland soils in Arkansas, for example, were simply more productive in soybeans than the old Piedmont soils abandoned by cotton farmers would have been.

Second, there was a general but very difficult to document movement toward better soils, even aside from change in the crop mix.[19] The massive outmigration of the rural farm population removed much of the local pressure to cultivate steep, eroded, or infertile soils. And various federal acreage control programs were set up in such a way that they encouraged farmers to take marginal land out of production and to concentrate on the most productive areas within their individual farms. Within any given area, the land remaining in cultivation tended to be the better land. Cotton, for example, was grown much less widely than before, but its production was concentrated in those areas where productivity was highest. Moreover, mechanization favored flatter areas where fields could be large and cultivation equipment could be easily turned. This had the effect of moving farming out of the steep, broken fields of the Piedmont and Uplands.

In general, the effect of both the shifting crop mix and the movement to better soils regardless of crop was to displace crop agriculture out of the Piedmont and Uplands and to increasingly concentrate it in the Delta and the South Atlantic Coastal Plain.

The Natural Foundations of Southern Agriculture

The great changes that have swept over southern agriculture in recent decades have erased much of what has been distinctive historically about the South's farming systems. To be sure, there are many important holdovers from former eras: a large (though much diminished) number of small farms, "neoplantations" that use hired labor to cultivate very large acreages, local areas based on traditional "southern crops" such as cotton and tobacco, and a troublesome legacy of degraded soils. But, in many ways, the South's agriculture currently is more like that of the rest of the country than at any time previously. In terms of acreage, its principal crops are the same as those of the nation as a whole: soybeans, corn, wheat, and hay. Today's southern farmer watches the international grain markets as avidly as his midwestern counterpart. And, at least on large-scale farms, the level of management and technology in the South differs little from that prevalent nationally.

We can therefore expect that the forces molding the future of crop agriculture in the South will be the same forces that deter-

Figure 2.5
Increase in Cropland Acreage, 1949-1969

   1 dot = 10,000-acre increase, in counties that had a net increase in cropland acreage.

Map excludes cropland used only for pasture.

Source: James Horsfield and Norman Landgren, *Cropland Trends across the Nation*, Agricultural Economic Report No. 494 (Washington, D.C.: U.S. Government Printing Office, 1982).

Figure 2.6
Increase in Cropland Acreage, 1969-1982

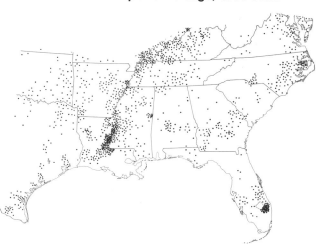

   1 dot = 5,000-acre increase, in counties that had a net increase in cropland acreage.

Map excludes cropland used only for pasture.

Source: Map drawn by H. Thomas Frey, U.S. Department of Agriculture, based on *Census of Agriculture* data.

mine the outlook for U.S. agriculture as a whole: export demand, new technology, government subsidy, and regulation. Increasingly, what makes the South's response to these forces different from the rest of the nation will not be tradition but natural endowments, the fundamental factors of land, sun, soil fertility, and water. These differ markedly from those found in other agriculturally important parts of the country, and understanding them is essential to understanding the potentials and limitations of future development of crop agriculture in the South.

Southern farming is still different in many ways, but today it is closer to the mainstream of American agriculture than it has ever been.

GEORGE L. ROBSON, JR., and ROY V. SCOTT,
Agricultural History, January 1979

Land

One of the South's most important agricultural assets is its potential to expand the area devoted to crops beyond the current level. Table 2.2 shows the actual 1982 cropland base for the United States, and for selected regions, as well as the amount of land identified by the U.S. Department of Agriculture as having high or medium potential for conversion to cropland. (The potential for conversion was estimated on the basis of physical soil characteristics and the commodity prices and development and production costs currently prevailing.)

For the United States as a whole, there are .363 acres of potential cropland for each acre now used for crops. The Corn Belt and the Lake States, center of the nation's corn and soybean production, have a much smaller expansion potential—fewer than .25 acres for each acre presently in crops. By contrast, the South is extremely well endowed with potential cropland, having .709 acres for each acre presently devoted to crops. Put another way, the Corn Belt and Lake States (combined total) currently have more than twice as much cropland as does the South. But because most of the land in the Midwest that is suited to crops is already in crop use, the Corn Belt and Lake States combined have only about two-thirds of the total expansion potential of the South.

Although all of the southern states are above average in the ratio of potential to present cropland (table 2.3), the ratio is much higher in the Southeast than in the Delta. Florida, Alabama,

Virginia, and North Carolina are particularly high in potential cropland, while in Arkansas, Mississippi, and South Carolina much of the land economically suitable for crop agriculture has already been converted.

Table 2.2

Arable Land, 1982
(thousand acres)

	Present cropland	Potential cropland	Potential cropland per acre of present cropland
U.S. (48 states)	421,402	152,974	.363
South (11 states)	61,758	43,769	.709
Corn Belt	92,394	17,878	.193
Lake States	43,924	10,716	.244

Current cropland data differ slightly from those used elsewhere in the text because of differences in sources. Potential cropland is land having "high" or "medium" potential for crop use.

Source: U.S. Soil Conservation Service, unpublished final data from 1982 National Resources Inventory, July 1984. Data do not include Texas or Oklahoma.

Table 2.3
Potential Cropland per Acre of Present Cropland, 1982

	Potential acres
U.S. (48 states)	.363
Florida	1.263
Alabama	1.138
Virginia	.994
North Carolina	.978
Georgia	.738
Tennessee	.709
Kentucky	.557
Louisiana	.531
South Carolina	.487
Mississippi	.473
Arkansas	.425

Source: See Table 2.2

The land from which the South can draw its potential cropland is currently about evenly divided between pasture- and forestland. Unfortunately, no data are available to describe how much this land produces in its current use. One might suspect that land sufficiently fertile to warrant conversion to cropland would be among the better pasture- or forestland. For example, pastureland with crop potential is likely to have deeper soils, flatter grades, and fewer soil nutrient limitations than would be true of ordinary pastureland.

How does the quality of potential cropland compare with that of land already in crop use? The U.S. Department of Agriculture classifies land into eight "land capability classes" based on soil characteristics and limitations to cultivation. Land in the top three classes is generally considered to be most naturally suited to crop production. In the United States, some 85 percent of current cropland is in capability classes I-III; of potential cropland, only 74 percent is in these classes.[20] In the South, potential cropland also has a lower average capability than land currently cropped, but the difference is not so large. Of current cropland in the South, 86 per cent is in classes I-III, compared to 79 percent for potential cropland.

Overall, it seems safe to say that, relative to national averages, the South has an unusually large supply of land that could, if demand for crops warrants, be brought into crop production and that this land does not appear to be markedly less productive than that already used for crops.

One important limitation on using the South's potential cropland is that a very large proportion of it either is subject to erosion or has excessive soil moisture. (It is impossible to say, however, how much of the latter is so wet as to be biologically classified as "wetland.") Soil moisture can be reduced by drainage and levee construction, though this can be extremely expensive and still may not offer complete crop protection against water damage in some years.[21] Erosion is a more subtle threat to soil productivity: its effects may not be apparent for many decades. Some 53 percent of the potential cropland in the South is considered subject to an erosion hazard. If this land were cultivated for crops and subject to the same level of erosion control as practiced on current cropland in the same soil class, we could expect average erosion of over 13 tons per acre per year.

This is more than double the 5 tons per acre per year that soil scientists consider "tolerable" without long-term damage to soil fertility.

Soil Fertility

Although the South is well endowed in terms of potential cropland acreage, it fares poorly in terms of native soil fertility. Except for Florida, most of the soils of the Piedmont and Coastal Plain belong to a family of soils called Ultisols. (Florida, unique in this as in so many other ways, has mainly sandy Entisols and Spodisols, types that for our purposes can generally be thought of as beyond the worst of the Ultisols on a continuum of negative intrinsic soil properties.)

Ultisols are relatively old soils developed under a warm, humid climate. Dozens of centuries of rainfall and high soil temperatures have weathered these soils, leaching away mineral fertility and making the soil acid. Most southern Ultisols are also limited by their physical structure. Over geological time, they slowly settle, forming a hard subsurface layer that interferes with plant rooting. They are low in organic matter and do not store water well. Overall, in most of the soil characteristics important to crop growth, southern Ultisols are quite inferior to the fertile soils of the Midwest. This difference is clearly reflected in crop yields. For example, in 1982 the average yield per acre for corn was 134 bushels in Illinois, only 66 bushels in Alabama; for soybeans, the yield was 38 bushels per acre in Iowa, 22 in South Carolina. (Not only are average yields in the South lower, they also vary more from year to year. This is mainly due to the weather, however, rather than to soil quality.) Soils in the Uplands and Delta are not in the Ultisol family, but they, too, have productivity problems, primarily connected with cooler temperatures and excessive slope, or poor drainage, respectively.

In addition to having naturally low fertility, millions of acres of southern soils are moderately to severely eroded, the result of decades of continuous corn and cotton production under poor soil management. Some of this land is still used for crops, though large areas have been planted in trees and are slowly recovering their fertility. (In the words of one long-time South Georgia farmer, now raising pine trees, his land was "cottoned to death.")

Despite these fertility problems, the South's cropland can be made quite productive under skillful management. In many places, yields can be brought up almost to midwestern levels, though this requires considerable care and sizable capital investment. Low mineral fertility and soil acidity can be corrected by applying fertilizer and lime. Subsoil "hardpans" can be broken up with special cultivating equipment. Careful management of crop residues can slowly build up the organic matter in soils. Overall, soil fertility problems are obstacles to capturing some of the South's other natural advantages for agriculture, but they do not appear to be insurmountable ones.

Growing Season and Sunlight

Another of the South's agricultural assets is its latitude and proximity to the warm Gulf and Caribbean maritime influence. Warm and humid air masses from these tropical waters flow generally into the region from the south and track northeastward. The ocean itself exerts a further moderating influence on areas close to the coast. As a result, the South as a whole is bathed throughout the year by mild weather. The entire Coastal Plain from Texas to North Carolina experiences fewer than 50 days yearly with minimum temperatures below 32° F. The frost-free period for much of the Piedmont and nearly all of the Coastal Plain extends from about March 30 to November 1, a growing season of at least 215 days annually (see figure 2.7). Even in the upper Delta and the Uplands, the growing season is generally above 200 days, except at the higher elevations. And from South Carolina to Texas, the frost-free period in the Coastal Plain is about 240 days, while immediately along the coast it reaches 270 days or more.

Overall, the South has a consistent 30- to 90-day seasonal advantage over the Corn Belt and Great Plains. On a weighted basis, the average advantage is considerably better than 60 days, since most southern crop production is concentrated in or near the Coastal Plain rather than near the region's northern limit.

Southern winters are relatively mild. The most severe isotherm encompassing the region is a 25° F. normal daily minimum temperature, occurring in January. The milder Coastal Plain has a corresponding normal daily minimum temperature of 35° F. or higher from Texas through North Carolina. These mild minimum temperatures have allowed most of the South to employ true spring wheat types for winter culture. This has permitted what is called "double-cropping," since a second warm season crop (usually soybeans) is planted following wheat harvest.

The relative distribution of solar radiation in the southern states has positive and negative sides. In theory, peak radiation intensities should compare favorably with the Corn Belt and Great Plains because of the higher clear-sky radiation intensities as one approaches the equator. However, the greater cloudiness of southern skies during the summer tends to reduce this advantage by intercepting sunlight before it reaches the ground. During the summer, therefore, the South gets about the same radiation accumulation at ground level as do the Corn Belt and the Great Plains and somewhat less than the Southwest. During the winter months, however, longer days in the South give it some advantage over other areas. The South also has the distinct advantage

Figure 2.7
Mean Length of Frost-Free Period

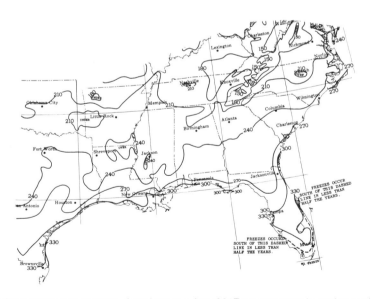

Numbers represent average days between last 32°F temperature in spring and first 32° temperature in autumn.

Source: U.S. Department of Commerce, Environmental Science Services Administration, *Climatic Atlas of the United States* (Washington, D.C.: U.S. Government Printing Office, 1968), p. 31.

at that time of milder temperatures, allowing this radiation to be used in double cropping. In the North, contrastingly, the winter radiation is wasted. On an annual basis, total solar radiation accumulation patterns put the South somewhat higher than the Midwest but lower than the Southwest. (Typical annual figures for mean daily solar radiation, in langleys, are 453 for Tampa, 404 for Charleston, 385 for Little Rock, and 396 for Atlanta, compared with 345 for Ames, Iowa, and 520 for Phoenix, Arizona.)

Water

The South has enormous supplies of fresh water in the form of rainfall, surface water flowing through streams and creeks, and groundwater. Water availability gives the South, vis-à-vis other regions, some substantial advantages in growing crops, including irrigation possibilities that have barely been exploited.

But the South's water supply is not unlimited and offers constraints on, as well as opportunities for, expanded crop production. The South's annual rainfall must be counted as a mixed blessing. Total annual rainfall in the region is roughly double that of the Great Plains and about 50 percent more than in most of the Corn Belt (see figure 2.8). This rainfall, however, is not meted out evenly over time or space. In the winter months, rainfall is usually less intense and occurs regionally. During these months, soil moisture is usually recharged even in the presence of a growing crop, since rainfall generally exceeds potential evapotranspiration. (Evapotranspiration is the sum of evaporation of water from the soil and the water vapor exuded by growing plants.) From late spring through early fall, rainfall intensities become severe, as rains become associated with intense localized thundershowers. Less water is stored in the soil, largely because the high intensities exceed maximum infiltration rates, resulting in runoff. In addition, the South's hot summer climate means that rainfall totals over this time period average less than potential evapotranspiration.

The South also has relatively wide year-to-year variability in rainfall. For example, while Fort Smith, Arkansas, has averaged a quite respectable 42 inches of rainfall annually over the last century, it has received as little as 20 inches (in 1917) and as much as 72 inches (in 1945).[22] Temporary drought is no stranger to the South. As recently as 1983, an almost complete lack of late summer rain reduced corn and soybean yields to a fraction of their normal level. Not atypically, the winter and spring of 1983 had seen heavy rains over much of the South. In Mississippi and Arkansas that year, many farmers suffered severe flood damage to their winter crops, then lost the summer crop to drought.

The South's seasonal and intraseasonal rainfall variations can be partially evened out through irrigation. Irrigation is not needed in parts of the South, and is not economically feasible in others, but it appears that there are many areas where irrigation would be worthwhile if the demand for crops warranted it. The capital costs of introducing irrigation are substantial and range from less than $200 per acre for furrow irrigation to about $500 per acre for center-pivot sprinkler systems. Nonetheless, because the need

Figure 2.8
Average Annual Precipitation

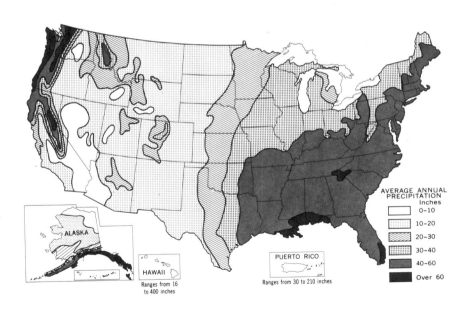

Source: U.S. Water Resources Council, *The Nation's Water Resources* (Washington, D.C.: U.S. Government Printing Office, 1968), p. 3-2-2.

for applying water is only intermittent and because systems can usually be supplied from runoff water collected in ponds, from nearby streams, or from shallow wells, the expenditure on pumping fuel is low compared to what it is in more arid areas.

High runoff, shallow water tables, and abundant streamflow provide substantial surface-water resources and water-storage capability in most parts of the South. Recharge of shallow aquifers is accomplished in most years by the high infiltration rates of most southern soils and the annual occurrence of prolonged wet weather in winter. Thus, less of the water pumped for irrigation in the South is "mined," that is, consumed and permanently lost, than in some western areas, such as the Ogallala aquifer region of the Great Plains. Nevertheless, in a few areas where irrigation is widely used, particularly in eastern Arkansas and southwestern Georgia, groundwater is being pumped in such quantities that aquifers are being depleted.

Pest Problems

The South's mild climate and frequent rainfall predispose the region to an array of agricultural pest and pestilence problems more serious than anywhere else in the nation. These include a profusion of plant-damaging insects, diseases, nematodes, and fungi. Many of these organisms are found only in the South; others affect agriculture nationwide but are particularly virulent in the warmer portions of the South, where winter temperatures do not get low enough to seasonally reduce pest populations.

Agricultural pests are an important factor in reducing crop yields or in raising costs, thereby limiting the competitive advantage of southern farmers. For example, compared to their counterparts in the Southwest, cotton farmers in the southern states expend more resources on insect control, lowering their net profits even when effective control has produced comparable yields.

In some areas, pests have made certain types of agriculture completely uneconomic. While southern beer consumption is sufficient to support a local base of malting barley production (highly profitable in the Great Plains), southern small grain breeders have never seriously attempted to produce adapted barley varieties due to the severity of smut and rust problems, which preclude meeting the quality standards required by the malting industry. Similarly, there is a reluctance to purchase white southern corn for use in the corn-chip snack industry due to contamination levels from disease and insects. In the same vein, use of southern corn supplies in preparation of animal feed rations is often a problem because of high levels of aflatoxin, a fungal contaminant that can be fatally toxic to animals at even low levels of contamination.

Because of the number and severity of these problems, the South would benefit more than other sections of the country if there is further progress in pest control. For example, the recent eradication of the boll weevil in parts of North Carolina has caused a modest resurgence in cotton cultivation and even has resulted in the conversion of some soybean fields to cotton. Similarly, the development of ways to control endemic cattle diseases and parasites was a major factor in the post World War Two expansion of the South's cattle industry (see chapter 4).

Another consequence of the South's pest problems has been an extremely high use of pesticides. Although the South accounts for only 14 percent of the nation's cultivated cropland, it consumes 43 percent of the insecticides and 22 percent of the herbicides used by farmers.[23] Not only does this greatly increase the southern farmer's production costs relative to those in other regions, it has impacts on environmental quality (see chapter 6) and makes southern farmers unusually vulnerable to economic loss when various substances are banned for health or environmental reasons or when pests acquire resistance to chemicals that had successfully controlled them in the past.

The South's pest problems are complex and serious. But pest problems tend to be easier to surmount, either by direct control or by new crop management systems, than even more fundamental constraints such as growing seasons or rainfall. Any future national progress in understanding and controlling agricultural pests should aid the South more than competing agricultural regions; conversely, any retrogression in pest control could differentially damage the South.

Projecting Cropland Demands

The future demand for southern cropland depends on a number of factors, each subject to uncertainty. The first is the future national and world demand for the crops that the South is suited

to producing. For simplicity, this discussion concentrates on four
of the South's major crops: soybeans, corn, wheat, and cotton.[24]
A large portion of the nation's output of each of these crops is
exported, with exports as a percentage of U.S. production
(1980-82 average) ranging from 60 percent for wheat to 45 percent for cotton, 43 percent for soybeans, and 27 percent for corn.

Although exports of these commodities have risen substantially over the last decade, U.S. domestic consumption has increased
much more slowly. Between 1970 and 1980, U.S. consumption
of corn rose by only 18 percent, while wheat and cotton consumption actually declined. Only soybeans showed substantial
growth—up 42 percent—though in this case, too, exports grew
more rapidly than did domestic use.

In the future, it seems likely that domestic consumption of these
commodities will go up little more than the rate of domestic
population growth, now a bit less than 1 percent annually. Most
Americans are so well fed and clothed that much additional
growth in direct per-capita consumption of these commodities
seems unlikely. Moreover, while a great deal of corn and soybean meal is consumed domestically in the form of livestock products, trends in meat consumption seem to be in the direction of
slow overall growth, with some tendency to shift toward types
of meat that require less grain feeding (see chapter 4).

If there is to be substantial growth in the total demand for the
crops now grown in the South, it will have to come mainly from
abroad. Although world population is expected to expand about
1.8 percent yearly over the next two decades, U.S. agricultural
exports are only tenuously linked with foreign population growth.
Most U.S. exports of agricultural commodities, despite the existence of chronic world hunger, are made to paying customers.
Thus, far more important than population growth is the rate of
foreign economic growth, both in the developed countries and
in the developing nations that now import about one-third of the
total value of U.S. farm exports. Also important are the performance of the agricultural sectors in countries that import U.S.
farm products, the exchange rate between the dollar and foreign
currencies (which helps determine how costly U.S. farm products
will be to foreign customers), and the competitiveness of the handful of other grain- and cotton-exporting nations, namely, Canada,

Farming the Federal Programs

Some of the crops traditionally associated with the South, among them cotton, peanuts, rice, and tobacco, have been prominent beneficiaries of federal programs aimed at supporting farm commodity prices. This leads one to speculate whether southern agriculture as a whole is unusually dependent on federal price supports—and to wonder whether current attempts to reduce the cost to the government of farm programs might differentially hurt farmers in the South.

The answer is "probably not," at least in terms of direct impacts. Overall, the South's crop mix is somewhat *less* skewed toward subsidized crops than is the national average.* This is to a large extent due to the importance in the South of soybeans, which receive little or no direct subsidy. Also, while cotton is the most highly subsidized major crop in terms of government price

support program expenditures per dollar of production, wheat and corn, which are less important in the South than they are nationally, also enjoy high levels of subsidy. (Tobacco does not receive a high subsidy by this cost-to-the-government measure, because the restrictions on planted acreage raise prices to the consumer but cost the government little.) Finally, for the individual crops, the percentage of southern farmers participating in federal commodity programs is about the same as that for the nation as a whole. Thus, while cuts in federal farm program expenditures would certainly hurt, southern farmers would most likely be hurt no more, and possibly less, than farmers nationally.

Indirect impacts of government price supports may also be significant, but they do not appear to have been studied systematically. For example, removal of the federal acreage controls on corn might stimulate Corn Belt producers to greatly increase their production, thus indirectly hurting southern soybean producers, whose output competes to some extent with corn as an animal feed.

---

*The impacts were calculated by weighting the 1982 southern and national values of output for major crops by a degree-of-subsidy measure calculated as the ratio for each crop of total government program expenditure 1970-82 to total value of output.

Australia, Argentina, Brazil, Thailand, France, and (for cotton only) the USSR. Of some significance is the possibility of any change in U.S. policy on food aid, which is not now very liberal but which could change in the future in the face of increasingly severe Third World food shortages.

Subject to these uncertainties, a number of forecasts of U.S. agricultural exports have been made, some quantitative and some only qualitative. One comprehensive and recent projection comes from

Resources for the Future (RFF), a Washington, D.C.- based research organization.[25] The projection assumes that world population growth, as well as economic growth, will slow between now and the year 2000 compared to rates of the past decade. This, combined with relatively good agricultural production in the rest of the world, would substantially reduce the rate of growth of U.S. agricultural exports. Even so, by the year 2000, total demand for U.S. grain is projected to be 31 percent greater than the 1979-81 average, that of oilseeds (mainly soybeans) 42 percent greater, and cotton about 20 percent greater. By the year 2000, export markets would be even more important to U.S. farmers than they are now. The projection also assumes that agricultural productivity will grow somewhat more slowly than in the past, though productivity growth would still be substantial.

Using RFF's "intermediate" projection (alternative projections are higher and lower), by the year 2000, the U.S. would need 10.2 million acres more in cereal grains, 13.3 million additional acres in oilseeds, and .9 million in cotton, for a total of 24.4 million more acres. For the year 2020, the projection is for 28.6 million added acres in cereals and 33.2 in oilseeds, for a total of 61.8 million additional acres (cotton acreage was not projected). This projection does not, of course, include vegetables, tree crops, hay, and other crops, which could either require more land or less, depending on demand and productivity. It also does not account for the possibility of multiple-cropping, which could reduce total acreage requirements.

Another recent projection has been made by the Economic Research Service, U.S. Department of Agriculture.[26] It indicates that the most likely prospect is for U.S. food exports to grow by about 3 percent yearly over the next two decades, a rate significantly lower than the 8 percent recorded in the 1970s. Combined with slow-growing domestic demand and expected productivity growth somewhat higher than in the last decade, this would imply about a 10 percent cumulative increase in cropland area by the year 2000, with most of the added acres in soybeans. The projection also stresses the possibility of increased year-to-year volatility in crop prices and growing dependence of U.S. farming on foreign markets.

A notably pessimistic view of the future of U.S. agriculture, including long-run projections, has been taken in a recent study by the Complex Systems Research Center of the University of New Hampshire.[27] The researchers point to the possibility that future technological change in agriculture could be low, that soil erosion might seriously reduce the productivity of agricultural land, and that the amount of fossil fuel energy available to agriculture could be limited. Under various scenarios assuming these conditions, the U.S. would be increasingly unable to meet even the current level of farm exports, much less expand them. By the early years of the 21st century, some runs of the Center's model indicate that U.S. food export capacity could drop to near zero.

The assumptions needed to reach such a result are quite extreme. But the analysis does highlight a major uncertainty in the future of U.S. agriculture. Much of the increase in output per acre recorded over the past two decades has been based on increasing applications of nonlabor inputs to the land, particularly water and energy. These inputs, plus a relatively high level of technological change, have masked declines (of unknown amount) in soil fertility associated with erosion, salinization, and expansion of farming onto marginal lands. Projections of future increases in agricultural productivity must make the somewhat dubious assumption that ever greater quantities of inputs will be available at a reasonable price or assume that technology will increasingly enable us to squeeze more output from the resources that we have.

Given the wide range of these projections, a qualitative view of U.S. export demand might be as accurate as one derived from a formal model. Most experts presently believe that U.S. food exports will grow, but at a rate moderately to significantly lower than that experienced in the last 10 years. Mark Drabenstott, of the Federal Reserve Bank of Kansas City, writes, "The 1980s may well turn out to be a decade of weak growth for U.S. agricultural exports. A sluggish world economy, a slow return of developing countries to financial strength, ample world food supplies, and relative strength in the dollar—all these point to slow growth for farm exports for the next few years."[28] Consultant Dale Hathaway argues that "the two parts of the world which accounted for almost all of the growth in world grain and oilseed exports during the last decade [the centrally planned economies and the middle income developing countries] will have limited growth and sharply curtailed capacity to pay for imports," while the United States now faces "competition for export markets far beyond what

we imagined or projected when we were making our estimates
of export markets only a few short years ago.''[29]

The level of export demand may be particularly important to
the South, where a high proportion of recent expansion in soybean, wheat, corn, and rice production is thought to have been
directly stimulated by foreign demand. No statistics are available
on the amount of agricultural commodities exported by each
region of the United States. Indirect, and not very satisfactory,
estimates of regional export dependence have been made by
assuming that each region's export dependence is proportional
to its crop mix. By this measure, the South exports 27 percent
of the total value of its farm sales, exactly the same as the U.S.
average.[30]

But the South's favorable geographic position relative to foreign
markets (the lower Mississippi area around New Orleans is by far
the leading point of exit for grain exports) could mean that the
southern share of exports is actually higher than average.
Economist Philip Raup notes that transporting grain by rail or
truck within the United States often costs much more than
transporting it by ship from the port of exit to points anywhere
in the world. As a result, ''Transport costs can be reduced if supplies can be located as close as possible to the Gulf [of Mexico
ports] not only because of distance but in order to permit quick
turnarounds and thus enable shippers to make the 45 trips per
year necessary to qualify for . . . lower unit-train leasing
charges.''[31] Grain producers in the Delta are unusually well located
with respect to both internal water transport (on the Mississippi
and tributary rivers) and to the port of New Orleans. Transport
costs are also favorable for growers on the South Atlantic Coastal
Plain. This transport advantage may mean that, in the event of
any future decline in exports, most of the reduction in acreage
would take place in parts of the Midwest not well served by water
transportation rather than in the South.

Another important factor to consider in projecting the demand
for southern cropland is the untapped production potential in
other parts of the country. This is considerable, though on many
counts it seems less extensive than it was only a decade ago.[32]
There is a great deal of potential cropland in nearly all regions
of the country, though opportunities for acreage expansion are

relatively slight in the Midwest, the nation's traditional agricultural heartland and the area of highest average productivity for most grain crops. Moreover, nationwide, a combination of land conversion to nonagricultural uses and continuing soil erosion is slowly but steadily reducing the productive potential of land already used for crops. Irrigation of arid lands in the Great Plains and West, which added at least 17 million acres to the agricultural land base between 1945 and 1974 alone, has become increasingly expensive. In some of those areas irrigated acreage is actually expected to decline in the face of urban competition for water and higher pumping costs.

Productivity per acre, which has been our most reliable source of output growth, grew more slowly nationally during the 1970s than in the 1960s. Experts are uncertain whether this downturn is a temporary aberration (productivity picked up again in the early 1980s) or whether a combination of lower growth in research budgets, scarcity of fossil fuels (the basis of many past agricultural advances), and a general failure of innovation will condemn U.S. agriculture to a relatively slow rate of future productivity growth.

Because of the limits on agriculture elsewhere in the United States, it is generally believed that the South will be called on to provide a greater share of national agricultural output in the future than it has in the recent past. Pierre Crosson and Sterling Brubaker projected that, comparing the period 1976-78 with the year 2010, the South's share of national wheat output will rise from 3.2 to 9.0 percent, of feedgrains from 7.0 to 9.0 percent, and of soybeans from 28.4 to 35.0 percent.[33] The South's share of cotton production, however, was projected to fall from 30.5 to 19.0 percent. After making assumptions about future national crop demand, and about future national and regional changes in yields, Crosson and Brubaker projected that the demand for cropland in the South will increase much more rapidly than will the demand for cropland nationally.[34] Comparing their projections for 2010 with the actual amount of cropland used for crops in 1981 shows a projected increase of 17 percent nationally, 18 percent in the Delta, 28 percent in the Appalachian states, and an extraordinary 80 percent in the South Atlantic states.

Opportunities for Expanding Crop Output

If there are additional demands for crop production, the South
can respond either by increasing the amount of land under cultivation or by raising output per acre. It has considerable opportunities
for doing both.

Cropping New Land

As already noted, the South has, by one estimate, some 44 million acres of "potential" cropland. Approximately half of this land
is now used for pasture and could be brought into crop production at relatively little cost, other than the value of the forgone
forage. The other half is forested and must be cleared before it
can be used for crops. Some of that land is also seasonally wet,
so drainage is necessary if crops are to grow well.

In the South, the first step in clearing land is to cut any salable
timber—though most of the really good timber is likely to have

*Land clearing in eastern Oklahoma. Starting in the 1950s, heavy machinery
made it economically feasible to clear forests and drain bottomlands on a
massive scale.*

been selectively removed long before. Then, the usual procedure is to use a bulldozer fitted with a special blade to push over the remaining trees and other vegetation. A bulldozer-drawn chopper is used to remove the roots. In most cases, it is cheaper to pile the fallen trees and roots in heaps ("windrows") and leave them to burn or rot rather than to try to recover any of the wood fiber for pulping. After clearing, the land is sometimes raked and leveled.

Land clearing is not cheap—a typical price, even aside from drainage, would be $200 to 300 per acre, less the cost of any timber that might be salvaged. The incentive for bearing this high cost of clearing is illustrated by the situation in the Mississippi Delta, where it is possible to buy bottomland forest for, say, $600 per acre, spend $300 per acre on clearing, and create cropland similar to that selling locally for $1,200 to $1,500 per acre. In fact, the newly cleared land may actually be superior in fertility, as it contains a layer of organic material resulting from its former forest cover. Says University of Arkansas economist Robert Shulstad, "new ground [made from clearing bottomland forest] responds fantastically well to cultivation. For cotton, the first year response is double usual yields, and there is some response over a 15-year period. For soybeans, the response is somewhat less."[35]

Small-scale clearing is often done by individual farmers, who may extend their existing fields onto wooded or low areas that they already own. This enables them to expand production without buying additional land and to spread the cost of large cultivating and harvesting machinery over a greater number of acres. Small-scale clearing is found throughout the South. No agency collects statistics about its extent, and the main evidence of its occurrence is the frequent sight of windrowed stumps and branches in the middle of now-cultivated fields.

Clearing is also done on a grand scale, particularly in the Delta, in central Florida, and in eastern North Carolina. In most cases, it is done in wet areas, which are often the only remaining large tracts of uncleared land in otherwise agricultural areas. Although elaborate drainage measures add to the cost of preparing for cultivation, the land is often quite inexpensive in its undrained state, making the draining and clearing operation economically feasible. Some large-scale clearing is done by corporate farmers, some by investors (Prudential Insurance Company and John Hancock Insurance have been active participants) who may subsequently rent the land to a local operator.

Land clearing is also encouraged by favorable federal tax treatment. Farmers are allowed to deduct up to $5,000 yearly in land-clearing expenses from taxable farm income. For drainage, farmers can deduct actual costs up to 25 percent of farm income in the first year and deduct the remaining costs in subsequent years; they also get an investment tax credit for the cost of installing drainage tiles.[36] Leonard Shabman has calculated that federal tax provisions lowered the cost of clearing bottomlands in eastern Arkansas from $312 to $218 per acre (in 1978 dollars).

Federal stream-channelization and levee-building programs, which reduce the annual frequency of flooding and make agricultural use practical on the newly protected area, have also served as subsidies to clearing. Such programs have involved the expenditure of hundreds of millions of dollars by the U.S. Army Corps of Engineers and the Soil Conservation Service. Although the pace of work on these programs has slackened since the mid-1970s, many projects remain authorized and some are still underway.[37]

University of Arkansas researchers have studied the potential for new cropland in the Mississippi Delta region, which includes 25.4 million acres in parts of Missouri, Arkansas, Kentucky, Tennessee, Mississippi, and Louisiana.[38] Millions of acres of woodland in the Delta have been cleared for crop use, primarily for cotton and soybeans. The Arkansas researchers determined that 86 percent of the nonflooded woodland and 74 percent of the nonflooded pastureland in the Delta could be physically converted to crops. Under nearly all of their 16 alternative combinations of assumed crop prices, clearing costs, and yields, the economics warranted converting all of the land, both woodland and pasture.

Land Retirement amid Expansion

Yet another way of improving crop output per acre in the South is by abandoning low-productivity cropland and replacing it with newly cleared land of higher quality. This process has been important historically, with worn-out cropland in the Piedmont replaced by flatter, more fertile land in the Delta and South Atlantic Coastal Plain. There appears to be considerable scope for this

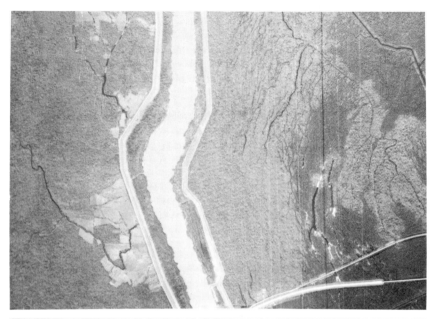

Clearing of wetland forest to create land on which soybeans and other crops can be grown has been widespread throughout the Delta. These photographs, taken in 1952 (top) and 1980, show an area along the Atchafalaya River, a few miles north west of Baton Rouge, Louisiana.

process to continue, for the South's current cropland inventory still contains large acreages of low-productivity land. For example, a recent U.S. Department of Agriculture study classified over 30 percent of present cropland in a large area of the southeastern United States as "marginal cropland" in the sense that the average economic return to using it for crops was negative.[39] (Because of this low return, some of the land is now idle, used for pasture, or placed in government land-diversion programs.) The Department of Agriculture is presently considering ways to encourage owners of such land to plant pine trees, partly to increase wood supply, partly to reduce erosion.

Retirement of marginal land from the cropland base would slightly reduce the South's total crop production potential, but it would raise average productivity per acre. To accommodate expected growth in total demand for southern crops, the retired land would likely be replaced by converting forest- or pastureland to crops. It seems reasonable to assume that this new land would be of higher productivity for crops than was the land where cropping was voluntarily abandoned. Thus, a long-standing trend in the South, the simultaneous retirement of marginal cropland and its replacement by new land, is likely to raise the region's crop output per acre, even if the total number of acres in crops remains unchanged.

The retirement-replacement process will cause further shifts in the location of cropland in the South. According to the U.S. Department of Agriculture, 72 percent of the current cropland in East Texas, northwestern Louisiana, and southwestern Arkansas is economically marginal, compared with 36 percent in the Piedmont and only 19 percent in the Coastal Plain.[40] This suggests that, over time, there will be a further net shift in cropland toward the more economically attractive portions of the Coastal Plain.

Yields and the "Learning Curve"

The obvious alternative to bringing more land into production is to raise yields per acre. Current southern yields of corn, wheat, and soybeans are all well below the national average. Cotton yields are about average, though far below those routinely achieved on irrigated lands in California, Arizona, and parts of West Texas.

Some of this lower-than-average yield can be attributed to limitations of soils and water. But part seems to be due to the fact that southern agriculture has changed so rapidly and so recently that the region's farmers and its agricultural researchers are still on a learning curve. Much of the technology for growing row crops was developed in the Midwest, a region with very different soils, growing season, and water regime from those prevailing in the South. Moreover, there is much less variation, particularly in soils, within the Midwest than within the South, where soils change dramatically from county to county, from field to field, and even within fields. While midwestern farmers have had several decades to develop cropping systems suited to their own situation, southern farmers are still experimenting with rotations, fertilization rates, and pest controls.

Because of this "learning curve" factor, one might argue that southern farmers have more scope to better their yields than do their midwestern counterparts. There also seems to be a more-than-average difference in the South between yields achieved by the top farmers and agricultural research stations and those achieved by average farmers. This means more possibility for improvement, even within existing technologies. Says pioneer Mississippi soybean breeder Edgar E. Hartwig, "I think we can do more to raise soybean yields [in the South] than they can in the Corn Belt."[41]

Irrigation

One of the most promising specific techniques of boosting per-acre yields is to expand the acreage under irrigation. In 1982, there were 5.6 million acres of irrigated land in the South, most of it cropland. This represents about 10 percent of the South's harvested cropland.[42] Irrigation is highly concentrated in the lower Coastal Plain and Delta (Florida, Arkansas, and Louisiana are the leaders), where the long growing season and water-responsive crop mix help justify the cost. Among the principal irrigated crops are rice, sugar cane, citrus, corn, soybeans, and vegetables.

During the 1970s, irrigation of crops in the South expanded rapidly, partly because of the growing acreage devoted to crops, partly because farmers became increasingly aware of the technological and economic possibilities for irrigation (see table 2.4).

Growth has slowed, but has not stopped, since 1980, the result of high interest rates and low crop prices. One area of particularly rapid expansion has been in southwestern Georgia, and adjoining northern Florida and southeastern Alabama, where more than a million acres have been newly irrigated since 1970. Approximately 55 percent of the irrigated acreage involves "center pivot" spray systems of the type previously found mainly in Nebraska, California, and Colorado.[43] These systems typically require large fields—in Georgia, fields irrigated with center pivots average 177 acres each. The bulk of the new irrigation is done on corn, peanuts, and soybeans.

Irrigation has also been spreading rapidly in the Delta, mainly because of the expansion of rice acreage (a crop that has always been irrigated) but partly because of the increasing use of supplemental irrigation on cotton and soybeans. In Florida, nearly all new citrus and vegetable operations are irrigated; there has also been a rapid increase in irrigation of field crops, such as soybeans and corn. Irrigation has also spread, if moderately, to areas

Table 2.4
Irrigated Acreage in the South
(thousand acres)

	1959	1964	1969	1974	1978[1]	1982[1]
Alabama	17	12	11	14	59	66
Arkansas	712	974	1,101	949	1,683	2,035
Florida	414	1,217	1,365	1,559	1,980	1,584[2]
Georgia	34	63	79	112	463	575
Kentucky	9	14	20	11	14	23
Louisiana	485	581	702	702	681	695
Mississippi	100	123	150	162	309	433
North Carolina	66	97	59	51	90	81
South Carolina	25	19	15	10	32	79
Tennessee	11	11	12	10	13	18
Virginia	31	51	37	28	42	43
Total	1,904	3,163	3,460	3,608	5,367	5,632

[1]Data are not directly comparable with other censuses as they include estimates from the direct enumeration sample for farms not represented on the mail list.

[2]According to a U.S. Department of Agriculture researcher, the apparent fall in irrigated land in Florida between 1978 and 1982 was due to a wet winter in 1982, which caused many farmers, particularly owners of irrigated pasture, to not apply water to their fields.

Source: U.S. Department of Commerce, Bureau of the Census, Census of Agriculture.

where it has heretofore been almost unknown, such as southeastern Virginia.

We would go to some counties in Southeastern Arkansas where they had 20 or 30 center pivot irrigation systems and come back the next year and find there were 200.

ROBERT SHULSTAD, agricultural economist,
University of Arkansas

Even though water may need to be applied only two or three times per year, irrigation can have dramatic effects on crop yields. A survey of Louisiana farmers who practiced supplemental irrigation found that they expected average cotton yields to be 278 pounds per acre above those achieved without irrigation. For soybeans, the expected increase was 14.1 bushels per acre, a differential of more than 50 percent over the usual Louisiana yield.[44] An experiment on corn in Georgia found that, in a situation where the unirrigated yield was 115 bushels per acre, application of 4 irrigations in a season could raise it to 160 bushels, while 11 irrigations could raise the yield to 190 bushels.[45]

A relatively new irrigation technology that may become important in the South is "subirrigation" or "controlled and reversible drainage." This practice, still largely experimental, involves draining wet soils in such a way that the subsurface water level just below the root zone of a crop can be raised or lowered at will through a series of ditches, gates, and underground pipes.[46] After heavy rains, water can be quickly moved offsite. But the control structures allow enough water to be retained to help plants during periods of drought. A recent review of irrigation and drainage research by a committee of the American Society of Civil Engineers described the technology as "in its infancy in the U.S." and assigned it a high priority for future research.[47]

Although subirrigation can be used only in areas of relatively flat land with a naturally high water table, it seems applicable to millions of acres in the Coastal Plain. Estimated capital costs are lower than those for center pivot systems, and, because the water moves mainly by gravity, pumping costs are lower.[48] Some forms of subirrigation might possibly improve the economics of draining wetlands by allowing irrigated crop production for not much more than the cost of drainage alone.

Land-forming

Another yield-raising technique, potentially applicable in large areas of the Delta and elsewhere in the Coastal Plain, is "land-forming" or "land-leveling." The purpose of land-forming is to correct field drainage and eliminate wet spots where crops grow poorly. It has recently become popular, partly because of large-scale farmers' desire for large, uniform fields in which to use heavy production equipment, partly because new laser-guided soil scrapers can create almost imperceptible slopes that help a field drain evenly. Land-forming is also used to fill in sloughs or ditches, increasing the farmable area of a field. For example, in one representative case, an 80-acre property contained only 72 arable acres due to the presence of an old slough through the middle

North Carolina farmer smoothing his land to promote better drainage and increase crop productivity.

of the field. After land-forming, nearly the entire 80 acres were farmable.[49]

One study put land-forming costs in the Delta between $130 and $278 per acre (in 1978 dollars).[50] This high cost is more than offset by yield improvements that, depending on the crop raised, range between 10 and 30 percent. Overall, the study estimated that (under a moderate level of future crop demand) there were 12.6 million acres of existing cropland in the Delta where land-forming was profitable.[51] That represents about half of the total acreage in the region and about three-quarters of the present cropland. The authors noted that, while economically feasible conversion of noncropland to cropland in the Delta could raise the region's total soybean output about 10 percent, economically feasible land-forming of existing cropland could raise soybean output between 18 and 22 percent.

Multiple-cropping

A final yield-increasing technique is multiple-cropping—raising two or more harvestable crops yearly on a single tract of land. A long growing season makes the South particularly suited to multiple-cropping, although the practice is feasible as far north as southern Illinois and has even been used in Michigan.[52]

The predominant multiple-cropping system now used in the South is a wheat-soybean system. In the fall, the farmer plants wheat (or another small grain, such as barley); this grows through the long frost-free season, goes dormant for a few weeks in winter, then produces a crop of grain for harvest in late June. After harvesting the grain, the farmer immediately plants soybeans, trying to lose not a day of summer growing time. After the 15th of June, each day of delay in planting a second crop of soybeans can reduce yields up to half a bushel per acre.[53] Frequently the beans are planted directly in the wheat stubble without preparatory plowing.[54] This ''no-till'' method conserves soil moisture and saves time. Herbicides are used to control weeds that would otherwise be eliminated by plowing. The winter-planted wheat may also be planted no-till, broadcast-seeded directly into the just-harvested soybean field.

Double-cropping of wheat and soybeans has spread rapidly over the South during the past several years. It is particularly common in the Delta, though it has been successfully practiced in the South

Atlantic Coastal Plain and Piedmont as well. Indeed, nearly all of the South's recent increase in wheat acreage has been due to double-cropping.

Agricultural researchers have been developing a wide variety of multiple-cropping combinations: corn/sorghum; wheat/sunflower; cotton/sorghum; and corn/soybeans, for example.[55] In the southernmost areas, triple-cropping may be feasible, perhaps alternating two grain crops with a winter vegetable. An agronomist in Florida underlines how the long growing season makes possible cropping systems drastically different from those of the nation's midwestern agricultural heartland, yet equally productive, despite the low native fertility of many southern soils. "We have learned much more about the specific limitations of soils and about how to overcome them. With modern technology and the proper amount of inputs, we can make beach sand outperform the best soils of Iowa."[56] He notes that over 300 multiple-cropping systems are now available for the South.

Not all of these are mixtures of grain crops. For example, corn or soybeans can be planted in Bermuda grass in late winter, then harvested in summer in time for the grass to take over again. Or corn can be interplanted with clover or bluegrass or double-cropped sequentially with hay.

Two major problems limit the spread of multiple-cropping in the South. First, the winter crop tends to deplete available soil moisture, so yields of the summer crop may be very low, especially in dry years. In some cases, total grain yield from two sequentially grown crops may actually be lower than what could be obtained from a single crop. More frequently, total yield may be higher with double-cropping but not by enough to justify the expense of growing and harvesting the second crop.[57] However, timely summer irrigation can deal with the soil moisture problem, and irrigation is frequently used on double-cropped fields. In fact, irrigation and multiple-cropping tend to reinforce each other, with irrigation making a second crop possible and the added income from more than one crop helping the farmer pay for the irrigation equipment.

Multiple-cropping also must contend with pest buildup. No-till residues may allow plant disease and insects to develop, while herbicides used on one crop may remain in the soil to damage the succeeding, biologically different crop.

Multiple-cropping offers considerable promise for raising crop output in the South without having to expand the cropland base. The practice tends to be most profitable on the best-quality land; thus, its spread could result in retirement of some marginal cropland. Multiple-cropping would also reduce erosion, partly by reducing the amount of land cropped, partly because having a growing crop on the land nearly year-round protects the soil. On the other hand, multiple-cropping is likely to require more irrigation water and greater per-acre chemical applications.

The Crop Mix

Most experts believe that the South's present mix of major crops will not change drastically in the medium-term future, but there is some room for relative shifts as well as overall expansion in acreage and output. The most dynamic crop in terms of acreage change will probably be wheat, with nearly all the increase associated with double-cropping. There may also be some potential for growing more corn. Currently, the South imports large quantities of corn from the Midwest for use as poultry feed. Southern feed mills now pay as much as 60 cents per bushel to transport corn by truck from the Midwest, a cost that might give local producers an advantage, even if their yields were lower than those in Iowa or Illinois. Expansion of corn production would be aided by development of varieties that are more closely suited to the South's climate and pest populations and that could be more easily adopted to some form of multiple-cropping system. Effective control of aflatoxin, which makes some southern corn unmarketable, could also increase the region's attractiveness as a corn producer.

Production of fresh vegetables, already important to the South in value, though not (except in Florida) by acreage, is widely expected to continue to expand in the Coastal Plain, partly as a result of increased per-capita consumption, partly because of the advantages, in cost and freshness, of producing close to expanding regional markets. Vegetable production may have been oversold, however, as a source of future growth in the South— for example, as a high value-per-acre substitute for tobacco. National acreages of most vegetable crops are rather small, and experienced producers in California, Arizona, and some midwestern states are not likely to yield their market share without a struggle. Another problem is the possibility of increased production in Mexico, where low labor costs and favorable winter climate may spur competition in some lines of vegetable production.

The availability of so many untapped agricultural resources in the South could stimulate the development of entirely new crops or cropping systems. Indeed, the fact that so much southern land, unlike that in the Midwest, is not "ideal" for traditional grain crops is a strong incentive to find some crop or combination of crops for which the land might be better suited. The history of the soybean, which over the course of only 40 years moved from an agricultural curiosity to the South's leading crop, underlines the potential land-use impacts that new crop development might have.

A handful of agricultural researchers scattered across the South have been experimenting with new crops or with systems that combine new crops with traditional ones. For example, rapeseed, an oil-bearing seed widely cultivated as a summer crop in Canada, might be raised in the South as a fall-planted crop following corn. Other examples of possible crops include sunflower, pulse crops (peas, beans, and lentils), or increased acreages of sorghum. All of these are short-season, warm-weather crops that can be used as alternatives in double-cropping systems or where more intensive use is made of the frost-free growing period. Sunflower, for example, which can be harvested in as little as 90 to 100 days from planting, is an oil crop that could be attractive to the southern oil-crushing industry. Demand for sunflower oil is on the rise both nationally and internationally, and sunflower meal provides a high-protein animal feed that can be substituted for soybean meal.

The diversity of the pulse crops, and their 60- to 90-day growing season may help them make inroads in southern agriculture as demands increase for suitable and diverse multiple-cropping systems. Sorghum, used primarily as a feed grain, is only a minor crop in most of the South, though it is important in the Great Plains. It can be grown in double-cropping systems and on relatively poor land. Southern acreage might increase if demand warrants.

Perhaps the greatest uncertainty in agricultural research today, in the South and outside it, is the potential for crop improvement offered by genetic engineering. Thus far, the techniques developed by molecular biologists have had virtually no impact on agriculture.[58] There are several reasons for this, among them the fact that the genetic material contained in plants is exceedingly complex (in many species more complex than that of mammals) and that the molecular structure of this material has been much less studied than that of other organisms.

Agricultural researchers foresee great opportunities for using genetic manipulation to improve plants, although one estimate puts improvements by deliberate transfer of single genes sometime in the late 1990s.[59] Significant improvements using cruder techniques may be much closer. One development is "somatic cell genetics," a set of techniques by which improved plants are reproduced through tissue culture rather than by breeding. This could greatly reduce the time needed to replicate improved traits. Another promising possibility is the use of genetic engineering to improve bacteria useful to plants—for example, transferring nitrogen-fixing bacteria from soybeans to corn, thus eliminating the need for nitrogenous fertilizer.

There is no way of telling whether genetic engineering would benefit agriculture in the South more or less than it would benefit other sections of the country. On one hand, greatly improved plant varieties would reduce the total demand for farmland, concentrating production on the nation's best land, found mainly in the Midwest. On the other hand, genetic techniques could make plants better able to use sunlight and more tolerant of disease, insects, and low-fertility soils, distinctly an advantage for the South.

Biomass: The Uncertain Competitor

Interest in producing energy from plant biomass—from agricultural crops, such as corn, sugar cane, or even sweet potatoes, or from trees, shrubs, and grasses—waxes and wanes with the price and availability of fossil fuels. At the height of the energy crisis, interest was high, and studies of biomass potential were commissioned by the score. Currently, with oil and gas in relatively good supply, commercial interest in biomass has faded.

Whatever the outlook for biomass energy, one thing is

certain—its production on any significant scale requires huge amounts of land. Even if there is only a remote chance that high oil prices or some technological breakthrough will improve the economics of biomass, the potential demand for land is so great that the implications for land use deserve serious consideration. One study estimated that to produce 1 percent of U.S. energy from biomass farming would require between 10 and 40 million acres![60]

Experts believe that economical biomass production will require fairly fertile land, with rainfall of at least 25 inches yearly, and preferably a mild, sunny climate.[61] Because all current cropland is likely to be needed to produce food, the most promising source of land for biomass culture is other relatively fertile land now in timber or pasture. Because there may be economies of scale in biomass culture—one study gave the optimal size of a wood biomass plantation as 37,000 acres—it would be useful if land were available in large contiguous tracts. There also appears to be a widespread belief that wood, not grain, is the most economically promising source of biomass on a large scale.

Taken together, these requirements are almost perfectly suited to the South.[62] (The northern Lake States contain a large area of the right kind of land, but they do not enjoy as favorable a climate.)

One energy-from-biomass technology already in fairly widespread use is the production of alcohol from corn by fermentation. (Fuel alcohol can also be made from other crops, from crop residues, or from wood, and research is now under way to develop more efficient ways of doing so.) Most of the corn-based alcohol now goes into a 90/10 blend of alcohol with gasoline (gasohol); because it has a higher octane rating than gasoline, alcohol may come into greater use as a lead-free octane booster. Alcohol from corn represents a proved technology, its costs relatively high but also relatively predictable.[63] Thus, it may very well be emphasized, as it was in the middle 1970s, in the event of a future sudden reduction of imported oil supplies.

The implications for the South are twofold. First, increased demand would stimulate corn production in the South, which has tens of millions of acres now in crops and pasture that have the soil, climate, and water conditions necessary for raising corn. Second, because the residue left after corn is fermented (distillers dried grain) makes a good substitute for soybean meal as an animal feed, the demand for southern soybeans would probably drop.

Overall, it appears that, although the amount of southern land physically suited to growing plant biomass for energy is quite large,[64] the present economics of biomass energy make it a rather unlikely competitor for southern land. This could change drastically, of course, in the event of another round of large increases in fossil fuel prices or major technological changes. The outlook for use of existing timber resources as fuel is more promising (see chapter 3); this use is already well developed in the home-heating and pulp-and-paper sectors. Given the present ample supply of burnable wood, the biggest impact on land of the use of wood for fuel is that it reduces the cost of agricultural clearing or of timber stand improvement by providing a modest market for woody waste materials that would otherwise be discarded.

The Outlook for Southern Cropland

The South's cropland base plays a role in U.S. agriculture similar to that played by a reserve force or national guard within a military system. Much of the South's productive capacity will be needed only in the event of a high level of demand for food and feed grains, a situation likely to occur only if exports experience a sustained and substantial rise. From the standpoint of immediate productivity, most southern cropland is inferior to that of the Midwest. The South's advantage is simply that a much higher proportion of the potentially arable land is not being cultivated and could be pressed into use if the need arose.

Southern cropland could be made more productive. In the short run, this means more intensive application of known technologies—irrigation, fertilizer, and pesticides. In the long run, there is great scope for productivity-increasing improvements in land management, including development of new crops and of new cropping systems that overcome the South's liabilities of low soil fertility and pest and disease problems and that take advantage of the region's natural assets.

These natural assets, particularly the South's long growing season and available water, offer some exciting possibilities for the development of new technologies. But the South's agricultural future depends to a large extent on what happens in other regions. For example, the South's *relative* water availability may be more significant as a determinant of its agricultural future than its absolute supply of water. "If there are to be increasing amounts of land and water going into southern agriculture," says one southern water researcher, "I think the key will be what happens in the Western U.S." He notes the sentiment for less federal support of water development in the West, the dearth of unexploited dam sites, competing residential and industrial demand for water as western population grows, and the possibility of major new demands on the West's water for steam-generated electricity and oil-shale processing. The future availability of western water "may be a powerful force toward the development of agricultural change and more production in the South."[65]

References

1. Official agricultural statistics offer several definitions of cropland. They

typically differ in whether or not they include "cropland pasture" (cropland temporarily used for pasture) and cropland held idle. I have tried where possible to indicate the precise definition used in any given case. In general, I have regarded "cropland pasture" as pastureland and have used the term "cropland" to refer to land actually used for crops or customarily used for crops but presently idle. The term "cultivated cropland" is used to indicate land actually used for crops in a given year.

2. U.S. Soil Conservation Service, unpublished final data from the 1982 National Resources Inventory, July 1984.

3. See Lewis Cecil Gray, *History of Agriculture in the Southern United States to 1860*, 2 vol. (Washington, D.C.: Carnegie Institution, 1933); James R. Anderson, *A Geography of Agriculture in the United States' Southeast* (Budapest: Akademiai Kiado, 1973); "Symposium on Southern Agriculture Since the Civil War," special edition of *Agricultural History*, vol. 53, no. 1 (January 1979) and references cited therein.

4. See Robert W. Fogel and Stanley L. Engerman, *Time on the Cross: The Economics of American Negro Slavery* (Boston: Little, Brown, 1974).

5. Donald L. Kemmerer, "The Pre-Civil War South's Leading Crop, Corn," *Agricultural History*, vol. 23, no. 4 (October 1949), p. 238.

6. Ibid., p. 236.

7. Gilbert Fite, "Southern Agriculture Since the Civil War: An Overview," *Agricultural History*, vol. 53, no. 1 (January 1979), p. 15.

8. See Merle Prunty, Jr., "The Renaissance of the Southern Plantation," *Geographical Review*, vol. XLV, no. 4 (October 1955), pp. 459-491.

9. U.S. Bureau of the Census, *Census of Agriculture, 1930* (Washington, D.C.: U.S. Government Printing Office, 1932).

10. U.S. Department of Agriculture, *Yearbook of Agriculture, 1938* (Washington, D.C.: U.S. Government Printing Office, 1938), p. 65.

11. Ibid., p. 145.

12. Pete Daniel, "The Transformation of the Rural South, 1930 to the Present," *Agricultural History* (July 1981), p. 231.

13. Gilbert Fite, "Southern Agriculture," p. 4.

14. Charles S. Aiken, "The Decline of Sharecropping in the Lower Mississippi River Valley," *Geoscience and Man*, vol. XIX (June 1978), pp. 151-65.

15. John Fraser Hart and Ennis L. Chestang, "Rural Revolution in East Carolina," *Geographical Review*, vol. 68, no. 4 (1978), pp. 435-58.

16. Prunty, "The Renaissance of the Southern Plantation," pp. 459-91.

17. Charles S. Aiken, "The Fragmented Neoplantation: A New Type of Farm Operation in the Southeast," *Southeastern Geographer*, vol. 11, no. 1. (1971), pp. 43-51.

18. See Henry D. Fornari, "The Big Change: Cotton to Soybeans," *Agricultural History*, vol. 53, no. 1 (January 1979), pp. 246-53.

19. John Fraser Hart, "Cropland Concentrations in the South," *Annals of the Association of American Geographers*, vol. 68, no. 4 (December 1978), pp. 505-87.

20. U.S. Soil Conservation Service, *Basic Statistics, 1977 National Resources Inventory*.

21. There are also important environmental impacts associated with drainage, which are discussed at length in chapter 6.

22. Jeanne L. Jackson and Leslie E. Mack, *Arkansas Water: Why Wait for the Crisis?* (Little Rock: The Winthrop Rockefeller Foundation, 1982), p. 9.

23. Unpublished data from Economic Research Service, U.S. Department of Agriculture. Data include West Virginia; exclude Texas and Oklahoma.

24. Because most hay is fed to livestock, either on the farm where it was produced or nearby, the demand for southern hay is directly determined by the level of southern livestock production. Therefore the demand for hay is treated in chapter 4 (animal agriculture) below.

25. Kenneth R. Farrell, et al., "Meeting Future Needs for United States Food, Fiber, and Forest Products," in U.S. Joint Council on Food and Agricultural Sciences, *Reference Document: Needs Assessment for the Food and Agricultural Sciences* (Washington, D.C.: U.S. Government Printing Office, 1984), pp. 9-100.

26. Clark Edwards, "World Food Perspectives: Implications for U.S. Agriculture," *Agricultural Outlook* (USDA), August 1984, pp. 26-28, and unpublished manuscript by Edwards and others at the Economic Research Service, U.S. Department of Agriculture.

27. John Gever, et al., *Beyond Oil: Ensuring Energy for America's Future* (Cambridge, Mass.: Ballinger, 1985).

28. Mark Drabenstott, "The 1980s: A Turning Point for U.S. Agricultural Exports?" *Economic Review of the Federal Reserve Bank of Kansas City* (April 1983), p. 14.

29. Dale E. Hathaway, "Agricultural Trade: 1984 and Beyond," address to 1984 USDA Agricultural Outlook Conference, Washington, D.C., November 1983.

30. U.S. Department of Agriculture, Economic Research Service, *U.S. Agricultural Exports by Region and State, Fiscal Year 1982* (Washington, D.C.: U.S. Government Printing Office, 1982).

31. Philip M. Raup, "Competition for Land and the Future of American Agriculture," in Sandra S. Batie and Robert G. Healy, *The Future of American Agriculture as a Strategic Resource* (Washington, D.C.: The Conservation Foundation, 1980), p. 71.

32. For general treatments of the constraints and opportunities for U.S. agricultural expansion see Batie and Healy, *The Future of American Agriculture as a Strategic Resource* and Pierre Crosson, ed., *The Cropland Crisis: Myth or Reality?* (Baltimore: Johns Hopkins University Press for Resources for the Future, 1982).

33. Pierre R. Crosson and Sterling Brubaker, *Resource and Environmental Effects of U.S. Agriculture* (Washington, D.C.: Resources for the Future, 1982).

34. Technically, their projections are points of supply-demand equilibrium and do not trace out a complete demand curve. They therefore implicitly include assumptions about crop supply and land supply in the South.

35. Interview, Morrilton, Arkansas, October 1983.

ter of the drainage deduction if the land is sold within 5 years, partial recapture if sold within 10 years. After that, any increase in value due to drainage is taxed only at capital gains rates.

37. See, for example, Jim Spencer, "The Clearing Goes On," *Fins and Feathers* (August 1983); Lonnie Williamson, "Wiping Out the Wetlands," *Outdoor Life* (August 1983); U.S. Soil Conservation Service, *Louisiana Watershed Progress Report* (Alexandria, La.: Soil Conservation Service, 1981).

38. Billy E. Herrington and Robert N. Shulstad, *Conversion of Delta Woodland and Pasture to Cropland: Economic Feasibility and Implications* University of Arkansas, Agricultural Experiment Station Bulletin 858 (Fayetteville: University of Arkansas, 1982).

39. U.S. Department of Agriculture, Office of Budget and Program Analysis, *Conversion of Southern Cropland to Southern Pine Tree Plantings* (Washington, D.C.: U.S. Government Printing Office, 1983), p. 48.

40. Ibid.

41. Interview, Stoneville, Mississippi, December 1982.

42. This figure is from the Census of Agriculture, 1982. The Soil Conservation Service's 1982 National Resources Inventory put total irrigated land in the South at 8.7 million acres. The higher figure is probably more accurate, but I use the Census of Agriculture figure here because somewhat more detail is provided on how water is used.

43. Merle C. Prunty and L. Carl Brandhorst, "Diffusion of Center Pivot Irrigation in the Southeastern Coastal Plain," presentation to annual meeting of Association of American Geographers, San Antonio, April 1982.

44. Lonnie R. Vandeveer and Michael E. Salassi, "What Does Supplemental Irrigation Cost?" *Louisiana Agriculture*, vol. 25, no. 3 (Spring 1982), pp. 10-12.

45. J. Troy Johnson and W. Franklin Congleton, *Growing Corn in Georgia*, Agronomy Bulletin 547 (Athens, Ga.: University of Georgia, 1981).

46. C.W. Doty, T.S. Currin, and R.E. McLin, "Controlled Subsurface Drainage for Southern Coastal Plains Soil," *Journal of Soil and Water Conservation*, vol. 30, no. 2 (March 1975), pp. 82-84.

47. Task Committee on the Status of Irrigation and Drainage Research, "Status of Irrigation and Drainage Research in the United States," *Journal of Irrigation and Drainage Engineering*, vol. 110, no. 1 (March 1984), pp. 55-74.

48. Brenda G. Worm, *et al.*, "Economic Evaluation of Subsurface and Center Pivot Irrigation Systems," *Proceedings of the Specialty Conference on Environmentally Sound Water and Soil Management*, American Society of Civil Engineers, Orlando, Florida, July 20-23, 1982, pp. 377-84.

49. Robert N. Shulstad and Billy E. Herrington, *Economic Potential for Land-Forming Existing Cropland in the Mississippi Delta Region*, Agricultural Experiment Station Bulletin 859 (Fayetteville: University of Arkansas, 1982) p. 6.

50. Ibid, p. 10.

51. Ibid, pp. 18-19.

52. Grant W. Thomas, "Multiple Cropping," in Yao-chi Lu, ed., *Emerging Technologies in Agricultural Production*, U.S. Department of Agriculture, Cooperative State Research Service (Washington, D.C.: U.S. Government Printing Office, 1983), pp. 71-92.

53. J.H. Palmer, *Growing Soybeans in South Carolina*, Extension Circular No. 501 (Clemson, S.C.: South Carolina Agricultural Experiment Station, 1983).

54. Stubble fields are usually burned, often disked once—sometimes both burned and disked.

55. Some southern farmers are also trying out these systems. For example, in 1982, a grower in Alabama obtained 130 bushels per acre of corn, followed by 21 bushels per acre of soybeans. See Harris Barnes, Jr., "Doublecrop Beans After Corn," *Soybean Digest*, vol. 43, no. 9 (September 1983), p. 115.

56. R. N. Gallaher, University of Florida, Gainesville, interview, April 1984.

57. W.M. Lewis and J.A. Phillips, "Double Cropping in the Eastern United States," in American Society of Agronomy, *Multiple Cropping* (Madison, Wisconsin: ASA, 1976), p. 47.

58. U.S. National Research Council, Board on Agriculture, *Genetic Engineering of Plants: Agricultural Research Opportunities and Policy Concerns* (Washington, D.C.: National Academy Press, 1984).

59. Ibid, p. 13.

60. Kathryn A. Zeimetz, *Growing Energy: Land for Biomass Farms*, Economics, Statistics and Cooperatives Service, Agricultural Economic Report (Washington, D.C.: U.S. Government Printing Office, 1979).

61. D.J. Salo, et al., *Silvicultural Biomass Farms,* McLean, Va.: The MITRE Corp., May 1977.

62. U.S. Department of Agriculture, *A Biomass Energy Production and Use Plan for the United States, 1983-90*, Agricultural Economic Report No. 505 (Washington, D.C.: U.S. Government Printing Office, 1983).

63. Ibid. Alcohol production for fuel use is now heavily subsidized, mainly through a congressionally authorized exemption, extending through 1992, of alcohol-from-biomass fuels from 5 cents of the 9-cent-per-gallon federal excise tax on gasoline. Because a 90/10 gasohol blend qualifies for the fuel exemption, the effective subsidy is a hefty 50 cents per gallon of alcohol.

64. For example, one study estimated that 10.1 million acres of land in Florida alone were physically suited to growing woody species commonly suggested as biomass sources. D.L. Rockwood, et al., *Energy and Chemicals from Woody Species in Florida: Final Report for the Period April 17, 1978–May 16, 1983* (Oak Ridge, Tenn.: Oak Ridge National Laboratory, 1983), p. 6-6.

65. Dr. Gary Lynne, Department of Food and Resource Economics, University of Florida, personal communication, June 1983.

Chapter 3

Wood Production's Claim on Southern Land

Toward the growth of trees, nature in most of the South can be considered generous, even profligate. You may clear-cut a dense southern forest, even burn off the debris and understory. Yet, before long, with no human intervention at all, the land will be revegetated. By the end of the first summer, a mat of grasses, shrubs, and seedlings will have taken over the site; by the fifth year, in most cases, small pioneer species of trees will be waist-high or taller.

The central issue in producing wood fiber in the South is not how to reproduce a forest, but how to populate it with trees of the most economically desirable species, at spacings between individual trees that will maximize annual wood growth per acre. This task, so simple conceptually, turns out to involve a complex mix of biological, economic, environmental and even social considerations. The difficulty is attested to by the fact that such a large number of expert observers are dissatisfied with the present growth and condition of the southern forest.

Southern forest covers some 207 million acres, or 61 percent of the total land area, making it the South's single largest land user. (The aggregate forestry statistics for the South used in this chapter, which follow the regional boundaries of the U.S. Forest Service, include portions of Texas and Oklahoma, but do not include Kentucky.) Of that 207 million acres, 188 million are considered "commercial forest" or "timberland," that is, capable of producing at least 20 cubic feet of industrial wood per acre annually and not set aside in parks or wilderness areas. Half of this acreage is in hardwood forest, with another 34 percent in pines, and 16 percent in mixed hardwood/pine stands. About one-third of the hardwoods are "bottomland" species (the oak/gum/cypress vegetation type), which grow on riverbanks, in swamps, and on other wet sites. The remainder are "upland" hardwoods, such as oaks, maples, and hickories.

Forces Shaping the Southern Forest

The present southern forest is the product not only of natural forces but of four distinct kinds of human intervention: fire control, land clearing and abandonment, timber harvesting, and silviculture. Each of these has left a visible mark on the kind of forest we see in the South today.

Fire helped create the great and economically valuable southern pine forests.[1] At the time of the first English settlement of the New World, vast stretches of southern pines—longleaf, shortleaf, slash or loblolly, according to latitude and soil drainage—predominated in the Coastal Plain and were found to some extent (experts disagree on how much) in the Piedmont. Much of this land would have been a hardwood forest were it not for the periodic occurrence of fires. Pine trees have a thicker bark than do most hardwoods; when a forest fire moves through the woods, it frequently kills the juvenile hardwoods but leaves most of the pines, young and old, intact. Even when the fire is sufficiently hot to kill all the trees regardless of species on a given site, the pine seeds, light enough to be easily wind-blown, are often first, along with certain grasses, to take over the site. American Indians knew this and sometimes deliberately set the woods afire—they cared little for the pines but wanted to encourage the grasses on which deer could feed. Between the fires set by the Indians and the wildfires started by summer lightning strikes, pure or nearly pure pine stands were quite common in aboriginal southern forests.[2] Later agriculturalists also used fire—to clear land, to drive game, and to "green up" the rangeland for their grazing animals. Often, forest fires were accidentally set or accidentally spread out of control.

By the third decade of the 20th century, however, alarmed by the frequency and destructiveness of wildfires, most of the southern states, with considerable financial help from the federal government, began increasingly effective programs of forest fire control. These programs have prevented the loss of tens of millions of dollars in timber annually, not to mention the savings in lives and structures. But effective fire control has removed a major force in the southern forest system and has thereby favored the spread of hardwoods at the expense of pines.

A second force molding the southern forest has been agricultural land clearing and land abandonment. Chapter 2 has already described the massive clearings by 18th- and 19th-century farmers, the abandonment of marginal cropland during and after the Great Depression, and the post-World War Two agricultural clearings in the bottomlands. There is no way of telling exactly how many of the South's presently forested acres were affected in these shifts, but they must number in the tens of millions.

Agricultural clearing and subsequent abandonment have had a significant impact on the species composition of the present southern forest. Provided there are some pine trees nearby to provide windblown seeds, an abandoned southern field will very often grow up in a nearly pure stand of pines. The clear, weed-free surface of an abandoned field, like the forest cleared by aboriginal fires, provides an excellent medium for reproduction of young pines. Beyond this natural regeneration, millions of acres of former croplands were planted in pines, some by the Civilian Conservation Corps in the 1930s, some under the Soil Bank program in the late 1950s and early 1960s. These now-mature stands of "old field" pines, whether natural or planted, are a major component of the present southern softwood timber inventory.[3] "People have underestimated the importance of this," says one long-time observer of southern forestry. "Literally millions of acres of cropland reverted to pine forest after World War Two, and right now we're reaping the benefits. It is this 'old field' pine that is running our mills."

Agricultural clearing and abandonment also affect the quality of forest *land*. Clearing away a forest is not a task lightly undertaken, whether one is a pioneer farmer felling trees with an ax and pulling stumps with a mule team or a modern land investor paying a bulldozer operator hundreds of dollars an acre to unleash his mechanical power. A landowner is likely to clear for crops only that land sufficiently productive to justify the trouble or expense. As a result, the better southern lands have become cropland, while the steeper, wetter, or less fertile lands have remained forested. Because cropland is generally of better quality than the land left in forest, when cropland is abandoned and reverts to forest, not only is the quantity of forestland increased, but the average quality of the forestland base tends to be augmented as well. Conversely, when forestland is cleared for crops, the average quality of the forestland base declines along with its quantity. I will elaborate on the implications of this process later in this chapter.

A third important influence on the southern forest has been timber harvesting. Although some commercial timber cutting has taken place in the South since colonial times, the attention of wood producers serving national markets did not really focus on the region until well after the Civil War. Many northern logging firms moved their operations southward around the turn of the century when production from the virgin pine forests of the Lake States began to wane. Between 1900 and 1925, the South ranked first among all the important lumber-producing regions.[4] As in the virgin forests elsewhere in the nation, volumes of wood per acre in the South were enormous. Loggers concentrated on extracting the best available trees of the species then most in demand—massive cypresses, oaks, and poplars and 80-year-old pines.

Trees that were crooked, or inconveniently located, or of less salable species, were left behind. This selective cutting, with no heed to its impact on the composition of the future forest, is popularly known by the now-pejorative term *high-grading*. Once a stand was high-graded, it was often abandoned. Sometimes it burned, perhaps occasionally and accidentally, perhaps yearly due to deliberate fires set by neighboring farmers who wanted to "green up" the land. Sometimes the unsalable residual trees on a high-graded site were simply allowed to grow, becoming larger, but not necessarily more valuable. Many stands were high-graded again and again, as loggers became less exacting about what kind of material was worth taking out of the forest. There is almost no virgin forest left in the South today, but many tree cutters are still carrying on the high-grading tradition, particularly in mixed-species stands and on swampy and inaccessible sites. The result of this removal of the biggest and best specimens has been a steady deterioration in the quality of the residual trees, as trees of inferior quality or economically less-valued species are left to grow and reproduce. On mixed pine and hardwood sites, moreover, high-grading has meant selective removal of the pine, which is much more easily marketable than most hardwoods, and has led to further hardwood dominance.

During the 1930s, millions of acres of southern forestland were restored to productivity through the efforts of Civilian Conservation Corps enrollees, such as this tree planter working near Spartanburg, South Carolina.

Even as high-grading continues, a fourth influence has been growing in importance. This is the deliberate practice of silviculture, the growing of trees as a crop. The South, in fact, can be justly credited as the ancestral home of silviculture in America, for it was at the Biltmore estate near Asheville, North Carolina, that a young forester named Gifford Pinchot (later the founder of the U.S. Forest Service) began in 1891 to oversee America's first scientifically managed forest.

Nonetheless, so seemingly inexhaustible were the South's timber stocks, it was not until the 1930s that more than a handful of

southerners began to think seriously about silviculture. Even today, it would be exceedingly generous to claim that good forestry
is practiced on even half of the South's commercial forestland.[5]

These deficiencies notwithstanding, enough acres are under active forest management to qualify silviculture as a major factor
molding the southern forest. During the period 1970-78, 10 million acres of trees were planted or direct-seeded in the South,
virtually all in southern pines.[6] An additional 6 million acres
received some sort of intermediate stand treatment, such as
eliminating less-desirable tree species or precommercial thinning
in young stands. The effect of nearly all of these silvicultural interventions has been twofold: to raise total fiber output per acre
and to encourage the growth of pines.

Paralleling the physical changes in southern forests have been
massive changes in forestland ownership. Unlike in the West,
where extensive government-owned forests have been carved out
of the unappropriated public domain, only 9 percent of the
South's timberland is in public hands. The largest part of this is
the 11 million acres in national forests, most of them created during the 1920s and 1930s from cutover land purchased at low
prices.

Forest industry firms own 19 percent of the South's timberland.
This ownership has been rising slowly over time. More important, since World War Two, holdings of smaller local lumber firms
have been acquired by large integrated lumber and paper producers, several of which own more than a million acres each in
the South.

The largest single category of timberland ownership in the South
is "nonindustrial private owners," who collectively own 134 million acres, or 71 percent, of southern timberland. As recently as
1952, nearly two-thirds of this land was owned by farmers, often
as a woodlot adjoining their cultivated fields. But the decline in
the number of farmers in the South has rapidly changed that situation; today, farmers own only two-fifths of the nonindustrial
timberland. The remainder is owned by a very diverse group—
retired farmers, urban residents who have inherited rural land,
nontimber corporations such as coal companies and banks, land
speculators, and large- and small-scale timber investors. Although
the increased ownership of land by the big timber firms, which
coincided with the advent of high-intensity forest management

in the South, may be the most significant event in the South's modern forest history, the change from farmer to nonfarmer ownership certainly has involved the greater number of acres. As we will see later in this chapter, it seems to hold the key to future wood production in the South.

Uses of Southern Timber

Southern wood fiber goes into a very large number of products, and listing them in any detail would likely prove more tedious than instructive. But the nature of the final product is so important to the kind of tree required that a few of the most important products should be mentioned. One is the southern pine two-by-four, about 12,000 linear feet of which are used in each new house. When harvested for lumber, southern pines are typically grown to 8-to-12-inch diameters on rotations of 30 to 35 years; the value at harvest can be several dollars per tree or well over $1,000 per acre.

Another product is paper, both the unbleached kraft paper used in grocery bags and shipping cartons and the finer grades used for printing. Paper can be made from hardwoods, softwoods, or a mix of the two. Softwoods are preferred for paper cartons and bags because the characteristically long fibers of softwoods improve the paper's strength; hardwoods predominate in the manufacture of printing paper, stationery, and other white papers. At present, the overall ratio of softwood to hardwood used in southern paper mills is about 3 to 1. Paper typically is made either from trees harvested in short rotations or from the waste material left from producing lumber. Recently, southern sawmills have begun to employ the "chipping saw," which wrests one or two pieces of lumber from a rather small log, then chops the edges into chips that can be used for making paper.

Another important product of southern forests is softwood plywood, most of which is used in construction. In 1982, the South for the first time surpassed the Pacific Northwest in softwood plywood output, accounting for about half of U.S. production.[7] Only 30 years ago, the South did not produce any plywood. Plywood is made by peeling wide strips from a log (called a veneer bolt) as it is rotated on what looks like a giant lathe. The strips are then laminated and glued together. Although some hardwood plywood is produced, the most desirable "peeler" log for making plywood is an 8-foot-long, perfectly straight, pine sawlog, the larger in diameter the better.

These three products—pine lumber, paper, and plywood—probably account for well over 75 percent of the value of the wood output of southern forests. This dominance means that the market for softwood stumpage is signficantly better than is the market for hardwoods. To be sure, the most valuable woods of all are furniture-grade hardwoods, the large, knot-free specimens of oak, hickory, or ash that can command hundreds of dollars per tree. But furniture accounts for only a small proportion of wood use, and most of the really magnificent trees have long ago been removed from the southern forest. The more typical hardwood tree is in demand, if at all, only for pulpwood or for low-value uses such as pallets and shipping crates.

The relative economic demand for hardwoods and softwoods can best be expressed by the fact that in the South as a whole hardwoods exceed softwoods in volume (105 billion cubic feet compared to 97 billion); yet the annual harvest of softwoods is more than double that of hardwoods. Another way to look at it is to note that predominantly hardwood ecosystems make up 47 percent of the commercial forestland in the South; yet they account for only 32 percent of the holdings of the forest products industry.

Forecasting Future Demand

In the future, demands for stumpage from southern forests will depend in large part on two things: the amount and kind of wood demanded nationally (and perhaps internationally) and the amount of fiber available from competing wood-producing regions.

The Forest Service periodically makes long-term national forecasts of wood demand.[8] The latest, released in 1984, looks toward a demand for softwood stumpage, assuming real prices rise at their 25-year historical trend, of 12.8 billion cubic feet in the year 2000 and 15.1 billion cubic feet in 2030. This compares with 10.7 billion cubic feet in 1980. The projection of increased demand depends on the assumption that growth in the number of households will raise the demand for lumber and plywood, while increased income and industrial activity will raise the demand for paper and containers. Hardwood demands are also projected

Softwoods, such as these young longleaf pines in Florida, grow rapidly in the South and find a ready market for lumber, paper, and plywood.

to increase substantially in the decades ahead, more than doubling by 2030. Crucial to this is the expectation that people and industry will greatly increase their use of hardwoods as fireplace, stove, or boiler fuel, and will continue to use large numbers of wooden shipping pallets, and that the proportion of hardwood fiber in the papermaking process will increase from 28 percent to 38 percent.

As with all long-term projections, these are subject to uncertainty. Indeed, the Forest Service has estimated several alternative levels of stumpage demand, based on varying assumptions about export demands, housing starts, processing efficiency, and stumpage prices. For softwood sawtimber, for example, changing assumptions from the base or standard case causes the projected demand level in 2030 to be as low as 52 billion board feet or as high as 64 billion.

According to the Forest Service, the most likely level of future demand is considerably above the amount of stumpage that U.S. forests are expected to supply, even given a continuation of the relatively rapid price rises of the past, so prices will have to rise still faster. Rising prices, in turn, will cause consumers to turn away from wood toward other products. For example, grocery stores might use plastic bags rather than the traditional kraft paper bag—unless the price of plastic rises even faster. Or homebuilders might space wall studs farther apart, economizing on the use of lumber.

Rising wood prices would also encourage wood producers to find ways to make the same products from cheaper grades or more plentiful species of wood. For example, several large companies are starting to produce "flakeboards" by laminating small fragments of either hardwood or softwood fiber, rather than making plywood, which requires expensive veneer logs.[9] This new product (also called "waferboard" or "oriented-strand board") is an acceptable substitute for plywood in some structural uses, though carpenters dislike the fact that it weighs more per square foot. Similarly, papermakers may react to rising softwood prices by using more hardwood in their processes. Newly developed technologies even make it possible to make a serviceable two-by-four by gluing together short lengths of wood that formerly would have gone to the pulpmill. Says one expert, "There's a revolution going on in wood utilization. We can expect much more use of low-quality fiber, including 'junk' hardwoods."

In addition to the level of national demand, demands on southern forests depend on the amount of wood available from other regions. In softwoods, the South's greatest domestic competitor is the fir, pine, and spruce area of the western United States, which stretches from the Black Hills of South Dakota to California, but which has its greatest current volume and growth potential on the moist west slope of the Cascades in Oregon and Washington and in parts of northern California. If one considers presently available trees, the West (Pacific states and northern Rockies) clearly surpasses the South, with more than two-and-a-half times the standing softwood timber and three-and-a-half times the stock of trees presently of sawtimber size. But if one considers the land itself, the West begins to look less dominant. In the West, there are 42.6 million acres of very good (site class 85 +) quality timberland. (Site class, a measure of potential timberland productivity, is defined later in this chapter.) Of those, 18.5 million acres are on national forests, and their availability for all-out wood production will be subject to the constraints of the other multiple uses for which national forests are managed. In the South, there are 60.6 million acres of very productive (site class 85 +) timberlands, only 2.7 million of which are on national forests. This difference between the South and the West in relative endowments of timber and land is the basis for widespread predictions that in the future the South will become even more important as a wood-supplying region.

Another possible source of softwood fiber is from abroad. W.N. Haynes, professor of industrial forestry at the University of Georgia, observes, "In the world, there are only six major softwood producing regions—Scandinavia, Russia, eastern Canada, western Canada, the Pacific Northwest, and the South."[10] He argues that each of the alternative suppliers, save the South, has limitations—ranging from biological limitations on growth in Scandinavia to likely Forest Service policy in the Pacific Northwest—that will restrict increases in output. "All of these factors," says Haynes, "will result in a greater demand on the South for softwood timber. In the whole world, you simply don't have any other place to go."

Bruce Zobel, of North Carolina State University, acknowledges the supply problems of traditional softwood-producing regions but is optimistic about long-run prospects for output from South America, where several countries have been planting hundreds of thousands of acres of pines yearly. "It will take 15 to 20 years," he says, "but after that the South will have a [foreign competition] problem."[11]

For hardwoods, the South's major competitor is the northeastern quadrant of the United States, including New England, the Middle Atlantic States, and the Lake States.[12] Both the South and the North have ample supplies of hardwoods, with annual growth in each region slightly more than double the annual harvest.[13] Because hardwoods are so plentiful, there has been little incentive in either region to increase levels of growth, and many opportunities for doing so remain unexploited. Given the increases in future hardwood demand projected by the Forest Service (driven in part by optimistic assumptions about fuelwood demand), the current oversupply could be greatly reduced by the year 2000. But the volume of wood in standing hardwood trees is still very high relative to demand. For example, the North alone has growing stock equal to 31 years of total national hardwood harvest and to 18 years' national harvest of hardwood sawtimber.

Because of the age and species composition of its hardwoods, the North probably could not by itself accommodate all of the country's hardwood demands, even if fuelwood requirements prove lower than projected. But its considerable hardwood resource will certainly be a major factor moderating the future need for hardwoods from the South.

There are also significant possibilities for importing hardwood pulpwood from South America.[14] Brazil already exports eucalyptus pulp to the Southeast, with low cost of production offsetting the added transportation cost. Both the short-run availability of hardwood chips and pulp from South America and the long-run potential for inexpensively growing hardwoods there in short rotations are very impressive.

Even as southern wood producers face potential competition from abroad, they are also looking abroad for new markets. At present, only 6.7 percent of the value of southern forest products output is exported.[15] But exports of both solid wood and paper products are now several times their level during the 1960s, and some experts see exports as a major growth area in forestry. Says the National Forest Products Association ebulliently, "If the U.S. export potential is properly handled, the United States can become to wood products what the Middle East is to oil."[16] The association has joined with the U.S. Department of Agriculture in an export promotion drive.

Much of the U.S. wood export growth during the 1970s took the form of shipping unfinished logs from the Pacific Northwest to Japan. This may fall off in years to come, as the Northwest's stock of old-growth timber becomes depleted. But, for the nation as a whole, there is likely to be greater export of softwood lumber, plywood, and pulp and paper to a wide range of international customers, including western Europe, the Caribbean, and the Far East. In 1980, for example, the People's Republic of China ordered 600,000 tons of U.S. paper goods, taking advantage of U.S. prices lower than those offered by Japanese suppliers.[17] The products in which export growth is most likely are precisely those in which the South has a long-term cost advantage. Predicts William R. Haselton, chairman of St. Regis Paper Company, "The South will rise again as the world's wood basket."[18]

Other observers are less confident, pointing to the existence of substantial tariff and nontariff barriers to U.S. lumber products, to a recently overvalued dollar, and to the reluctance of U.S. producers to make a permanent commitment to the world market.[19] Perhaps the most important limitation is the projected high price of softwood stumpage as a result of growing domestic demand. Says one economist, "U.S. firms become enthusiastic about foreign markets whenever domestic demand is soft, then look away when the U.S. market improves."

The Forest Service's long-range planners have the unenviable task of making regional demand projections amid all this uncertainty. They project that once wood prices have been allowed to adjust fully, and allowing for output from all other regions, the demand and supply for softwood stumpage in the South will reach equilibrium (the level of output and price at which supply is equal to demand) at a year 2000 output 51 percent higher than the 1976 level.[20] By 2030, the equilibrium southern output will be 74 percent higher than in 1976. For supply to equal demand, the real (constant dollar) price of southern pine stumpage will have to rise substantially, with sawtimber stumpage selling in 2030 at triple its current price and pulpwood somewhat less than double.

Equilibrium demand for southern hardwoods is projected to rise even more rapidly than that for softwoods, to 260 percent of its 1976 level by 2000, and 366 percent by 2030. Prices of hardwood sawtimber in the South are expected to rise about 75 percent by 2030, much less than softwood sawtimber prices. So abundant are low-quality hardwoods that, despite the tremendous projected increase in demand, real prices for southern hardwood pulpwood (stumpage value) are projected to stay around their present relatively low level until the end of the century and then to rise only modestly.

My own qualitative evaluation leads me to suspect that, with respect to total timber demand, the Forest Service is more likely to have slightly overestimated demand than to have grossly underestimated it. It is much easier to foresee technological changes that substitute other materials for wood (for example, plastic packaging) than those that would create whole new uses for wood. There has been much discussion of using wood as non-conventional chemical feedstock, but it is difficult to see its advantage over coal, which is easier per ton to collect and transport.

On the other hand, it is difficult to foresee anything that would really devastate the market for wood. It is a versatile material, and the systems for harvesting and processing it are well-organized and sophisticated. Moreover, wood processors have been very attentive to energy conservation and use of waste-wood for fuel, making them relatively immune to surprises in the energy area.

I am somewhat less sanguine than is the Forest Service about the prospects for demand growth in softwood sawtimber relative to pulpwood, particularly in view of the projected growth in the ratio of sawtimber prices to those of pulpwood. There are tremendous possibilities for substituting small logs for large ones and for substituting hardwoods for softwoods. The huge investments in current mills and machines will limit substitutions in the short run, but it is likely that 50 years from now there will be less distinction made between types of wood fiber than there is today.

In looking at the South relative to its competitors, one has to be impressed with the South's location relative to national and European markets, its excellent transportation network, its familiarity to forest products firms, its favorable and predictable tax structure, and its political and labor stability. Each of these factors makes the South attractive as a location for sawmills and pulp and paper operations, not only to serve domestic markets but also to export.[21] The fact that intensively managed forests in Brazil or Chile can annually grow two or three times as much wood per acre as can the South is impressive, but such areas present major risks for investors, either as plant sites or as dominant fiber suppliers for U.S. mills.

To my mind, there is only one major factor that could severely restrict growth in the South's share of future timber markets—a greatly increased liquidation of old-growth timber on national forests in the West.[22] I suspect that a policy allowing greater year-to-year variation in old-growth sales may be quite likely in the event of future drastic increases in softwood lumber prices. But a really major increase in old-growth liquidation I think unlikely. Not only would there be objections on environmental grounds, but faster harvesting of old-growth timber would greatly threaten investments in timber growing by individuals and companies in both the Northwest and the South. Moreover, much of the old-growth timber may prove expensive to harvest because of steep terrain and distance to mills.

My overall assessment, like that of the Forest Service, is that

Burning Wood as Fuel

Wood is used as a primary or secondary heating fuel in many southern homes, particularly in rural areas. Most of this is cut from small hardwood or softwood logs, essentially the same material that is harvested for pulp. Another major user of wood for energy is the forest-products industry itself, particularly the paper mills. These enterprises have found themselves with huge quantities of wood residues, including bark, rotten wood, and spent pulping liquors, as well as a substantial need for steam and electricity for processing purposes. Since the increase in oil prices in the mid-1970s, pulp mills all over the South have come to generate an increasing proportion of their energy from wood. A few even generate surplus electricity, which is sold to local power companies.

As onsite wood residues are becoming fully utilized, a few companies are seeking additional supplies of wood to burn. One alternative is "whole-tree chipping," whereby tops, limbs, and trees not desirable for lumber or pulp are chopped up in the course of harvesting operations and the resulting chips trucked to the mill. There has also been experimentation with raising trees specifically for fuel—densely planted pines or eucalyptus are the favored species—but the wide availability of existing trees suitable for chipping tends to dampen the economic potential of these efforts.

In North Carolina, there is a brick factory that is fueled by hardwood chips made available when low-grade hardwood stands are cleared for future pine plantations. Although the stumpage value of the hardwoods is only $1 to $2 per ton, the harvesters are happy to sell what would otherwise be worthless fiber. A North Carolina forest economist argues that, "*Growing* timber for biomass in the South is unlikely to be economic, but *mining* [existing] hardwood timber is."[1]

southern timber will be in increasing demand, both absolutely and relatively. There may be some long-run convergence in the prices for various types and species, though the big softwood log will still be the most sought-after commodity. I believe that demand for southern fiber will be high, despite very substantial increases in real prices. But I also believe that substitution possibilities—among species, between timber and nontimber materials, and among regions—are an ever-present limit to the rise in southern stumpage prices.

Determinants of Forest Output

How does the demand for wood translate into demands on southern land? In the short run, the volume of trees now standing on the land, what foresters refer to as "growing stock," is

Table 3.1

Timberland Changes in the South
(acres)

	Date of latest survey	Timberland at latest survey	Change since previous survey	Gain or loss to agriculture	Gain or loss to urban and water	Gain or loss to non-commercial
Alabama	1982	21,659,000	+ 326,000			
Arkansas	1978	16,615,600	- 1,591,100	- 557,200	- 1,036,300	+ 2,400
Florida	1980	15,664,177	- 597,000	- 135,900	- 549,700	+88,600
Georgia	1982	23,733,684	- 1,092,700	- 525,500	- 472,400	- 94,800
Kentucky	1975	11,901,900	+ 189,100			
Louisiana	1977	14,526,600	- 1,509,900	- 1,058,500	- 451,400	
Mississippi	1977	16,504,300	- 387,600	+ 75,400	- 464,700	+ 1,700
North Carolina	1984	18,450,269	- 1,094,600	- 474,800	- 597,100	- 22,700
Oklahoma (part)	1976	4,323,400	- 494,000	- 508,000	- 74,500	
South Carolina	1978	12,502,906	+ 76,300	+ 215,100	- 145,700	+ 6,900
Tennessee	1980	12,879,000	+ 59,200	+ 415,200	- 356,000	
Texas (part)	1975	10,901,500	- 554,300	- 227,000	- 328,000	+ 700
Virginia	1977	15,972,793	+ 148,400	+ 276,800	- 211,200	+82,800

Source: U.S. Forest Service.

most important. The amount and location of today's growing stock is the result of management decisions made many years ago; not much can be done to augment it. But, over a longer period, the supply of wood from the South is highly variable and depends both on the size and quality of the timberland base and on the intensity of forest management.

The Timberland Base

The size of the South's timberland base has historically been closely related to the expansion and contraction of the region's cropland. To a great extent, trees have occupied the land that farmers didn't want. Thus, timberland expanded as cropland was abandoned during the early post-World War Two years, then started to decline in the mid-1960s as the cropland base began to grow again. By 1977, southern timberland had declined a full 12 million acres (to 188.0 million) from its postwar high—and it seems quite likely to have declined still further since that time.

Table 3.1 shows where recent changes in southern timberland have taken place and some of the reasons for their occurrence. Between the most recent forest survey and the one immediately preceding it (generally 10 years earlier), the amount of timberland fell in eight southern states and increased in five. Of the five states having surveys taken since 1980, two (Alabama and Tennessee) showed a gain in timberland, and three (Florida, North Carolina, and Georgia) showed a loss. Interim surveys of Louisiana (1980) and Oklahoma (1981) also showed a loss, but at a slower rate than in preceding years.

Nearly all of the states lost substantial amounts of timberland to urbanization and to water impoundments. Some, such as Arkansas and Louisiana, lost large amounts of timberland to agriculture; Tennessee, Virginia, and a few other states gained as agricultural land reverted to forest.

The figures shown here are net changes, which tend to understate the extent to which land in the South has actually been shifting use. For example, the net loss of timberland to agriculture in North Carolina is the product of 722,200 acres of forest going into agriculture and 247,400 acres of agricultural land going to forest. The types of agriculture involved in land shifts also varied from state to state, with land clearance for pasture being of particular importance in Alabama, Texas, Oklahoma, and Florida, while clearance for crops was particularly important in Mississippi, Louisiana, and North Carolina. Both pasture and crops were responsible for the very large amount of net forestland clearance in Arkansas.

A few states had varying amounts of land transferred into the timberland category because the estimated productivity of forest-land considered too poor in quality to be timberland was reevaluated (as in Florida and Virginia) or transferred out of timberland because it was set aside in parks or wilderness (as in Georgia and North Carolina).

For the future, the official Forest Service projection is for a southern timberland base of 182.5 million acres in 1990, with steady decline to 172.9 million in 2030.[23] The loss of timberland is projected to occur in all of the southern states except Kentucky, with the greatest percentage declines in Oklahoma, Florida, and Louisiana.

This projection, of course, rests on some assumptions about the degree to which other uses of land will be expanding in the South—precisely the subject of this book. I will return in chapter 7 to a new, more elaborate projection by the Forest Service. For the moment, it is sufficient to note that the general expectation of southern foresters is that the area of southern timberland is likely to be smaller in the future than it is at present.

The future productivity of the South's timberland, as well as its acreage, is important. At the simplest level, assume that land is used to produce undifferentiated wood fiber, with no distinction made between hardwood and softwood, pulpwood and saw-timber. Table 3.2 shows how many acres of southern forestland would be needed at alternative levels of demand and at alternative levels of output per acre.

In 1976 (the latest year for which such data have been published), southern timberlands grew wood at an average rate of 56.9 cubic feet per acre—thus, the 188.0-million-acre land base grew 10.70 billion cubic feet of wood. But only about half of this wood was sold, and the amount sold could have been produced on fewer than 100 million acres. (Most of those "excess" acres were growing hardwoods, which were in lesser demand than pine.)

If southern forests maintained their 1976 average level of productivity, and inflation-adjusted product prices were to rise at

Table 3.2

Timber Demands and Land Requirements in the South
(all species)

Year	Timber demand (billions of cubic feet per year)	Land required at alternative productivity levels (million acres)			
		56.9 cu. ft./ac.	70.0 cu. ft./ac.	80.0 cu. ft./ac.	100.00 cu. ft./ac.
1976	5.66 (demand)	99.5	----	----	----
	10.70 (growth)	188.0[1]	----	----	----
2000	10.62 (historical trend)	186.6	151.7	132.8	106.2
	10.14 (rising prices)	178.2	144.8	126.8	101.4
2030	13.97 (historical trend)	245.5	199.6	174.6	139.7
	12.69 (rising prices)	223.0	181.3	158.6	126.9

[1]Present timberland base.

Unlike most projections, projections by the U.S. Forest Service do not include a "baseline projection" in which prices remain constant. Rather, projections are made assuming (1) that timber prices will rise at the same rate at which they have risen over the past 25 years and (2) that prices will rise fast enough to make demand and supply come to equilibrium. A baseline or constant price assumption would involve a higher timber demand than is shown here, and hence a larger land area would be needed at any assumed level of productivity.

Source: U.S. Forest Service.

no more than the historical trend rate, by the year 2030 the region would require 245.5 million acres of forestland. This is 57 million acres *more* than the South's 1977 forest area. If prices were to rise as steeply as the Forest Service expects, the demand for southern forestland (at a constant level of productivity) would be 223.0 million acres, still well above the current average.

But there are many ways now available by which landowners can raise productivity per acre. And general progress in society's knowledge about silviculture will most likely give them additional options in the future. These factors could make it possible to meet projected timber demands on a smaller total acreage. For example, if by the year 2030, average output on southern forestland can be raised to 100 cubic feet per acre, only 139.7 million acres will be required to meet historical-trend demand and only 126.9 million if prices are allowed to rise more rapidly than the historical trend. Increases in forest productivity could release tens of millions of acres to meet the demands of agriculture.

The Land Quality Issue

An important influence on forest productivity is the soil's inherent ability to grow wood. This is measured in terms of "site class"— the number of cubic feet per acre of commercially valuable wood that can be grown in a "fully stocked natural stand." In 1977, southern timberlands were classified as follows:

Site class (cubic feet per acre)	120 +	85-120	50-85	20-50
Acres (000)	12,681	47,900	98,302	29,163

Given the continual shifts of land into and out of forest, is the average quality of the South's forestland base getting better or worse over time?

This issue seems particularly apt in light of the apparent slowdown in the amount of farmland abandoned and allowed to revert to forest. In past decades, farmland reversion was probably an important force raising the average quality of the timberland base, because land marginal for farming often makes relatively good timberland. But there are indications that this replenishment of forest quality has declined markedly from its peak in the 1950s and 1960s.

Moreover, clearing for agriculture and for urban uses has continued or even increased. A Forest Service researcher in North Carolina describes the possible implications for forestland quality:

> Better, flatter, higher quality forestland is always being looked at for other uses—for housing, for pasture, for crops, for fruit growing. Forests are always being pushed back into the mountains and the swamps. Meanwhile, abandonment of farmland has almost stopped, and what is reverting to forest now is coming from very miscellaneous sources.[24]

It might seem easy to check the impacts of this process by comparing the average site class of land in the South at two points in time. Unfortunately, persons responsible for collecting these data indicate that relatively large areas of land have been reclassified from one site class to another between surveys as a result of changing estimates of their potential productivity. For example, tens of thousands of acres of low-quality land in Florida have been moved in and out of the timberland category as a result of changing ideas about their timber potential. The result of this kind of reclassification is to obscure any changes in land quality that may be due to forest clearing and reversion.[25]

Perhaps the most relevant, though partial, data are figures for the state of Georgia, where forest surveys were taken in 1972 and 1982.[26] Between those two surveys, 1,152,200 acres of privately owned forestland were diverted to other uses, while only 347,500 acres of land that was not in forest went into forest. The land taken out of forest was of markedly lower-than-average quality, as measured by site class.[27] On the other hand, the land going into forests was also of lower-than-average quality.[28]

The most that can be said of the land quality issue is that it is a potentially important concern that cannot be resolved with existing data. Given the ever increasing importance of land quality to intensive forestry, one can only hope that the Forest Service will give more attention to collecting consistent information on how the quality of the South's forestland base may be changing over time.

Forest Management

The amount of wood fiber that an acre of southern forestland actually produces relative to its biological capacity depends primarily on two aspects of forest management: (1) the economics of alternative management practices and (2) how different classes of forest landowners respond to economic opportunities.

Forest Economics—The Tyranny of Time. The farmer, planting a crop, expects to harvest within 3 or 4 months. The livestock raiser need plan on no more than 2 years between a calf's conception and its sale as an adult beef animal. But the essence of forestry is waiting. Even on the more fertile southern soils, one who invests in growing trees must wait at least 12 to 15 years for a crop of pulpwood, 25 to 30 years for pine sawlogs, and 50 or more for hardwood sawlogs.

Planting a tree, therefore, requires an implicit belief that there will be a market for that species, in that location, decades hence. And even given the ability to forecast the market with perfect certainty, the forestry investor must bear the financial costs of waiting. These include the costs of carrying the land for the entire growing period, both the forgone interest on the land's initial purchase price and the recurring costs of property taxes, boundary maintenance, and fire protection. If the initial establishment of the stand requires site preparation or planting, that investment must also be carried over a very long period of time.[29]

Assuming that the forest owner instead put money into a bank account with a real (net of inflation) compound return of 3 percent, each dollar of the initial investment would be worth $1.56 in year 15, $2.43 in year 30, and $4.38 in year 50. In the bank, the investment would be federally insured. Moreover, it would be always available at no greater trouble than a visit to the bank. An investment in trees, by contrast, might be wiped out physically at any time by fire or insects or voided economically by the closure of a local mill. And, although a growing timber stand does have some market value, it takes time and trouble to liquidate.

On the other hand, if all goes well, a dollar's worth of planted pine seedlings will (using current prices for comparison) be worth perhaps $2 as pulpwood at age 15 and $17 to $20 as lumber at age 30. The returns from forestry can be substantial, provided the investor is willing to wait for them.

Land fertility has a crucial, and often unappreciated, relationship with waiting time. A high-fertility site not only can grow more wood per acre than a site of poorer quality, it can bring each of its trees to maturity considerably faster. For example, consider loblolly pine seedlings planted on each of two sites, one of high quality and the other of medium-to-poor quality. By age 20, the poor site will have produced 14.5 cords of pulpwood, worth perhaps $145. But the better site will at the same age contain not only 32.5 cords of pulpwood (worth $325) but also 3,700 board feet of lumber, worth an additional $555. In this hypothetical—but realistic—example, an investor who intended to plant trees could get a higher return on his investment by choosing the high-quality site, even if buying the land cost $600 per acre, while the poor quality land could be used for free.[30]

Using high-quality land is only one of the ways by which foresters try to overcome the tyranny of time. A major reason for planting seedlings in the first place is to get a head start on establishing a new stand, rather than waiting until nature produces a good seed crop. Another way of shortening the time needed until harvest is to use genetically superior seedlings. For example, after only two generations of genetic selection, loblolly pine seedlings are available that produce 24 percent more wood annually than do ordinary seedlings.[31]

Still another method of raising per-acre wood production is precommercial thinning, removing from a juvenile stand perhaps a third of the individual trees. This reduces the amount of wood per acre in the short run, but it allows the remaining trees more room to grow and lets them reach sawtimber size much sooner than trees in an unthinned stand. Later "commercial" thinnings have the same effect, though they pay for themselves by providing salable pulpwood. More agricultural methods of speeding tree growth, such as fertilization and irrigation, have been tried, but high cost limits their application.[32] Other widely used approaches to speeding wood growth are drainage to remove subsurface water and the use of chemical herbicides on undesirable vegetation.

All of these techniques for speeding the growth of trees may be subsumed under the general title of "intensive silviculture." But there is another, quite different, way in which a landowner might deal with forestry's tyranny of time. Instead of investing substantial sums of money in an attempt to speed the day when financial return begins, the investor can try to minimize his initial investment, then simply accept the longer wait. With little capital at stake, the delayed return could represent a healthy percentage return on investment. Thus, rather than clear-cutting and replanting, a forest owner may decide to harvest only a portion of the

The Weyerhaeuser Way

Weyerhaeuser Company, the forest products giant based in Tacoma, Washington, is the nation's largest lumber company and among its largest papermakers. Its 3.0 million acres of southern forestland, principally in Oklahoma, Mississippi, Arkansas, and North Carolina, rank it second (to International Paper's 4.6 million acres) among the South's industrial forest landowners. Although most of the South's large timber firms are firmly and energetically committed to intensive management of their company-owned forestlands, Weyerhaeuser has embraced the goal of higher forest productivity with particular fervor. Millions of its corporate dollars annually go into research on intensive silviculture in the South, and tens of millions into translating research results into forest management on the ground. Officially, the company refers to its efforts as "the Weyerhaeuser high yield forestry program," but some southern foresters simply call it "the Weyerhaeuser way."

I spent a hot June day with two Weyerhaeuser foresters inspecting some of the company's 600,000 acres in eastern North Carolina. Most of the land, which they described as having been "impenetrable swampland," was acquired (sometimes from other forest products companies) during the 1950s and 1960s. "At that time," one of the foresters observed, "people would say to lumber companies, 'You cut my timber and I'll give you the land.' We turned down many thousands of acres at $5 to $15 an acre even into the 1950s." Now, after more than a decade of silvicultural investment, Weyerhaeuser has 320,000 acres of its North Carolina holdings in pine plantations, with 15,000 more added each year.

The area that I visited was near New Bern, North Carolina, a tract of several tens of thousands of acres that feeds a medium-sized pulp mill, much of its product eventually being used in disposable diapers. The plant is set up to make maximum use of all of the wood fiber that comes off the land. Of the trees consumed by the mill, 80 percent are pines. Large trees are sawed into lumber or peeled for plywood veneer; the small trees and lumber-mill residues are chipped and fed into the pulping process. Bark and spent pulping liquors are burned in the powerhouse boiler (the plant is close to completely energy self-sufficient).

The company-owned land that supplies the mill is primarily a "pocosin," a seasonally wet area with peaty, poorly drained soils. Because of the poor drainage and lack of certain nutrients, the natural forest is a mix of hardwood scrub and thinly stocked pond pines and cypress. "Without drainage," says one of the foresters, "some of the company land would not even grow timber. Or, if it did, it might grow 40 cubic feet per acre."

Weyerhaeuser's forestry prescription for this land involves massive investment and massive ecological change. "This is one of the few areas [in the South]," explains the forester, "where we can actually manipulate the site." The company's total investment in silviculture, aside from land costs, may exceed $300 per acre. The first step is drainage. Canals are cut with a large dragline ($50 to $75 per acre), causing the water table to fall below the root zone and rainfall to move off the land instead of pooling on it. Roads accompany the drainage. After drainage and road building, any merchantable timber is harvested (producing some revenue) and the stumps are sheared off ($70 to $75 per acre) with a huge Caterpillar-type tractor fitted with a special attachment called a "K-G blade." Remaining woody material is chopped into pieces ($35 per acre) by another machine, raked into piles, and burned ($8 per acre). At this point, the land looks like nothing other than a huge level field, awaiting its spring planting in crops. The land having been prepared, it is hand-planted ($35 per acre) with genetically superior trees ($15 per acre) and fertilized ($20 per acre). Once or twice during its early years, the plantation is treated with herbicides to control hardwoods and other vegetation that might compete with the young pines. The final result is impressively agricultural looking —thousands of acres of trees in even-aged blocks that allow the experienced eye to accurately guess the date of planting. The result is also an impressive wood-producing forest. "The average North Carolina nonin-dustrial forest," says one of the Weyerhaeuser men, "produces 50 cubic feet per acre per year. With some management this can be increased to 100. We average 150 to 200 and sometimes as much as 300."

According to Weyerhaeuser's present plans, a new plantation will be given its first commercial thinning at 12 to 15 years, with two more thinnings preceding the final harvest at age 27 to 30. But even with its massive landholdings and equally massive investment, Weyerhaeuser still relies on nonindustrial lands for a significant portion of its mill's fiber requirements. As a result, the company has employed several foresters to promote intensive silviculture throughout the procurement area of its North Carolina mills. To date, more than 600 owners, with over 250,000 acres of land, participate in Weyerhaeuser's North Carolina "Tree Farm Family."

mature pines, leaving others behind to drop seeds that will revegetate the site. (Once the new stand has been established, the mature trees may be harvested in a second cut.) The resulting forest is unlikely to be as productive as a carefully planted site, but the cost of establishing it will be minimal, so the return on investment may be quite satisfactory. Some foresters and many forest landowners believe that low-investment management, dubbed "soft silviculture" by one expert, is more profitable and more compatible with the needs of the typical nonindustrial owner than is intensive management.[33]

The trickiest aspect of soft silviculture is how to keep hardwoods from taking over after pines are cut. Hardwoods are tough competitors for light and water, and unless they are "knocked back" by fire or herbicides or mechanical cultivation, they have a strong tendency to crowd out the economically valuable pine reproduction. The more fertile the site, the more vigorous the hardwoods tend to be, and the more effort must be expended to control them. Thus, the economic rationale for concentrating intensive silviculture on the higher quality sites is reinforced by a biological rationale.

Aerial view of windrowed debris on a recently cleared and drained (note drainage ditches) pocosin wetland in eastern North Carolina. This land will be replanted in genetically improved pine seedlings.

Interestingly, to implement soft silviculture properly requires a higher level of forestry skill than does the blanket application of intensive forestry practices. It takes little knowledge of forest ecology to clear-cut a site, plow it, and replant with trees at a uniform spacing. A much more subtle perception is required to time cutting to the production of a good seed crop or to carefully select which trees to cut and which to leave behind for further growth. Says a Duke University silviculturist, "It requires a truly professional forester to apply soft silviculture with skill." And it takes a good understanding of both forestry and economics to know when some mix of intensive and "soft" methods is most suitable to a particular site or to the goals of a particular owner.

The choices that landowners make between intensive silviculture, with its high costs and high productivity, and soft silviculture, with its lower productivity but potentially higher net return, are central to judging the adequacy of the timberland base in the South. If all southern forestland were managed intensively, there is little doubt that there would be an adequate supply of softwood fiber, although wood prices would almost certainly have to rise considerably to make this intensification occur. More intensive management would permit a fairly significant shrinkage of the commercial forestland base, freeing land for alternative uses. There might still be problems, however, if competing uses took too much of the highest quality lands.

On the other hand, if, at current stumpage prices, many landowners are wiser to practice low-intensity management, the total acreage in southern forests, and particularly the land devoted to softwoods, becomes a very central and important concern.

Owners and Choices. A number of studies and surveys have pointed out that the southern forest products industry, which owns 19 percent of the South's commercial forestland, is undertaking high levels of investment in both reforestation and intensive management, while nonindustrial private owners, who own 71 percent of the acreage, are not For example, of 2.6 million acres of Florida forest harvested between 1970 and 1980, only one-third was artificially regenerated in pine. On private nonindustrial land, only 8 percent of the harvested land was so regenerated. Studies in several other southern states have found similar results, with nonindustrial owners much less likely than forest industry firms to replant after harvest.

Nonindustrial lands also rank below industrial lands in their total rate of tree growth. Across the South, annual growth on industrial timberlands averages 60.4 cubic feet per acre, against 56.1 cubic feet for private nonindustrial lands.[34] Moreover, a disproportionate amount of the growth on nonindustrial lands is in hardwoods. When only softwood growth is considered, industrial lands are approximately one-third more productive than those held by nonindustrial owners (41.4 cubic feet versus 30.4).

The alleged poor performance of nonindustrial private timberlands in the South has been an issue for decades, although the relatively recent intensification of silviculture on industrial lands has brought the matter into sharper focus. Initially, it was assumed that nonindustrial owners did not invest in forest management because they were ignorant of either the silvicultural techniques or the economic opportunities available. To correct this, the federal government and the states have for many years undertaken forestry extension programs aimed at "educating" nonindustrial landowners (though forestry extension programs have not been nearly as well funded as have the agricultural extension programs directed at crop and animal producers).

Virtually every forested county has an office where a forestland owner can go to get literature, advice, even an inspection and management plan for his land. These offices may also offer low-cost seedlings, the loan of planting equipment, and cost-sharing monies. In addition, the forest products industry has since 1941 supported a program called the American Tree Farm System, which offers advice to landowners, as well as a system of certification and awards for well-managed properties.

Given the effort that has gone into landowner education, and the relative ease with which most owners can get free advice about forestry, it is difficult, I believe, to make a case that owner ignorance is the primary reason why nonindustrial owners overwhelmingly choose low-intensity management.

Part of the explanation may lie in the fact that some nonindustrial owners are hampered by small-sized management units. A survey of landownership found that 11.4 percent of forestland in the South was held in units of fewer than 50 acres.[35] Moreover, an ownership unit may not be uniform in the age or species of its trees, so that the size of the ownership may overstate the size of the logical management unit. For example, a 1977 inventory of the Piedmont of South Carolina revealed that about 30 percent of the commercial timberland was broken up into stands (defined as groups of trees of similar age and species composition) smaller than 10 acres in size.[36] This problem of small stand area was especially pronounced on pine stands owned by nonindustrial private owners. Most industrial stands, by contrast, were larger than 50 acres.

Small management units adversely affect both the economics of timber harvesting and, especially, the economics of intensive management.[37] In addition to making it more costly to actually implement most forestry practices, small ownership size and small stand area present real obstacles to decision making. Even if the percentage return to investment in a given forest management practice is high, owners of small sites may simply find the total profit too small to be worth the trouble. The government or consulting foresters who might advise the owners are likely to feel the same way.

Another factor that could hamper nonindustrial owners is that their land is on average of lower quality than industry-owned land. In the South, 40 percent of industry land has a site class of 85 (cubic feet per acre) or higher; only 31 percent of nonindustrial land is of such high quality. As already noted, land fertility has a very large impact on the economic returns to tree planting.

These two characteristics of the land—stand area and land quality—no doubt explain part of the difference between industrial and nonindustrial investment patterns. But there are reasons to believe that, even when land characteristics are identical, nonindustrial owners may not find intensive forestry as attractive as do industrial firms. As one forester put it, "Intensive forestry makes perfect sense for the big timber companies, but it may not make any sense at all for 'Mr. Jones.'" There are at least four reasons why this is so.

First, a forest products firm regards at least part of its land base as a strategic investment rather than one that needs to be economically justified acre by acre. Before a firm invests several hundred million dollars in a mill, it usually makes sure that it has control over a certain percentage of its fiber requirements (about 50 percent is a common target). Without being able to demonstrate this control, the firm may find it difficult to secure from banks the financing needed for mill construction or expansion. Faced with a choice of buying new land, or intensifying the management of land it already owns, the firm frequently chooses intensive management. This is particularly likely when the firm owns good land close to its mills.

Second, firms may be more able than an individual to endure the relative illiquidity of timber during the growing period and to bear (by virtue of geographically diversified holdings) the risks of fire and disease. A firm is more easily able to borrow on the strength of its growing timber than is the owner of a single tract. The firm is also better able to generate a steady income stream from its holdings, some of which may be mature, while others

A Georgia tree farmer. The future of southern wood production depends heavily on management decisions by such nonindustrial private forest owners.

are seedlings. These factors may make the industrial firm more inclined than an individual owner to make the long-lived investments in reforestation that intensive forestry generally requires.

Third, forest industry firms may have an advantage when stumpage markets are not fully competitive. Because raw wood is a heavy commodity relative to its value and cannot be economically shipped over long distances, the owner of a given piece of land often finds only a handful of potential bidders for his stumpage. In some cases, there are only one or two. This kind of market power may be used by timber firms to depress the price of purchased stumpage relative to the price of the finished lumber or paper product. The firm, on the other hand, is able to get true market value for its own stumpage by processing it into products that can be sold in national markets, giving it a proportionately greater return on investment in intensive management.

Finally, the firm is likely to be interested almost entirely in wood production and will judge investments on the basis of how well they further that objective. The nonindustrial owner, however, may be interested in hunting or camping as much as in wood production. He may even intend eventually to use the land as a homesite or to sell it to someone else for that purpose. Because of these multiple objectives, the nonindustrial owner may prefer a mixed oak-pine forest to a pine plantation, because the former produces more palatable food (mainly grasses and acorns) for deer or squirrels. Or perhaps a stand with trees of several age classes, because it seems more attractive than a stand of evenly spaced, even-aged pines. Or the owner may resist clear-cutting, because it might reduce the land's market value as a dwelling site. These decisions can be considered "economically irrational" only if we fail to consider the owner's multiple objectives in owning forestland.

Intensive forestry pays off handsomely on the extremely good sites, but not so well on the average or poorer sites. If a man is restricted for capital, if he owns land of modest productivity and if he doesn't want to risk a great amount, and if timber production is not his lust in life, he is not foolish at all in not adopting intensive silviculture.

FRED M. WHITE, chief of research, development,
and planning, North Carolina Forest Service

Because of these differences between industrial and nonindustrial owners, it is likely that each will respond differently to changes in the demand for wood products. The timber firm is likely to react quickly to new profit opportunities, probably by intensifying management of its current land base, but occasionally by buying new land when the price is right and when large tracts are available. The nonindustrial owner will probably also respond positively to higher wood prices but is likely to favor wood production methods that require modest cash investment, that promise relatively quick returns, and that involve little interference with nontimber uses. Even though an increase in wood demand is likely to evoke greater output from both classes of owners, at any given level of demand, the average industrial property will almost certainly be more intensively managed than the nonindustrial property.

The "Pine Reforestation Problem"

The reluctance of nonindustrial owners to spend the money necessary to replant pines, and the reliance of these owners on methods of soft silviculture that are often carelessly implemented, have led a number of observers of southern forestry to worry that even present levels of pine production may not be maintained in the future.[38] Without either massive replanting or extremely widespread and careful application of low-investment methods of regeneration, they argue, millions of acres of southern timberland now in pine will regenerate after harvest in hardwoods, not pine. One study of loblolly pine, the South's leading softwood timber species, observes that, unless considerable effort is made to reforest, "the productivity of the [loblolly] ecosystem may [now] be at a peak."[39]

Forest Service analysts Stephen G. Boyce and Herbert A. Knight note that the lack of aggressive reforestation, coupled with high rates of harvest of pines that had grown up (often in abandoned farm fields or in Soil Bank plantations) during the 1950s and 1960s, has caused a decline in the number of pines 2 to 4 inches in diameter. "This decline," they report, "will [in coming years] reduce the number of pines in the 6-inch and larger diameter classes, especially on the nonindustrial private forests."[40] Their observation is underlined by a recent study of forest conditions in Georgia, the South's leading wood-producing state. Between 1972 and 1982, the study found, the number of southern pines dropped 45 percent in the 2-inch class, 29 percent in the 4-inch class, and 18 percent in the 6-inch class. Although the number of pines of sawtimber size is now higher than it was in 1972, the study concludes that the reductions in new pine seedlings "suggest that losses in pine volume in the 8-inch to 10-inch diameter classes will likely occur in the coming one to two decades."[41]

The prospective threat to future pine production is generally referred to as the South's "pine reforestation problem." A task force convened in the late 1970s to study the problem concluded that, "unless a substantial percentage of the independently owned acreage is placed under management and pine reforestation increased, there will be a shortage of sawtimber in the year 2000."[42] Pulpwood supplies were expected to be adequate, though it was thought that mills might have to enlarge their procurement areas. Many experts emphasize that the prospective shortfall in pine supply is more serious when local areas are considered than when only aggregate statistics are used. As the task force observed:

> The region's net annual cubic volume growth of softwood still exceeds the drain by 45 percent (5,752,000,000 vs. 3,964,000,000 cubic feet), and the sawtimber growth exceeds the drain by 30 percent (21,881 [million] vs. 16,817 million board feet). However, the sawtimber cut [now] exceeds the growth in the Coastal Plain of Virginia, in the north Coastal Plain of North Carolina, and in southeast Georgia south of the Altamaha River. And the situation bears watching in southwest Alabama, south Mississippi, east Texas, and southwest Arkansas.[43]

When taking my ecology classes on field trips around here, I've found it harder to find "old field" pines in the younger age classes. The places I used to visit are either grown up in houses or have been cut and are not regenerating well.

ARTHUR W. COOPER, professor of forestry, North
Carolina State University

A recent overview of timber growth data revealed that net annual growth of softwood timber in the South, which had been rising for many years, seems recently to have peaked and turned downward.[44] Several possible reasons have been advanced for the downturn, including the continuing decline in timberland area, inadequate pine regeneration on nonindustrial private lands, a sharp increase in annual mortality of pines, possibly due to insects or disease, and a recently noted reduction in the rate of individual tree diameter growth in parts of the Piedmont and Uplands. The last factor introduces a new uncertainty to long-range projections of forest productivity. To date, the growth reduction is not adequately understood, with some experts attributing it to drought and other natural cycles, while others attribute it to atmospheric pollutants. (For discussion of the latter, see chapter 5).

The Policy Context

Much effort has been expended over the years to raise the level of forest output in the South. Most of the attention has been directed toward increasing pine production. The major financial contributors to this have been state and federal governments, with continuous, though mainly verbal, support from the forest-products industry. However, in the last decade, the industry has become so concerned about future fiber supply that it has started to spend its own money to encourage nonindustrial owners to increase the productivity of their timberlands.

Nearly all of the policy initiatives taken so far have addressed the management of southern forestland, not the land base itself. The bulk of the effort has come through state forestry departments—each southern state has one—along with some technical assistance and funding from the U.S. Forest Service. The amount spent annually on these activities is substantial. In 1982, the Forest Service spent more than $25 million on "state and private forestry" programs in the South, while the southern states expended $163 million of their own.[45] The largest share of these expenditures was to protect forests from fire. In fact, state forestry departments have become, often by default, a major line of defense against rural fires of all types.

States also offer advice, and even some management services, to forest landowners. In most states, an owner with questions can go to a conveniently located office and secure, free of charge or for a small fee, a written management plan for the land, a rough estimate of the worth of the standing timber, advice on selling timber, and access at cost to pine seedlings produced in state-owned nurseries. Sometimes the state will lend the owner equipment for use in replanting or in timber stand improvement. State forestry agencies try to pay special attention to smaller land-owners; the owners of really large tracts are encouraged to buy management services from private consulting foresters.

The state forestry offices try to help landowners qualify for reforestation subsidies under various state and federal programs. For example, under the federal government's Forestry Incentives Program (FIP), a landowner may obtain a subsidy of up to 75 percent (the actual percentage is generally less) of the costs of reforestation or timber stand improvement. In 1982, the federal government spent about $10 million on FIP assistance in the southern states. In most places, there is an excess of applicants for FIP and other subsidies, so a landowner must decide whether to wait in line, losing valuable growing time, or to do the work immediately, without subsidy.

An indirect way of promoting timber growth in the South is through research. The federal government spends $22 million annually (FY 1982) on wood-related research at its research centers in Asheville, North Carolina, and New Orleans, as well as at smaller locations scattered throughout the South. Southern states also spend millions on forest research, principally through forestry departments at state universities. Several of the universities have cooperative research projects with industry—for example, North

Carolina State University has multicompany cooperatives on forest fertilization, loblolly pine genetics, and hardwood management, while Auburn has one on forest herbicides.

Perhaps the greatest subsidy to forestry in the South is through the federal tax system. For decades, owners of forestland have been able to write off annual expenses for stand management (though not reforestation) and to treat the income from a timber harvest as a long-term capital gain. In 1980, Congress passed legislation providing for a 10 percent investment tax credit and amortization over a seven-year period for up to $10,000 yearly of reforestation expenditures. This measure remedied a long-standing inequity that had allowed an investment tax credit and accelerated depreciation to people making long-term investments in machinery but denied them to people investing in trees. The impact of this new law was blunted somewhat by the passage the following year of still further tax concessions to nonforest investments. However, the subsidy to small-scale forestland owners is still very substantial, and foresters in the South report considerable enthusiasm for the program among their clients. It remains to be seen how much new reforestation will result. (In 1985, major changes in federal tax treatment of timber investments were proposed as part of the Reagan administration's initiative for general tax revision. The status of those proposals at this writing is unresolved.)

A final governmental approach to raising forest productivity is regulatory. The state of Virginia has, since the 1940s, had a so-called seed tree law.[46] The Virginia law, as it presently reads, requires that, when any stand containing more than 10 percent pine is harvested, eight 14-inch pines must be left per acre as seed trees to ensure reforestation in pine. Leaving these trees would deprive the owner of about 2,000 board feet of wood per acre, worth about $200 (though the seed trees could be cut after three years). Because of this cost, and because regeneration by seed tree is quite uncertain, nearly all owners choose another option allowed by the law—a promise to reforest the land so that there is survival of at least 400 pine seedlings per acre. This usually involves site preparation and the planting of seeds or seedlings. Expenditures in compliance with this law vary from $15 to $175 per acre, with the average about $130.[47] Partly as a result of the requirement, Virginia leads the South in number of pines planted yearly on nonindustrial private land.[48]

While effective, the regulatory approach is not popular in the South, where land-use regulations of all kinds tend to be resisted on ideological grounds. Mississippi has a similar regeneration requirement, though enforcement is said to be much less effective than in Virginia. Even in Virginia, says a state forestry employee,

"It's very questionable that such a law could be passed today."

A recent and potentially very important development in southern forestry is the increased commitment of forest industry firms to raising the productivity of nonindustrial forestland within the procurement areas of their mills.[49] Few of the companies are self-sufficient in timber—most buy 50 percent or more of the wood they process from private owners. Many firms perceive the South's pine reforestation problem as a major threat to their softwood fiber supply.

As a result of this concern, several major southern firms have begun programs for assisting nonindustrial owners, variously called "Tree Farm Families," "landowner assistance programs," or "cooperative forest management programs." For example, International Paper Company (IP) offers landowners within hauling range of its mills a free field inspection and written forest management plan, then recommends a contractor to provide needed services. If a contractor is not available, the company performs the service at cost. In return, the company is given right-of-first-refusal when the landowner wants to cut the timber. By 1983, IP had about 974,000 acres enrolled in the program, 917,000 in the South.

Westvaco Corporation provides not only advice and a written management plan but also free seedlings worth $15 to $20 per acre. It employs several full-time foresters, each of whom advises approximately 100 owners whose holdings total 80,000 acres. One of its foresters in South Carolina points out that a major advantage to the landowner is that the forester's constant involvement ensures that cutting and reforestation work will be done correctly—a major concern of owners who may live many miles from their forest property. In return for its help, Westvaco receives right-of-first-refusal on both land and timber. The South Carolina forester notes that from the company's standpoint the program is "the next best thing to owning land."

Timber firms' landowner assistance programs are likely to increase in the future, as firms become more concerned about fiber supply and as opportunities for management intensification on their own land are exhausted. These programs are targeted to the larger landowners—most firms will deal only with 100 acres or more—and, while somewhat sensitive to nontimber values, are mainly oriented to maximizing fiber output.[50] Landowner

Can Intensive Forestry Survive?

Intensified forest management frequently entails a major simplification of the forest ecosystem: trees of a single species and uniform age are grown, with vigorous measures taken to control competing vegetation. It also may mean the application on the site of herbicides, insecticides, and fertilizers. Harvest is more frequent than in a less intensively managed stand, and as much wood material as possible is taken from the site, sometimes including branches, tops, and even stumps.

A number of forest scientists, biologists, and environmentally concerned laypersons have expressed fears about the long-term side-effects of these practices. "What is going on in the root zone with repeated pine cropping?" wonders Fred M. White, chief silviculturist with the North Carolina Division of Forest Resources. "You can put fertilizers back in the soil, but you can't replenish the soil texture." There is also concern about the damage that measures intended to increase wood output are doing to other values of the forest. In 1980, the National Wildlife Federation brought a stockholder action against the Weyerhaeuser Company, charging that wildlife habitat was being degraded by clear-cutting and hardwood-to-pine conversion on the company's 900,000 acres of timberland in Oklahoma.[1] And, in Arkansas and western North Carolina, the Forest Service has faced strong local opposition when it tried to use chemical herbicides to kill hardwoods.

Concern about the long-term sustainability of short-rotation forestry has prompted the establishment of two comprehensive research projects, one at North Carolina State University (NCSU), the second at the University of Florida. The NCSU in-vestigators believe that the major impact on forest soils is likely to be not nutrient depletion, but compaction from heavy harvesting machinery.[2] Severely compacted soils resist plant rooting and show sharp reductions in productivity on the second rotation. But compaction, the researchers say, can be corrected—the forest owner may need only plow up the skid roads to reaerate the soil. One NCSU researcher believes that uniformity of species may be less of a problem than it appears. He notes that it is actually very difficult to maintain a single species forest monoculture in the South, and even an intensively managed site will have a fair amount of plant diversity. Controlled burning, for example, kills the hardwood reproduction only above ground level and thus slows but does not prevent its regrowth.

The Florida researchers found that in intensively managed slash-pine plantations there were some measurable ecological changes, but these changes seemed neither serious nor long term.[3] For example, water runoff rose after clear-cutting but quickly returned to normal as the new trees grew. The researchers also found that some impacts could be ameliorated by adjustments in management practices, such as not placing cutting debris in large piles or windrows (which tends to redistribute nutrients on the site) and leaving a few older trees to provide wildlife habitat on clear-cut sites. But one researcher did emphasize that the monitoring had been under way for only seven years; hence, the study could not be conclusive about impacts over several short rotations.[4] Nor did the investigators evaluate the impacts of really drastic management practices, such as whole-tree harvesting or stump removal, which remove from the forest large quantities of organic material and nutrients that in conventional harvesting systems are left behind to replenish the soil.[5]

Intensive forestry may also involve use of chemical herbicides to manage hardwood competition.[6] A given piece of land may be sprayed once or twice over the course of a rotation. Although it is possible to apply these chemicals with hand-operated spray rigs, or even by injecting individual trees, in most cases they are applied by aerial spraying. As a class, herbicides are usually considered less dangerous to nontarget species than insecticides, but there is still considerable argument over their safety.[7] Prescribed burning and mechanical brush control are alternative methods of controlling hardwoods, particularly on the flatter sites.[8]

Finally, there is increasing concern about the quality of lumber produced under conditions that encourage very rapid annual growth.[9] Trees harvested at an early age may produce weak lumber that tends to warp or crack under stress. As this problem becomes more widely known in the building industry, it could lead to lower prices for intensively grown wood that would partly or entirely offset the advantages of more rapid growth.

assistance programs may play a role in a future specialization among those trying to increase nonindustrial forest productivity in the South, with private consulting foresters dealing mainly with the very largest owners; landowner assistance programs with the large to medium-sized owners; and state forestry agencies with those owning the smallest properties.

The South's Forestry Outlook

Viewed from one perspective, southern lumber and paper producers seem likely to eventually face very serious constraints on the availability of softwood fiber. Demand for forest products will be rising, particularly if exports are strong. Mill wastes are increasingly well used, so it will be much more difficult than in the past to raise product output simply by more efficient processing of the material taken out of the woods. The softwoods that grew up in abandoned fields and in Soil Bank plantations during the first two post-World War Two decades are now being harvested; yet, in many cases, these softwoods are not being replaced. And, although forest industry firms are intensifying the management of their land, the nonindustrial owners who control more than two-thirds of the South's timberland are continuing to adopt low-investment methods of silviculture or are practicing no silviculture at all. As a result, millions of acres formerly stocked with pines are regenerating in hardwoods or mixed stands. Finally, the timberland base itself is under pressure, both in terms of acreage and possibly in terms of land quality. Because of this combination of forces, it is widely believed that prices for southern wood products will rise substantially in the years ahead.

This rise in price, however, will help southern forests increase their productivity. Even allowing for a declining land base, there are a number of options for raising the output of wood products in the South. One direction that will surely be adopted is greater substitution in final products of abundant hardwood fiber for soft-woods. A slight lowering of strength and brightness standards for paper, for example, could permit more use of low-quality hard-woods in the pulp mix. And hardwood-based flakeboards could substitute for softwood plywood in many applications. Advanced manufacturing methods will make it possible to make lumber out of trees now considered too small or crooked for that purpose.

There are also other opportunities. Although mill wastes are close to being fully used, there is more opportunity for making economic use of tops, branches, and saplings that are now left in the woods (an estimated 10 to 50 percent of forest biomass).[51] Increased use, of course, must be balanced against possible damage to soil fertility. In plantation forestry, greater use of genetically improved planting stock is likely to raise productivity per acre significantly. The gains may be particularly impressive if recombinant DNA techniques are successfully applied to tree genetics.

The crucial variable in assessing the future of the South's timberland is the behavior of the nonindustrial private owners. Until recently, it was assumed that the most appropriate goal of forest policy was to find ways to make the nonindustrial owners adopt the intensive forestry practices of industry. Debate among foresters centered not on this goal but on whether the very obvious failure to reach it was due to ignorance on the part of the nonindustrial owner or lack of economic incentive. Increasingly, foresters are becoming aware of the variations within this nonindustrial group: it consists of large-scale, economically motivated nonindustrial owners, who may indeed respond to price incentives with more intensive management; of owners hampered by small plots, short time horizons, and aversion to risk, who will only consider forest practices that require low front-end investment; and of multiple-objective owners, who will practice forestry only if it does not interfere with hunting, esthetic, or homesite uses of the land. For many of the last two groups of owners, hardwood or mixed pine/hardwood management makes much more sense than does softwood plantation forestry.

The long-term task for southern forest policy is to increase forest productivity, while recognizing that each group of owners will do what best meets its own objectives. Industry and the larger-scale nonindustrial owners will produce an increasing proportion of softwood fiber, with increasingly intensive management of short-rotation plantations. Ways must be found to do this without excessive damage to long-term land productivity or to nontimber values (see chapter 6). The smaller-scale nonindustrial owners will still play an important (perhaps even a predominant) role in fiber supply, but, unless economic incentives change radically, their supply of low-cost softwoods will dwindle, as poorly managed stands revert to low-grade hardwoods. Ways must be found to increase both hardwood and softwood productivity on these nonindustrial lands, with considerable sensitivity to problems of scale and of multiple objectives.

References

1. For an excellent account of the historical uses and results of fire in the South, see Stephen J. Pyne, *Fire in America* (Princeton, N.J.: Princeton University Press, 1982). See also Thomas D. Clark, *The Greening of the South* (Lexington: University Press of Kentucky, 1984), pp. 7-10.

2. See Thomas C. Croker, Jr., "The Longleaf Pine Story," *Journal of Forest History*, vol. 23, no. 1 (January 1979), pp. 32-43.

3. Boyce, McClure, and Sternitzke state flatly that "The [commercially important] loblolly pine ecosystem is a byproduct of land use changes in agriculture. Only 12 percent of the ecosystem is in plantations and most of these were established on retired croplands." Stephen G. Boyce, Joe P. McClure, and Herbert S. Sternitzke, *Biological Potential for the Loblolly Pine Ecosystem* (Asheville, N.C. and New Orleans, La.: U.S. Forest Service, 1975), p. 18.

4. Clarence F. Korstian, *Forestry on Private Lands in the United States* (Durham, N.C.: Duke University School of Forestry, 1944), p. 64.

5. A survey of nonindustrial private landowners in the South found that 63 percent did not use a forester to determine which trees were to be cut. See R.S. Fecso, et al., *Management Practices and Reforestation Decisions for Harvested Southern Pinelands* (Washington, D.C.: Statistical Reporting Service, U.S. Department of Agriculture, 1982). Since nonindustrial owners own 71 percent of southern forestland, this means that *at least* 45 percent of all southern forestland is harvested without a forester's help. Most, but certainly not all, of the public and industry-owned land is probably managed by professional foresters. Some private owners, no doubt, practice good forestry

without a forester's help, but, it is also certain, not all foresters practice good forestry.

6. U.S. Forest Service, *An Analysis of the Timber Situation in the United States, 1952-2030* (Washington, D.C.: U.S. Government Printing Office, 1982), pp. 231-32.

7. "Timber Firms Moving to the South as Supplies in Northwest Diminish," *Wall Street Journal*, July 18, 1983.

8. See U.S. Forest Service, *An Analysis of the Timber Situation in the United States, 1952-2030*; U.S. Forest Service, *America's Renewable Resources: A Supplement to the 1979 Assessment of the Forest and Range Land Situation in the United States* (Washington, D.C.: U.S. Government Printing Office, 1983); and unpublished U.S. Forest Service Data.

9. Most present production takes place in the Lake States, New England, and Canada, using aspen. But two new plants, in Louisiana and Texas, will use abundant southern hardwoods. See Peter Koch and Norman C. Springate, "Hardwood Structural Flakeboard—Development of the Industry in North America," *Journal of Forestry*, vol. 81, no. 3 (March 1983), pp. 160-1.

10. Interview, Athens, Georgia, January 1983.

11. Interview, Raleigh, North Carolina, February 1983. See also Bruce J. Zobel, "The Southeast Timber Supply: How Will It Be Affected by Changing Forestry in South America, Canada, and the Northeast?" *Southern Journal of Applied Forestry*, vol. 3, no. 2 (May 1979), pp. 37-42.

12. The northern states contain (1977) 129 billion cubic feet of hardwood growing stock, against 105 billion in the South. Annual growth is 4.2 billion cubic feet in the North and 4.6 billion in the South, with annual removals at 2.0 billion and 2.1 billion, respectively. U.S. Forest Service, *An Analysis of the Timber Situation*, various tables.

13. Despite the general abundance of hardwoods, large, select trees of species used in some types of furniture or for veneer have become increasingly scarce.

14. See Bruce J. Zobel, "Timber Supply Trends in South America" (unpublished paper, March 1979) and interview, Raleigh, North Carolina, February 1983.

15. Data are from U.S. Department of Commerce, *Annual Survey of Manufactures, 1980*. They do not include Arkansas or Kentucky. Eighty percent of southern forest products exports are paper products; 20 percent are lumber products. The value of exports would be much higher (13.3 percent of production in 1980) if indirect exports (for example, cartons used in shipping exported products) were considered. For changes over time, see Harold W. Wisdom, James E. Granskog, and R.J. Peeler III, "Southern Exports of Wood Products 1967-80," unpublished manuscript prepared for U.S. Forest Service, Southern Forest Experiment Station, New Orleans, Louisiana, 1983.

16. *U.S.A. Wood for the World* (Washington, D.C.: National Forest Products Association, 1983).

17. *Industry Week*, July 27, 1981, pp. 38-42.

18. *Business Week*, September 13, 1982, p. 72.

19. See, for example, D.R. Darr and G.L. Lindell, "Prospects for U.S. Trade in Timber Products," *Forest Products Journal*, three-part article, March, May,

June 1980.

20. Unpublished U.S. Forest Service data.

21. Foreign markets are likely to be particularly important in taking up any excess supply of wood that might occur if domestic demand fails to live up to projected levels. If domestic demand is strong, however, U.S. wood may be priced out of world markets.

22. For an exposition of some of the issues involved in accelerating harvest of old growth, see Con Schallau, "Departures from What?" *Western Wildlands*, University of Montana (Winter 1983).

23. Brian R. Wall, *Trends in Commercial Timberland Area in the United States by State and Ownership, 1952-1977, with Projections to 2030*, General Technical Report WO-31 (Washington, D.C.: U.S. Forest Service, 1981).

24. Joe McClure, Project Leader, Southeastern Forest Experiment Station, Asheville, North Carolina, personal communication, July 1982.

25. Inspection of site class data for 10 recent surveys taken around the country bears this out, with many surveys showing large shifts in the number of acres in any given site class, but with no apparent pattern.

26. Data provided by Herbert Knight, U.S. Forest Service, Southeastern Forest Experiment Station, Asheville, North Carolina.

27. Average site class for converted land was compared to the average for all nonindustrial private owners, on the assumption that relatively little of the land converted was owned by timber industry firms.

28. For example, only 25 percent of the land going out of forest had a site class of 85 or greater, compared with 47 percent for all Georgia forests. Of land going into forest, 16 percent was of site class 85 or greater. It is possible, however, that, because of the difficulty of measuring the site class of cleared land, the quality of land going into forest is systematically underestimated.

29. Federal legislation passed in 1980 makes it possible for investors to recoup some of their investment through tax benefits, by allowing a 10 percent investment tax credit and seven-year amortization of up to $10,000 in qualifying reforestation expenses incurred in any given year. However, general tax legislation passed in 1981 gave even more generous depreciation treatment to other forms of investment, so reforestation must still be considered in a relative sense an investment that ties up capital for a very long period of time.

30. The example assumes stand establishment (site preparation and planting) costs of $105 per acre or higher in each case. See J. Michael Vasievich, "Loblolly Pine Plantation Returns with Land Costs Included," U.S. Forest Service, unpublished paper, April 1982.

31. Peter Farnum, Roger Timmis, and J. Laurence Kulp, "Biotechnology of Forest Yield," *Science*, vol. 219 (February 11, 1983), p. 699.

32. Fertilization seems profitable on some sites in the South, such as pine plantations on poorly drained sites low in phosphorus. A good response may also be obtained by applying nitrogen to 10- to 25-year-old pine stands. One survey estimated that, in the 10 years ending in 1978, 900,000 acres of forest had been fertilized in the South, nearly all of them softwoods owned by timber companies. George W. Bengtson, "Forest Fertilization in the United States:

Progress and Outlook," *Journal of Forestry* (April 1979), pp. 222-29.

33. Although the concept has been advanced by several southern foresters, the term *soft silviculture* was to the best of my knowledge coined by Fred M. White, chief of research, development, and planning with the North Carolina Division of Forest Resources. Other foresters have used the terms *naturalistic silviculture* and *natural regeneration* to refer to this general approach.

34. These figures understate the actual difference because the Forest Service does not measure annual growth for trees less than five inches in diameter and therefore does not count the rapid growth being achieved on the industry's younger pine plantations.

35. Thomas W. Birch, Douglas G. Lewis, and H. Fred Kaiser, *The Private Forest-Land Owners of the United States*, U.S. Forest Service Resource Bulletin WO-1 (Washington, D.C.: U.S. Government Printing Office, 1982).

36. Herbert A. Knight, *Sizes of Timber Stands in the Piedmont of South Carolina*, U.S. Forest Service Research Note SE-67 (Asheville, N.C.: Southeastern Forest Experiment Station, 1978).

37. See Clark Row, "Economics of Tract Size in Timber Growing," *Journal of Forestry*, vol. 76, no. 9 (September 1979), pp. 576-82.

38. See, for example, Herbert A. Knight, "Southern U.S. Timber Supplies," paper presented to meeting of the International Institute for Applied Systems Analysis, Victoria, B.C., Canada, April 1985.

39. Boyce, McClure, and Sternitzke, *Biological Potential for the Loblolly Pine Ecosystem*, p. 23.

40. Stephen G. Boyce and Herbert A. Knight, *Prospective Ingrowth of Southern Pine beyond 1980* (Asheville, N.C.: U.S. Forest Service, 1979), p. 1.

41. John B. Tansey, *Forest Statistics for Georgia, 1982* (Asheville, N.C.: U.S. Forest Service, 1983), p. 1.

42. Hamlin Williston, "The South's Pine Reforestation Problem," *Journal of Forestry* (April 1979), p. 235.

43. Ibid., p. 235.

44. Knight, "Southern U.S. Timber Supplies."

45. Data from U.S. Forest Service and National Association of State Foresters. Federal funding for state and private forestry was severely cut in the 1982 and 1983 budgets. Initially, southern states made up the shortfall from their own resources, but in 1983 they too were cutting back forestry programs.

46. Virginia Seed Tree Law, Title 10, Article 6, Virginia Code, as amended 1972.

47. Interview with Richard Woodling and Frank Burchinal, Virginia Division of Forestry, Portsmouth, Virginia, June 1983.

48. Virginia Division of Forestry, *Virginia's Pine Resources—Problems and Opportunities* (Charlottesville, Va.: Virginia Division of Forestry, 1981), p. 8.

49. Some of the programs described below have antecedents that go back to the 1950s. But, since the mid-1970s, most companies have committed much more substantial amounts of money to them.

50. The letter of agreement that one company executes with landowners in its program notes that "The management plan generally will be designed to maximize the present value to owner of probable future economic returns

from use of the land for commercial timber production.''

51. For detailed estimates of the biomass distribution by species, see Joe P. McClure, Joseph R. Saucier, and R.C. Biesterfeldt, *Biomass in Southeastern Forests* (Asheville, N.C.: U.S. Forest Service, Southeastern Experiment Station, 1981).

Burning Wood as Fuel

1. Interview with J. Michael Vasievich, Duke University, Durham, N.C., January 1983.

Can Intensive Forestry Survive?

1. Dick Cook, ''Weyerhaeuser and Wildlife: NWF Finds a Key,'' National Wildlife Federation *Leader*, May 1980, p. 13.

2. Interviews with Jim Gregory and Russ Lea, School of Forestry, North Carolina State University, Raleigh, North Carolina, February 1983.

3. Sandra S. Coleman, Arnett C. Mace, Jr., and Benee F. Swindel, eds., *Impacts of Intensive Forest Management Practices*, Proceedings, Fourteenth Annual Spring Symposium, March 9-10, 1982, School of Forest Resources and Conservation, University of Florida.

4. Interview with Dan Neary, School of Forest Resources and Conservation, University of Florida, Gainesville, Florida, April 1983.

5. Coleman, Mace, and Swindel, eds., *Impacts of Intensive Forest Management Practices*, p. 4.

6. Among the herbicides commonly used on southern forest land are 2,4-D, Velpar[R] (hexazinone), glyphosate, Garlon[R] (triclopyr), and picloram. 2,4,5-T was once commonly used for hardwood control, but its EPA registration for forestry use has recently been suspended.

7. *Proceedings of the Symposium on the Use of Herbicides in Forestry*, Arlington, Va., February 21-22, 1978. (Washington, D.C.: U.S. Government Printing Office, 1978); Bette Hileman, ''Herbicides in Agriculture,'' *Environmental Science and Technology*, vol. 16, no. 12, 1982, pp. 646A-650A.

8. These methods are sometimes more costly than herbicides and can involve dangers of their own, such as carcinogens present in wood smoke and injuries suffered by workers using chain saws or driving tractors. Ibid.

9. John F. Senft, B. Alan Bendtsen, and William L. Galligan, ''Weak Wood: Fast-Grown Trees Make Problem Lumber,'' *Journal of Forestry*, vol. 83, no. 8 (August 1985), pp. 476-84.

Chapter 4

Animal Agriculture's Claim on Southern Land

Raising animals for meat, milk, eggs, and other products is a very important form of agriculture in the South, with annual sales about two-thirds as large as those of crops.[1] Beef cattle, dairy cattle, racing and pleasure horses, poultry, swine, sheep, and even pond-raised catfish contribute to this total, each creating both direct and indirect demands for rural land. In terms of total acreage, however, no form of animal agriculture comes close to making the claim on land made by the grazing of the South's 14 million beef cattle.

On today's southern farm, pigs and poultry are raised in pens or confinement houses, eating corn or soybean meal, much of it shipped in from the Midwest. Although dairy cattle, horses, and sheep do get much of their nutrition from pasture, their numbers are relatively small.[2] Southern beef cattle, however, get most of their food by grazing and require the services of tens of millions of acres of pasture and rangeland.

In addition to the sheer magnitude of this demand for land, beef cattle are of special interest for two reasons. First, by virtue of their multichambered stomachs, cattle (and other ruminants such as sheep, bison, and deer) are able to digest cellulitic plant materials that cannot be eaten by humans. They can thus make economic use of native grasses and shrubs, as well as of planted forage crops that may be grown on land unsuitable for other crops. Quite adaptable in their dietary requirements, beef cattle may be fed with surplus grain held off the market in times of low prices, with cottonseed hulls, with cornstalks and other crop residues, or with hay. Thus, beef cattle represent a major source of flexibility in the agricultural system, with the number of animals and methods of feeding fluctuating with relative prices of alternative feeds.

Second, southern beef-cattle raising has become relatively more important in recent years, with animal numbers more than triple what they were in 1950 and methods of production in flux. There appear to be significant opportunities for further expansion, should the demand for beef warrant it. Future cattle numbers and the technologies employed to feed them will have a complex impact on the South's land resources. Beef cattle will not only affect the demand for pasture and rangeland but also the demand for cropland, which produces hay and feed grains consumed by animals, and forestland, which holds the promise of offering forage among the growing trees.

The South's Beef-Cattle Economy

The foundation of the South's present beef cattle industry is the "cow-calf" operation.[3] In its classic form, this means that southern cattle raisers keep a herd of female animals on pasture and breed them each summer to produce a calf early the following spring. Calves remain with their mothers for 7 to 11 months, getting some

Every week during the early fall, an assortment of farm vehicles converges on livestock auctions, such as this one in Morrilton, Arkansas, where southern-born calves are sold as stocker cattle.

of their nutrition from mother's milk and some from their own grazing. By fall, the cattle raiser has a 300- to 500-pound calf that has required virtually no purchased feed and that can be sold for 50 to 70 cents per pound. Once a week, an assortment of vehicles, ranging from dusty pickup trucks carrying a calf or two to large trailers hauling dozens, will converge on auction barns in small towns all over the cattle-raising area of the South.

The predominant buyers of these animals have traditionally been midwestern grain farmers and western ranchers who purchase truckloads of southern-born calves to feed over the fall and winter on Oklahoma hay and winter wheat, Iowa corn silage, or Arizona winter grasses. Other buyers come from within the South —owners of land in coastal Texas and Louisiana who have lush winter pastures, Mississippi soybean growers who can turn cattle loose on a field of double-cropped winter wheat, and local farmers who have an excess of hay or crop residues. This period of a beef animal's life, when it is from 9 to 15 months of age, is potentially a period of very rapid growth. There are significant opportunities for profit if a cattle buyer can combine a reasonably priced calf with inexpensive forage to produce weight gains of one to two pounds per day. This phase of the animal's life is called the "stocker" period; the animals involved are called stocker cattle.

By 15 months of age, a beef animal weighs 600 to 800 pounds and is ready for "finishing." An animal raised entirely on grass or hay does not have enough fatty tissue to produce the tender cuts of meat that grade as USDA Choice or Prime and command a premium price at slaughter. Thus, most beef cattle gain their final 250 to 500 pounds by being fed corn or other grains over a three- to six-month period.

Traditionally, most southern cattle were finished on grain farms in the Corn Belt, then slaughtered in market centers such as Chicago or Omaha or St. Louis. Starting in the mid-1960s, however, a highly important structural change revolutionized the cattle-feeding business.[4] A number of aggressive entrepreneurs discovered that cattle could be fed in confinement pens or "feedlots" on a large scale in the dry climate of North Texas, the Oklahoma Panhandle, Kansas, Nebraska, or Colorado and produce faster weight gains than in more humid areas. The huge scale (100,000 animals per year from a single feedlot is not uncommon) made it possible to mechanize the feeding process and to introduce sophisticated formulation of the feeding ration, while supplies of sorghum and other feed grains were newly available from nearby land irrigated from the Ogallala Aquifer. Animals could be slaughtered in modern, automated plants near the feedlot and the meat shipped to market in refrigerated rail cars or trucks. Recently, more than half of the fed cattle marketed in the United States have been fed in only about 420 large commercial feedlots, nearly all in the southern part of the Great Plains.[5] As a result of this shift in feedlot location, the annual flow of southern calves to pasture and feedlot has turned distinctly westward in the last 10 to 15 years.

Looking at the beef production system then, two economic characteristics soon become apparent. First, cattle move from owner to owner and from place to place in response to the availability of cheap food. It is not unusual for an animal to be trucked 500 miles to gain 300 extra pounds.[6] The average southern steer may travel 1,500 miles during its lifetime.[7] Because a beef animal can gain weight on such a wide variety of feedstuffs, cattle raisers are quite opportunistic in the mix of feeds used. When grain prices are low, animals go to the feedlot at a younger age and consume cheap grain; when grain is expensive, they spend more time on grass. If summer rainfall is low, southern calf producers will draw down their herds, even selling some breeding cows so that fewer animals will have to be fed over the winter on expensive purchased hay or grain. On the other hand, if fall pastures are lush, southern producers will market fewer calves in the fall and do the further development of the animals on their own pastures. The following spring the heavier animals can be shipped directly to a feedlot. Most of the profit in the southern cattle business comes from a finely tuned sense of when to sell an animal and when to hold it back for a few more months on forage.

The South has a consistent comparative advantage over other regions as a supplier of calves, partly because of the seasonal pattern of its forage, partly because of low labor costs. But its advantage in the stocker phase varies from year to year according to the availability of feed and forage in other parts of the country. Thus, the South has a well-developed cow-calf industry; its stocker-cattle activity waxes and wanes depending on conditions elsewhere in the country.[8]

A second important economic characteristic of cattle raising is that the economic value of pasture and range is essentially determined (and limited) by the cost of producing the equivalent amount of weight gain by feeding an animal grain or a harvested forage such as hay or silage.[9] Although there are many ways of using land to produce forage (see below) and some are much more intensive than others, almost never do the per-acre returns to grazing approach those of using land for crops. The net return from an acre of grassland is generally only a few dollars per year, and returns of $50 per acre are exceptional.[10] Grazing is a use of land that flourishes on land too steep or too infertile to be profitably used for crops or that can be introduced as an adjunct to a cropping or timber operation. The South has a great deal of such land, particularly hilly land in the Piedmont and Uplands, coastal grasslands too wet for crops, and worn-out former cotton fields. "The only justification for the beef cow is as a scavenger," says Dr. Charles Lassiter, head of the animal science department at North Carolina State University. "But 60 percent of the land in the U.S. is unsuitable for row crops and that's what you use to feed cattle."[11]

The Varieties of Southern Grasslands

Roughly 50 million acres of southern land are presently used to provide forage for farm animals, perhaps 90 percent for beef cattle. One must use the qualifier "roughly" because some grazing activities overlap with crop and forest uses and because grassland statistics come from more than one government agency and tend to be inconsistent, even contradictory.[12] The imprecision of available statistics is oddly appropriate, since grazing is by nature a flexible use of land, which probably expands and contracts from year to year by more than do crop uses, and certainly by more than does forest area.

Southern grassland comes in a bewildering profusion of types, with yields per acre extremely variable and dependent on soils, rainfall, temperature, and intensity of management.[13] There are five principal ways of managing land to produce forage for animals.

Table 4.1

Forage-Producing Land in the South, 1982

(acres)

	Harvested forage (hay, grass silage)[1]	Fertilized pasture and rangeland	Unfertilized pasture and rangeland	Farm woodland grazed	Total grazing land
Arkansas	878,203	470,875	3,088,892	1,241,835	4,801,612
Alabama	568,456	655,334	1,991,221	1,219,880	3,866,435
Florida	281,747	1,069,974	5,109,846	1,965,900	8,145,720
Georgia	482,438	538,596	1,655,401	1,036,749	3,230,746
Kentucky	1,466,050	458,236	4,057,640	1,054,505	5,570,381
Louisiana	348,497	321,363	1,615,772	500,986	2,438,121
Mississippi	607,011	582,072	1,983,929	1,259,043	3,825,044
North Carolina	375,940	323,747	931,725	605,843	1,861,315
South Carolina	216,153	234,203	516,809	391,166	1,142,178
Tennessee	1,127,138	624,441	2,941,258	1,229,016	4,794,715
Virginia	948,741	328,018	2,438,607	821,941	3,588,566
Total South	7,300,374[2]	5,606,859	26,331,100	11,326,864	43,264,833[2]

[1]Because of definitional problems that might have produced double-counting, several hundred thousand acres of southern land producing corn silage and sorghum silage are excluded.

[2]Total forage-producing land (harvested forage plus total grazing land)—50,565,197 acres.

Source: U.S. Department of Commerce, Bureau of the Census, *Census of Agriculture 1982.*

First, one can grow a grass (such as tall fescue), a legume (such as alfalfa or clover), or even a grain-bearing plant such as oats or corn, then harvest the entire plant for hay or silage. This is a relatively expensive way of producing forage, but it results in a product that can be stored and fed to animals when pasturage is not available. In 1982, some 7.3 million acres of southern land were used for this purpose (see table 4.1). These acres are counted as "harvested cropland" rather than grazing land, but they represent an important supplement to the diet of the grazing animal.

Second, one can grow grass under relatively intensive management, harvesting the resulting material by grazing. Intensive management can involve application of fertilizer and lime, control of weeds with herbicides or by mechanical means, planting of nonnative grass, and fencing of the land into small units. Given the unavailability of data on all of these practices, I will define intensively managed pasture as that to which fertilizer is applied. In 1982, there were 5.6 million acres of such land in the South. The intensity of management of this land is probably quite variable. It may be heavily fertilized in years when fertilizer prices

Cattle grazing on a large plantation, Colfax, Louisiana.

are low and beef prices high but not fertilized at all when the reverse is true. To justify the expense of fertilization, land quality must be relatively high. In fact, much fertilized pasture is actually cropland temporarily or permanently taken out of production.

A third way of producing forage is with unfertilized pasture and rangeland. In the past, one could distinguish between rangeland and pasture by the fact that the former grew native grasses and was unfenced, while the latter grew nonnative grasses or legumes and was fenced. But there is now hardly any open range left in the South, and much lightly managed pasture consists of a variable mixture of grasses. Whether or not fertilizer is applied is probably the more helpful way to distinguish among important types of pasture management. Unfertilized pasture is generally much inferior in production per acre either to fertilized pasture or to land harvested for hay. To support a cow and her calf for one year would require between 1 to 3 acres of fertilized or harvested pasture, while with unfertilized pasture between 1 and 10 acres would be required, with the average probably above 5 acres. (The difference in productivity is not merely due to fertilization but also to the fact that fertilizer can profitably be applied only to fairly good-quality land.) Unfertilized pasture, or "extensive pasture," amounts to some 26.3 million acres in the South. It is by far the largest type of pasture use by acreage but may provide no more annual feeding value than do the more intensively managed pastures.

A fourth type of grazing is forest grazing. A dense forest, whether pine or hardwood, generally shuts out so much light from the forest floor that little forage is produced, even for wildlife. But open forestlands, whether they are sites of recent clear-cuts, forests interspersed with meadows, or pine plantations with relatively wide spacing, can produce as much as 2,000 or 3,000 pounds of forage per acre per year. In most cases, forest grazing blends with the less-intensive types of pasture management. Typically, a farmer will have wooded areas adjoining a grassland pasture; animals will be free to graze among the trees or in the open grassland as they please. Considering only forest owned by farmers, the South provides some 11.3 million acres of forest grazing; if one also includes nonfarm forest, one might count as many as 49 million acres (excluding Oklahoma and Texas) of grazed forest. Some grazed forest, particularly in the better soils of the southern Coastal Plain, may produce enough forage to allow one cow/calf unit for each 10 acres of land. But many other forests would require 100 acres per unit, and the average is probably close to 50.

A final way of producing forage is to let animals graze on crop residue, such as cornstalks or wheat stubble. The animals probably get little food energy from so doing, but the cost is minimal. A more productive method, which is increasing in popularity in the South, is to allow cattle to graze winter wheat fields during the early stages of the crop's growth.[14] If grazing is terminated before the wheat begins to produce its seed stalk, the size of the wheat harvest will be little less than if the field had not been grazed at all. No regionwide data are collected on the extent of crop-residue grazing.

The Seasonality Problem

What mix of these forage systems will be used by a given farmer depends on the land available, either owned or leased from someone else. It also depends on the marginal costs of fencing, fertilizer, labor and other inputs that are applied to land. But regardless of the system chosen, the southern farmer has to face another problem—the seasonality of forage. Much of the South is sufficiently mild in winter so that snow rarely covers fields for long. And, while there are summer droughts, one rarely finds periods in which lack of water actually kills the grass crop. However, even within these mild extremes, no single species of grass grows uniformly over the course of the year.

Farmers might plant "cool season" grasses such as bluegrass or tall fescue, but the growth of these grasses slows drastically in summer. Alternatively, farmers might grow "warm season" grasses such as Bermuda grass, which stays green in the hottest summer weather (as long as it gets sufficient water) but turns brown and unpalatable when the weather turns cool. Naturally, the seasonal performance of grasses differs with latitude; monthly performance is different, for example, in Piedmont Virginia and southern Alabama. The principle, however, is the same—a mixture of grasses must be used to provide forage year around. Moreover, except in the southernmost portions of the South, for two or three winter months no forage crop is very productive, and grazing must be supplemented with hay or even grains.

The seasonality of grasses causes southern graziers to grow several different kinds of plants, each with a different seasonal distribution, in individually fenced fields or occasionally simply mixed together in the same field, with one type of plant accelerating its growth as other species begin to falter. Seasonality also leads to the yearly sale of stocker calves born in the upper South to owners of winter pasture farther South. Florida's mild winter climate gives it an unusual advantage in producing good-quality forage year-round. This high total productivity has yielded one of the South's most intensely managed livestock industries. Florida has more fertilized pasture than any other southern state; its 569,000 acres of irrigated pasture represent more than 90 percent of all irrigated pasture in the South.[15] (Florida also has the South's only large area of native rangeland, so its beef-cattle industry is an interesting mixture of very intensive and very extensive use of land.)

The Sociological Dimension

The availability of forage is the foundation of southern cattle raising, not a full explanation of it. Nearly 300,000 southern farms (about half of all farms) have some beef cattle; 90 percent of these operations have fewer than 50 animals, although these small herds contain half of all southern beef cattle. There are also huge operations, concentrated mostly in Florida, where there are 158 farms that each contain more than 1,000 cattle. Some of these Florida farms devote more than 10,000 acres of mostly native rangeland to grazing.

One cannot understand the southern beef-cattle economy without appreciating its sociological dimension. Cattle raising is, on one hand, a romantic, high-rolling enterprise that appeals to wealthy enthusiasts whose willingness to bear risks is enhanced by abundant tax advantages (see box). Geographer John Fraser Hart describes the southern cattle farm as

> a pleasant place to invite friends for the weekend, [which confers] upon its owner a special distinction, the pleasure of wearing cowboy regalia. No insignia distinguish the cotton planter, the hog farmer, the forester, the businessman or the industrialist, but the man who owns a cattle farm is entitled to wear the ten-gallon hat, high heeled boots, western shirt,

and longhorn tie clasp, which make him the envy of his colleagues and all small boys.[16]

The cowboy image is relatively unimportant in the upper South, though it is replaced in such areas as Kentucky and Piedmont Virginia by the "gentleman squire" equivalent. It is quite evident in Florida, Louisiana, and Texas. People seldom enter the cattle

Taxes and "The Farmer's Friend"

"Sophisticated investors today have their eyes on cattle for a number of sound financial reasons."[1] Thus begins a chapter on tax planning in a popularly written guide to the beef-cattle business. Although tax considerations are by no means the only reason why so many southern landowners are in the cattle business, the abundant advantages possible under current federal income tax law have played a significant role in attracting part-timers and nonfarm investors into the cattle business.

Some tax advantages are peculiar to livestock, chief among them Section 1231 of the Internal Revenue Code, sometimes called "the farmer's friend."[2] This provision allows the owner of a breeding cow (the basis of the South's cow-calf operation) kept more than two years to qualify for capital gains treatment when the animal is sold. Since the expenses of raising a heifer to maturity are deductible as ordinary business expenses, this provision essentially allows the cattle breeder to convert ordinary income into capital gains (as well as deferring the tax liability over time) should the breeder ever decide to sell breeding cows from a herd. A cattle raiser who buys cows for breeding purposes, rather than to raise personally, is allowed a 10 percent investment tax credit and depreciation over a five-year period. (The 1981 Tax Act improved these from a 7 percent

credit and seven-year depreciation.) Favorable tax treatment is also allowed for fencing and for other types of fixed capital commonly used in the cattle business. Tax subsidies available to nonfarm investors owning cattle fed in feedlots have indirectly helped cow-calf operations by increasing the amount feedlots are willing to pay for cattle.[3]

Other tax provisions applicable to farming in general are also heavily used by cattle operators. Provided they generate a certain level of farm income, farmers in many states are allowed preferential assessment of land for real-estate tax purposes. Substantial estate tax benefits are allowed for people who inherit operating farms. And there are a host of small but valuable opportunities for income tax savings. For example, farmers can use favorable rules on reporting of income and expenses to shift tax liability from one year to another. Or farmers might pay their children a (tax-deductible) wage for tending livestock in lieu of an allowance. Tax preferences are probably not the sole motivation for most southern cattle farmers, but they represent an important source of financial return, particularly to those who have relatively high incomes from other sources. In effect, tax preferences are a government subsidy of cheap beef and a particular way of life.

business intending to lose money, but for many affluent investors the romance of the business is at least as important as the simple economic return. (The business of raising purebred horses, which is important in several southern states, is often similarly motivated.)

On the other hand, the South contains many part-time cattle raisers who also have a mix of economic and noneconomic motives. Beef cattle-raising is one of the least labor-intensive forms of agriculture. The cattle feed themselves most of the year. Even in winter, an owner might safely leave them unattended for several days, simply making sure that there is enough hay in the field for the cattle to eat. Cattle do not have to be attended when they drop calves (although a certain death loss is avoided by doing so). The low labor requirement makes cattle raising ideal for the part-time farmer with a nonfarm job, or even for the weekend farmer. It is also a good sideline for the full-time crop farmer who may have a few hours to spare and who wants to do something with land too poor for row crops. As one southern beef-cattle expert puts it, "People inherit 100 acres of land and like the country life and, if they can get $5,000 or so a year from raising cattle, they are content. The only real cost they have is buying a bull."

The heavy participation by both wealthy enthusiasts and part-time farmers has contributed to low profit margins and high cyclicality in the cattle business. It is a business easy to enter on a small scale, and there are enough people who want to do so that each uptick in the beef market tends to encourage over-expansion of herds and a subsequent fall in prices. As one stock-raising magazine has put it, "A businessman cannot compete with a man enjoying a lifestyle."[17]

The wide differences among the types of southern cattle raisers, in size, wealth, and sophistication, are reflected in an array of management practices. Some southern cattle farms have an almost manicured look, with improved, lavishly fertilized pasture and cattle of uniformly good genetic stock; others, even in the same county, have rough, unfertilized pasture and animals whose breeding is obviously inferior.[18] There is much more variance in intensity of management and in technologies employed within the cattle business than there is within crop agriculture. In this respect, grazing is comparable to forestry, where intensive man-agement and "soft silviculture" coexist. As in forestry, the most intensive form of management is not always the most profitable one, even if it results in the highest wood output per acre or the greatest weight gain per calf. What is important is the return relative to the inputs needed to produce it. One animal scientist points to the financial flexibility available to the small or part-time southern stock raiser, who "may do everything wrong but still has wads of hundred dollar bills in his pocket. He doesn't get overextended; he can produce cheaply by not using a lot of inputs; he doesn't have high expectations for his own consumption [and so can cut it back when times are hard]."[19]

The Future of Grazing in the South

Just as the demand for southern cropland depends on the demand for soybeans, the demand for the South's grazing resource depends in great part on how much beef will be demanded by consumers.[20] In this case, the relevant demand is domestic, not domestic plus foreign, for only a tiny fraction of U.S. beef production is exported. Even at a static demand for beef, there are indications of change in the economics of beef production that could increase the relative amount of pasture used in the South. Still, an overall expansion of the U.S. cattle herd over current levels would probably be needed before pressure on the South becomes noticeable.

The Demand for Beef

For many years, it appeared that the American consumer's demand for beef was insatiable. Although consumption would fall somewhat whenever short supplies caused a rapid increase in prices, the long-term trend in demand was clearly upward. The observation that affluent people eat more beef than do poorer ones seemed to characterize U.S. society, as rising affluence was translated into a demand for more beef. In 1976, per-capita beef consumption reached a record of 94.4 pounds (retail weight), up from only 64.2 pounds in 1960. In response to rising demand, the number of U.S. beef cattle also rose, though with considerable cyclical variation, and reached an all-time high in 1975.

The years since the mid-1970s, however, have been difficult ones for the cattle industry. By 1982, per-capita beef consumption had fallen to 78 pounds, and, in response to lower demand, the number of beef cattle had fallen by 14 percent. Part of the falloff in demand might be attributed to slowing growth in consumer incomes. But other forces seemed to be at work as well and to suggest a long-term change in consumption patterns.

A recent and unusually frank appraisal of the beef-cattle industry's prospects by the National Cattlemen's Association observes that, barring a substantial increase in consumer incomes, "the rise in average per capita consumption of meat is at an end."[21] Well-fed Americans seem to be reaching the limits of overall meat consumption, and many have actually begun to cut back on calories for health reasons. With the U.S. population now growing at less than 1 percent per year, this seems to indicate very slow potential growth in total meat consumption in the years ahead.

A plateauing of total meat consumption means an intensification of competition for the consumer dollar among producers of various types of meat. Beef faces two problems in this competition. First, it is perceived as "heavier" and more fatty than many other animal protein foods, such as poultry, cheese, and fish. This perception appears to be particularly strong among young people and persons with higher than average levels of income and education. Second, the price of poultry has fallen dramatically relative to that of beef, in both the last few years and over a span of several decades. In 1950, the price per pound of chicken averaged 80 percent of the price per pound of beef; by 1981, chicken was only 30 percent as expensive as beef.[22] Pork prices have also fallen somewhat relative to beef, although the long-term trend is not nearly so pronounced. For both chicken and pork, the price has been held down by widespread adoption of labor-saving confinement methods of raising the animals and by genetic improvements in the animals themselves.

Some have argued that the poultry industry has now exhausted most of the available opportunities for productivity improvement, while the beef industry has barely scratched the surface of what is possible. Yet there are basic limitations that will make it extremely difficult for beef to compete on a price basis with chicken and other meats. For one thing, chickens are very efficient converters of grain into meat protein. A pound of chicken can be produced from only 2.1 pounds of grain; the conversion ratio for beef is about 7:1. (Various forms of aquaculture are more efficient than poultry, raising the possibility of long-term competition from this entirely new area.)

The Broiler Industry:
A Southern Livestock Phenomenon

In 1982, the southern states produced the startling total of 2.95 *billion* broiler chickens. This was about three-quarters of total national broiler production and was worth just over $3 billion. (For comparison, the value of annual sales of cattle in the South was $2.9 billion and of soybeans $3.6 billion.)

The chickens themselves occupy only a tiny amount of land, because nearly all are raised in confinement structures, the long white-washed wood or prefabricated metal buildings so often seen from rural roads. But the broiler industry has two important indirect effects on how land is used.

First, broilers (as well as eggs and turkeys) are a major source of income for many small and part-time farmers in the South. The modern broiler industry developed during the 1930s, when many small southern farmers were casting about for an alternative to crop production.[1] Because of the relatively high capital requirements for raising broilers in confinement, a system developed whereby entrepreneurs (some of whose operations developed into huge vertically integrated firms) would furnish a farmer with baby chicks, feed, and medications, then truck the mature broilers off to the packing plant. Because of the disparity in bargaining power between the farmer and the broiler owner, the farmer's return was usually meager. But it was often enough, perhaps when combined with income from a few cattle or a tobacco allotment, to keep a farmer on the land.

A second impact is through the feed ration. Broilers eat a carefully compounded diet that is mainly corn and soybeans, with the addition of other grains and small amounts of vitamins and antibiotics. Although chickens are extremely efficient feed converters—only 2.08 pounds of feed are required to produce a pound of poultry—the huge numbers of chickens on southern farms equate to a huge demand for feed. One can calculate that, for a feed ration that is 60 percent corn and 20 percent soybean, the South's annual broiler population would require 104 million bushels of soybeans and 294 million bushels of corn. At the South's average per-acre production of these crops, feeding the region's broilers would require more than 11 million acres of land.

However, southern chickens do not necessarily eat southern grain. Each fall and winter hundreds of big tractor-trailers move back and forth between the grain farms of Iowa, Illinois, and Missouri and the South's poultry-raising centers in the Georgia and Alabama Piedmont and in northwest Arkansas, bringing in corn and soybeans that, even after factoring in the relatively high cost of hauling, can be sold more cheaply than they can be produced locally. No agency keeps track of how much of the South's poultry feed is locally raised and how much is imported from other regions. Grain consumption by poultry is equal to about a quarter of the South's soybean output and more than half of its corn output, but it appears that the region exports much of its grain overseas, while its broilers get much of their food from outside the South.

Subregionally, the centers of corn and soybean production in the South do not correlate well with its centers of poultry raising. The latter tend to be found in some of the poorer crop-raising areas, tending to confirm the hypothesis that lack of alternative opportunities pushed farmers into chicken raising. One U.S. Department of Agriculture poultry expert says that there is a historical relationship between the development of the South's broiler industry and that of its grain production, but not a close one. "Chickens didn't go to the South because the grain was there," he says, "but there isn't any doubt that it has encouraged grain production locally in places, such as North Carolina, that were well suited to raising grain."[2]

The nation's broiler industry is likely to grow by 2 to 3 percent yearly, and the South is expected to retain its historic predominant share.[3] Thus, broilers represent a significant and growing potential market for the South's corn and soybeans, but only if the grain can be produced at competitive prices.

The cattle industry is also hindered by the fact that a cow can give birth to only 1 or at most 2 calves yearly, while a female pig can produce 30 offspring yearly and a hen well over 100. These fundamental biological factors mean that beef is always likely to be more costly than other meats. Cattle producers' principal hope to remain cost competitive is the ability of the beef animal to use forages of no direct food value to humans.

Beef producers probably have a better chance of adapting to consumer concerns about calories and fat. A number of supermarket chains have begun to sell ungraded or "house brand" beef in addition to or instead of "USDA Choice" cuts. This meat sells for slightly less per pound than does Choice, and it contains less fat. There may also be opportunities to sell more hamburger (where lack of fat commands a premium price) and entirely new products manufactured from low-fat, ungraded beef. At the same time, there is pressure to change the grading system to allow a less fatty, and hence often less tender, animal carcass to grade as Choice.

The easiest way to produce lower-fat beef is for an animal to get a greater portion of its total weight gain from pasture rather than from eating grain in a feedlot. This has obvious appeal to beef producers in the South, which is rich in forage but not in feedgrains.

Regional Impact of the Demand for Beef

Even if we accept the likelihood that the national demand for beef will rise by no more than, say, 1 to 2 percent yearly, there remains the possibility that the various economic forces determining how cattle are raised will cause the industry to expand disproportionately in the South. There is some historical precedent for believing this might occur. In 1982, the South (excluding Texas and Oklahoma) contained 17.8 percent of the nation's total cattle herd and 23.6 percent of its beef cows. (A beef cow is a female animal that has calved during the year and is not kept for dairy purposes.) The South's beef-cow population per square mile was actually slightly higher than that observed in the Great Plains and western states, the traditional home of the cattle industry. Moreover, over the last three decades, the South has been gaining in relative share of total beef-cow population.[23] Between 1950 and 1978, over 32 percent (7.1 million animals) of the net addition to the national beef-cow herd took place in the South. A number of reasons have been given for this relative growth in the South, including the abandonment of cropland, mechanization, and the rise in part-time farming—all of which have tended to make both land and labor available for cattle raising.[24]

Adjustment to these forces has probably more or less ceased, so there does not seem to be much reason to believe that the South will gain relative market share in its traditional cow-calf specialty. Perhaps more likely is the possibility that the availability of inexpensive forage in the South, combined with increasing acceptance of low-fat, grass-fed beef, will cause southern cattle to get relatively more of their total weight gain from southern grass. In effect, this would mean that the South would be selling calves at heavier weights, expanding into the "stocker" phase of beef production.

The period between 1971 and 1981 might seem to have been an ideal decade over which to observe such effects, given that it encompassed marked increases in the prices of feed grains and energy, as well as the suspected change in consumer tastes. Unfortunately, several variables that might affect the economics of southern beef production were changing simultaneously, and often in different directions. For example, over this 10-year period, the price farmers paid nationally for animal feed rose by 139 percent. This, by itself, would encourage more forage use in the South. Yet, over the same period, the price of fertilizer rose 188 percent and the cost of farm labor 130 percent. The costs of fencing and tractor fuel also rose. Thus, it is unclear whether the net change in relative prices favored southern pasture or greater grain feeding. Moreover, prices of energy and feed grains fluctuated widely from year to year, so short-run variations have tended to obscure possible long-term adjustments.

There is no direct measure available of the amount of forage consumed annually by southern beef cattle. Thus, it is impossible to measure directly the impact that these complex forces have had over past years. But many grazing experts believe that southern beef calves are going to auction barns at somewhat heavier weights than in the past, a sign that they are consuming more forage. The data indicating this were described by one researcher as "very skimpy," but he, too, suspects that the phenomenon is real.[25]

Perhaps the best way to forecast the future demand for southern forage is to look at the South's competitive position relative to other regions, much as we did in the discussion of crops and forestry. One major competitor is the corn- and sorghum-based cattle-feeding industry of the southern Great Plains and the Corn Belt. As noted in chapter 2, the Corn Belt no longer has the great reserve of uncultivated cropland that enabled it to expand feed-grain output so dramatically in the 1970s. In "normal" years, this reserve is already in production. Therefore, most of the future expansion of corn output will depend on raising yields per acre. In the southern Great Plains, sorghum and corn production have depended heavily on water pumped from the Ogallala Aquifer, a nonrenewable resource. Already, as water table levels have declined and energy costs have risen, some areas have shifted out of irrigated agriculture and into dry farming.[26] Experts differ on the ultimate future of feed-grain production in the Plains, but one of the most comprehensive and recent studies indicates that a combination of irrigation in untapped portions of the Ogallala and improved yields from dry farming will result by 2020 in total grain production that would be substantially above that region's current levels.[27]

The other major national source of cattle feed is forage from western rangeland. Much of this land is already producing at its maximum sustainable level. Because the land has no alternative economic use, beef can be produced there quite cheaply. But if the national cattle herd were to expand much beyond its 1975 high point, expensive investments would be required in water and forage-grass development to expand production on western rangeland. Better opportunities for economic expansion probably exist on some of the higher-quality rangeland and pastures in Texas and western Oklahoma. Expanded forage output there would require more water and more fertilizer, and may be somewhat more expensive than in the more humid South.

Overall, one might conclude that regions of the country outside the South have ample physical capacity to supply the nation's present level of demand for beef. At higher levels of demand, however, there will be some relatively severe cost pressures, unless either international demand for Corn Belt feed grains falls, or feed-grain productivity per acre rises rapidly. Conditions appear favorable for a slowly increasing demand for forage from the South, provided that it can be produced at a reasonable cost.

Production Opportunities in Southern Grazing

There are many opportunities for expanding the output from southern grazing land, provided there is sufficient demand to warrant it. The virtually unanimous view among grazing experts, both those looking at the question from the forage side and those working on animal physiology, is that southern cattle production could easily be expanded to at least half again its present size by better herd genetics and by greater inputs of fertilizer, fencing, and management. Naturally, this would involve higher production costs than the present low-input, low-output system; yet it would not require new scientific discoveries, and the slope of the curve of incremental cost per pound of beef would be smooth and not too steep.

Genetic Improvement. One way of raising cattle output would be to improve the average genetic quality of the southern beef-cattle herd. Historically, southern cattle were grazed in an open range situation. There was, in consequence, a complete lack of selectivity in breeding.[28] Southern beef cattle were noted less for their meat-production qualities than for their ability simply to survive in a totally unmanaged situation. During this early range-grazing period, a full-grown southern beef animal might have weighed only 400 to 500 pounds and was sometimes described as being of the "4H" type—little more than hide, hair, hoofs, and horns.[29]

The movement of the South away from open-range grazing in the early part of this century—hastened by growth in crop acreage and the frequent collisions of automobiles and wandering cattle—gave beef producers an incentive to begin improving their herds. So did control of endemic diseases and parasites, which, after about 1940, greatly reduced death loss and made it worthwhile to begin breeding for quality rather than mere survival. A number of large farms producing purebred stock have sprung up in the South, including some that raise newly developed breeds (for example, the Santa Gertrudis and the Brangus) specifically adapted to hot, humid weather. These new breeds, as well as substantial upgrading of longer-established ones, have helped to greatly raise herd quality. But there is still a substantial difference between the practices of the more sophisticated cattle raisers and the average ones, particularly those who have only a few animals.

The opportunity for genetic improvement over the level currently prevailing in most herds is substantial. Much improvement could be obtained if cattle raisers simply kept better records of the performance of their calves and culled their herds to retain cows that consistently produced superior offspring. In some ways, this option is more practical for the small-scale stock raiser than for the larger operators, as the former often "knows his animals" better than the overseer of a big herd. The widespread use of microcomputers, even among small farmers, is likely to enhance this approach to herd improvement.

Improving Forage Quality. Even more promising than the potential genetic improvement in beef cattle is the opportunity for raising per-acre output of forage, thereby raising grazing capacity. Southern stock raisers are well aware that additions of fertilizer and lime and more frequent reseeding can greatly increase the forage output of their pastureland.[30] That they do not now apply more of these inputs is mainly due to the fact that it is unprofitable at current cattle prices. If beef demand were to increase, more would be done, provided that prices of fertilizer, lime, and seed did not also rise proportionately. Installation of fencing is another purchased input that can raise output per acre by better distributing grazing pressure and by allowing the seasonal rotation of pasture. A related measure is "creep grazing," a system in which unweaned calves are given access to supplemental pasture by means of a fence through which they can pass, while the mother cow cannot. It is important to note that forage im-

I was brought up in Texas, in a military family, not on a farm. But when I was a child, my family lived for several years in a rural area in France. Now I work as a maintenance electrician in Arkansas Kraft's paper mill. Eight years ago I built a house on the mountain, and two years ago I went into the cattle business. I've just always wanted to have a farm.

There are 8 acres of land around my house and 80 under lease a couple of miles away. At the present time, there are 30 cattle on this land—1 bull, 19 cows, and 10 calves. I'm strictly a cow-calf operation and sell the calves at the end of the summer. But this year calf prices are so low and the drought has left them so light that I will keep the ones that are left through the spring and sell them as heavy stockers.

At the mill where I work there are maybe 20 or 30 men who are in the cattle business part-time. Some people talk hunting and fishing, but we get together and talk cattle. I'd quit the mill if I could afford it and work cattle full-time, but nobody I know can make a living from a small farm. There are some tax benefits in raising cattle, but it's too much work to do only for that. I just love working with the animals and doing general farm work. It's peaceful work. Cattle raising has to be something you enjoy doing, because there isn't any money in it.

The person I lease my pasture from is over 70 years old and wouldn't be interested in giving me a long lease that would allow me to put money into the land. As it is, I have a five-year lease on 80 acres for $600 a year. You don't do much improvement to a leased farm. I do just enough fencing to keep the cows in.

I built a corral on his land but used cheaper materials than I would have on my own farm. The land next to this pasture belongs to another old man who now lives in town. He didn't have anyone to bale the hay that grows on it, so I bought a baler and offered to bale it on shares. His field needs fertilizer badly but he won't fertilize it.

BILL GALLOWAY, part-time stock raiser, Morrilton, Arkansas

provements often require greater labor and management input as well as simply the expenditure of additional money. Adoption of these improvements is limited not only by direct cost but also by the low labor and management input presently characteristic of the cattle business.

There are also great opportunities for introducing new forage crops, including crops that can help reduce the seasonality problem. Much less research effort has been expended on southern forage crops than on row crops, mainly because of a perceived lack of need. A new surge of demand for southern grazing would eventually change that situation and would probably have a high, though delayed, return. The demand for forage crop improvement is closely connected with the intensity of pasture management. Many new forage crops are highly responsive to fertilizer and give greatest returns when nutrients (and water) are most available.

A very significant trend in southern grazing has been the increased use of winter wheat and other small grain crops. In most cases, these are double-cropped and sometimes irrigated. With these crops, a farmer can use land in a single year to produce a late summer crop of soybeans, allow for winter grazing, and have an early summer harvest of grain.

Feeding and Finishing in the South

It has long been the dream of the southern beef cattle industry to maintain animals all the way through to slaughter weight. "There is no biological reason why we cannot produce slaughter beef in Georgia," says a University of Georgia agronomist. "People in the Midwest are buying our calves at low prices, fattening them, and then shipping the finished beef back here at a profit. The Georgia consumer picks up the tab for transportation costs. This can be changed, but it will require new thinking among producers in the state."[31]

The recent growth of the southern population—and hence of the South's market for meat—the increased cost of truck and rail transportation, and the dramatic increase in feed-grain prices that followed the massive 1973 Soviet wheat purchase have all encouraged southerners to think that it might in the long run be cheaper to produce finished beef regionally rather than to ship calves out and meat in. So has the well-publicized depletion of the Ogallala Aquifer, which supports irrigated production of much of the grain used in Great Plains feedlots.

There are two versions of the "finished in the South" scenario. One possibility is to take the heaviest calves raised on southern grass and feed them grain in feedlots within the South. These feedlots might possibly use southern corn, soybean meal, and milling by-products, but it is more likely that they would use corn shipped in from the Midwest, probably by barge. The heavier the calf, the less grain would have to be shipped. Today, despite signs that southern cattle are going to market at heavier weights, there does not seem to be a trend toward increased feedlot finishing in the South. On January 1, 1982, some 345,000 southern cattle were being fed on grain, some of them on feedlots and the rest on individual farms. This was only 3.4 percent of the national total and was fewer than half the number of cattle found on feedlots in Colorado alone.

A second version of the "finished in the South" scenario is to produce a totally grass-fed animal of slaughter weight. This would require a marked shift in consumer preferences toward very lean, undoubtedly tougher, beef or further development of ways to tenderize meat after slaughter. It also probably would require some change in grazing methods (or consumer preferences) to avoid the characteristic yellow fat and "stronger" taste of grass-fed beef.

Both of these scenarios are technically feasible but economically unlikely. Agricultural economist Richard O. Wheeler points out that western feedlot owners presently have a huge excess capacity in both feeding facilities and packing plants. It would simply not be profitable for the South to replicate these capital facilities so long as western capacity is available. "Even if it could be shown that the South has a comparative advantage in feeding," says Wheeler, "it will be many years before this could be decapitalized."[32] He concedes, however, that "nevertheless, gradually over a 20-year period, you may see more cattle feeding in the South."

The key variable in any long-run scenario of increased southern beef feeding is clearly the availability and price of grain in the Corn Belt and Great Plains. A problem for "finished in the South" enthusiasts is that grain prices high enough to reduce cattle feeding in other regions would probably also be high enough to move some of the best southern pastureland (cropland pasture) into grain production. Similarly, an increase in the price of energy, which would raise the costs of transporting southern calves to western stocker operations or feedlots, would also raise the price of nitrogen fertilizer (made from natural gas) and hence the cost of producing southern forage. Also problematic is the South's humid

Aquaculture

One of the fastest-growing of all agricultural activities in the South is aquaculture. This consists mainly of raising catfish, crawfish, and baitfish commercially in ponds. When intensively managed, aquaculture allows exceptionally high per-acre yields of fish—over 5,000 pounds per acre has been achieved with catfish and 3,000 pounds per acre with crawfish. It is a risky enterprise, but one that provides potential economic returns frequently higher on a per-acre basis than those from any other agricultural use of land.

Catfish are the South's best-known aquacultural product. They are generally raised in shallow ponds, often on heavy clay soils not very productive for crops. In 1982, there were about 71,000 acres of commercial catfish ponds in the South, of which 50,000 were in Mississippi and most of the rest in Arkansas and Alabama.[1] In recent years, farm-raised catfish production has been expanding by almost 20 percent annually.[2] One attraction is the fish's extremely high feed efficiency—catfish convert a feed ration of corn, soybean meal, and fish meal into body weight at a ratio approaching 1:1. This is even better than a broiler chicken's 2.1:1 ratio, and is made more impressive by the fact that the wholesale value of a pound of catfish is about twice that of a pound of chicken.

Like broilers and cattle, catfish offer crop farmers a way to make use of family and hired labor at times when it is not needed for the crops. Says one expert, "Catfish farmers can keep their workers occupied [full-time]—they can take a worker out of a cornfield and have him seine a pond."[3]

There are about 115,000 acres of crawfish ponds in the South, of which 90,000 are in Louisiana. Until very recently, the market for this tasty staple of Cajun cooking was almost entirely confined to the region where it is produced. Crawfish are mainly double-cropped with rice; the rice season stretches over spring and summer, while the crawfish season occupies fall and winter. Crawfish feed on decomposing rice stubble and, unlike catfish, do not have to be fed grain. Harvesting them, however, entails a major cost, as they must be trapped almost as if they were in the wild.[4] So time-consuming is this operation that it is common for a trapper to be paid half or more of the value of a harvest. Because of this factor, the harvesting of wild crawfish, mainly from Louisiana's Atchafalaya River Basin, is highly competitive with farm production, though the Atchafalaya's wild harvest is highly variable from year to year.

The ability to double-crop crawfish and rice means that there is a large area of rice-producing land available for expanding crawfish production should demand warrant it. Crawfish have also been double-cropped with soybeans, as well as triple-cropped with rice and cypress trees.[5]

Baitfish production has expanded along with sportfishing in the South. Arkansas produces more than half the national total of such fish as minnows and golden shiners—using an astonishing 56,300 acres of land. Just one baitfish farm occupies more than 6,000 acres in intensive culture, with a production of 3 million pounds per year.[6]

As with broilers, aquaculture production is more important as a source of farm income than as a source of demand for land. Prospects for future aquaculture expansion in the South are quite promising, particularly given the increased pressure on ocean fish stocks and the possibilities of promoting such southern delicacies as crawfish etouffé and fried catfish in other parts of the country. There seems to be an ample supply of land suitable for aquaculture to meet any foreseeable demand, with most of it coming from marginal cropland rather than forest use. (This saves the fish farmer the cost of land clearance.) There may be a potential threat to wetlands, particularly by crawfish farming, though fish farmers prefer to avoid the very wet areas because of the danger of uncontrolled flooding. Moreover, fish ponds do have some habitat value for waterfowl.

One possible resource limitation on aquaculture's expansion in the South may be the fact that it requires large amounts of high-quality water. It has been estimated that 1 acre of highly intensive catfish pond requires 40 to 60 acre-feet of water yearly.[7] Because the water must be free of pesticides and unwanted fish eggs, well water is preferred. This demand could accelerate localized drawdown of groundwater, a problem that has already occurred in Lonoke County, Arkansas, where large baitfish and rice farms compete for water with urbanization and industry.[8]

Catfish ponds under construction near Pine Bluff, Arkansas.

climate. Because animals use grain more efficiently in the hot but dry climate of the West, even high grain prices may not be enough to shift cattle feeding to the South.

New Lands for Grazing

Although the bulk of the South's opportunities for increased grazing will probably be found in intensifying management on land already grazed, there is some scope for introducing grazing where it has not previously been practiced. Much of the land on which this could be done is probably technically classified as forest, though it is stocked (if at all) with low-value trees and is essentially unproductive in that use. North Carolina State University's Charles Lassiter observes, "In North Carolina we estimate that there are a million acres of [potential] grazing land west of Raleigh—rolling land, perhaps with scrub tree cover."[33] The University of Georgia's Carl Hoveland sees new grazing opportunities on the Georgia Piedmont, on land that "should not be cropped because of the erosion produced."[34] Vivian Allen, of Virginia Polytechnic Institute, is seeking ways to use low-quality, hilly land, such as scrub timberland, in that state.[35]

Many southern forage experts argue that, except in very special cases, grazing simply cannot compete economically with either crops or intensive forestry for the sole use of land. Returns to grazing may be competitive with those from extensive forestry, but converting forestland to pasture costs several hundreds of dollars per acre. The best opportunities for expanding the South's grazing land base therefore appear to lie either in using land not suitable for forestry or crops or in combining grazing with some simultaneous and complementary use.

Agroforestry. In terms of acres potentially affected, the greatest opportunities for complementary use lie in managed grazing of timberland, often called "agroforestry." Some form of forest grazing has been widely practiced in the South since the earliest European settlement.[36] Mostly, it was done on an open range basis, with cattle simply allowed to roam freely through the woods, often grazing land not owned by the cattle owner. Traditionally, cattle owners would set fires to "green up" the forest floor; thus, forest grazing became closely associated in the minds of foresters with the problem of wildfires. Foresters also observed that uncontrolled grazing damaged trees, as cattle ate hardwood shoots, trampled young pines, and compacted the soil around the bases of mature trees.

In the 1930s, the open range began to be fenced in, and foresters made a concerted effort to eliminate both forest fires and forest grazing. The process was not an easy one. The "revenge fires" set by graziers newly excluded from privately owned forests tended to reinforce the association between grazing and forest fire. Today, forest grazing in the South is practiced primarily on farmer-owned land not actively managed for wood production or on large tracts owned by timber companies. The companies are not particularly enthusiastic about the practice—the lease revenues they receive from it are quite modest—but tolerate it for public relations purposes and to avoid further arson.[37]

Data on the economics of forest grazing in the South are scarce. However, all indications are that present returns are quite low. For example, one unit of measurement in the grazing business is the "animal unit month" (AUM), the amount of forage required to support a 1,000-pound cow for one month. Even good-quality forested grazing land seldom yields more than one AUM per acre annually. But the market price of an AUM of forest grazing in Florida recently was only $1.25.[38] Timber companies generally charge grazing leaseholders only $0.50 to $2.00 per acre annually, and some make no charge at all. One researcher attributes the willingness of southern graziers to use the forest range despite low returns to the fact that woodland grazing is "mainly opportunistic," with few management inputs, so that even a very small gross return is mostly profit.[39]

From a strictly biological standpoint, it appears possible to practice grazing on several of the South's important forest ecosystems without interfering with wood growth: open coastal forests where stands of trees are interspersed with forage-producing wetlands, pine plantations where the trees are sufficiently high to resist damage by the cattle, and mature pine and hardwood forests (though these tend to produce very little forage). In pine plantations, grazing may actually benefit tree growth by removing some of the understory that competes with the pines for water and by making it economic to fertilize for the benefit of both grasses and trees. On the other hand, cattle are incompatible with young hardwood forests, where they tend to eat or otherwise damage the smaller trees.

Provided that cattle numbers are controlled and their grazing limited to stands where they will not damage young trees, the main trade-off between grazing and wood production is the spacing of the trees. The greater the distance between trees, the more sunlight will reach the ground and the more forage will be produced. Up to a point, wide spacing may even benefit total wood growth, by allowing each tree relatively more sunlight and growing room. But, well before the point of maximum pasture productivity in most stands, widening the spacing means smaller total wood production. A certain amount of flexibility is possible, because one can start with a relatively dense planting of trees, then use pulpwood cuts to thin the stand so that forage production remains high. Many studies have tried to determine the optimal balance for pine plantations.[40]

There is considerable intellectual appeal in the agroforestry concept. It would, in effect, extend the land base by allowing more than one simultaneous, but complementary, use of the same acre. Perhaps more important, it would provide the forest owner with an annual stream of income (in the form of grazing revenues) from the forested land, thus dealing directly with the time horizon problem that appears to be so important in inhibiting timber management by nonindustrial private forest owners. However, there are both economic and social obstacles to agroforestry.

On the economic side, the projected returns even to rather sophisticated forest grazing systems are often quite low on a per-acre basis, both in absolute terms and in comparison to the returns obtainable from good timber management. One of the few studies done on the economics of forest grazing simulated average annual returns to grazing on the most common southern forest ecosystems. Gross returns were between $0.52 per acre and $5.95 per acre, depending on intensity of management.[41] Net returns ranged from $0.03 per acre to $3.43 per acre annually. Another study found simulated net grazing returns per acre (after capital costs) ranging under a variety of assumptions from negative to $483 per acre. The latter figure seems quite impressive, but it is unclear how much timber value had to be given up to achieve it. Perhaps significantly, the author of the study notes that the contribution of the *cattle* investment to total return per acre in integrated cattle/timber situations ranged only from 4 to 20 percent of total net return.[42]

There are also some social obstacles to agroforestry. Cattle farmers are frequently uninformed and uninterested in growing trees, and foresters are in the main uninformed and sometimes even hostile toward grazing. If economic returns were high, it is likely that some rapid learning would occur in both cases. With grazing returns of only a few dollars per acre per year, and returns from forestry often quite a bit higher, it seems likely that cattle growers would be more attracted to forest management than foresters to cattle raising. The combination of low grazing returns and lack of management familiarity probably explains why the large forest-products companies in the South, while they may tolerate grazing by local farmers, almost never engage in cattle raising on their own account.

> *One problem with grazing [forestland] is that native grasses are short season and with low nutritive value. It takes an average of 10 hectares [of forest range] to support a cow-calf unit, but for developed pasture you can get a cow-calf unit on 1 hectare. It's harder to check on breeding when cows range over a large area. You also have to fence the land, and that can cost close to $2,500 per mile. It seems to me to be a very expensive system, and it seems to make more sense to intensify on a small area and leave the rest to pine.*
>
> CARL HOVELAND, agronomist, University of Georgia

Overall, forest grazing appears to be a technically feasible means of providing a considerable amount of forage output in the South. One estimate puts the upper limit on forest grazing capacity under intensive management at over 11 million animals yearly.[43] This is enough to support more than two-thirds of the South's present beef-cattle herd. At current cattle and feed-grain prices, increased use of this resource does not seem particularly profitable. However, the availability of the forest grazing alternative means that southern forage-fed beef production could expand greatly should demand warrant it.

Other Integrated Production Systems. In addition to the possibilities for grazing cattle on forested land, there are other ways in which beef-cattle might be integrated into various sorts

of multiple-output farming operations. As mentioned above, the low labor demands in raising beef cattle are compatible with the intense, but seasonal, labor demands of crop agriculture. A crop farmer can spend minimal time with beef cattle during the planting and harvest seasons, then use slack periods to do postponable chores such as mending fences or developing water sources for the animals. Another integrated operation, very popular in parts of Arkansas and Oklahoma, is for a farmer to engage in both cattle and broiler-chicken production. The labor and land requirements are compatible, but there are other links as well. According to one poultry expert, "Some of the land in northwest Arkansas was just worn out from continuous cotton cultivation and erosion. But the spreading of poultry manure on the land brought back enough fertility to make a beef-cattle industry possible."[44] Poultry manure and bedding can also be fed directly to cattle and provide a usable source of high-nitrogen feed.

Near Bradenton, Florida, an integrated operation combines cattle grazing with thousands of acres of tomatoes. Cattle are used to graze fields after tomato harvest, as well as to feed on grass on fields taken out of production in the course of a rotation. Cattle can also be grazed alongside sheep, as they use somewhat different forages. The most widespread, and apparently flourishing, form of integrated production is grazing beef cattle on double-cropped winter grains, as already discussed.

Grazing and the Demand for Land

Within the range of reasonably anticipated variations in beef demand, grain prices, climate, and competing land uses, it is most likely that the amount of southern land grazed in the future will be approximately what it is today. If future southern area in row crops expands, some of what is currently the region's most productive grazing land will be lost. This has been occurring recently in some areas in the Delta and Coastal Plain, where land going out of cotton production, which would in years past have become pasture, is moving directly into soybeans.

The "lost" acreage, however, will most likely be replaced by somewhat greater grazing on forestland and on marginal lands not presently grazed. Total land grazed, therefore, should remain more or less constant. In terms of forage production, lost output due to conversion of pasture to cropland will be made up by the intensification of production on the better-quality remaining pasture, both through fertilization and through better management of animals and grasses. There will also be considerable forage added through integrated management, particularly by the introduction of a grazing component in double-crop systems.

References

1. In 1982, sales by southern farms were $17.3 billion for crops, $12.0 billion for animals and animal products. Of the latter, approximately $3 billion came from sales of broiler chickens.

2. Only about 10 percent (1.5 million) of southern cattle are kept for milking, and their number has fallen greatly as milk production per cow has increased. There are only 223,000 sheep and lambs in the South, more than half in Virginia. There are more than 400,000 horses and ponies on southern farms and thoroughbred horse-raising is economically important in parts of Kentucky, Tennessee, and Florida.

3. This discussion is drawn from interviews with Dr. Frank H. Baker, Winrock International, and other beef-cattle experts. See also, U.S. Department of Agriculture, Economic Research Service, *Cattle Raising in the United States*, Agricultural Economic Report No. 235 (Washington, D.C.: U.S. Government Printing Office, 1973) and University of Arkansas, Cooperative Extension Service, *Beef Cattle Production* (Fayetteville: University of Arkansas, 1981).

4. J. Rod Martin, "Beef," in Lyle P. Schertz, ed., *Another Revolution in U.S. Farming?* (Washington, D.C.: U.S. Government Printing Office, 1979) pp. 75-118.

5. Ibid., p. 100.

6. Although cattle do lose some weight in transit, shipping animals to the feedlot is not as inefficient as it appears. A beef animal would require an average of 7 pounds of grain or approximately 15-20 pounds of hay to gain 1 pound of meat. It would thus be even more costly to ship the feed to the animal.

7. Interview with H. Allan Nation, editor, *The Stockman*, Jackson, Mississippi, November 1982.

8. See Charles Y. Liu and Donald A. West, *A Spatial Analysis of Beef Feeding and Slaughtering with Emphasis on the South*, Bulletin No. 177, Southern Cooperative Series (Raleigh: North Carolina State University, Department of Economics, 1973).

9. Hay is a generic term for harvested and air-dried grasses and legumes; silage is a product made by storing green harvested material (corn is commonly used) so that it ferments and becomes more digestable to animals.

10. Returns to hay and silage or to grazing small grain crops (such as wheat) may be much higher, but these are more like crops than "grassland" uses.

11. Interview, Raleigh, North Carolina, January 1983.

12. For a description of some of the data problems, see Evert Byington, "Livestock Grazing on the Forested Lands of the Eastern United States," in *Impacts of Technology on U.S. Cropland and Rangeland Productivity*, vol. 2, paper 3 (Washington, D.C.: U.S. Government Printing Office, 1982).

13. See Maurice E. Heath, Darrel S. Metcalfe, and Robert F. Barnes, *Forages: The Science of Grassland Agriculture,* 3rd ed. (Ames: Iowa State University Press, 1973).

14. "Wheat for Winter Grazing and Grain," Agronomy Notes, No. 150, October 7, 1983 (University of Florida, Florida Cooperative Extension Service).

15. The figure is for 1978. In 1982, probably because of sufficient natural rainfall, Florida pasture owners irrigated only 282,000 acres of "pastureland and other land," a figure far below their capacity to irrigate.

16. John Fraser Hart, *The South* (New York: Van Nostrand, 1976), p. 62.

17. H. Allan Nation, "Welcome to Grass Farming," *The Stockman*, vol. 40, no. 7 (July 1983), p. 3. The statement was made in the context of a discussion of southern grass farmers competing with amenity-minded western ranchers, but the sentiment is equally true of competition among various sectors within the cattle business in the South.

18. Good genetic stock does not mean that a commercial beef cow must be purebred. In fact, crossing two purebred lines can result in a calf whose "hybrid vigor" contributes to rapid and profitable growth. Good genetics does mean that animals are bred to enhance desirable traits and that good records are kept of the performance of calves born to particular matings within the herd.

19. Interview with Will Getz, Winrock International, Morrilton, Arkansas, December 1982.

20. For an overview of the expected demand for both beef and grazing land, see John Fedkiw, "Demand for Red Meat and Range Grazing," presentation to Soil Conservation Service National Range Workshop, Wichita, Kansas, June 18-22, 1984.

21. National Cattlemen's Association, Special Advisory Committee, *The Future for Beef* (Denver: National Cattlemen's Association, 1982), p. 6.

22. Ibid., p. 10.

23. See Martin, "Beef," pp. 85-118. The total beef-cow herd dropped slightly between 1978 and 1981, as did the proportion in the South. We must caution that "beef cows" refers to heifers that have calved during the year; it does not include stocker animals or cattle on feedlots.

24. Ibid., p. 96.

25. Telephone interview with Henry C. Gilliam, Department of Agricultural Economics, North Carolina State University, November 1983.

26. See Philip M. Raup, "Competition for Land and the Future of American Agriculture," in Sandra S. Batie and Robert G. Healy, *The Future of American Agriculture as a Strategic Resource* (Washington, D.C.: The Conservation Foundation, 1980), pp. 66-69.

27. Raymond J. Supalla, Robert R. Lansford, and Noel R. Gollehon, "Is the Ogallala Going Dry?" *Journal of Soil and Water Conservation*, vol. 37, no. 6 (November-December 1982), pp. 310-14.

28. For a fuller account of the historical development of grazing in the South, see Evert K. Byington, "The Use of Southern Forest and Associated Pasture and Range Lands in Historical Perspective," unpublished manuscript, Winrock International, July 1983.

29. Ibid., p. II-9.

30. Considering only fertilizer, for example, one Oklahoma study found that heavily fertilized Bermuda grass pasture produced 2.7 times as much dry forage matter, 3.8 times as much crude protein, and 9.1 times as much beef per acre as similar but unfertilized pasture. See Lelan Kim Martin, *Fertilizer Responses of Common Bermuda Grass* (Poteau, Okla.: The Kerr Foundation, 1975).

31. Dr. Steven Fales, quoted in Jack Reeves, "New Thinking Needed in Southeast," *The Stockman*, vol. 40, no. 8 (August 1983), p. 27.

32. Interview, Winrock International, Morrilton, Arkansas, October 1983.

33. Interview, Raleigh, North Carolina, January 1983.

34. Interview, Athens, Georgia, January 1983.

35. Interview, Blacksburg, Virginia, August 1983.

36. An excellent review of the history of forest grazing in the South is found in Byington, "The Use of Southern Forest and Associated Pasture."

37. See, for example, Harold E. Grelen, "Forest Grazing in the South," *Journal of Range Management*, vol. 31, no .4 (July 1978), p. 248; John A. Goodwin, "Oklahoma Region of Weyerhaeuser Company's Cattle Allotment," in R. Dennis Child and Evert K. Byington, *Southern Forest Range and Pasture Resources* (Morrilton, Ark.: Winrock International, 1980), pp. 201-4.

38. Interview with Clifford Lewis, University of Florida, Gainesville, January 1983.

39. Evert K. Byington, "Livestock Grazing on the Forested Lands of the Eastern United States."

40. See Clifford E. Lewis, "Grazing Considerations in Managing Young Pines," in *Proceedings, Symposium on Management of Young Pines, Alexandria, La., October 22-24, 1974* (Atlanta, Ga.: U.S. Forest Service, Southeastern Area State and Private Forestry, 1974), pp. 160-70.

41. Byington, "Livestock Grazing on the Forested Lands of the Eastern United States," pp. 36-40.

42. Harry L. Haney, Jr., "Economics of Integrated Cattle-Timber Land Use," in Child and Byington, *Southern Forest Range*, pp. 165-84.

43. Byington, "Livestock Grazing on the Forested Lands of the Eastern United States," p. 10.

44. Interview with Richard Sellers, Winrock International, October 1983.

The Broiler Industry: A Southern Livestock Phenomenon

1. See generally, Bernard F. Tobin and Henry B. Arthur, *Dynamics of Adjustment in the Broiler Industry* (Cambridge, Mass.: Harvard Business School, 1964) and Floyd A. Lasley, *The U.S. Poultry Industry: Changing Economics and Structure*, Agricultural Economic Report No. 502 (Washington, D.C.: U.S. Government Printing Office, 1983).

2. Interview with Floyd Lasley, Economic Research Service, U.S. Department of Agriculture, July 1983.

3. Interview with William Roenigk, director of economic research, National Broiler Council, Washington, D.C., July 1983.

Aquaculture

1. U.S. Department of Agriculture, Statistical Reporting Service, *Catfish* (February 1982).

2. U.S. Federal Coordinating Council on Science, Engineering and Technology, Joint Subcommittee on Aquaculture, *National Aquaculture Development Plan*, vol. 2 (Washington, D.C.: U.S. Government Printing Office, 1983), p. 15.

3. Interview with Bill Hougart, aquaculture coordinator, U.S. Department of Agriculture, Washington, D.C., December 1983.

4. U.S. Federal Coordinating Council, *National Aquaculture Development Plan*, vol. 2, pp. 25-39.

5. Information on crawfish/rice/cypress rotations was obtained from Frank Shropshire, U.S. Forest Service, interview, Jackson, Mississippi, December 1982.

6. U.S. Federal Coordinating Council, *National Aquaculture Development Plan*, vol. 2, p. 2.

7. U.S. Soil Conservation Service, *Catfish Farming*, Farmers' Bulletin No. 2260 (Washington, D.C.: U.S. Government Printing Office, 1982).

8. U.S. Federal Coordinating Council, *National Aquaculture Development Plan*, vol, 2, p. 3.

Taxes and "The Farmer's Friend"

1. William Laas, *Make Money in Pure-Bred Cattle* (New York: Popular Library, 1972), p. 77.
2. Charles A. Sisson, *The U.S. Tax System and the Structure of American Agriculture* (Washington, D.C.: National Rural Center, 1980), p. 2.
3. H. Allan Nation, "Grazer and Feeder: Uneasy Partners in a World of Change," *The Stockman*, vol. 40, no. 8 (August 1983), p. 16.

Chapter 5

The Landscape of Human Settlement

The South is home to more than 50 million persons, or slightly under one-quarter of the total U.S. population. During the 1970s, the South's population increased by nearly 21 percent, well over twice the rate of increase in the rest of the United States. Once the source of massive exodus to other parts of the United States, the South has now become a destination for migrants. During the 1960s, 8 of the 11 southern states had more people moving out than were moving in. During the 1970s, all of the southern states experienced net in-migration.[1] The impact of this change was magnified by the fact that the number of housing units in the South increased between 1970 and 1980 by 40.7 percent, a reflection not simply of population growth but of the trend to smaller families and more single-person households.

The patterns of human settlement—and how those patterns have been changing—can have important effects on the availability of land for the rural productive uses described in earlier chapters. This chapter is concerned mainly with patterns of primary residential settlement, though some space will be devoted to industrial and commercial uses of land, surface mining, land-consuming infrastructure (such as reservoirs, highways, and airports), and second-home developments.

All of these uses affect land in two ways. First, they physically occupy sites, thereby preempting the land from other uses. Second, they reduce the production options available on nearby land, either by physical spillovers, witness the chronic battles between farmers and suburbanites, or through economic impacts such as parcel division and land speculation.

The Geography of Residential Settlement

Although there are tremendous variations from one state to another within the South in patterns of residential settlement, the region as a whole has several distinctive features. First, although the South compared to the rest of the country has a more or less average number of metropolitan centers,[2] it has few very large ones. The four largest Standard Metropolitan Statistical Areas (SMSAs) in the South (again, as defined in this book) are Atlanta, Miami, Tampa, and New Orleans. These rank 16, 21, 24 and 33 in population among all the nation's SMSAs. However, several larger SMSAs lie on the periphery, with parts of their outskirts reaching into or very close to the South: Washington, D.C. (7 in population nationally), Dallas (8), Houston (9), and St. Louis (12).

The typical large southern metropolitan area is in the 500,000 to 1 million population range—Memphis, Nashville, Jacksonville, Birmingham, Charlotte, Norfolk. Most of these areas have specialized functions within the national system of cities—Norfolk's port and military functions, for example—but they also perform important regional commercial functions for a large hinterland. It is likely that their populations are larger than they might otherwise be if the South had a more evenly distributed set of SMSAs of the largest size.

A second distinctive feature of the southern settlement pattern is the persistence of a large rural population. From its earliest settlement, the South has had a much larger proportion of its population in rural areas than the nation as a whole (figure 5.1). The gap has been closing since 1940, but it is still substantial. Today, all of the southern states except Florida contain a larger percentage of their population in rural places than the national average; in most cases, the differential over the national average is large (table 5.1). In Mississippi and North Carolina, more than half of the population is rural.

Traditionally, the South's large rural population has been associated with its large number of persons employed in agriculture. In recent decades, however, farm population in the South has been falling even more rapidly than in the rest of the country, while nonfarm rural population has been increasing. Not only

Figure 5.1

Growth of Urbanization in the U.S. and the South, 1790–1970

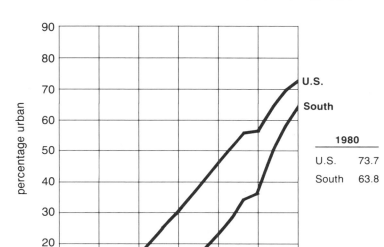

Source: U.S. Department of Commerce, *Census of Population* and *Census of Population and Housing*, 1790–1970.

are farm residents a minority in the South (in 1980, 1 southerner in 39 lived on a farm), they are a minority even within rural areas. In 1980, only 1 rural southerner in 15 lived on a farm, compared with the national average of 1 in 10. The large number of nonfarm rural residents is one of the most striking demographic characteristics of the contemporary South.

A third distinctive characteristic of the South is the somewhat greater importance of the nonsuburban town or small (less than 50,000 population) city. Nationally, 12.3 percent of the population lives in such places, while the southern states average 14.7

Table 5.1

Population, by Size of Place, 1980
(percent of total)

	Urban		Rural		
	Inside urbanized area	Other urban	Place of 1,000 to 2,500	Place of less than 1,000	Other rural
Alabama	45.3	14.7	3.5	2.3	34.1
Arkansas	24.6	27.0	5.4	5.2	37.9
Florida	76.2	8.0	1.9	0.4	13.4
Georgia	47.6	14.8	3.1	2.3	32.2
Kentucky	33.7	17.2	3.6	1.9	43.7
Louisiana	52.3	16.3	3.2	1.6	26.6
Mississippi	23.4	24.0	4.3	2.6	45.8
North Carolina	34.0	14.0	3.8	2.0	46.2
Oklahoma, eastern (18 counties)	0.5	35.7	8.6	7.0	48.1
South Carolina	38.1	16.0	4.3	1.6	40.0
Tennessee	45.4	15.0	3.3	1.4	34.8
Texas, East (36 counties)	27.6	24.1	5.7	2.6	40.0
Virginia	56.9	9.1	2.4	0.9	30.7
Total U.S.	61.4	12.3	3.1	1.7	21.4

Source: U.S. Department of Commerce, Bureau of the Census, *1980 Census of Population*.

percent.[3] Arkansas and Mississippi have a particularly large proportion of people living in places of this type.

Finally, urban densities in the South are very low compared with the national average. In 1980, for the country as a whole, the average amount of urban land per urban-area resident was .28 acres.[4] In the South, each urban-area resident occupied .40 acres, almost half again as much. At least part of the South's low urban density is explained by its relative lack of very large cities, which tend to have particularly high densities, and by the relative youth of many southern cities, which experienced much of their growth since the advent of the automobile made a sprawling settlement pattern possible.

A Demographic Convergence?

Although settlement patterns in the South differ from those found elsewhere in the country, there is evidence of a long-term convergence toward national norms. Ironically, this sometimes means that the South is becoming more like other regions even as the other regions have begun to diverge from their own historic patterns. For example, in the period 1970-80, the South showed a continuing trend toward increasing the proportion of its population in urban areas. In the rest of the country, a strong revival of rural population growth meant that the proportion of urban areas (while still much higher than in the South) remained steady.

Table 5.2 shows the 1970-80 change in the distribution of population by size of place for the southern states and for the United States as a whole.[5] Across the South, the number of people living in large "urbanized areas" (over 500,000 population) rose faster than the national average. Growth was highest in the suburban fringes of these areas. Although populations fell in some of the very largest central cities, such as Atlanta, New Orleans, and Norfolk, in most southern states even central city populations showed considerable increase. Despite the move to the cities, the South's rural population also rose, with 6 of the 11 states showing higher rural growth than the national average. And the population of the South's nonsuburban towns and small (under 50,000) cities fell, but by less than the fall experienced nationally.

Calvin Beale, chief demographer for the U.S. Department of

Florida: A Special Case

Human settlement has occurred over the past 30 years in Florida, particularly in the lower half of the state, at a more rapid rate and on a more massive scale than it has occurred anywhere else in the South. Florida's growth has been fueled not only by tourism and a continuing influx of retirees but by a major industrial expansion, both in low-wage sectors such as apparel and in high-technology sectors such as electronics and aerospace equipment. As older growth areas—the Miami to Palm Beach corridor, Tampa-St. Petersburg, Orlando—have become congested, the highest rates of growth have been found in such smaller centers as Ocala and Fort Myers. Dense beachfront development, once confined to the lower Atlantic and Gulf coasts, is now particularly intense in the Panhandle, which has become a recreational mecca for vactioners from Alabama, Georgia, and other southern states. And, although by far the most highly urbanized state in the South, Florida had during the 1970s the most rapid rate of rural growth in that section of the country.

Large-scale subdivisions and "new communities" are found around the edges of most southern large metropolitan areas, as well as in resort areas in many parts of the South, but they are particularly frequent—and particularly large—in Florida. "Ten Thousand Acres of Living Room," reads a billboard advertising one development in South Florida—and it is only one of many. Florida had responded to the rapid development of the early 1970s with a series of state and local laws regulating land development and protecting environmentally sensitive lands. By 1984-85, dissatisfied with the results of past regulation, the state was again in the midst of a major debate over "growth management," one given particular impetus by the widely publicized prediction that, by the year 2000, Florida could be the nation's third most populous state, with a total population of over 17 million.

Agriculture, finds the South's continuing urbanization to be the unsurprising result of economic development in a region that had been "underurbanized" in the past.[6] He notes, however, that Census figures probably overstate the attractiveness of central cities in the South, because liberal annexation laws in some southern states allow central cities to expand their boundaries over time. He also points out that the South experienced in its own way the rural population revival that was so noticeable in the Northeast and West during the 1970s. "If you look at the South's metropolitan areas," he says, "you certainly find continued growth. But in rural areas you find a real turnaround. Hundreds of rural southern counties declined in population during the 1960s; in the 1970s decline was limited mainly to the Delta and the Alabama Black Belt."

Over the past several decades, the South has been converging

Table 5.2

Population Change, by Type of Place, 1970–1980

(percent)

	Urban area			Rural area			
	Central city	Suburb[1]	Other urban	1,000 to 2,500	less than 1,000	Other rural	Total rural
Alabama	+ 19.6	+ 39.1	− 7.0	+ 3.9	+ 3.3	+ 10.1	+ 9.1
Arkansas	+ 29.3	+ 195.8	+ 5.8	+ 14.3	+ 3.8	+ 16.8	+ 15.0
Florida	+ 15.7	+ 92.3	− 3.6	+ 24.5	− 20.7	+ 25.3	+ 23.2
Georgia	+ 5.8	+ 77.6	− 9.2	− 0.6	+ 0.8	+ 15.2	+ 12.8
Kentucky	+ 4.5	+ 15.2	+ 11.8	+ 11.1	+ 0.4	+ 18.6	+ 17.2
Louisiana	+ 8.2	+ 54.3	+ 6.9	− 1.0	+ 19.4	+ 8.8	+ 8.2
Mississippi	+ 56.6	+ 168.6	− 9.3	− 6.2	+ 8.8	+ 9.4	+ 7.9
North Carolina	+ 19.8	+ 130.7	− 13.0	− 1.5	+ 4.0	+ 11.8	+ 10.4
South Carolina	+ 27.7	+ 88.6	− 5.3	+ 8.4	− 3.6	+ 7.2	+ 6.9
Tennessee	+ 30.4	+ 160.7	− 4.4	+ 28.8	− 6.7	+ 12.9	+ 13.2
Virginia	+ 5.6	+ 45.5	− 9.8	+ 34.8	− 19.8	+ 5.5	+ 6.3
Total U.S.	+ 4.9	+ 32.3	− 9.7	+ 5.7	+ 0.3	+ 12.0	+ 10.4

[1]Urbanized area fringe.

Source: U.S. Department of Commerce, Bureau of the Census, 1970 and *1980 Censuses of Population.*

on the national average in such social indicators as per-capita income, proportion of the population nonwhite, and proportion of the population employed in agriculture. It is perhaps unsurprising that the spatial distribution of its population would also move toward national norms.

The most interesting question for the future is whether this convergence will continue until the South's population distribution is identical to that of the rest of the country, or whether the forces that encouraged the rural population revival of the 1970s are sufficiently strong to offset the urbanization process. Before analyzing these prospects, it seems appropriate to describe the South's settlement patterns and how they evolved.

Historical Development of Settlement Patterns

Habits of settlement tend to persist over time, as do buildings themselves. At any given moment, the South's stock of buildings is a mixture of the old and the new, of structures built specifically to serve the needs of its present economy and the present tastes of its people and of structures built originally to serve very different needs and tastes. Given the popular image of the South as a region steeped in history, it may be surprising to note that only a quarter of its present housing units were built before 1950.[7] But even some of the new construction reflects longstanding habits or patterns of settlement that have deep historical roots.

The original settlement of the South, in the 18th and 19th centuries, was, of course, based on agriculture. The living patterns of the small farmers (the people whom W. J. Cash called "the pioneer breed")[8] were not much different from those found anywhere on the American frontier. A farm unit contained a crude shack, a few outbuildings (the South's mild winters made a barn for the livestock unnecessary), and as much land as the owner and his family could wrest from the woods. The other type of southern agricultural unit, the plantation, was sometimes little more than a pioneer farm with a few slaves. The larger plantations, however, were virtually villages, producing on the premises not only cash crops and most of the food they consumed but many of the processed and manufactured goods they needed as well.

With so much of the population living on farms or plantations, towns in the pre-Civil War South were less numerous than elsewhere in the United States. Landscape historian John Stilgoe emphasizes the role that roads played in the antebellum South— providing places for a dispersed population to interact socially, whether along the road itself or at crossroads churches, courthouses, or stores. "Strangers," Stilgoe writes, "especially Europeans or 'Yankees,' failed to understand the extraordinary importance of the road in southern culture because they searched for the towns and hamlets so uncommon south of Pennsylvania and ignored the roads and waterways that substituted for them."[9]

After the Civil War, many plantation owners divided their holdings into small subunits, each worked by an individual tenant farmer and each occupied by the tenant's cabin.[10] A dispersed rural settlement pattern resulted, giving the impression of numerous small farms, when in reality these farms were often part of a larger landholding.[11] Thus, the entire South took on the appearance (though not necessarily the economic reality) of a region of small farms, from the owner-operated farms of the Uplands to the sharecropper or tenant-operated plantations of the Piedmont and the newer agricultural region of the Mississippi

Valley.

The last half of the 19th century brought to parts of the South, primarily in the Piedmont, a belated surge of industrialization and with it a heavy sprinkling of new industrial towns and even (as in the case of such places as Durham and Birmingham) industrial cities. Cash describes the late 19th-century Piedmont as a place with "four hundred mills. . .smoking upon its hills and in its plains," where "sleepy villages were growing. . .into towns, indistinct hamlets into villages; and new villages and towns were rising out of the earth beside the flow of rivers and in the midst of fields."[12] The economic opportunities afforded by industrialization, added to the chronic difficulties of agriculture, drew rural southerners, particularly of the entrepreneurial sort, to the towns and cities. "By the early 1900's," writes Cash, "the migration had gone so far that in many districts of the South the larger number of the 'big houses' had become merely the shabby dens of overseers or tenants. . .or, standing empty and abandoned, were falling into staring-eyed ruin."[13]

The 20th century brought further economic and technological changes to the South, each with an impact on settlement patterns. During the first few decades of the century, the South became

Abandoned sharecropper cabin on the Georgia Piedmont.

a healthier place in which to live, as malaria, yellow fever, and other diseases were eradicated. A little later the South became a more comfortable place in which to live, as mosquito control was improved and air conditioning was introduced. Despite these improvements, the South's rural population began to decline rapidly. The post-1930 agricultural changes (detailed in chapter 2)—the shift away from cotton and the mechanization and consolidation of farm units—caused a massive abandonment of rural dwellings, particularly the tenant houses. Even today in the Georgia Piedmont, as in many other traditionally crop-producing parts of the South, "a walk through pine forests often reveals former housesites, overgrown roads, cemeteries and terraced woodlands."[14]

Geographer John Fraser Hart, among the most prolific writers on southern landscape change, has done a detailed study of dwelling patterns in rural Carroll County, Georgia, as they have changed since 1921.[15] He discovered that houses lying off paved roads were more likely to be abandoned than those fronting the road and that two-thirds of the post-1921 dwellings have been built along a paved road. Hart has dubbed the process "migration to the blacktop." As another analyst describes the same phenomenon, "The scattered society became the linear society."[16]

Very few of the people living "along the blacktop" today are farmers. Noted University of North Carolina sociologist Rupert Vance observed decades ago, "The South has developed a definite pattern of living in the open countryside and working in urban-oriented occupations."[17] This pattern has been associated with a preference for low-density living, a need for low-cost housing, an attachment to place of birth, and a desire to continue part-time farming. The abundant and low-cost labor supply released by the mechanization of southern agriculture and the abandonment of unprofitable small farms proved strong attractions to manufacturing plants, particularly plants performing routinized functions that do not require close proximity to suppliers, customers, or specialized services. Much of the South's manufacturing is in industries where there are few economies of scale, so that small plants can effectively compete with large ones. The South's rural factories often draw workers from a very large commutershed[18] and have made it possible for people to continue to live in a dispersed pattern despite the decline in agricultural employment.

One southern economist, who grew up in the textile and furniture-making territory of rural North Carolina, advances yet another reason why southern factory workers have preferred rural living. "The major southern industries," he says, "have been highly cyclical. The cyclical employment pattern caused rural people to want to hang on to their rural places, where they could grow their food and live inexpensively, especially during unemployment."[19]

The most evident phenomenon to the careful observer of [the Georgia Piedmont] landscape is that most of the population is neither urban in residence nor rural farm in function.

> JAMES S. FISHER, in James Heyl, ed., *The South: A VadeMecum* (Atlanta: Association of American Geographers, 1973)

Particularly since the middle 1960s, rural areas in the South have experienced a population turnaround based on amenities as well as jobs. Retirees have returned to their place of origin, bringing their pensions with them. Television, better highways, and improved schools have substantially reduced rural isolation in the South, at the same time that crime and congestion have made large cities seem less desirable. This has encouraged new migrants to come to rural places, as well as making it more likely that young people born there will stay. "Rural areas have become more attractive to live in," says a Georgia sociologist.[20] He also notes lessened job discrimination against blacks, which means that they no longer have to leave the South to find decent jobs.

New factories, as well as job- and nonjob-related population growth, have brought significant changes to the settlement landscape. For example, a study of recent growth in rural counties of Eastern North Carolina reports that

> . . .new job opportunities have been scattered, apparently in random fashion, throughout the region, with little or no thought to the long-term implications of such a pattern. . .[new residents] are spread out over the landscape along major and minor roads, in new houses erected in subdivisions and in mobile homes located on scattered sites or within mobile home parks.[21]

As the houses of nonfarm rural residents spread along the road-sides, their builders in most cases abandoned traditional or "vernacular'' architectural forms. One impetus to this was the builders' guides, plan books, and even complete blueprints that the person seeking to build a house could order by mail. Another was the appraisal practices of the Farmers Home Administration, which has been a major lender for new rural construction and which has favored simple, modern styles of dwellings. Also influential were prefabricated homes (which could also be mail-ordered) and the ubiquitous mobile homes.

The new rural houses represented a massive improvement in housing quality for the occupants.[22] But they failed to make use of some of the good ideas that had evolved from vernacular design traditions, such as ample front porches for sitting, cooling off, and socializing; opposing front and rear doors for natural ventilation; roof overhangs to shade walls from the summer sun; and a fireplace for low-cost heating.[23] The new dwellings were also much less successful esthetically. Rarely did they reflect even a hint of southern vernacular traditions—though such dwellings have become so widespread in the rural South that they threaten to *become* a sort of vernacular.

A Mississippi architect criticizes the ''tract houses of the 1950's through the 1970's'' as having been ''imposed on our countryside.'' ''These houses,'' he writes, ''lack any socio-cultural ties to the rich traditions of the South. They are equally out of context in the Northeast, the Northwest, or Middle America. Appropriate regional differences have been neglected and forgotten.''[24]

At the extreme of standardization is the mobile home, a mass-produced artifact that rarely makes even a token acknowledgment of regional tradition. Costing only about half as much per square foot as site-built structures, mobile homes have proliferated in the South since 1960, particularly in rural areas. In some places, they have become the dominant type of new rural dwelling—during 1970-80, over half of the new rural residential structures in South Carolina, Florida, and Louisiana were mobile homes.[25]

The increase of modern rural dwellings and mobile homes in the South has been accompanied by continued abandonment of old farmhouses and tenant dwellings. A North Carolina study notes that:

In rural communities across the state, people build new houses—many of poor quality construction—and purchase mobile homes, while older, usable dwellings often of excellent quality materials and craftsmanship not affordable today are left to fall into ruin. Not only is our history wasted, but valuable housing stock is wasted.[26]

Sometimes, the older structures are torn down to accommodate the consolidation of farm fields; often, they are simply left to rot or be vandalized. Along with the farmhouses, there has also been a considerable abandonment of farm outbuildings, such as the picturesque flue-curing barns so common in tobacco-growing regions. Overall, the replacement of old farm structures by new, nonfarm ones has reinforced the visual impact of other landscape changes such as field consolidation and the shifts of crops and forests. The net result is a virtual revolution in the "look" of the South's rural landscape.

The combination of linear sprawl and "placelessness" that characterizes rural residential patterns in the South also afflicts commercial structures. The roadside general store has evolved into the highway commercial strip, dominated by the franchised outlets of national fast-food, motel, restaurant, and convenience-store chains. In the last decade or so, in the larger towns and small

Edge-of-town commercial strips, such as this one outside Greenville, Mississippi, are often visually unattractive and take business away from stores in the downtown area. Note the "rollaway billboards" topped with flashing lights.

cities, this linear sprawl has increasingly been supplemented by the self-contained shopping center, invariably set well back from the highway. In larger places (known in the retailing business as "the middle markets"), the center may feature an enclosed mall, movie theatre, and one or more "big city" department stores. The overall effect of sprawling residential and commercial growth has been a blurring of the distinction between town and country and a reduced—or at least not expanded—role for the old town center.

In the last several years, there has been a reaction against both sprawl and placelessness, in the form of public and private efforts to revitalize downtowns, to preserve and reuse old urban and rural structures, and to create new regional architectural traditions. Examples are widespread, though some parts of the South are virtually unaffected by the reaction; and the balance still seems to be in the direction of loss of regional identity in the built environment.

Preservation of single buildings of exceptional interest, such as Mount Vernon or the great plantation houses along the Natchez Trace, has long been commonplace in the South. The nation's first historic districts were created in Charleston, South Carolina (1931) and New Orleans (1936). But it has been only recently that southerners have taken—as have people elsewhere in the country—a significant interest in their legacy of "ordinary" residential and commercial structures. Medium-sized cities such as Little Rock and Winston-Salem have experienced a wave of private renovation of housing in neighborhoods bordering the downtown. There has also been widespread recycling of old commercial structures, such as the railroad station in Knoxville, Tennessee, tobacco warehouses in Richmond, Virginia, and Durham, North Carolina, and dozens of buildings in downtown Savannah, Georgia.

Among the South's greatest architectural assets are the downtown areas of its small towns. Many of these developed as county seats and farm-service centers, reaching their greatest prosperity in the early years of the 20th century. Then began a long decline, paralleling the South's decline in agriculture. Because of this lack of growth, many downtowns escaped the tendency, so widespread in other regions during the 1950s and 1960s, to modernize old stores with false fronts or to tear them down entirely. "Our small towns didn't change," says one Alabama planner, "because they were too poor to change."

Now, as old buildings are again in fashion, many southern towns offer ensembles of late 19th- and early 20th-century buildings rarely found in more prosperous places. Dozens of southern towns have used federal urban aid monies and their own funds to build on old design traditions rather than simply to "modernize." Some of this activity has been inspired by the Main Street Project of the National Trust for Historic Preservation; much is simply due to a growing appreciation of local history and of the architectural merits of older buildings.

The economic position of many of these downtown areas is still precarious. Commercial buildings may be occupied on the first floor but be entirely vacant on the next two stories. And edge-of-town commercial strips and regional shopping malls continue to siphon away customers. But there seems widespread recognition that the old downtowns have something unique to offer their communities, and interest in their preservation has increased.

Although much of the post-World War Two building in the South, whether commercial, residential, or governmental, has completely turned its back on regional architectural traditions, there are some exceptions. In Louisiana, the election in 1972 of the state's first governor of Cajun ancestry helped precipitate a

---

Athens [Georgia] now has a regional mall, and the old downtown has been thinking about its future. Another effect has been new peripheral development around the mall, an aesthetic blight and a traffic hazard. Even the green strip in the middle of the highway was wiped out to provide a turn lane. Ironically, the mall hasn't diversified shopping opportunities—the mall has 16 shoe stores, but the merchandise is no different from what we had downtown. It has taken business from the small towns, which were themselves impacted by smaller edge-of-town shopping centers.

BERT SPARER, regional planner, Institute of
Government, University of Georgia

---

revival of interest in ethnic culture. One aspect of this is a striking revival of design traditions drawn from early French and Spanish colonial days (many are actually of Caribbean origin). The results are evident in many neighborhoods in Baton Rouge and surrounding communities: new houses raised from the ground,

Comfortable dwellings with all modern conveniences can still borrow many design elements from the South's traditional rural architectural styles, as is evidenced by this house in Alabama.

rather than on slab foundations; widespread use of balconies and porches; roofs and overhangs of traditional shapes, greater use of wood and ornamental ironwork. Even banks and small shopping centers have been built in "neo-Cajun" style.

Another minor, but apparently spreading, trend is the relocation and renovation of old rural structures. A farmer near Fitzgerald, Georgia, for example, bought an abandoned small town railroad station and, after moving it several miles to his farm, renovated it into an attractive Victorian home. And just outside Auburn, Alabama, developers have collected farmhouses from around the countryside and aggregated them into clustered subdivisions to be modernized and renovated.

Future Population and Job Growth in the South

Future demands on land in the South from human settlement depend on the amount of population and job growth, as well as where that growth is located. Once noted for its high birth rates, particularly in rural areas, the South now has an average birth rate close to the national average of 15.8 per 1,000 residents.

There is, however, considerable variation from state to state, ranging from a high of 19.1 per 1,000 in Louisiana to 13.6 in Florida. This natural increase is an important component of population growth, but much depends also on whether the South can retain its young people when they reach maturity and whether it can attract new migrants from other parts of the country. U.S. Census Bureau estimates indicate that during the 1970s net migration to the South (that is, the excess of people moving in over people moving out) was 3.7 million.[27] Although more than half the net inflow was to Florida, all of the southern states had positive net migration.

Future net migration to the South is likely to depend heavily on the availability of jobs. Economist Herman Bluestone, in recent studies of regional patterns of job growth, found that the relative performance of the South in creating jobs has been declining in recent years.[28] During the economically difficult 1979-82 period, employment in metropolitan areas in the South did quite well by national standards, but it still failed to keep up with a higher than average increase in people looking for work. The South's nonmetropolitan areas, however, had virtually no net increase in jobs and faced a soaring unemployment rate.

Bluestone points out that the low-wage, labor-intensive industries that had earlier been mainstays of southern growth are

---

There is a sort of three-legged stool supporting the rural economy in some parts of Tennessee—unemployment insurance, part-time farming, and manufacturing jobs.

TED SCHMUDDE, geographer, University of
Tennessee

---

facing increased competition from foreign countries, where wages are even lower. Moreover, other traditional advantages of the South, such as aggressive industrial promotion and low levels of unionization, have increasingly been imitated by other parts of the country eager to lure new employment sources. And, although the South has benefited in the past from a disproportionate share in federal expenditures, future growth in defense expenditures, which tend to be beneficial, is likely to be offset by expected cuts in domestic programs important in the South. "While it may be too early to draw firm conclusions," Bluestone writes, "recent

changes in the industrial structure of southern employment
growth and recent changes in the national economy suggest that
the South may be hard pressed to duplicate its [past] relatively
good growth performance in the 1980s.''[29]

Beyond the influence of jobs, population growth in some parts
of the South—including much of Florida, the Ozark-Ouachita
region of Arkansas, mountain resorts in Tennessee, North
Carolina, and Georgia, parts of East Texas, and coastal areas
throughout the South—is dependent on retirees. The retirement-
age population nationwide is certain to rise in the future, and the
South's moderate winter climate and low living costs are likely
to prove a continued attraction. One interesting question is the
extent to which crowding and rising land prices in central and
southern Florida will push potential retirees to other parts of that
state or elsewhere.

The most recent Census Bureau population projection for the
South is based primarily on extrapolation of demographic patterns of the recent past and does not account for possible changes
in the South's ability to generate new jobs. It shows the region's
population increasing by over 15 million persons (31 percent) between 1980 and 2000, well above the national average growth
rate (18 percent). According to the Bureau, Florida would be the
South's fastest-growing state (up 79 percent to a staggering year
2000 population of 17.4 million), while Alabama would be the
slowest growing, with an increase of 13 percent.[30]

Future Demands for Land

Accommodating Population Growth

The combination of a large rural population and lower than
average urban densities means that human settlement in the South
occupies more land than might the equivalent population in other
parts of the country. Measuring human occupancy of land is more
difficult than measuring areas of cropland or forestland, both conceptually and practically.[31] The two statistical measures commonly
employed to approximate land used for human settlement come
from two different federal agencies—the U.S. Census Bureau and
the Soil Conservation Service (SCS), U.S. Department of
Agriculture—and count somewhat different aspects of human occupancy of the land.

The Census Bureau tries to measure the amount of land occupied by "urban" people, that is, by persons living in places of over 2,500 in population. This obviously underestimates the amount of land devoted to settlements by ignoring all rural residents; on the other hand, it overestimates settled land to the extent that undeveloped land is included within urban boundaries. According to the Census measure, in 1980 urban land in the South amounted to 12.5 million acres, or 4.11 percent of all nonfederal land in the region.[32] This proportion was one-third higher than for the nation as a whole, for which 3.14 percent of nonfederal land was urban.

The Soil Conservation Service did an inventory of "urban and built-up" land as part of its 1982 National Resources Inventory.[33] This survey counted not only land in urban settlements but also all areas of one-quarter acre or larger occupied by houses, farm and ranch buildings, industries, commerce, airports, golf courses, and similar development. By this measure, the South had 16.5 million acres of built-up land, or 5.42 percent of its nonfederal land area. (For the United States as a whole, 4.17 percent was built-up.) An additional 2.00 percent of southern land was in "rural transportation" uses, such as rural highways, railroads, and logging roads.

Combining the built-up and rural transportation acreages, Florida and North Carolina have proportionately the largest ratio of developed land to total nonfederal land area (11.40 percent and 10.08 percent, respectively), while Arkansas, Louisiana, and Mississippi have the smallest.

How might the South's future population and nonfarm economic growth affect the demand for land? The Census figures show that during the period 1970-80, the South added 6.5 million urban people, while its urban land area grew by 4.4 million acres. This means that each new urbanite required .67 acres of urban land.[34] Extrapolating on the basis of this relationship, one might hazard the very rough guess that, when the United States reaches a national population of 300 million (an event the Census Bureau projects might occur by 2030), the South will need another 18 million acres of urban land.[35] This would mean another 6 percent of its nonfederal land might be diverted to built-up uses and hence be unavailable for farming, forestry, and other rural endeavors.

Using Soil Conservation Service data gives a broadly similar result—as the U.S. population grows to 300 million, between 8 and 21 million additional acres of southern land might be built up.[36]

Using the shorter range (year 2000) official regional projections for the South prepared for the U.S. Census Bureau, various assumptions about land consumption indicate between 5.0 and 12.6 million additional acres would become built-up by the year 2000. It is hard to imagine that southern population growth will halt after 2000, so the amount of land ultimately affected would almost certainly expand beyond that level.

These very rough estimates of future settlement demand for land are based on the assumption that both the South's share of the nation's population growth and the amount of land "built-up" per capita will follow the patterns of the recent past. It is not hard to envision scenarios in which future densities are either higher or lower than those recently prevailing. Higher densities could be brought on by high energy costs, environmentally based local growth regulations, or the changing residential preferences of an aging population. Densities could go still lower if southern cities are perceived as unsafe or otherwise unattractive or if the ideal of "country living on a few acres" increases its pull.

If we content ourselves with the guess that long-run demand for new built-up land in the South will be in the range of 8 to 21 million acres, the next question is, How significant is such an expansion for the traditional rural uses of land? The potential amount of new built-up land is between 3 and 7 percent of the South's total stock of nonfederal land. Looked at as an aggregate, I consider this a significant claim on land but one that need not reduce the South's production of food or timber. For example, if the full 21 million acres of new built-up land came out of crops, forests, and grazing in proportion to their current occupancy of land, the impact of the loss could be compensated by an 8.9 percent increase in average productivity per acre.

However, there are some features of the settlement demand for land that make it rather more important than its overall acreage seems to merit. For one thing, built-up uses are unusually strong competitors for land—they typically can pay per-acre prices far higher than can crops, forests, or animal agriculture. For example, I have calculated that, under a typical production regime in

The Great Citrus Freeze

The massive and destructive freezes that hit Florida's citrus groves in December 1983 and January 1985 added an entirely new element potentially affecting the state's settlement pattern. Despite the growth of Orlando during the 1970s, much of central Florida has remained in citrus, a crop with an unusually high profitability per acre. Although the central Florida citrus area (centered on Lakeland and Claremont) is exceptionally attractive for hobby farms or rural residential development, and land prices have long been rising, many citrus growers found that the relatively high income available from citrus production overcame any temptation to sell producing groves for development. But the massive loss of trees to the recent freezes, combined with the competitive pressure from imported citrus, may cause many growers to look more closely at opportunities for subdividing or developing their land. Moreover, even if some former grove land is replanted in vegetables or other annual crops (a strategy suggested by a University of Florida task force), the absence of a fixed investment in mature trees is likely to make farmers much less reluctant to sell if they see the possibility of a good offer from a developer.

the Northern Virginia Piedmont, corn would have to sell for nearly $11 per bushel for agriculture to be able to offer the $15,000 per acre that suburban tract-home developers are able to bid for raw land.[37] That is well over three times the current price of corn.

Away from the suburban fringe, homesites are larger and people are much less willing to pay $15,000 per acre for them (though such a figure is not unusual for a well-located rural industrial plant site). But the fact remains that, given current levels of net returns to rural production uses of land, the person intending to introduce a built-up use of the land can nearly always outbid the farmer or forester. This means that, unless food or wood prices rise dramatically, it will be the production of these commodities that will have to adjust to human settlement, not settlement patterns to the needs of commodity production.

Another important feature of built-up uses of land is the high cost of terminating them. It has been customary to treat human settlement as an *irreversible* use of land, but this claim is contradicted by the evidence of abandoned settlements in fields and forests all over the South. On the other hand, even if future scarcity brought food or wood prices to levels high enough to compete for raw land with development, the amount of capital invested in structures and the hard-to-remove physical alterations to the land militate against much deliberate conversion of built-up land back to farming or forest. Much more likely is the possibility that very high food or wood prices would cause more commodity production on land classified as "built-up" but not actually occupied by a structure. For example, more food might be grown in home gardens or more commercial trees grown along highway rights-of-way. The low densities characteristic of urban settlements in the South probably mean that they contain a great deal of vacant urban land, some of which may be in tracts large enough for commercial agricultural production.

A special concern about the demand for land for human settlement is whether it disproportionately affects land of the best quality. One formulation of this argument posits that human settlements have historically been sited in areas of good agricultural land; as settlement expands over time, it inevitably spreads onto

---

There are few cities in the state large or small that haven't burst their seams in the last few years. The prosperity that came with the state's industrial boom brought the need for more housing and more shopping areas. People have known for a long time that indiscriminate development contributes to flooding, which in turn causes erosion. But the biggest problem of sprawling urban development is that it gobbles up farm land. You can't grow corn in the middle of a shopping center.

EDITORIAL, *Jackson* (Tennessee) *Sun*,
October 6, 1982

---

high-quality land. Another perspective rests on the fact that it is generally cheaper to install utilities, build roads, and grade house pads on sites that are flat and well-drained. This is particularly true where septic tanks are used, because they demand soils through which water can percolate easily. Unfortunately, the qualities that make land most suitable for building also tend to make for fertile farmland. Offsetting these forces is the fact that good cropland, and to a lesser extent good grazing and timber land, sells for a premium. The builder must therefore determine whether, for example, the greater costs of grading hilly land offset its lower purchase cost.

Surveys taken by the Soil Conservation Service permit an evaluation of the quality of land converted to built-up uses during the period 1967-75.[38] The SCS has developed "land capability classes" based on the degree to which a particular soil is physically suited to agricultural use. Nationally, 44 percent of all nonfederal land lies in the top three classes. But of land converted to built-up uses over the 1967-75 period, 58 percent was in the top three capability classes. Thus, the data support the proposition that built-up uses differentially claim the better land. Considering only the southern states, 47 percent of the land was in the highest capability classes; but 58 percent of the land urbanized was in those classes. The small sample size of the SCS surveys unfortunately makes figures for individual parts of the country subject to large sampling errors; so the national comparison but not the southern one is statistically significant.[39]

Two studies of areas within the South support the same conclusion. A statewide survey in Louisiana found that 107 of the state's 115 municipalities with populations of over 2,500 were located on prime agricultural land, though such land made up only 43 percent of total state land area.[40] According to the study, as of 1977, some 9.1 percent of Louisiana's prime agricultural land was urbanized, used for highway or railroad rights-of-way, or used for an extractive purpose (for example, mining or oil and gas).

In the Greenville, South Carolina, area, past urban and industrial development were found to have occurred disproportionately on prime agricultural land. This was also true of land considered most likely to be developed by 1990. In two of the three counties considered, more than half of the prime land not already developed was designated by local plans for future development.[41]

Second Homes and Premature Subdivisions

Several areas of the South have large concentrations of weekend and vacation homes. These are generally termed "second homes," though many are eventually occupied full-time when the owner retires. The homes may be in large-scale developments (as in many coastal areas and in the Blue Ridge and Smoky Mountains), in communities of individually built homes (the area around Hot Springs, Arkansas, for example), or may be isolated structures in picturesque rural areas (horse-oriented hobby farms in the Virginia Piedmont and parts of Kentucky and Tennessee, hunting camps in the Louisiana bayous, restored 19th-century farmhouses in rural Georgia).

The amount of land occupied by these structures is probably not large. Although the U.S. Census does not enumerate second homes, their number may be approximated by the number of "year-round units held for occasional use" plus "vacant seasonal and migratory units" (the latter includes some farm labor housing). By this measure, the South contains 648,000 second homes—about 3 percent of all houses in the region. Nearly half of these units are in Florida, with lesser concentrations in North Carolina, South Carolina, and Virginia. If it is assumed that these units occupy one acre each (a generous estimate given that many of them are in condominiums or on tiny beachside lots), they would collectively occupy only two-tenths of 1 percent of the South's total nonfederal land area. In any case, the land occupied by second homes is already included in the "urban and built-up" category of the SCS data.

From the standpoint of land demand, second homes are significant for two reasons other than the amount of land they occupy. First, they are concentrated in the South's most scenic areas, particularly its beaches and mountains. They thus are likely to compete for the limited supply of this special sort of land with other uses such as outdoor recreation, landscape protection, or wildlife habitat. It is easy to find examples of such conflict: the disputes over growth of the Gulf Shores area along the Alabama coastline; the controversy over the erection, in 1983, of a 10-story condominium atop a North Carolina mountain; the long-standing battles over residential development of mangrove wetlands in Southwest Florida.

Second, playing on the widespread interest in owning a second home as well as on buyers' speculative instincts, real estate developers have subdivided millions of residential parcels, ranging in size from houselots to several acres apiece. A few of these subdivisions, particularly near beaches or ski areas, have become recreational communities. But most of them can be classified as "premature" subdivisions—that is, subdivisions built far in advance of actual demand for structures and unlikely to be built-out for many years, if at all.

Records of the Office of Interstate Land Sales of the Department of Housing and Urban Development list some 6,600 subdivisions in the South, with 3.2 million lots covering 2.3 million acres.[42] Unsurprisingly, the largest acreage (1.5 million acres) is in Florida, followed by North Carolina and Arkansas. Florida, with its large number of vacant platted lots and its unusually sensitive natural systems, has had a particularly difficult time managing the

Rural lots in eastern North Carolina subdivided as future sites for mobile homes.

huge number of small rural lots created prior to the enactment of tougher environmental laws in the mid-1970s. These older lots do not meet contemporary environmental standards, yet are "grandfathered" under later laws. Florida is now studying ways to replat and combine lots so that future population growth can be accommodated without causing intolerable environmental and esthetic damage.[43]

Water Impoundments

In addition to the human settlement uses of land already described, two other forms of development occupy significant amounts of southern land. Man-made water impoundments can range from farm ponds to local water storage reservoirs to large multi-purpose lakes, such as South Carolina's Lake Marion and Texas' Toledo Bend Reservoir. Better measures exist of how much water area there is (including both natural and man-made water bodies) than of how it is changing. In 1980, the Census Bureau measured 11.4 million acres of permanent inland water in the southern states; the Soil Conservation Service measured another 3.0 million acres of water bodies and streams too small to have been counted by the Census.[44]

Neither Census nor SCS data allow reliable comparisons of change over time.[45] This may not be much of a loss, because it is unlikely that future development of water impoundments will closely parallel that of the recent past. The large-scale dam projects so popular throughout the South in the 1950s and 1960s are becoming rare, partly because the best sites are already utilized, partly because federal funding is less readily available, and partly because of environmental opposition. Tennessee's Tellico Dam, though eventually ordered by Congress to be completed, was delayed for years by a potent coalition of environmentalists concerned with wildlife impacts and farmers upset because the reservoir pool would flood their land. The continued likelihood of such opposition will inhibit new dam proposals in the years ahead.

Although few large dams are now being built, two long-planned exceptions, the Richard B. Russell Dam on the Savannah River and the Tennessee-Tombigbee waterway in Alabama affect 59,000 and 104,000 acres, respectively.[46] Moreover, the search for a dependable water supply for fast-growing urban areas is likely to lead to many smaller reservoir projects, such as those recently completed or underway in the Raleigh-Durham, North Carolina, area.

Water impoundments tend to claim a great deal of land of poorer than average quality but also some very good land. Streamside land inundated by reservoirs is frequently either too steep or too wet for agriculture. But the edges of the reservoir pool may extend onto fertile bottomlands, which are generally the South's finest cropland.[47]

Mining

Another source of development demand for southern land is from the mining industry. Many of the minerals found in the South are extracted by surface mining or open pit methods, which not only occupy land during the course of the mining operation but also may degrade or even permanently eliminate the land's natural fertility. Moreover, even when a mineral is extracted by pumping or deep-mining (as in the case of petroleum and some coal), there is a potential impact on land productivity and amenity through the pollution of surface water or groundwater.

Table 5.3 shows the impressive number of commercially valuable minerals found in the South. Only a small fraction of these deposits are now being mined. At the present time, the most

Table 5.3

Known Mineral Deposits in the South

Bauxite—Arkansas, Alabama, Georgia
Bituminous Coal—Arkansas, Alabama, Georgia, North Carolina, Kentucky, Oklahoma, Tennessee, Virginia
Clays—Georgia, North Carolina, South Carolina, Tennessee
Copper—Alabama, Georgia, North Carolina, Tennessee, Virginia
Gold—Alabama, Georgia, North Carolina, South Carolina, Tennessee, Virginia
Iron—Alabama, Arkansas, Georgia, Louisiana, Mississippi, North Carolina, Tennessee, Texas, Virginia
Molybdenum—Alabama, South Carolina, North Carolina
Nickel—North Carolina
Lignite—Alabama, Arkansas, Georgia, Louisiana, Mississippi, Tennessee, Texas
Oil Shale—Alabama, Arkansas, Georgia, Oklahoma, Tennessee
Peat—Florida, Louisiana, North Carolina, South Carolina
Petroleum and Natural Gas—Louisiana, Texas, Kentucky, Alabama, Oklahoma, Arkansas, Florida, Mississippi
Phosphate—Florida, Georgia, North Carolina, Tennessee
Sand, Gravel, and Cement—Ubiquitous
Silver—North Carolina, Tennessee, Virginia
Tar Sands—Alabama
Titanium—Florida
Uranium—Virginia, North Carolina
Zinc—Tennessee

Source: U.S. Department of Interior, *Minerals Yearbook* (Washington, D.C.: U.S. Government Printing Office, 1982); Robert A. Honig, Richard J. Olson, and William T. Mason, Jr., *Atlas of Coal/Minerals and Important Resource Problem Areas for Fish and Wildlife in the Coterminous United States* (Kearneysville, W.Va.: U.S. Fish and Wildlife Service, 1981); miscellaneous sources.

important mining operations in the South from the standpoint of land use are the strip-mining of bituminous coal in Kentucky, Virginia, and Alabama; strip-mining of lignite in East Texas; strip- and pit-mining of phosphates in eastern North Carolina and central Florida; and the extraction of sand, gravel, limestone, and clay in hundreds of scattered locations throughout the South.

The latest available estimate of the amount of land disturbed by surface mining is a cumulative total up to the year 1977.[48] It indicates that in the South 1.56 million acres had been surface-mined, with 1.01 million of these acres still in need of reclamation. The largest areas of unreclaimed lands were in phosphate mines in Florida and coal mines in Kentucky and Alabama. Visual comparison of maps of principal mining areas in the South with maps of land use indicate that most of the present mining areas are of less than average importance for agriculture and forestry.[49]

Data on current and projected *rates* of land disturbance are available only for coal. During 1977, strip-mining for coal affected 19,700 acres in the South, more than half of them in Kentucky.[50] Although the total national demand for coal may increase greatly in the future, many experts believe that the high sulfur content of much Appalachian coal, and the cost of restoring strip-mined land to original contour (as required by the 1977 Federal Surface Mining Act), will hold back the expansion of strip-mining in the South, except in the lignite-producing area of the Gulf states. For example, the Office of Technology Assessment projects that even if national coal production doubles or triples by the year 2000, output of Appalachian strip-mined coal will actually be below its 1977 level.[51]

At present, there are several areas of new or expanded mining activity in the South, some of which are the subject of local controversy. In Virginia, the Marline Uranium Company has leases on 40,000 acres in Pittsylvania County that appear to contain some of the richest uranium ore in the country. Pittsylvania is also one of Virginia's most important agricultural counties. The company also has options on nearly 16,000 acres in the Rappahannock Basin in north-central Virginia. Although the uranium would be mined through an open pit covering only 100 acres, there is concern that possible radioactive pollution of groundwater and surface water could affect agriculture over a much larger area.[52] According to one leading Virginia environmentalist, "Tobacco and dairy farmers are concerned that even the suspicion that their products might be contaminated could make them unmarketable. Already, the trade association of Virginia's new wine grape industry has passed a resolution opposing such mining."[53] Thus far, Marline has not formally applied for a permit to mine its deposits. But both Virginia and North Carolina (where uranium also is found) have started to study possible regulatory regimes.

The phosphate industry has major plans for expansion in both Florida and North Carolina, states that in 1981 produced $1.3

billion of the mineral, an important constituent of fertilizer and a major export. In eastern North Carolina, the North Carolina Phosphate Corporation plans to open a large new strip mine in the late 1980s, not far from Texas Gulf Company's phosphate operation, which is one of the largest nonfuel mines in the United States. Several new mines have been proposed in Florida, including one in Manatee County, which has raised the ire of county supervisors (see box), and some on national forest lands, where companies have argued that discovery of the mineral entitles them to development leases.

In East Texas, continued expansion is forecast for the lignite (a soft coal) industry, which expanded several-fold during the 1970s, mainly to fuel new mine-mouth electric generating plants. Although lower in heating value than bituminous coal, the lignite deposits are much closer to fast-growing urban and industrial areas

Florida's Phosphate "Nightmare"

In addition to its beautiful bays teeming with fish, luscious groves laden with fruit, and wild unspoiled mangrove islands, Florida also has the distinction of being the state with the largest contiguously mined-out area in the country. Over 200 square miles of central and southern Florida land are permanently scarred as a result of phosphate mining.

Massive upheavals of earth, acres of green slime ponds, and large expanses of barren, pock-marked earth greet the Florida visitor. Huge mountains of radioactive gypsum wastes silently leach deadly poisons into ground and surface waters, and nearby phosphoric acid factories emit clouds of radionuclides, fluorides, and other toxics into the air. . . .

Hardest hit by phosphate pollution is Florida's Manatee County, where Mobil [Corp.] controls some 95,256 acres—nearly one-fourth of the entire county. Proposed mining sites in the county cover about 42 percent of the Manatee River's 135 square mile watershed, which contains the primary drinking water supply for approximately 250,000 people in Manatee and Sarasota counties. There is no backup supply.

One of these sites, proposed by Estech [Mining Co.], will generate 90,000 gallons per minute of phosphatic slime waste water, which is to be stored on site in over 6,000 acres of above-grade slime ponds. According to Estech, between 1.44 and 2.5 million gallons per day of waste water will seep into the Manatee aquifer. This seepage can contain high levels of radionuclides, fluorides, chromium and other toxics. Levels of radium as high as 2,000 picocuries per liter (ppl) in slime ponds are not unusual. (The drinking water standard for radium-226 is five ppl.)

—Jay Blucher, "Florida's Phosphate 'Nightmare,' " *Resources*, Environmental Task Force, vol. 2, no. 3 (Fall 1982), p. 1.

along the Gulf Coast and thus enjoy a significant transport cost advantage. Besides those in Texas, two major lignite mines are expected to open soon in Louisiana and two more in Arkansas.[54]

Southern minerals also have possibilities as a source of synthetic fuels. Exxon once planned a multi-billion-dollar lignite gasification plant in East Texas, though falling oil prices caused the project to be scrubbed. Plants gasifying bituminous coal were proposed in Kentucky. There was also a proposal for a synthetic methanol plant in eastern North Carolina, based on the region's widespread peat deposits.[55] Although the initial proposal covered 15,000 acres, the company involved controlled over 100,000 acres of peat deposits. And hundreds of thousands of additional acres of peat are found in the "pocosin" wetland areas of North and South Carolina. Opposition to the North Carolina peat-mining proposal came not only from environmentalists and farmers but also from the state's important seafood industry, which is concerned about changes to water quality in the nearby estuaries that provide breeding grounds for many commercially valuable marine species.[56] The first of the peat-to-methanol projects was to rely on a loan and price guarantee from the U.S. Synthetic Fuel Corporation, an arrangement that a North Carolina environmentalist called, "a direct federal subsidy of the destruction of wetlands."[57] The subsidy application was withdrawn by the developer in 1984, and the project apparently has been abandoned. Not far away, however, another firm is planning a facility to burn peat to generate electricity. Peat mining has also been recently under consideration on timber company land in Florida.[58]

Conflicts between "Developed" Uses and Other Uses

In addition to the land physically occupied by human settlements and other "developed" uses, uncounted millions of acres in the South are affected by nearby urbanization or by expectations related to urbanization. The conflicts caused by the spatial proximity of developed and traditional rural uses of land may be even more important to the South's resource and environmental future than is the amount of land actually paved over or mined or devoted to buildings and lawns.

Spillovers

One consequence of the spread of low-density urbanization into a formerly rural area is the potential for conflict when two very different uses of land are adjoining or near each other. Not all of the interactions or "spillovers" between activities are negative (after all, farms and forests can produce an attractive visual setting for a housing development), but the list of possible problems is long.[59] A major problem for farmers is their residential neighbors' free-roaming pets, which chase and even sometimes

> *Urbanites that locate contiguous to farm operations complain about odors from dairy farms, poultry farms, hog farms and feed lots. Urbanites complain about the noise from irrigation pumps during the night or from a strawberry farmer shooting robins early on a Sunday morning.... Conversely, farmers dislike urbanites because of increased vandalism and thefts, trespassing, trail bikes, and the lack of animal [dog] control. Sometimes, urbanites view agricultural areas as exclusive residential areas and they attempt to rid the area of obnoxious farm activities that were "there first."*
>
> HILLSBOROUGH, FLORIDA, COUNTY PLAN, draft
> agricultural element, April 1982

kill livestock. Children may vandalize the farmer's property; careless adults may leave gates open. The wells that serve new developments may, in times of drought, compete with irrigated crops for water. As rural areas develop, roads and powerlines can cut across fields and forest tracts.

A growing problem in forest land management in urbanizing areas is the prevention and control of wildfires. Says the director of Virginia's state forestry service:

> We have a new form of "string development" in this state—houses strung out along rural roads with huge blocks of forestland behind them. . . .There are more people to start fires and now there are homes to burn. We're not just protecting the woods anymore. We're protecting people and property.[60]

He notes that a fire that broke out in the summer of 1982 in a roadside dump in southeastern Virginia spread into a housing subdivision and burned 17 houses. "This is the kind of thing that we didn't worry about 20 years ago."

Many traditional agricultural and forestry practices prove objectionable in a mixed urban/rural setting. During planting and harvest season, farmers tend to run noisy machinery at inconveniently early hours. Slow-moving farm machinery proves less than welcome on suburban roads. Odors from manure spreading, hog and chicken operations, and dairy pens may offend residential neighbors. Burning crop stubble and prescribed forestland burning produce smoke that may drift across roads or into homes. In an age of pervasive concern about the dangers of toxic materials, persons whose homes or well fields adjoin agricultural or forest areas are likely to object increasingly to the application (particularly by aerial spraying) of herbicides and pesticides.

"The people who live in rural areas now just aren't like the ones who lived there before," says the head of forest management for the Texas State Forest Service. "They don't have any connection with agriculture or forestry. . . . You're going to have a lot more 'people conflicts' in trying to manage the natural environment."[61]

In general, when conflict arises between agricultural and ur-

A nonfarm house on a 10-acre lot in rural Virginia. Local zoning for very large lots can have unintended effects, actually increasing the amount of farmland taken out of production and spreading the nonfarm population over a very wide area.

ban users of land in an urbanizing region, the urban user ultimately prevails. The late University of Georgia geographer Merle C. Prunty described what he called the "zone-out process," which occurs when neighbors of livestock operations decide they "don't like the smell of animal manures, flies they attribute to animals, truck traffic to and from farms, and cows that moo in the night."[62] As suburbanites gain a numerical majority, they may incorporate the area, then enact zoning regulations to ban the livestock.

To defend agriculture against such conflicts, several southern states have recently enacted "right to farm" laws that exempt farmers from nuisance suits brought by nonagricultural neighbors. Louisiana (1978) and North Carolina (1979) were the first states in the nation to do so; by 1981, such laws were on the books in all of the southern states.[63] North Carolina's law, which served as a model for most state laws, provides that "agricultural operations" (the term includes livestock farms, but not forestry activities) that have been in place for more than one year may not be subject to nuisance suits because of "changed conditions" in or about the locality. The North Carolina law does not apply to farm-generated water pollution nor to problems that are the result of "negligent or improper operation" of a farm.

"Right-to-farm" laws are likely to prove more difficult to implement than they were to enact. The laws do not necessarily protect existing farms that try to change production methods or adopt new technologies. For example, in Georgia, a chicken house built on a former pasture was held by a court to be not protected by the right-to-farm statute.[64] Moreover, given the numerical superiority of nonfarm rural residents, it is likely that there will be continuing pressure throughout the South for statewide regulation of agricultural chemical use and of similar generic activities likely to produce nuisances.

The Economic Shadow

Besides producing physical spillovers, human settlement casts an economic shadow that may affect the use of land over a wide area. This impact takes several forms.

First, when farmers or forest owners notice that their land is in the path of urban development or that similarly situated properties have gone into rural nonfarm use, they may change their expectations about the future use of their land. They may become reluctant to make long-term investments, say in specialized farm machinery or in planting pines. They may neglect to control soil erosion, on the grounds that the future fertility of the soil is unimportant if the land will eventually be developed. And owners may resist land-use controls that would designate their land as permanently agricultural. At the same time, implement dealers, gin operators, and seed companies in urbanizing areas are likely to let their investments depreciate. Overall, the response of agriculture to the prospect of increased human settlement has been aptly described as "the impermanence syndrome."

Second, as property values rise to reflect development value, real estate taxes go up. In most of the southern states, assessments on farmland or forestland in excess of "current use value" may be reduced or deferred, though the landowner must sometimes accept restrictions (rarely onerous) on development in exchange for the tax reduction.[65] But even if farm assessments do not rise, the public services required by new nonfarm residents may push up the rates applicable to all properties. Farmers may also be liable

Central Florida's citrus grovelands, already threatened by spillover of growth from fast-growing Orlando, were devastated by severe freezes in 1983 and 1985. Many groves seem destined to become subdivisions or hobby farms.

for special assessments to pay for adjoining roads or sewers.

Third, the structure of landownership starts to change.[66] More land is bought by speculators, by hobby farmers, or by people who intend to eventually build nonfarm residences. Parcel sizes also fall, frequently to levels below those usable for agriculture or forestry, even as part of a "fragmented neo-plantation" such as was described in chapter 2. Although these impacts have long been observed in tracts of land on the urban fringe, the spread of increased human settlement over the countryside has greatly widened the amount of land affected. For example, a recent survey of persons knowledgeable about the farmland market in North Carolina found that, statewide, 51 percent of respondents thought that nonfarm uses were the primary determinants of demand for rural farmland.[67] Moreover, the respondents also estimated that about 34 percent of all farmland sold in the state was purchased for nonfarm use.

Pollution and Land Productivity

A possibly serious threat to the productivity of the South's rural land, only recently being recognized, is air pollution. This emanates from a wide range of human activities. The greatest concern is over the deposition of airborne sulfates and nitrates (usually called acid rain, though dry deposition is also significant). Although acid rain is popularly thought of as a problem limited to New England and parts of the Midwest, the measured acidity of rainfall is also increasing in many parts of the South (see figure 5.2). Some of the acidity comes from urban areas and coal-burning power plants within the South; some drifts in from the highly industrialized Ohio Valley.

Scientists are presently uncertain about what impact levels of acid rain comparable to those observed in the South might have on crops and forests.[68] Some southern soils are deficient in either sulfur or nitrogen; thus, moderate amounts of airborne deposition of these chemicals may actually increase plant growth. On the other hand, controlled experiments have shown that high levels of acid rain reduce plant growth, sometimes by injuring foliage, sometimes by mobilizing toxic metals in the soil, perhaps sometimes by interfering with soil microbial processes. Aside from experimental evidence, some scientists believe that acid rain is responsible for recent severe declines in forest growth in moun-

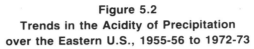

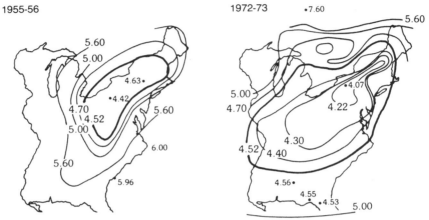

Figure 5.2
Trends in the Acidity of Precipitation
over the Eastern U.S., 1955-56 to 1972-73

Numbers indicate average pH of annual precipitation. Normal rainfall has a pH of 5.6.

Source: U.S. Department of Energy and U.S. Environmental Protection Agency, *Energy/Environmental Fact Book* (Washington, D.C.: U.S. Government Printing Office, 1977), p. 71

tain areas of New England and in parts of Europe.

One characteristic that may be particularly important in the South is the low acid-buffering capacity of some southern soils (see figure 5.3). Acid ions deposited on these soils are less likely to be neutralized and are, therefore, more likely to immobilize essential plant nutrients, thereby reducing crop or forest growth.

Large parts of the South also have a problem with ozone, though levels in some areas are expected to fall as statewide pollution control plans are put into effect.[69] The area around Houston, with its concentration of automobiles and of petrochemical plants, seems to have the most intractable problem and is projected to exceed the federal primary ozone standard even in 1987. Ozone is a powerful oxidant that in high concentrations damages leaf surfaces. Studies have shown that chronic exposure to ozone in concentrations well below the national ambient standards (which much of the South does not meet) can cause yield reductions in many crops, including cotton, soybeans, peanuts, and vegetables.[70] One Department of Agriculture researcher concludes that ozone pollution may be a factor in the lack of improvement in cotton

Figure 5.3
Acid-Sensitive Soils in the Eastern U.S.

Hydrogen loading equivalents per square meter.

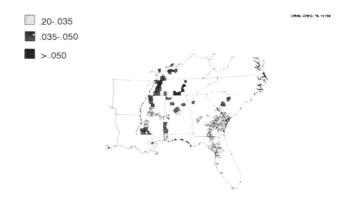

.20-.035

.035-.050

> .050

ORNL-DWG 79-15159

Source: Jeffrey M. Klopatek, W. Frank Harris, and Richard J. Olson, "A Regional Ecological Assessment Approach to Atmospheric Deposition: Effects on Soil Systems," in David S. Shriner, Chester R. Richmond, and Steven E. Lindberg, *Atmospheric Sulfur Deposition* (Ann Arbor, Mich.: Ann Arbor Science Publishers, 1980), p. 548. Map by Oak Ridge National Laboratory.

yields since the mid-1960s, despite the development of better varieties.[71] Ozone also reduces growth in many species of trees, though there seems to be considerable variation from tree to tree in response to a given level of pollution.[72]

Very recently, scientists and foresters have begun to observe troubling physical symptoms among some species of southern trees, including the economically important loblolly and shortleaf pines.[73] The latest forest survey data for thousands of sample plots in Alabama and the Piedmont of Georgia and South Carolina indicate that these species have not been growing as fast as in previous decades. "It is obvious something is happening," says one Forest Service researcher, "but it is very complex to sort out just what it is that is happening." Some observers attribute the growth slowdown to pollution, perhaps some combination of acid deposition and ozone.

A long-term, very uncertain, but potentially quite important, phenomenon is the continuing buildup of carbon dioxide in the global atmosphere as a result of combustion of fossil fuels.[74] A doubling of CO_2 relative to 19th-century levels, which may come before the year 2050, could cause a global warming of several degrees Celsius, with the warming becoming greater with distance from the equator. Two projected impacts seem most relevant to southern land use. First, projected lower rainfall could reduce the productivity of rainfed agriculture in the Midwest and sharply limit the availability of irrigation water in the West.[75] This could give the South a relative advantage in both rainfed and irrigated agriculture. Second, a rise of several meters in the level of the ocean (a result of melting polar ice) would inundate large portions of the South Atlantic Coastal Plain and Delta. Many coastal cities would have to be relocated; large portions of Florida might be covered by seawater.

These impacts would most likely occur very slowly, and there are many ways in which they might be mitigated or avoided. It is possible, in fact, that policies taken to avoid CO_2 buildup might have more impact on the South than the buildup itself. Consider, for example, a massive program of tropical reforestation, meant to reduce CO_2 but having the incidental effect of providing a huge new source of subsidized pulpwood that could compete with southern producers. Or consider the impact on the South of massive interbasin water transfers designed to protect the agricultural economy of the Midwest from climate-induced drought.

The Outlook for Settlement and Development Demands on the Land Base

Since the end of World War Two, the South has experienced impressive growth in both its population and economy. Although there are many reasons for this growth, four seem to be particularly important: (1) a low wage structure and lack of unionization, which made the region attractive to labor-intensive manufacturing firms; (2) low living costs, especially for housing and taxes; (3) a convergence with the rest of the United States in racial and other social attitudes, which made the South less intimidating to new in-migrants, both black and white; and (4) a warm winter climate, which attracted retirees and others seeking amenities.

Each of these factors is likely to continue to exert its pull in the years ahead. But it seems plausible to expect a modest weakening of some of these advantages. For example, wages in the South have been getting closer to those in the rest of the country, while the expansion of international trade makes international wage comparisons as important as interregional ones in determining where labor-intensive industry will locate. And the South is likely to have a difficult time in maintaining low housing costs and low taxes, particularly in those regions attracting the most new growth.

Earlier in this chapter, I described the potential demand for additional urban and built-up land in the South as significant but unlikely to reduce production of agricultural and forest products. A slowdown in regional growth would make the demand for land still smaller. And the amount of new land demanded would be further reduced by anticipated rates in construction of water impoundments and highways lower than those experienced in the 1960s and 1970s.

Overall, I suspect that the impact of human settlement on the South's land base will be not so much the number of acres of new land paved over or flooded or built-on as it will be problems stemming from the proximity of human settlements to crop, forestry, and grazing uses. I have described these problems as consisting of both physical spillovers and a more subtle "economic shadow."

The competition of human settlement uses of land with other uses will be mediated in part by the automatic operation of land and product markets. It can be argued that the relatively lavish current use of land in the South for settlement activities is a consequence of the fact that the urban value of land is high relative to its value in other uses. But if urban and other settlement uses of land begin to reduce significantly the agricultural land base, prices of crops and timber will rise. With higher product prices, agricultural and forestry users of land will be able to offer more to rent or buy land.

As I noted earlier, agricultural product prices would have to be almost unimaginably high to bid land away from traditional suburban growth. But there is greater opportunity, I believe, for agricultural users to bid land away from some of the more spread-out forms of human settlement. For example, many rural properties in the South are bought for retirement, recreation, or simply the satisfaction of landownership. When land prices are very low, land purchasers with these motivations may buy tracts of 50 or 100 acres or more. But as agricultural land uses bid up land prices, these purchasers may reduce their expectations about what size of parcel is most suitable.[76]

The automatic operation of economic markets also causes agricultural uses to adjust to spillover effects. If product prices are quite high, agricultural users seem willing and able to tolerate fairly crowded conditions. (The adjustment of the horticultural and dairy industries to urbanization in California and Florida is a case in point.) In general, however, an efficient resolution of the sort of complex spillovers peculiar to land use seems to require a combination of market adjustments and strategic public interventions through land-use controls or other public policies. The South's continued growth will make these adjustments and interventions increasingly necessary.

References

1. Between 1980 and 1983, however, Kentucky, Alabama, Mississippi, and Arkansas again experienced net outmigration.

2. The South has 21 percent of U.S. population and 24 percent of the total number of U.S. Standard Metropolitan Statistical Areas.

3. Excluding Florida, 16.2 percent of the South's population lives in small towns. Technically these figures represent persons living in places with populations between 2,500 and 50,000 and lying outside the boundaries of Census Bureau-designated "urbanized areas." The latter are places with populations of 50,000 or greater and the closely settled territory, including suburban towns, surrounding them.

4. See H. Thomas Frey, "Expansion of Urban Area in the United States: 1960–1980" (unpublished report, Economic Research Service, U.S. Department of Agriculture, 1983).

5. It is important to point out that the change figures represent percentage changes in the number of people living in places of a given size at two points in time, 1970 and 1980. They do not represent the percentage rates of growth for places that were in a given category in 1970. Thus, the figures show that fewer people lived in small cities in 1980 than in 1970. This does *not* mean that small cities declined in population; indeed, some grew above 50,000 persons and became "urbanized areas."

6. Calvin L. Beale, telephone interview, Washington, D.C., June 1985.

7. U.S. Department of Commerce, Bureau of the Census, *State and Metropolitan Area Data Book, 1982* (Washington, D.C.: U.S. Government Printing Office, 1982). Florida has the newest housing stock, with only 14.3 percent of units built before 1950. But all of the other southern states are below 30 percent. (The national average is 37.4 percent.)

8. W. J. Cash, *The Mind of the South* (New York: Vintage Books, 1941), p. 9.

9. John R. Stilgoe, *Common Landscape of America, 1580 to 1845* (New Haven: Yale University Press, 1982), p. 74.

10. James S. Fisher, "The Piedmont: Old and New," in James Heyl, ed., *The South: A Vade Mecum* (Atlanta: for 69th annual meeting of the Association

of American Geographers, 1973), p. 77. See also John Brinckerhoff Jackson, *American Space: The Centennial Years* (New York: W. W. Norton, 1972), pp. 156-57, and Merle Prunty, Jr., "The Renaissance of the Southern Plantation," *Geographical Review*, vol. 45, no. 4 (1955), pp. 459-91.

11. Fisher, "The Piedmont," p. 78.

12. Cash, *The Mind of the South*, p. 198.

13. Ibid., p. 194.

14. Fisher, "The Piedmont," p. 79.

15. John Fraser Hart, "Migration to the Blacktop: Population Redistribution in the South," *Landscape*, vol. 25, no. 3 (Fall 1981), pp. 15-19; see also John Fraser Hart and Ennis L. Chestang, "Rural Revolution in East Carolina," *Geographical Review*, vol. 68, no. 4 (1978), pp. 435-58.

16. Doug Swaim, *Carolina Dwelling* (Raleigh: North Carolina State University, School of Design, 1978), p. 44.

17. John Shelton Reed and Daniel Joseph Singal, eds., *Regionalism and the South: Selected Papers of Rupert Vance* (Chapel Hill: University of North Carolina Press, 1982), p. 182.

18. For a detailed study of nonmetropolitan commuting in a 40-county area in Georgia and South Carolina, see James S. Fisher and Ronald L. Mitchelson, "Extended and Internal Commuting in the Transformation of the Nonmetropolitan Periphery," *Economic Geography*, vol. 57, no. 3 (July 1981), pp. 189-207.

19. W.W. McPherson, Gainesville, Florida, personal communication, June 1985.

20. Quoted in *Atlanta Journal and Constitution*, April 15, 1984, p. 12-A.

21. Richard R. Wilkinson and Robert M. Leary, *Conservation of Small Towns* (Raleigh: North Carolina State University, School of Design, for Coastal Plains Regional Commission, 1976), pp. 20-21.

22. For example, the percentage of housing units in the South lacking complete plumbing fell from 28 percent in 1960 to only 3 percent in 1980.

23. A survey of low-income families in Alabama found that 90 percent spent a substantial amount of their at-home time sitting on their front porch. They also preferred some features of their "substandard" dwellings to the "improved" design of modern tract housing. See Alabama-Tombigbee Rivers Regional Planning and Development Commission, *Housing Needs Perception* (Camden, Ala.: The Commission, 1976).

24. Robert M. Ford, *Mississippi Houses: Yesterday Toward Tomorrow* (Starkville, Miss.: Mississippi State University, 1982), pp. 16-17.

25. Richard R. Gardner, "The Mobile Home Challenge," *American Land Forum Magazine*, vol. 5, no. 2 (Spring 1985), p. 8.

26. Kathleen Pepi Southern, *Historic Preservation in Rural North Carolina: Problems and Potentials* (Raleigh: Historic Preservation Society of North Carolina, 1982), p. 1.

27. U.S. Department of Commerce, Bureau of the Census, "Provisional Projections of the Population of States, By Age and Sex: 1980 to 2000," *Current Population Reports*, Series P-25, no. 937 (Washington, D.C.: U.S. Government Printing Office, 1983).

28. Herman Bluestone, "Economic Growth of the South versus Other Regions: Past Trends and Future Prospects," *Southern Journal of Agricultural Economics* (July 1982), pp. 43-52; Stan G. Daberkow and Herman Bluestone, *Patterns of Change in the Metro and Nonmetro Labor Force, 1976-82*, Rural Development Research Report No. 44, Economic Research Service, U.S. Department of Agriculture (Washington, D.C.: U.S. Government Printing Office, 1984).

29. Bluestone, "Economic Growth of the South," p. 43.

30. U.S. Bureau of the Census, "Provisional Projections."

31. For example, how does one treat a vacant tract of land surrounded by urban development? Should the extensive grounds of a rural industrial plant be counted as "built-up"? In most cases, such uncertainties are resolved in the direction of overestimating the amount of built-up land.

32. Census data presented in Frey, "Expansion of Urban Area."

33. U.S. Soil Conservation Service, unpublished data from 1982 National Resources Inventory.

34. This figure for the *marginal* acreage required per urban resident is more than double the 0.32 acres per person that was the South's *average* in 1970. Interestingly, although the South's urban areas are less dense than the national average, the region's marginal urbanization rate of 0.67 acres per person is below the national marginal rate of 0.72 acres per person. Calculated from Frey, "Expansion of Urban Areas," pp 14-15. Frey argues that marginal acreage may be increasing because a higher proportion of vacant land may be included in Census Bureau-defined urban areas.

35. This very crude estimate assumes that as the nation grows from its 1980 population of 226 million to 300 million, the South will garner the same share of growth (35.3 percent) that it did during the period 1970-80. It also assumes that the South's additional rural population will require the same area (0.67 acres per person) as has its urban population.

36. The lower estimate was obtained by multiplying the population projection in reference 35 by 0.32 acres per person, which is the *average* per capita amount of urban and built-up land as defined by the U.S. Soil Conservation Service (SCS). The higher figure was obtained by using a figure (0.80 acres per person) for *marginal* land consumption in the South over the period 1967-75 drawn from U.S. Soil Conservation Service, *Potential Cropland Study* (Washington, D.C.: U.S. Government Printing Office, 1977). The higher figure represents some statistical approximations and cannot be regarded as precise. Moreover, the use of SCS data for measuring interperiod land-use changes has been severely criticized by some scholars. See W.A. Fischel, "The Urbanization of Agricultural Land: A Review of the National Agricultural Lands Study," *Land Economics*, vol. 58, no. 2 (May 1982) pp. 236-59; H. Thomas Frey, "Farmland Conversion: Some Comments on the Potential Cropland Study," *Professional Geographer*, vol. 34, no. 3 (August 1982), pp. 342-45.

37. Robert G. Healy, "Land Market Issues," in Max Schnepf, ed., *Farmland, Food, and the Future* (Ankeny, Iowa: Soil Conservation Society of America, 1979), p. 72.

38. Most of the objections to using SCS data for interyear comparisons that

were made in articles cited in reference 36 do not vitiate a comparison of *relative changes in land quality*, as distinct from land quantity, between the two years.

39. The national result is statistically significant at the 0.05 level. Because SCS defines its regions somewhat differently than I do, the South as denoted here includes Kentucky and West Virginia, but no part of Texas or Oklahoma. See U.S. Soil Conservation Service, *Potential Cropland Study*.

40. A. Frank Ramsey and Floyd L. Corty, *Prime Agricultural Lands of Louisiana: Location and Losses to Nonagricultural Uses*, D.A.E. Research Report No. 596 (Baton Rouge: Louisiana State University, Department of Agricultural Economics and Agribusiness, 1982). Eleven of the municipalities, in the New Orleans area, had apparently consumed all the available prime land and had expanded onto nonprime marshland.

41. Charles F. Cousins and B.L. Dillman, *Prime Agricultural Land Conversion in the Greenville-Spartanburg-Pickens Area* (Clemson: South Carolina Agricultural Experiment Station, 1982).

42. Information from Office of Interstate Land Sales Registration (OILSR) Computerized Management Information System as of September 30, 1983. The OILSR data, which cover both registered subdivisions and some unregistered ones, probably understate the total number of lots, particularly those in subdivisions of fewer than 50 parcels.

43. See *Platted Lands Press* (Lincoln Institute of Land Studies), various issues, 1984-85, and Frank A. Schnidman, "Resolving Antiquated Subdivision Problems," *Florida Environmental and Urban Issues*, vol. 12, no. 1 (October 1984), pp. 20-27.

44. Census figures from U.S. Department of Commerce, Bureau of the Census, Geography Division; SCS figures are from U.S. Soil Conservation Service, *Basic Statistics, 1977 National Resources Inventory*.

45. U.S. Soil Conservation Service, *Potential Cropland Study,* indicates that well over 3 million acres of southern land were inundated during 1967-75. The small sample size on which this figure is based, the fact that more than 80 percent of the change supposedly occurred in Florida, and some inconsistencies with other data convince me that this figure is simply not reliable.

46. U.S. Army Corps of Engineers data.

47. Nationally, SCS figures show that 39 percent of land inundated during 1967-75 was in the two lowest (poorest for agriculture) land-capability classes; 22 percent of all land was in those classes. Thirty-nine percent of inundated land was in the three highest classes, against 44 percent for all land. These differences are only indicative, as they are not statistically significant. Soil Conservation Service, *Potential Cropland Study*.

48. U.S. Soil Conservation Service, *Soil and Water Resources Conservation Act: Appraisal, Vol. 1* (Washington, D.C.: U.S. Government Printing Office, 1981), p. 181. Total does not include Texas and Oklahoma, where 256,303 and 86,311 acres, respectively, were mined or disturbed statewide.

49. This impression is confirmed by data on land use for coal-producing counties in the South in U.S. National Academy of Sciences, *Surface Mining: Soil, Coal, and Society* (Washington, D.C.: National Academy of Sciences,

1981), p. 33.

50. U.S. Soil Conservation Service, *Soil and Water Resources*, p. 180.

51. Office of Technology Assessment, *The Direct Use of Coal—Prospects and Problems of Production and Combustion* (Washington, D.C.: U.S. Government Printing Office, 1979).

52. *Richmond Times Dispatch*, August 12, 1982, and December 22, 1982; *Norfolk Virginian-Pilot*, October 3, 1982.

53. Interview with Robert Dennis, Piedmont Environmental Council, Warrenton, Va., September 1983.

54. Peter Galuszka, "Lignite: Once Scorned Fuel Powers Gulf Coast Energy Drive," *Coal Week*, July 25, 1983, pp. 3-5.

55. Carol Polsgrove, "Conflict Along the Carolina Coast," *Oceans* (May 1983), pp. 65-67.

56. Gary Govert, "The Wetlands War," *Carolina Lifestyle*, vol. 2, no. 7 (July 1983), pp. 46-52.

57. Derb Carter, National Wildlife Federation, quoted in *Raleigh News Observer*, December 15, 1982.

58. Theresa Waldron, "Florida's Santa Fe Swamp: To Mine or Not To Mine?" *Journal of Soil and Water Conservation,* vol. 38, no. 2 (March/April 1983).

59. Another possible benefit is that farmers in an urbanizing area can lease land cheaply from absentee owners or speculators. See "How He Farms in the Suburbs," *Progressive Farmer* (December 1981), p. 24. This increases profitability for remaining farmers, but does not raise overall farm output.

60. Interview with James Garner, Virginia Division of Forestry, Charlottesville, Va., August 1983.

61. Telephone interview with Ed Barron, College Station, Tex., October 1984.

62. Merle C. Prunty, "Agricultural Lands: A Southern Perspective," paper prepared for Agricultural Lands Study Workshop, Memphis, Tennessee, October 3, 1979 (Mississippi State, Miss.: Southern Rural Development Center, 1979).

63. Edward Thompson, Jr., "Defining and Protecting the Right to Farm" *Zoning and Planning Law Report*, vol. 5, nos. 8-9 (September and October 1982), pp. 58-70.

64. *Herrin* v. *Opatut*, 281 S.E. 2d 575 (Ga. 1981), cited in Ibid., p. 62.

65. For provisions of applicable state laws in the South see, for farmland, Robert E. Coughlin and John C. Keene, *The Protection of Farmland: A Reference Guidebook for State and Local Government*, National Agricultural Lands Study Report (Washington, D.C.: U.S. Government Printing Office, 1981), and, for forestland, Patricia Dusenbury, *Report on the Duke/SGPB Forest Policies Project* (Raleigh, N.C.: Southern Growth Policies Board, 1982).

66. See, generally, Robert G. Healy and James L. Short, *The Market for Rural Land: Trends, Issues, Policies* (Washington, D.C.: The Conservation Foundation, 1981), which includes case studies of land ownership patterns in Loudoun County, Virginia, and Tyler County, Texas.

67. Leon E. Danielson, *The North Carolina Rural Real Estate Market*, Economics Information Report No. 66 (Raleigh: North Carolina State University, Department of Economics and Business, 1981).

68. See, generally, David S. Shriner, Chester R. Richmond, and Steven E. Lindberg, *Atmospheric Sulfur Deposition* (Ann Arbor, Mich.: Ann Arbor Science Publishers, 1980); George H. Tomlinson II, "Air Pollutants and Forest Decline," *Environmental Science and Technology*, vol. 17, no. 6 (1983), pp. 246A-255A; Arthur H. Johnson and Thomas G. Siccama, "Acid Deposition and Forest Decline," *Environmental Science and Technology*, vol. 17, no.7 (1983), pp. 294A-305A; Soil Conservation Society of America, *Acid Precipitation: A Position Statement* (Ankeny, Iowa: Soil Conservation Society of America, 1983); National Clean Air Coalition, *Acid Rain in the South: Its Impact and Its Threat* (Washington, D.C.: National Clean Air Coalition, 1984).

69. U.S. National Commission on Air Quality, *To Breathe Clean Air*, (Washington, D.C.: U.S. Government Printing Office, 1981), pp. 3.4-6, 3.4-27.

70. See Walter W. Heck et al., "Assessment of Crop Loss from Ozone," *Journal of the Air Pollution Control Association*, vol. 32, no. 4 (April 1982), pp. 353-61.

71. "Disappointing U.S. Cotton Yields Due to Ozone Air Pollution, According to USDA," *Journal of the Air Pollution Control Association*, vol. 32, no. 4 (April 1982), p. 398. One might speculate, however, that given the intractability of air pollution in California, a major cotton-growing state, ozone pollution might actually improve the *comparative* advantage of the South in cotton production.

72. See William H. Smith, *Air Pollution and Forests* (New York: Springer-Verlag, 1981).

73. *New York Times*, February 26, 1984.

74. See Roger Revelle, "Carbon Dioxide and World Climate," *Scientific American*, vol. 247, no. 2 (August 1982), pp. 35-43; Paul E. Waggoner, "Agriculture and Carbon Dioxide," *American Scientist*, vol. 72, no. 2 (March-April 1984), pp. 179-84.

75. William W. Kellogg, "Impacts of a CO_2-Induced Climate Change," in W. Bach, et al., *Carbon Dioxide: Current Views and Developments in Energy/Climate Research* (Boston: D. Reidel, 1983), pp. 379-413.

76. Previous research on the rural land market (see Healy and Short, *The Market for Rural Land*) convinces me that much of the satisfaction that nonagricultural buyers obtain from rural land is not closely related to parcel size so long as the parcel is 2 or 3 acres or larger and privacy and view protection are assured. Moreover, many landbuyers seem more certain about the maximum dollar amount they are willing to spend than about the precise acreage of land they wish to buy.

Chapter 6

Unpriced Values

A farmer who is deciding whether to buy a hundred acres of Louisiana bottomland forest and turn it into a soybean field presumably compares the price of the land and of bulldozer rental, labor, and diesel fuel against the net return available from the land in soybean production. In effect, the farmer considers the forestry value of the land, because that helps determine the price he must pay for it in an uncleared state.

Yet the land to be cleared has other values that have no market prices. It may provide habitat for endangered species of animals, birds, or plants that will not survive after the forest cover is removed. When cleared and planted in soybeans, the tract may contribute sediment to nearby streams, or increase downstream flooding, or leach pesticides into groundwater. If the farmer chooses to irrigate the land, the decision will be made only on the basis of the price of pumping equipment and the cost of fuel to run it—the water itself is free for the taking.

Each of these commodities—the wildlife, the sediment damage, the groundwater—has a value, which may be very large though difficult to determine with any exactness. What all lack is a price to the user.[1] This chapter is about these "unpriced values" affected by land-use change. Because they lack prices, they do not necessarily influence the land-use decision maker. The word "necessarily" is used here with some deliberation. Decision makers may care about soil conservation for altruistic reasons, or conserve water because of some moral aversion to "waste," or protect wildlife because of some personal satisfaction from doing so. But the powerful force of profit motivation is not engaged where these values are concerned, so it is more than likely that private decision making will underproduce some things that society wants (for example, wildlife habitat) and overproduce some things that society does not want (for example, water pollution).

Water Resources

Many of the expanding land uses in the South require water. It is needed for urban homes and businesses, for farm residents and their livestock, for industry and, above all, for irrigation. Although the total consumptive use of water in the South as a whole is only a minuscule fraction of what is available, there are local areas in which some aspect of water supply is currently a problem. There are many more where water availability is seen as a possible long-term issue and where users are taking steps to establish legal rights to water in anticipation of a future competition among potential users. And there are also many places throughout the South where surface water or groundwater has become severely polluted as a result of unwise land-use practices.

As of 1980, the largest single use of water in the South was for irrigation, which accounted for 58 percent of total consumptive use.[2] (Table 2.4 in chapter 2 shows how irrigated acreage has grown over time.) All of the southern states have at least some irrigated land, though it is minor in Kentucky and Tennessee.

Although the greatest amount of irrigated land is found in Florida, the largest water demand (see table 6.1) is in Arkansas and Louisiana, primarily because of the huge quantities of water applied to rice fields. In most states, irrigation water comes from both surface water and groundwater, with the latter predominating in all the major irrigated states except Louisiana.

The next-largest demand for water comes from industry, which accounts for 23 percent of consumptive use. About a third of this is consumed in the course of cooling thermal electric power plants. Actually, a far larger quantity of water than that is drawn into the plants' cooling systems, but 98 percent of it is returned to a stream. Other large industrial uses of water in the South are for petroleum refining, chemicals, and pulp and paper. (As many as 82,000 gallons of water may be needed to make a ton of Kraft paper; even more for printing papers.)

The remaining water consumers are public water systems (10 percent of total consumptive use) and rural domestic and livestock uses (8 percent). The rural users get nearly all of their water from wells; the origin of water going into public systems varies from place to place. In Florida and Mississippi, it comes mostly from groundwater; in Kentucky, the Carolinas, and Virginia, mostly

Table 6.1

Consumptive Use of Fresh Water, 1980
(million gallons per day)

	Irrigation	Rural domestic and livestock	Public systems	Self-supplied industrial	Total
Alabama	33	190	44	300	567
Arkansas	3,100	110	64	300	3,574
Florida	1,500	100	330	500	2,430
Georgia	580	110	180	180	1,050
Kentucky	5	87	23	180	295
Louisiana	1,600	57	350	870	2,877
Mississippi	500	45	100	69	714
North Carolina	130	170	110	340	750
South Carolina	54	87	53	83	277
Tennessee	9	54	55	150	268
Virginia	17	91	32	90	230
11–state South	7,528	1,101	1,341	3,062	13,032
	57.7%	8.4%	10.3%	23.5%	100.0%

Source: Wayne B. Solley, Edith B. Chase, and William B. Mann IV, *Estimated Use of Water in the United States in 1980*, Geological Survey Circular 1001 (Alexandria, Va.: U.S. Geological Survey, 1983).

from surface water. The other southern states get their drinking water from both surface and ground sources.

Total use of water in the South has been growing rapidly in the last two decades, more than twice as fast as the national average (see table 6.2). Water consumption for irrigation, in particular, rose by 207 percent between 1960 and 1980. The South's rural domestic and public water use also grew faster than the national average. Industrial use, though it more than doubled, grew much less rapidly in the South than elsewhere. This appears

Table 6.2

Change in Consumptive Use of Fresh Water, 1960–1980
(percent)

	Irrigation	Rural domestic and livestock	Public systems	Self-supplied industrial (including thermo-electric)	Total
South	+207	+46	+133	+118	+151
U.S.	+60	+39	+105	+212	+69

Source: K.A. MacKichan and J.C. Kammerer, *Estimated Use of Water in the United States, 1960*, Geological Survey Circular 456 (Washington, D.C.: U.S. Geological Survey, 1961); Wayne B. Solley, Edith B. Chase, and William B. Mann IV, *Estimated Use of Water in the United States in 1980*, Geological Survey Circular 1001 (Alexandria, Va.: U.S. Geological Survey, 1983).

to reflect increased water conservation in Louisiana, Florida, and Tennessee, the states that had been the region's largest industrial water users in 1960.

Among the southern states, total growth in water use was particularly rapid in Georgia (+525 percent), Arkansas (+373 percent), and North Carolina (+299 percent); in these states, irrigation, public, and industrial uses were all growing very rapidly. Despite these increases in use, supplies of water in the South overall are far above any conceivable level of demand. In 1980, total consumptive use as a percentage of renewable water supply was estimated at 1 percent for the Tennessee Valley, 2.4 percent for the South Atlantic-Gulf water resources region (which includes most of the Piedmont and Coastal Plain), and 9 percent for the Mississippi River region (entire basin).[3] Yet one expert on water law told a recent conference on southern water policy, "Across the South we have localized water shortages that in some instances approach crisis proportions."[4]

The problem, even at a very local level, is almost never an absolute shortage of water. Rather the "crisis" consists of cases in which the increased demand for water by one user raises the cost of water to that user and to other users. The pumping of groundwater for agricultural irrigation provides a good example.

In several of the principal irrigated areas of the South, increased rates of groundwater pumping have lowered subsurface water levels by anywhere from 50 to several hundred feet. In the Grand Prairie area of eastern Arkansas, for example, irrigation pumping since the 1930s has caused water level declines of more than 60 feet in the Mississippi River Alluvial Aquifer.[5] Water levels are presently falling by as much as 1 foot per year.[6] Declines in water tables, or at least "cones of depression" (of reduced water pressure) around individual wells, have been reported in irrigated areas in southeast Alabama, in northern and southern Florida, in Mississippi, and in southwest Georgia.

In nearly all cases, abundant water can be obtained by pumping from somewhat greater depths. Often, there is also sufficient unused surface water within a reasonable distance that could be used for irrigation if required channels and pumping stations were constructed. But these alternatives would raise the cost of irrigation, in some cases by enough to make a particular crop uneconomic.

The lowered water level or cone of depression frequently is not permanent but occurs locally only during prolonged drought. This was the case in the Dougherty Plain in southwest Georgia, a center of center-pivot irrigation, where high levels of agricultural pumping during a drought in 1977 temporarily lowered water levels in the Principal Artesian Aquifer, even though it is one of the largest aquifers in the world.[7] By the end of the year, rainfall had returned the water level to normal. Although this problem was only temporary, it remains important, because drought periods are the very time when a dependable water supply is most critical.

Most southern groundwater is a renewable resource, recharged by rainfall, though the area of recharge may not coincide with the area of greatest withdrawal. This contrasts with the situation in some areas of the West, such as the southern Great Plains,

The South as a whole has abundant supplies of both surface and ground-water; yet it increasingly faces localized shortages.

where aquifers receive little annual recharge and where withdrawal of water means essentially permanent depletion of the
supply. There is also often a high degree of interrelation between
surface water and groundwater in the South; withdrawals from
groundwater may reduce the flow of nearby streams. This occasionally causes problems. "During the 18-month drought of
1980-81," says a University of Georgia researcher, "the interrela-
tionship of surface and ground water became apparent. The largest
spring in Georgia went dry, for the first time in history, and many
attributed it to agricultural irrigation nearby."[8]

Figure 6.1 shows some of the principal areas of groundwater
drawdown in the South. In addition to the predominantly rural
irrigated areas already mentioned, there are a number of places
where greatly increased industrial and municipal demands, sometimes compounded by irrigation demands, have had noticeable
impacts. In southwest Louisiana, there has been a 180-foot decline

Figure 6.1
Areas of Water-Table Decline or
Artesian Water-Level Decline

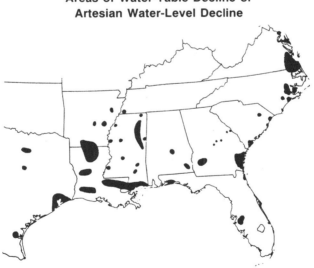

Map indicates decline in excess of 40 feet in at least one aquifer since
predevelopment.

Source: U.S. Geological Survey, *National Water Summary 1983—Hydrologic Events and Issues*, Water-Supply Paper
       2250 (Washington, D.C.: U.S. Government Printing Office, 1984), p. 40.

in the Chicot Aquifer, which has been used to irrigate rice as well as to supply the municipal and industrial complex at Lake Charles, Louisiana.[9] A large area along the Georgia coast, between Savannah and Brunswick, has experienced cones of depression and subsequent infiltration of saltwater so severe that some wells have had to be abandoned.[10] The same is true in Florida, particularly around Tampa and Jacksonville. In central Florida (not shown on map), increased urbanization and water use has lowered the water level of many lakes near centers of major groundwater development.[11]

Farmers are drilling more and deeper water wells, and they are using more and more water for irrigation and freeze control. Typically, farmers will pump excessively during freezing weather, resulting in lower water tables which in turn "dry up" shallow wells. Farm families accept this occurrence as a price to pay for living on the farm; however, a dry well is unacceptable to adjoining non-farm residents. Because of this type of conflict, farmers are increasingly skeptical about urban competition for water.

HILLSBOROUGH, FLORIDA, COUNTY PLAN, draft
agricultural element, April 1982

Because aquifers, like surface waters, do not respect state boundaries, the increased competition for southern water sometimes has interstate ramifications. North Carolinians are concerned about declining groundwater levels in coastal counties in the northeast corner of their state, the result of withdrawals of water in neighboring Virginia.[12] Arkansans have long worried about the designs that Texas may have on their state's water. (Engineering studies of diverting water from the Arkansas River hundreds of miles into Texas were commissioned by the Texas Water Board in the mid-1970s.)[13] And the heavy pumping of groundwater around Savannah has produced a cone of depression that affects wells in Beaufort County, South Carolina.[14]

Although more than a third of the South's irrigation water comes from surface streams, most reported surface-water shortfalls are associated with municipal or industrial users. Several southern cities—for example, Atlanta, Georgia; Lexington, Kentucky; and Asheville, North Carolina—have put such pressure on nearby surface streams that they are having to develop more expensive alternate supplies.

There are also major conflicts between withdrawals of surface water and so-called instream uses—navigation, fisheries, dilution of pollution, and so on. "In the spring of 1981," says a University of Georgia researcher, "effluent from a paper plant turned the Flint River black when the river's flow was reduced below normal by a combination of drought and agricultural withdrawals."

In South Florida, the Everglades National Park has been severely affected by water demands of agricultural and urban activities lying in its upper watershed[15] (see figure 6.2). At one time, the main worry was that these users would demand so much water that the Everglades would dry up. Ironically, after that issue was addressed (by 1971 federal legislation guaranteeing the park a minimum flow), it became apparent that the Everglades were also threatened by the prospect of too much water in times of flood, the result of flood-control works outside the park's borders. "Water used to arrive in the park according to biological rhythms," says the assistant superintendent of the national park. "Now it arrives by man's rhythms and life in the Everglades doesn't dance as well to that rhythm."[16]

Figure 6.2
Wetlands in the Florida Everglades

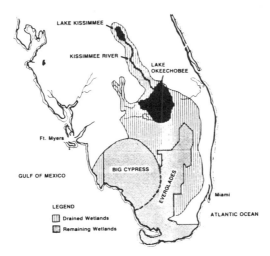

Source: U.S. Department of the Interior, Fish and Wildlife Service, National Wetlands Inventory *Wetlands of the United States: Current Status and Recent Trends* (Washington, D.C.: U.S. Government Printing Office, 1984), p. 41.

The Right to Use Water

Water is allocated among users partly by law, partly by economic considerations. Economics has an influence because, even when a water user need pay nothing for the water itself, the costs of transporting it to a field and applying it to the crops can be considerable. Typical initial costs for a distribution system range from $350 to $1,000 per acre, with annual operating and fixed costs of $80 to $155 per acre.[17] Moreover, as water tables decline or more distant streams must be tapped, the cost of getting water to the point of consumption rises. Thus, the water user faces a "price," even if access to the water is free.

Access to water at its original source, whether streamside or aquifer, is also subject to legal regulation.[18] The system of water rights in the South is presently in flux, partly because of current demands but even more in anticipation of increased competition for water in the future.

Southern water laws differ from state to state, but, most commonly, surface water is allocated by judicial application of the "riparian doctrine." This legal principle gives owners of property bordering a watercourse the exclusive right to take water from it, provided they put it to "reasonable use" and do not unreasonably interfere with the amount of water available to downstream users. Unlike in the West, rights are not lost if the water is not used. In theory, persons who do not own property along a watercourse have no legal right to water, nor can an owner of riparian rights transfer them to nonriparian land. In practice, however, surface water has been so plentiful that water is freely available to offstream land, provided a riparian owner permits the water to be conveyed across his property.

Not all southern states use the riparian doctrine. Mississippi, Oklahoma, and Texas subscribe to the western practice of "prior appropriation," that is, priority among users is determined by the date they began using the water. Kentucky (1966) and Florida (1972) have set up systems that allocate surface water by permit. Only large users must obtain a permit; virtually no one is, at present, turned down.

Groundwater use in the South is generally governed by the principle of "reasonable use." Any landowner may draw as much groundwater from beneath his land as is needed for a reasonable use, regardless of what this does to others who pump from the same aquifer. Because of the growing number of instances where high rates of pumping have drawn down water levels, several southern states have instituted groundwater permit systems. As with surface water, permits are usually quite easy to obtain, and many states see the permits as much as a reporting mechanism as a regulatory one.

As individual water users and units of government have become more aware of the growing competition for water, they have paid closer attention to establishing secure water rights. Many water users have supported state permit systems as a way of confirming the legal rights of present users, who are generally granted permits automatically.

Anticipation of possible future problems has sometimes led to conflict among users even when present water supplies seem more than adequate. "Current water problems in Virginia are problems of political boundaries," says a researcher at Virginia Polytechnic Institute. "Many urban areas are looking for water beyond their political boundaries, but because of the recent hysteria about resource scarcity, other users are objecting." In the Norfolk area, he points out, there has been a major battle over moving water from one political jurisdiction to another even though the total quantity of water seems sufficient for all.

Elsewhere in Virginia and in other states, farmers are worried that satisfying urban or industrial demand will imperil their ability to irrigate in times of drought. For their part, nonfarm interests wonder if the continued growth of irrigation might eventually constrain water supply for other types of development. "Falling water tables are something we don't like to talk about around here," says an Alabama extension agent. "How do you think the county officials in a place like this would feel if they were trying to attract new industries and it were to get out that they wouldn't have any water after 10 or 12 years?"

Soil Erosion

Soil erosion has been a chronic problem in many parts of the South. Much of the land on which steep slopes were cropped has gone out of production since the 1930s. But erosion can be severe

Many of the South's soils are highly susceptible to erosion by water, as in the case of this field in Georgia.

even when terrain is fairly flat, because of the South's frequent conjunction of erosive soil types and violent rain storms. Soils that "melt like sugar and flow like water" are found in abundance in such places as West Tennessee, the Georgia Piedmont, and southwestern Mississippi. Severe gullying is even possible—in one famous Georgia case, a tiny gully started by poor farming practices in the early 19th century has grown into a canyon 150 feet deep.

In general, erosion is a greater threat in the Piedmont, Uplands, and parts of the Delta than in the South Atlantic Coastal Plain. This is due partly to the South Atlantic Coastal Plain's flat terrain, partly to its predominance of sandy soils.

The amount of erosion that will occur on a given piece of land also depends closely on the kind of vegetation that covers the land during various times of the year. In Tennessee, for example, erosion from cultivated cropland as of 1982 averaged 11.5 tons per acre per year, more than twice the level considered "tolerable" by soil scientists.[19] In many cropped areas of the state,

erosion rates of up to 100 tons per acre per year were not uncommon. But Tennessee pastureland averaged only 1.3 tons per
acre annually; grazed forestland 2.2 tons; and ungrazed forestland
only 0.4 tons.

Different uses of cropland can greatly change erosion rates as
well. Experimental data indicate that, for a given soil and location, erosion from soybean cultivation may be less than half that
of cotton. If the soybeans are grown no-till, erosion falls by
another 50 percent or more. And if no-till soybeans are double-
cropped with wheat, the latter shielding the soil from winter
erosion, expected erosion falls by half again.[20]

The water-caused erosion typical of the South has three types
of undesirable impacts. First, runoff carries nutrients away from
growing plants and frequently washes out some of those plants
or covers them with silt. This reduces the current year's production, giving the farmer some immediate incentive to control the
rate of erosion. Second, over a period of time, erosion permanently reduces soil productivity, as part or all of the topsoil layer
is washed away. In severe cases, gullies are created, reducing the
usable area of the field. Third, erosion can cause water pollution
and sedimentation off the farm.

The state of the art in predicting the long-term impacts of erosion on productivity is not very good. One of the few studies
available for the South estimates, for common soils in South
Carolina and Georgia, how much soybean yields will be reduced
if various rates of erosion are allowed to continue over a 50-year
period.[21] For an annual soil loss of 3.2 tons per acre, the cumulative loss of topsoil depth after 50 years would be only 1.1 inches;
there would be no discernable impact on yields. For a 6.2 ton
loss, the yield reduction would be only 1 percent. But at an annual
erosion rate of 22.2 tons per acre, the cumulative topsoil loss
would be 7.4 inches, and soybean yields would be 44 percent
below those otherwise expected. For cotton growing on the same
soils, an annual erosion rate of 6.2 tons per acre would reduce
productivity by only 2 percent; but erosion at a rate of 22.2 tons
per acre would, after 50 years, lower productivity by 30 percent.

The ultimate productivity losses for the higher rates of erosion
seem great. However, given the long period of time involved,
these future losses will not have much impact on the decisions
that profit-motivated farmers make. Many farmers, of course, are

driven not just by profit but by ethical considerations or by a desire to hand their land on to their descendants. But, the unfavorable cost-price conditions in agriculture in the last several years have put severe pressure on farmers to maximize current revenue, regardless of future consequences.

Erosion, as indicated, also has an impact off the farm.[22] Waterborne (and to a lesser extent airborne) soil particles clog irrigation ditches, wash across roads, silt up reservoirs and wetlands, and carry with them residues of herbicides and insecticides. Fertilizers and other farm chemicals are washed from beneath the crops into streams and lakes, where they add an excess of nutrients to the water.

Reelfoot Lake, a shallow body of water in western Tennessee, provides a dramatic example of many of the off-farm impacts of soil erosion.[23] Formed by an earthquake in 1811, the lake once covered 50,000 acres. But the relatively recent introduction of soybean cultivation to the rolling hills east of the lake has caused severe erosion and a high rate of sedimentation. The lake has shrunk to only 18,000 acres and will, at present rates of sedimentation, be filled in entirely by the year 2032. It is also burdened by chemical pollution associated with the agricultural runoff, and both fishing and birdlife seem to have suffered as a result.

A recent study of soil erosion in Georgia makes it possible to estimate, though far from precisely, how the private gains from bringing new land into crop production compare with the social costs of erosion.[24] Between 1973 and 1976, favorable crop prices brought 724,000 acres of new cropland into production in Georgia. Nearly all of the land went into corn and soybeans. Three quarters of the newly cropped land was in the Coastal Plain, with most of the rest in the Coastal Flatwoods and the Piedmont.

The private gain from conversion was estimated at an average of $36 per acre annually. It was calculated as equal to the difference in net income between crop production and the net income from the land in its previous use in pasture or forest. But, when the land was cropped, average sediment yield rose from .21 tons per acre to 4.38. (In the Piedmont, where topography is rougher and soils more erodible, the rise was from .41 tons to 11.86 tons.) Cultivation was also associated with environmental loadings of 7.45 pounds of nitrogen per acre, 1.30 pounds of phosphorus, and an indeterminate amount of pesticides.

It is impossible to assign a precise value to these social costs. But, during the early 1970s, the Department of Agriculture's conservation subsidies to farmers cost the government an estimated $2.22 per ton of soil loss avoided.[25] Thus, the cost of extra erosion associated with bringing an acre of Georgia cropland into production might be estimated at $9.26 per acre (4.17 tons per acre x $2.22 per ton) or about a quarter of the farmer's net income gain.[26] In the Piedmont, the imputed cost of erosion would be $25.42 per acre, not too much below the average farmer's total net return from putting land into crop use.

A serious soil degradation problem other than erosion is the oxidation of the organic or "muck" soils of southern Florida. Centered on the vast Everglades Agricultural Area south of Lake Okeechobee, this land was developed for agriculture after drainage districts were formed early in the 20th century. The muck soils are extremely productive, and the area's mild winter climate has made it one of the nation's leading centers of vegetable production. Since the cutoff of Cuban sugar supplies in the early 1960s, sugar-cane plantings have also increased greatly.

In the period 1979-81, Florida's organic soils grew a yearly average of 330,000 acres of sugar cane with a gross value of $500 million, 97,000 acres of vegetables (including sweet corn, carrots, lettuce, and celery) worth $135 million, and 10,000 acres of sod worth $25 million.[27]

Drained organic soils are notoriously susceptible to oxidation, compaction, and subsidence. Luther Carter reports, "Every ten years about one foot of decayed organic matter that had taken at least 400 years to accumulate was lost."[28] Although the organic layer was initially fairly thick, this rapid rate of loss has continued to the point that significant impacts on productivity are in sight. One recent study indicated that, of the 700,000 acres of organic soils in the Everglades, 99 percent intially had a depth of over 36 inches. It projected that, largely because of oxidation, by the year 2000 only 13 percent will have over 36 inches of depth, while 45 percent will have 0 to 12 inches.[29] Thus, says a University of Florida expert, "We have a vegetable industry worth hundreds of millions of dollars a year that is based on an exhaustible resource of muck soils."

The costs of degradation of muck soils are largely borne by their owners. But there is a potential social cost as well. So limited is the zone where sugar cane and winter vegetables can be successfully grown that exhaustion of presently cultivated areas will cause great pressure for agricultural expansion elsewhere in South Florida, an area that contains one of the nation's most prized and most delicate ecological systems.

Agricultural Chemicals and Drinking Water

Use of agricultural chemicals of all kinds has traditionally been high in the South. The region's inherent pest problems (see chapter 2), the cultivation of cotton, a particularly insect-prone crop, and the frequent introduction of exotic pests, such as the fire ant, have encouraged heavy application of potent insecticides. Low soil fertility meant that fertilizers were needed if reasonable yields were to be obtained. And the post-World War Two loss of the cheap agricultural labor force that had been used for weeding by hand led the South's farmers to eagerly embrace chemical herbicides as soon as they were developed.

In 1982, southern states accounted for 43 percent of the insecticides and 22 percent of the herbicides used nationally.[30] The insecticide proportion was down from 56 percent in 1976 due in part to the decline in cotton acreage and to a fall in the proportion of cotton acreage sprayed. The decrease in spraying may be partially explained by the spread of integrated pest management, which limits the use of chemical treatments. Even with reduced use of pesticides on cotton, however, chemical use in the South remains high. One study found that soybean farmers in the Southeast used up to two and a half times as much fertilizer as their counterparts in the Midwest, and far greater amounts of insecticides. (Herbicide use on soybeans, however, was slightly lower in the South.) Soybean farmers in the Delta were intermediate between the Southeast and Midwest in fertilizer and insecticide use.[31]

In tonnage terms, insecticide use has fallen sharply in the South in recent years, while herbicide use has risen modestly.[32] The fall is due mainly to a change in the nature of the chemical agents used—the new chemicals are so potent that smaller doses are required to achieve the same result. The new insecticides tend to be less persistent in the environment than those compounds (such as DDT) that they replaced. Nonetheless, it is unclear whether these factors translate into any decline in environmental toxicity.

Agricultural chemicals do not always remain at the point where they are applied. They can be lost by spray drift, by solution in groundwater or surface runoff, by volatilization, and by adsorption onto soil particles that are later eroded. Although some farm chemicals quickly break down and lose their potency, others remain chemically active for months or even years.

An issue of growing concern in the South is the tendency of chemicals used on farms and forests to find their way into drinking-water supplies. The problem received national attention in 1983-84 when the pesticide EDB was found in numerous wells in central Florida. The chemical, used primarily as a soil fumigant to control nematodes (very small, soil-dwelling worms) in citrus groves, had apparently worked its way through the soil and infiltrated the groundwater. A suspected carcinogen, EDB was found in approximately 400 of 3,500 wells sampled, about 300 of which were contaminated to the point that their 50,000 users were advised not to drink or cook with the water.[33] Minute amounts of EDB have also been found in Virginia's Blackwater River, an auxiliary source of Norfolk's drinking water.[34] Another nematicide, aldicarb (Temik) was suspended from use in Florida in 1983 after it, too, was found in drinking water.[35]

Several commonly used farm pesticides have been found in wells in Georgia's Dougherty Plain.[36] There is also concern in some parts of the South about contamination of water with nitrates leached from fertilized fields or from poultry manures. High nitrate concentrations in drinking water are considered extremely dangerous, even fatal, for infants and may form carcinogens in the human stomach.[37]

Herbicides used on farms and forests may also reach water supplies. In the rice-growing region of eastern Arkansas, there is considerable concern about the possibility that cancers and other serious illnesses are being caused by the residues of herbicides, long used for controlling aquatic vegetation in rice fields. The herbicides contained minute amounts of the highly dangerous substance dioxin.[38] Recent controversies over herbicide application on forestland have flared in Rabun County, Georgia, and Cherokee County, North Carolina.[39] One experiment with three forest herbicides has revealed no stream contamination if a 10-foot buffer strip is used. In the study, however, the chemicals were sprayed by hand, whereas aerial application (where much less control is possible) seems to be the most commonly used technique in southern forestry.[40]

A water researcher in Georgia reports "a fairly widespread practice of drilling drainage wells in wetlands to drain water directly into the limestone aquifer in South Georgia."[41] This has a double negative impact on the environment in that it not only results in wetland loss but also drains any agricultural chemicals that are applied into the region's major aquifer.

Although farm chemicals have been found in both surface water and groundwater in the South, pollution of aquifers seems particularly problematic because the extent of the pollution is so hard to measure and because underground pollution is so difficult to clean up once it occurs. "Very little is known about the water quality problems resulting from [groundwater] recharge in agricultural lands treated with chemicals," writes one southern geologist.[42] "This is a potentially serious problem, particularly in areas of highly fertilized [fields], heavy pest control treatments and permeable soils where groundwater recharge occurs." The possibility of contamination may be especially great in multiple-cropped, irrigated agriculture because of the quantities of chemicals applied to the land over the course of a year.

Another scientist who has studied groundwater pollution points out that the soil type, as well as the nature of the chemical is crucial in determining whether groundwater will be polluted. "The Dougherty Plain has sandy soils directly overlaying an aquifer recharge area," he says. "The use of a chemical like EDB in that area is more dangerous than using it in central Georgia where soils are different and it is less likely to get into an aquifer."

There are also major uncertainties with respect to how chemicals move in the soil and in the water table. It is thought, for example, that some cases of chemical pollution of farm wells could be avoided at a very low cost by simply casing the well bore for 25 feet or so below ground level, thus avoiding pollution from pesticides that have been sprayed nearby and transported laterally on the surface or through the upper soil layers.

Perhaps the most troublesome thing about chemical pollution of drinking water in the South is how little is known about the extent of the problem. In January 1984, at the height of the national controversy over EDB, the chief of the groundwater section in North Carolina's Division of Environmental Management was quoted as saying that North Carolina had not tested any water samples for this chemical "to my knowledge," although it was planning to do so.[43] The same has been true all over the South. One obstacle is the cost of testing. Florida spent $1 million in 1983-84 testing water samples for EDB, at costs of up to $850 per sample.[44] Yet EDB is only one of literally scores of chemicals that might potentially be found in a water sample from an intensively cultivated agricultural area. The task of evaluating the problem, much less dealing with it, is formidable.

Wildlife and Ecosystems

Land-use changes almost invariably affect the numbers and composition of wildlife present on the land. Because "wildlife" means different things to different people, the degree to which a particular land-use change presents problems can vary greatly depending on whose interests are being considered. For many southerners, wildlife consists of the species sought by hunters and by recreational and commercial fishermen. These are principally deer, turkey, squirrel, waterfowl, and various warm- and cold-water fish and shellfish. A more inclusive view of wildlife would encompass songbirds, reptiles, wildflowers, and so on. Especially significant in this view are the relatively uncommon species, including those listed by federal or state governments as threatened or endangered. The most inclusive view of wildlife is the ecologist's conception of communities of living things, encompassing not only individual plant and animal species but groups of life forms having intricate relationships with one another.

Game Species

Hunting and fishing are major forms of outdoor recreation in the South, particularly among men. According to a national survey, about 12 percent of adult southerners hunt and 29 percent fish; both figures are somewhat higher than national averages.[45] The percentages increase in rural areas and in some subregions of the South. For example, a survey of residents in 11 counties in North Central Florida indicated that more than 40 percent of adults considered themselves hunters, ranking hunting as the most important form of outdoor recreation.[46] Moreover, for those who do participate, hunting and fishing are more than just enjoyable ways of spending time—they are part of southern culture and southern myth.

The species currently hunted are a quite small proportion of total species and are primarily ones that do well in areas modified by man—open areas and second-growth forest. The last several decades have seen major increases in populations of most of the South's principal hunted species, partly due to favorable habitat changes, partly due to better game management.

Deer populations, for example, which had been reduced by unregulated hunting to very low levels by the 1920s and 1930s, made a dramatic comeback after World War Two. This was partly due to state restocking programs and licensing of hunters but was aided by the large number of abandoned farms—overgrown fields make ideal deer habitat. Mississippi, for example, which had only an estimated 2,500 deer in 1941, had a deer population in the late 1960s of 275,000.[47] For the South as a whole (excluding Texas and Oklahoma), the annual deer kill by hunters rose from about 60,000 in 1950 to 274,000 in 1967.[48] In 1980, it had reached 932,000.[49]

Wild turkeys, once all but exterminated over large portions of the South, have also made a dramatic comeback. Squirrels, raccoons, and waterfowl, always fairly abundant, have thrived over the last few decades.

Despite this impressive record, many wildlife experts in the South are concerned about the future, even of game species. Their worries focus not on poaching or on lack of management knowledge but on anticipated land-use changes affecting habitat. Says an official of Arkansas' Game and Fish Commission, "Someone asked me what I perceived to be the most serious threat to wildlife in our state. . . . My unequivocal reply was *habitat loss!*"[50]

Habitat requirements differ greatly from one game species to another. For example, quail require a mainly open and brushy habitat, while wild turkeys need a greater percentage of dense forest. Moreover, game animals require a variety of habitat qualities—mature hardwood trees to provide acorns and other nuts (mast), dense forest to shelter them from predators, openings to provide grasses, and small bushes for food. Many species find some habitat value in farm fields, where they can feed on the grain left after mechanical harvesting of corn or soybeans. Indeed, for most game species, the single most important factor affecting populations is *diversity* of habitat.[51] Few game species thrive in dense forests; few thrive in a landscape consisting only of cultivated fields or improved pastures.

Because of this need for diversity and because of the differing interspecies patterns of habitat preferences, it is not easy to say whether a given type of land-use change is good or bad for "game." The effect will depend on the species and on the scale of the change. Small-scale, clearcut timber harvests, for example,

---

There has been a total change in the ecosystem of plant and animal species [on the Pamlimarle Peninsula, North Carolina] ... the black bear is gone; there is no bear season in Hyde County anymore. Deer have begun to graze on crops because their natural food is gone. On one corporate farm they shot two hundred deer out of one soybean field last summer.

STEVE FRICK, manager, Lake Mattamuskeet National
Wildlife Refuge, North Carolina, quoted in Thomas
J. Schoenbaum, *Island, Capes and Sounds: The
North Carolina Coast* (Winston-Salem: John F. Blair,
1982)

---

can be very beneficial to deer if openings are provided in a dense forest; clearcuts can be devastating if they remove the last available cover in a predominately agricultural region.

On balance, the land-use changes that have taken place in the South since about 1935 have probably improved carrying capacity for many game species by creating a more diverse local habitat. Field abandonment, more frequent timber harvest, and the change from cotton to soybeans, for example, have done more help than harm. Even activities such as establishment of pine plantations and clearing of hardwood forests, which are generally undesirable in their habitat effects, did not for a long time have much impact on game. These changes took place within the context of both a relatively diverse landscape and other, offsetting changes, such as the growth of unmanaged hardwood forests. There are likely two major exceptions to this statement; squirrels, which have suffered from the continued loss of mature, acorn-producing hardwood forests, and quail, whose numbers are augmented by timber harvests but fall quickly as brushy fields grow up in trees.

The reason for widespread concern about habitat loss is not so much what has happened to date but what might result if two particular types of land-use changes continue to occur—namely, the clearing of bottomland hardwood forests (primarily for soybeans) and the replacement of mixed pine-hardwood forests by monocultures of planted pines.

The bottomland hardwood ecosystem is among the most productive of all natural habitats for southern game species. Although clearing has already been very substantial, deer populations at least have generally not suffered, since the loss of hardwood cover was offset by the increased food provided by the cultivated area. But total clearing has now reached such an extent that total carrying capacity is threatened. Says a Louisiana wildlife biologist, "You need openings in a forest for deer, but 10,000 acres of soybean fields is not the ideal size of an opening." He explains that,

> As you clear, the additional food provided by the soybean fields initially compensates for the lack of cover and food provided by the forest. There appear to be more deer, too, because they are concentrated and clearly visible. But beyond a certain point, clearing could produce a dramatic drop-off in deer population.

Creation of pine monocultures, particularly on a very large scale, can also greatly reduce wildlife populations. Deer tend to flourish in the first 3 to 5 years after pines are planted, as the open landscape encourages the growth of small bushes and herbs on which the deer feed. As the trees grow older, however, particularly if densely planted, their closed canopy shades the ground and greatly reduces forage production.[52] Quail and rabbit populations also decline as the canopy closes. The 30-year rotations and elimination of hardwood reproduction common in intensive pine cultivation also do not permit the growth of mature, mast-producing hardwoods. Therefore, this source of food for deer and other species does not become available as the stand gets older.

A recent report by a "blue ribbon" panel of scientists evaluated the impacts on wildlife from the Weyerhaeuser Company's operations in Oklahoma and Arkansas, where "the entire area of southeastern Oklahoma and southwestern Arkansas is [being] transformed into a pine monoculture."[53] Although the scientists found that "Weyerhaeuser is generally doing a good job of timber management," they concluded that the reduction in the number of acorn-producing hardwoods as a result of species conversion was likely to have negative impacts on such species as deer and wild turkey. The report also found that the improvement in the road network was greatly increasing illegal hunting pressure. Moreover, the scientists expressed concern for what might happen to aquatic food chains as the annual leaf fall from the hardwood trees was replaced by less nutritious needle fall from the pines.[54]

If pine plantations are managed in relatively small units, a substantial deer and quail population can still be maintained, because the units where the canopy has closed will be offset by recent clearcuts and by older units where repeated thinning has opened the understory to sunlight. The Piedmont National Wildlife Refuge, near Macon, Georgia, which manages its pines in even-aged blocks averaging about 25 acres, is an example of how large deer populations can coexist with pine timber management.[55] (In addition, the refuge has left 20 percent of its forest in hardwoods.) Unfortunately, many of the South's pine plantations are managed in much larger even-aged blocks, greatly reducing the overall forest's diversity. "I've always frowned on big (300-400 acre) blocks of solid planting as the companies do," says the manager of a hunting preserve in South Carolina. "You can have a pine desert or a sand desert. Wildlife need variety, and you don't get that with a large pine forest."

Another problem with pine plantations is that maximization of pine production implies the elimination of woody and brushy vegetation other than the growing pines, even in the early stages of regeneration. Use of controlled fire for this purpose tends to leave a considerable amount of forage for wildlife and can even augment the amount of palatable vegetation. But use of herbicides, which more effectively reduce the understory, appears to be spreading. Fortunately for game, complete understory removal is rarely feasible, either economically or technically. But to the extent that it is achieved, deer and other wildlife suffer. According to the National Academy of Sciences, using herbicides in forests "may be detrimental to many species of wildlife because of their impact on food plants (particularly legumes) and the insects that live on them."[56]

From the standpoint of game species, at least, wildlife experts appear to be less concerned about present forestry practices than about what they see as the ultimate goal of wood-growing technology in the South. According to an Alabama zoologist,

> The forestry establishment here—the companies and the state forestry commission—would like to see every piece of land capable of growing a pine tree converted to pine. And they would like to see the hardwood sites and bottomlands coverted to a single species of hardwood like sycamore.

The impacts of land-use change on fishing in the South are somewhat more subtle than are those on hunting. The large number of reservoirs built since World War Two throughout the South have vastly increased opportunities for warm-water fishing for such species as bass, catfish, and panfish. In some cases, the damming of streams was associated with the loss of cold-water fishing (for example, for trout), but on balance the South's fishing is probably better than it has ever been.

Other than reservoirs, the greatest impacts of land-use change on the South's fishing have been sedimentation from soil erosion, pollution of fishing waters with agricultural chemicals, and changes in the pattern of runoff. Sediment impairs fishing either by harming the fish directly or through destroying their habitat. For example, eggs may be covered, or there may be a reduction in the growth of plants and algae that the fish consume.[57] The sediment affects not only streams but also the estuaries located at the mouths of major southern rivers. Oyster production in Florida's Appalachicola Bay, for example, has been threatened by sediment from second homes and timber clearcuts far upstream.

In 1980, the death rate of juvenile shrimp following application of the farm pesticides toxaphene, methyl parathion, and endosulfan in coastal counties led South Carolina's Shrimpers' Association to express concern over the "possibility of great damage" to commercial fishing.[58] Sediment and farm chemicals may also threaten on-farm aquaculture. Catfish require clean water and hence may be affected by sediment and chemicals from adjoining lands.[59] In Louisiana, the herbicide paraquat has been found to kill juvenile crawfish, an important economic resource.[60]

Even if farm chemicals do not actually kill fish, they may still make the fish unsafe to eat. One study of rural watersheds in the lower Mississippi Valley found that, because of "the combination of current agricultural practices, climatic factors, and prevailing soil conditions...fish from the Yazoo River, which drains the Mississippi Delta, contain higher toxaphene, DDT and endrin residues than fish from any other station in the National Pesticide Monitoring Program, along with substantial residues of other organochlorine insecticides and arsenic."[61]

Another study analyzed 361 samples of fish tissues collected at various locations in Louisiana between 1977 and 1981.[62] Virtually all of the samples contained residues from one or more of 23 pesticides or chlorinated hydrocarbons, particularly DDT, dieldrin, toxaphene, chlordane, and endrin. Of the samples, 23 percent contained at least one residue exceeding the EPA alert level. The greatest amount of contamination was found in fish from northeast Louisiana, where agricultural pesticide use is heaviest. "Many of the pesticide problems we see are the result of some very ruinous recommendations to farmers by the state department of agriculture in the early 1970s," says one of the study's authors. "Many of these substances remain in the environment for years. Now the substances they recommend are probably somewhat safer, such as the synthetic pyrethroids [used extensively on cotton]. But new chemicals are coming out all the time and we don't know what we're going to see in the environment. In fact, our monitoring is now being cut back."[63]

Finally, fish can be affected by changes in the water regime due to drainage or irrigation. In coastal North Carolina, for example, commercial fishermen have protested the draining of coastal wetlands for crop agriculture, arguing that drainage canals cause sudden surges of fresh water into estuaries, reducing salinity enough to kill saltwater fish and crustaceans.[64] A popular bumpersticker in the area reads, "No Wetlands, No Seafood."

Access for Hunting and Fishing

Even as physical changes in the landscape have been affecting habitat for game and fish, changes in landownership have affected access to land by hunters and fishers. Tending to increase access has been the acquisition of millions of acres of land by timber companies, most of which have historically opened large amounts of their land without charge for public recreation. In some cases, companies even invest in modest facilities to improve recreational

Agricultural use of low-lying coastal areas can cause chemical runoff and can change the mix of fresh- and saltwater in estuarine systems, leading to lower productivity of fish and shellfish. This intensively farmed area lies adjacent to Pamlico Sound in eastern North Carolina.

access (hiking trails and boat ramps, for example), and several of the larger companies employ wildlife biologists to improve habitat.

Offsetting this trend, however, has been an increase in posting against trespass on nonindustrial private lands, by far the most common category of landownership in the South. This has been due partly to increased hunting pressure on those woodlands remaining after agricultural clearing and partly to acquisition of land by owners who object to hunting or who wish to reserve all recreational use to themselves. The upshot has been more and more hunters concentrated on public land, timber-company land, and whatever private land remains unposted.[65]

Leasing of hunting rights was historically widespread in western and southern Texas and in some of the prime Atlantic Coast water-fowl areas. But it was relatively uncommon in most other parts of the South, though timber companies often leased particular tracts to hunting clubs. The timber-company leases were generally at quite modest rents, and were entered into less for raising revenue than for public relations and because club members could be relied on to police the land against arson, trash dumping, and other undesirable activities.

In recent years, however, competition for hunting access has led to greatly expanded leasing of hunting rights and to substantial increases in the cost of those leases. A researcher who surveyed 187 firms managing 20 million acres of forestland in the South reports that "the amount of income that can be derived by selling access to wildlife is substantial and increasing."[66] Overall, he found an average payment of $1.38 per acre on the 6.3 million acres for which complete lease information was available.[67]

Even higher payments are commonly made for lands with particularly large game populations or for lands that are managed to favor game. An Alabama wildlife specialist notes, "I could put you in touch with a dozen clubs in Alabama that are paying $5 per acre for deer [leases], and in Louisiana rice farmers are getting $1,000 per blind for duck hunting." In Mississippi, landowner returns from hunting leases rose from 40¢ per acre in 1968 to more than $2 in 1981.[68] Prime bottomland hardwood tracts in the Delta are leased to deer hunters for as much as $10 per acre yearly.

The increase in demand for hunting leases has presented timber companies and other locally dominant landowners with a dilemma. The prospect of increased revenues from their land is attractive, but maximizing revenue is not the best way of keeping the goodwill of local residents. One company forester in eastern North Carolina observed that his company only rents to local clubs, even though it could probably get much more revenue by leasing to groups of doctors and lawyers from Raleigh. He noted that another timber company in the area had had hundreds of acres of valuable trees burned by arson after it increased rental rates only slightly.

Even at present levels, fees for hunting rights frequently compare favorably with returns from forest grazing. This may discourage forest landowners from putting cattle or sheep on their land. As a Forest Service handbook puts it, although game and grazing animals can coexist, for optimum results "determined efforts in resource coordination are required."[69] Many owners may not wish to make the effort, and hunting clubs may balk at leasing heavily grazed land.

I used to hunt on land owned by a local hardwood lumber company here [in Eastern Oklahoma]. It was always open for hunting, as though it were yours or mine. The company cut selectively, and you couldn't tell they had been there except for a few stumps. People used to paint "welcome deer hunters" on their windows during deer season. The hardware store owner here says he makes most of his money during deer season, selling guns, clothes, ammunition, etc. I left for college and came back in 1974. The land had been sold to a large timber company, which was clear-cutting and converting to planted pines. The old people who went in the woods were all concerned about what was happening. Forty thousand acres of timber were being cut every year. They could see the creeks and fishing holes filled up, and the clear rivers were flowing red clay. They knew that removing that much timber would remove that much wildlife. The forest was disappearing in big chunks, and the people who lived out there were concerned.

ODIE HALEY, Broken Bow, Oklahoma

In most cases, potential hunting revenues are so far below the yearly returns from timber management that they should not much affect management style. But small modifications in intensive management can substantially improve habitat, with only minor loss of fiber production. ("For deer [management], an owner might lose 5 percent of timber production," says a South Carolina game manager.) On the other hand, the yearly revenue from a hunting lease, along with the benefits from personal hunting use, is often just enough to cause a smaller landowner to keep an old hardwood stand, even though the strict economics of the situation would favor conversion to planted pines.

Nongame Species

The South has a wealth of nongame wildlife species—from the impressive American alligator and osprey, to thousands of plant species and dozens of snails and mussels. Some nongame species, such as most of the South's songbirds, are widespread; others occur only very locally: the Ozark big-eared bat is found only in a few Ozark Mountain caves; the watercress darter, a tiny fish whose entire population is only several hundred, is believed to be confined to three small Alabama springs.

In addition to their value as a gene pool and as a resource for scientific study, nongame species provide an immense amount of outdoor recreation. They also contribute strongly to local and regional identity. It is hard to imagine Louisiana without pelicans or South Carolina without palmettoes and spanish moss. Interestingly, the number of southerners who engage actively in "nonconsumptive use" of wildlife (observing, photographing, and so on, either game or nongame species) is well below the national average, though still above 40 percent of the adult population.[70]

Human-induced land-use changes have had, and are having, dramatic impacts on nongame species in the South. Naturally, some nongame species flourish best in deep forests, others in farm fields, still others in pastures. Some of the important impacts of human activity on these habitats are subtle. For example, mechanical harvesting has increased the grain supply in farm fields, reducing winter mortality for such birds as the brown-headed cowbird and the common grackle.[71] (This has undesirable secondary impacts because the cowbird is a predator of songbird eggs, while the grackle has become an agricultural pest.) On the other hand, breeding populations of wood storks, found in parts of Florida, Georgia, and South Carolina, have declined from an estimated 20,000 pairs in the 1930s to fewer than 5,000 pairs since 1978, mainly due to alteration and destruction of their feeding habitat.[72]

In summer 1982, some 95 percent of the alligator nests in South Florida's Everglades National Park were destroyed when excess runoff was diverted to avoid flooding adjoining agricultural and residential areas.[73] The Florida panther once roamed several southern states, but there are now perhaps only 20 left. Their remaining habitat in remote parts of South Florida is threatened by oil drilling, new roads, and agricultural land clearing.[74]

Fish populations change drastically when fast-flowing, shallow streams are dammed to create reservoirs (as in the case of the snail darter, wiped out in its known range in the Tennessee River by Tellico Dam[75]) or when summer flows are reduced by irrigation diversions. Spraying of farm and forest pesticides can change both target and nontarget insect populations.

The myriad land-use changes that have taken place in the South over the past two centuries—an individual tract of land going from climax forest to cotton field to broomsedge wildland to pine plantation, for example—have had a cumulative impact on wildlife. Such changes have favored the most adaptable and omnivorous species at the expense of those with highly specific requirements for food and habitat.[76]

Extensive land clearing, whether for housing, industry, mineral exploitation or agriculture, takes a heavy toll of many forms of reptile and amphibian life. Increasingly, our forest lands are being clear-cut and prepared for row-crop production of pine pulpwood, a practice that is devastating to many forms of low mobility and to those that require a humic, forest-floor habitat.

ROBERT H. MOUNT, *The Reptiles and Amphibians of Alabama* (Auburn, Ala.: Auburn University, Agricultural Experiment Station, 1975)

From a policy standpoint, most of the concern about nongame species has focused on those listed by the federal government as "endangered" or "threatened." In 1983, the official U.S. Interior Department list contained 73 southern species, including 9 species of mammals, 10 birds, 7 reptiles, 11 fish, 24 snails, clams, and crustaceans, 2 insects, and 10 species of plants.[77] By virtue of their listing, these species are given certain protections against both publicly and privately sponsored habitat changes; in some cases, federal and state lands are actively managed to benefit the species.

One example of such management applies to the red-cockaded woodpecker, which was once common throughout the Southeast. This bird nests in over-mature pine trees (average age about 70 years) infected with red heart disease. Because of active timber harvesting and shorter rotations, such pines have become increasingly scarce in the South. As a result, the red-cockaded woodpecker population had by 1979 fallen to between 5,000 and 6,000.[78] In an attempt to reverse the march toward extinction, several of the National Forests in the region have set aside special management areas, where trees are kept past economic maturity solely for the woodpeckers' use. Some private timber companies have done the same, as has the Piedmont National Wildlife Refuge, said to be the largest breeding area for the species.

Inclusion on the federal list does not, however, guarantee a species' survival. It is apparently too late for Florida's dusky seaside sparrow, for example. The known population has fallen to only five individuals—all males.

The federal list also fails to contain large numbers of species, particularly insects and plants, but including fish and reptiles, that are widely believed to be threatened. For example, according to Arkansas' Natural Heritage Inventory Program, 458 of that state's 2,350 plant species are considered rare or worthy of special consideration.[79] Of the 458, 14 may already be extirpated from the state and 106 are known from only one occurrence. Yet Arkansas has no plants on the federal list.

The situation is worse in some other southern states which, unlike Arkansas, have not even systematically studied their less obvious species. "We don't really know what's growing in Louisiana," says the curator of the higher plant collection in the botany department of Louisiana State University. "There is not even a complete guide to the flora of the state." She notes that amidst this ignorance considerable loss of rare plants is taking place. "One species of trillium is found in only one place in Louisiana, though it is also found in Texas. It occurs in one low wet area along a stream in a hardwood forest. When we went there recently to collect a specimen, we found that the area had been staked out for some sort of development." "There was blue and orange flagging right down the center of the patch," added a colleague.

Even some of the South's showier and better-known plant species are severely threatened by habitat loss due to land conversion for agriculture and forestry. The pitcher plant is a carnivorous plant with several very attractive varieties, found in poorly drained areas along the Gulf and Atlantic coasts. One expert calculated that, until the late 1800s, pitcher plant bogs stretched almost continuously from Pensacola, Florida, west to Pascagoula, Mississippi, with some bogs covering thousands of acres.[80] Yet today even a liberal estimate indicates that at least 97 percent of the former bogs have been destroyed or seriously altered.[81] The most damaging factors have been draining of land and restriction of natural summer fires. Even grazing causes major changes in the composition of the bog flora, because cattle trample the pitcher plants; continued intensive grazing results in a rapid decrease in species diversity and eventual destruction of the bog. Development also exacts a toll. "People are putting houses right in the middle of pitcher plant bogs here," says a South Carolina biologist. "The plants just don't mean anything to them."

The survival of endangered plants is not entirely a matter of scientific curiosity or esthetic enjoyment. The economic value of unstudied species can't be determined, but it seems very likely that some of the species now being lost have properties we may one day regret losing. An agricultural researcher, interviewed at the large federal research station at Tifton, Georgia, expressed great concern about the accidental impact of land-use change on the South's native sunflowers—30 of the nation's 50 species are found in the South. He was unaware that agricultural researchers elsewhere in the South were experimenting with sunflower as an oil seed crop, emulating Canada and North Dakota, where it has become a major agricultural commodity. Genetic material from native southern sunflowers could be of great help in adapting commercial sunflower varieties to southern disease, climate, and pest conditions, provided that the native varieties remain in existence. If one takes a long-term view, the line between those things that have an economic value and those that do not is not always clear.

Ecosystems

In addition to considering the status of individual species, whether game or nongame, it is useful to consider wildlife communities or ecosystems. One advantage of this approach is that the area in a given ecosystem is often easier to measure than are the numbers of the many species contained therein. Moreover, protection of ecosystems protects not just a single target species but other associated species, including insects, plants, and aquatic life. Among the ecosystems presently considered in most danger from land-use change in the South are floodplain and bottomland forests, pocosins, coastal wetlands, and the longleaf/wiregrass ecosystem.

The first three of these systems are wetlands, which range from the daily tidal inundation of most coastal wetlands to the wet but rarely flooded soils of the pocosins. It is no accident that wetlands should be so prominent among the South's threatened ecosystems. As use of the South's land spread and intensified, its wetter areas were usually skipped over. Settlers not only found wet areas expensive to drain and clear and frustrating to farm but perceived them as unhealthful for man and beast. The introduction of railroad logging in the late 1800s made it possible to extract most of the wetlands' valuable timber, but this was generally done by selectively harvesting the largest trees, not by clearcutting. Thus, the South's wetlands tend to have preserved wildlife species and communities that have been modified or eradicated elsewhere. They provide much of the habitat for black bear, for example, and for the exceedingly rare eastern mountain lion (also known as the "panther"), two species that require large areas of relatively undisturbed land free from human habitation. Moreover, wetlands tend to be "high-energy" ecosystems, supporting a large biomass and considerable biological diversity. Wetlands also have the added benefit of helping to regulate water levels, both in times of flood and times of drought.

Times have changed for the wetlands. The solution of health problems, introduction of draglines for drainage and bulldozers for clearing, and the increased economic value of cleared land have, since the 1920s, made southern wetlands much more economical to put to other uses. Millions of acres have been converted since that time, and millions more are under threat of conversion.[82]

The most widespread of the South's wetland systems, and the one that has been proportionately most reduced in size, is the floodplain and bottomland forest.[83] These wetlands lie along the myriad streams and rivers of the Piedmont, Delta, and Coastal Plain. The portion that is most regularly flooded, or that has standing water, tends to support stands of tupelo and cypress; the slightly higher and drier areas, which may extend a considerable distance from the main river channel, have mostly "bottomland hardwoods," such as oaks, sweetgum, and ash. Floodplain and bottomland forests support a large number of forms of wildlife, both game and nongame.

Historically, the floodplain and bottomland forest had their greatest extent along the Mississippi River and its tributaries, perhaps as much as 24 million acres. But the level land and relatively fertile soils have been attractive candidates for large-scale clearing, particularly for soybeans. The most comprehensive study of clearing in the region estimated that, of the 11.8 million acres of bottomland hardwood forests existing in 1937, only 5.2 million acres were still in hardwood forest in 1978.[84]

The resulting loss of wildlife habitat has been dramatic. Says a Baton Rouge hunter, "Louisiana's license plates have for years had the slogan 'Sportsman's Paradise.' Maybe we should change that to 'Soybean Paradise.' " In eastern Arkansas and western Mississippi, huge areas have been so thoroughly cleared that only after referring to historical photographs does an observer realize that the cleared fields, their openness reminiscent of the Corn

---

Ten years ago, it wasn't so noticeable unless, of course, you had the occasion to fly the Louisiana delta region in a light plane. Today, a plane is not necessary. The change is dramatic and readily observed from the roadside.

The story is told by muddy waters, lost hunting grounds, and wide open spaces punctuated by smoldering woodpiles left by the big machinery—the last vestiges of a great hardwood forest. The high price brought by soybeans and the fertile, albeit sticky, soil of these delta timberlands have encouraged their devastation at the hands of large land management corporations.

LOUISIANA OUT-OF-DOORS, August 1981

Belt, were 20 or so years ago a dense hardwood forest. Among the especially severe impacts, writes one wildlife biologist, have been those on small insectivorous birds:"entire populations of these birds have been eliminated in major portions of the Delta because of destruction of habitat."[85]

In the southern states bordering the Atlantic, there are about 7.3 million acres of bottomland hardwood forest in stream margins and in cypress ponds and channels.[86] There has been little large-scale clearing of these ecosystems in recent years, though there has been a moderate amount of small-scale disturbance by farmers enlarging fields. "Satellite photographs show that South Carolina from the central Piedmont to the coast is primarily agricultural cleared land," says a U.S. Fish and Wildlife Service employee in Charleston, "and the wetlands and bottomland forests are like arteries stretching through this land. They are the only remaining areas of sanctuary for wildlife—and I'm afraid we are at the point where these areas are starting to be encroached upon."

Pocosins (the term is derived from an Algonquin Indian word which translates as "swamp on a hill") are distinctive ecosystems found in eastern North and South Carolina.[87] They sometimes extend unbroken over thousands of acres. Pocosins owe their status as wetlands not to inundation by flowing water but to poor drainage, principally because of peat soils. Pocosins generally support a shrubby evergreen vegetation, with occasional pond pines; selective harvest of the large pines has historically been the only economic use of pocosins. They are unusual among wetlands in that their vegetation is heavily influenced by the fires that sweep

---

Pocosins are a very important component of the estuarine system in North Carolina.... They capture rainfall and keep it from reducing the salinity of the sounds that breed shrimp and shellfish. I don't think anyone could say that if you clear a square mile of pocosins you get x percent reduction in shrimp. But there is a connection between the salinity of water and the productivity of the shellfishing. There are a lot of pieces to this puzzle, and the pocosins fit in somewhere.

LANCE PEACOCK, ecologist, Chapel Hill,
North Carolina

---

across them in dry periods. Although pocosins are nutrient-poor systems, they contain a fairly good selection of wildlife, particularly those species that are sensitive to human disturbance and are rare elsewhere in the Carolinas.

Although some pocosins were drained as early as the 18th century, their development for agriculture or for pine plantations appears to have accelerated starting in the 1960s.[88] The principal attraction of the pocosins seems to have been their low price and their availability in very large blocks, an ideal situation for a corporate farmer or timber company seeking to operate on a large scale. Conversion, which involves drainage and clearance of the vegetation, is so complete as to obliterate the pocosin as an ecosystem, both biologically and hydrologically. After conversion, the result is a flat field dissected by drainage ditches, often covering many hundreds or even thousands of acres.

It is estimated that of 1.9 million acres of pocosins that were found in eastern North Carolina in the 1940s, 26 percent are now totally developed, 28 percent are "in transition" (partially altered or held for development), and only 28 percent are still in a natural state.[89] The rapidity of conversion within recent decades, and the large acreages owned by corporate farming and timber in terests, has made the preservation of this system a leading cause among environmentalists, particularly in North Carolina. One ecologist who has inventoried pocosins argues that successful preservation requires very large blocks of undisturbed land. ''The way [pocosins] function,'' he argues, ''they can't be maintained except on a large scale. For example, you can't let wildfire burn randomly in a small tract, you can't have the same large game species, you lose the hydrologic integrity. . . .You need maybe 15,000 acres if you want to preserve a pocosin system.''

In 1984, some 120,000 acres of pocosins and marshlands located on the tip of North Carolina's Albemarle-Pamlico Peninsula were donated by the Prudential Insurance Company to the Nature Conservancy.[90] The property, valued at $50 million, will be managed by the U.S. Fish and Wildlife Service as the Alligator River National Wildlife Refuge. The donation settled a suit brought by the National Wildlife Federation and other environmental groups to stop Prudential from the planned drainage of 23,000 acres for agricultural purposes. In addition to the donation, the settlement allowed agricultural development to proceed on 3,000

Draining a pocosin wetland in eastern North Carolina. The land will be converted to a pine plantation.

acres, subject to various easements to protect wildlife.

Coastal wetlands ring the entire South, frequently extending inland for many miles. They are often very attractive visually and support an unusually diverse terrestrial and aquatic life. These wetlands are currently being modified by a variety of new uses. Immediately along the Atlantic and Gulf coasts, the major pressure is for recreational and residential development. Because of state coastal management laws and the floodplain zoning requirements of the federal flood insurance program, such development tends to be less ecologically destructive than in the 1970s, but it still introduces structures, roads, causeways, marinas, and sewage plants into what had formerly been completely natural areas.

In Louisiana, where the lower third of the state is wetland, major ecological changes have occurred as a result of oil and gas production. To gain access to the wells that dot the state's wetlands by the thousands, oil companies have cut extensive systems of canals. An estimated 9 percent of the total wetland area is occupied by the canals and their spoilbanks alone.[91] The canals also enable salt water to infiltrate deep into freshwater areas, killing freshwater fish and vegetation. Moreover, they increase the pace of erosion, which swallows 50 square miles of Louisiana marshland each year. A rising sea level, combined with reduced sediment coming down the Mississippi because of dam and reservoir construction, compounds the problem of land loss.[92] A recent study by the U.S. Army Corps of Engineers estimates that, if present rates of wetland loss in Lousisiana continue, by the year 2040 commercial and recreational harvests of fish and wildlife will fall by 32 percent.[93]

In Georgia, the owners of an old coastal plantation have requested state permission to rebuild a dike around a former rice field, now a tidal wetland.[94] The owners plan to see if modern techniques would permit rice-growing there, in a region where it had long been abandoned. If successful, the project could be a precedent for altering 30,000 to 50,000 acres of Georgia wetlands for similar purposes.

In South Carolina, where there are tens of thousands of additional acres of old rice fields, an interesting conflict is brewing between hunters and fishermen.[95] The former are trying to expand duck habitat by rediking the fields, cutting them off from tides and creating freshwater impoundments. But removal of these lands from tidal action would end their contribution to the estuarine systems on which many marine organisms of commercial and recreational importance depend.

A dryland ecosystem that has increasingly been changed by human activity is the longleaf pine forest. Found primarily on sandy soils in a broad belt stretching across northern Florida and southern Georgia into Alabama and Mississippi, the longleaf forest is characterized by relatively open stands of longleaf pine, with a low layer of scrub oaks and an understory of saw palmetto and wiregrass. The existence of this distinctive southern ecosystem depends on frequent summer fires, which keep the oaks from becoming dominant.

Two land-use practices of increasing importance in the last 20 years or so are slowly changing the character of the longleaf ecosystem. First, timber companies are impatient with the growth habits of the longleaf pine which, although an excellent timber tree, tends to grow very slowly during its first several years. When longleaf stands are clearcut, they are frequently replaced with loblolly or slash pine seedlings, which reach an earlier maturity. Second, forest wildfires, which were usually started by lightning or by human accident during the dry late summer, have either been eliminated or replaced by controlled burning. For safety's sake, the latter tends to be done during the late fall or winter. The result is an entirely new fire regime to which native plants and animals are not adapted. Lack of burning can greatly reduce numbers of many species of reptiles, including the endangered eastern indigo snake and the gopher tortoise.[96] And the wiregrass, which needs a hot summer fire to reproduce, is being gradually replaced in the understory by bracken fern, a plant poisonous to cattle.[97]

The Outlook for "Unpriced Values" in the South

As economies and societies develop, several things can happen to their many unpriced values. Some values may remain unpriced over long periods of time, because they are based on resources found so abundantly that very high levels of consumption, and even a measure of abuse, can be maintained. In the South, this has been true of such resources as water and wetlands—they were originally found in great abundance, and many southerners still consider them in little danger of depletion. But, as I have pointed out in this chapter, many signs of scarcity are appearing as the intensity of use increases and as what should be renewable resources sustain permanent damage.

Other unpriced values start to acquire prices as they become more scarce. For example, as available habitat for hunting has shrunk in the South, landowners have started to find it profitable to lease shooting rights to individual hunters and to hunting clubs. Prices not only tend to limit overuse, they also give resource owners an incentive to make investments (for example, in wildlife management) that increase the total quantity of the resource in question.

Still other resources become managed or regulated by public authorities as their quantity diminishes. Severe soil erosion, particularly when it has impacts off-site, brings forth calls for government regulation of farming and forest practices. Diminishing open space causes various levels of government to set aside parks and reserves.

Each of these paths of development can be found in the South today. It is difficult to predict how far various unpriced values will be depleted before they are either priced or regulated. Envi-

ronmental history, in the South and elsewhere, has tended to show that many important values have been reduced from exceptional abundance to extreme scarcity, and sometimes to extinction, before they have been transformed into marketable commodities or protected by government. It does appear, however, that for many of its resources—its topsoil, its water, its wildlife habitats, its scenic and historic resources—the South has moved far down the path of depleting once abundant supplies. The impacts from the competition for land by the various economic uses may bring southerners to a sudden, perhaps belated, realization that many values can remain unpriced or unregulated only at the expense of eventual diminution far below the levels of abundance that the South has historically enjoyed.

References

1. Some, but by no means all, of the "unpriced values" could be allocated by market prices if certain public and private institutional arrangements were changed. Chapter 8 contains my own views on some areas where greater use of the price system would be desirable (for example, salable water rights). A few of the unpriced values discussed in chapter 6 currently have prices in some circumstances (for example, hunting rights), but these are presently the exception rather than the general case.

2. Wayne B. Solley, Edith B. Chase, and William B. Mann IV, *Estimated Use of Water in the United States in 1980*, Geological Survey Circular 1001 (Alexandria, Va.: U.S. Geological Survey, 1983).

3. U.S. Geological Survey, *National Water Summary 1983—Hydrologic Events and Issues*, U.S.G.S. Water Supply Paper 2250 (Washington, D.C.: U.S. Government Printing Office, 1984), p. 27.

4. Jake Looney, dean of University of Arkansas Law School, quoted in Southern Rural Development Center, *Proceedings of the Conference on Water Policy in the South, November 18-19, 1982, Memphis, Tennessee* (Mississippi State, Miss.: Southern Rural Development Center, 1983), p. 1.

5. U.S. Geological Survey, *National Water Summary*, p. 89.

6. Falling water tables not only increase the cost of raising water to the surface; they may also so reduce the saturated area of an aquifer that some users find it impossible to obtain the minimum desired discharge from a given well, making it unusable. Richard C. Peralta and Aminollah Yazdanian, "Projected 1972 Groundwater Levels on the Arkansas Grand Prairie," *Arkansas Farm Research*, vol. 33, No. 2 (March-April 1984), p. 3.

7. James E. Kundell, ed., *Georgia Water Resources: Issues and Options* (Athens, Ga.: Institute of Government, University of Georgia, 1980), pp. 15-16.

8. James E. Kundell, Institute of Government, University of Georgia, interview, January 1983.

9. U.S. Geological Survey, *National Water Summary*, p. 135.

10. Ibid., p. 110.

11. Ibid., p. 106.

12. Interview with Dr. James W. Stewart, Water Resources Research Institute, North Carolina State University, Raleigh, North Carolina, February 1982.

13. Interview with Dr. Kenneth Young, Winrock International, Morrilton, Arkansas, October 1983.

14. *Southeast Water Resources* (Chapel Hill, N.C.: Water Resources Research Institute, University of North Carolina), vol. 1, no. 2 (Spring 1979), p. 12.

15. Luther J. Carter, *The Florida Experience: Land and Water Policy in a Growth State* (Baltimore: Johns Hopkins University Press, 1974); Denis Collins, "Okeechobee: Damming a Lake, Then the Future," *Washington Post*, February 13, 1983; Kerry Gruson, "Flooding Poses Threat to Everglades' Ecology," *New York Times*, July 25, 1983.

16. Gruson, "Flooding Poses Threat."

17. Eugene W. Rochester and Larry M. Curtis, "Potential for Irrigation," *Alabama Agribusiness*, vol. 22, no. 3 (December 1983), p. 3.

18. See Sandra S. Batie, "Water Rights and Water Law in the Southeast" (unpublished paper); David H. Howells, *Summary Report: Southeast Conference on Legal and Administrative Systems for Water Allocation and Management* (Raleigh: University of North Carolina, Water Resources Research Institute, 1978); Roopchand Ramgolam and Floyd L. Corty, *Water Use and Water Rights in Louisiana*, D.A.E. Research Report No. 593 (Baton Rouge: Louisiana State University, Department of Agricultural Economics and Agribusiness, 1982).

19. U.S. Soil Conservation Service, *1982 National Resources Inventory* (unpublished final data, July 1984).

20. R.E. Sojka, G.W. Langdale, and D.L. Karlen, "Vegetative Techniques for Reducing Water Erosion of Cropland in the Southeastern U.S.," *Advances in Agronomy*, vol. 37 (1984), pp. 155-181. Another study, however, found little difference in erosion between conventionally tilled cotton and soybeans, though the erosion for soybeans was far less for no-till and double-cropping. Ivery C. Clifton et al., *Agricultural Production Patterns and Resultant Soil Erosion in the Altamaha River Basin*, Agricultural Experiment Station Research Report No. 407 (Athens: University of Georgia, 1982).

21. U.S. Soil Conservation Service, *1980 RCA Program Report and Environmental Impact Statement* (Washington, D.C.: U.S. Government Printing Office, 1980), p. 3-5.

22. See Edwin H. Clark II, Jennifer Haverkamp, and William Chapman, *Eroding Soils: The Off-Farm Impacts* (Washington, D.C.: The Conservation Foundation, 1985).

23. See Sandra S. Batie, *Soil Erosion: Crisis in America's Croplands?* (Washington, D.C.: The Conservation Foundation, 1983), pp. 51-52.

24. Fred C. White et al., "Relationship Between Increased Crop Acreage and Nonpoint-Source Pollution: A Georgia Case Study," *Journal of Soil and Water Conservation*, vol. 36, no. 3 (May-June 1981), pp. 172-77.

25. American Farmland Trust, *Soil Conservation in America: What Do We Have to Lose?* (Washington, D.C.: American Farmland Trust, 1984), p. 67.

26. The comparison is a crude one, because the $2.22 per ton figure apparently refers to soil savings during the first year the conservation practice is in place. Since many practices last for more than one year, the figure overestimates the cost per ton ultimately saved. On the other hand, $2.22 represents only the government's share of the cost of erosion control, generally about 50 percent of total cost.

27. *Organic Soils (Histosols)*, Research Report 435 (East Lansing: Michigan State University, Agricultural Experiment Station, 1982), p. 33. It should be noted that sugar-cane production is valued at U.S. market prices, which are supported at a level significantly above the world market level.

28. Carter, *The Florida Experience*, p. 85.

29. *Organic Soils (Histosols)*, pp. 62-63.

30. Unpublished data from U.S. Department of Agriculture, Economic Research Service. Data include West Virginia but exclude Texas and Oklahoma.

31. Michael Duffy and Michael Hanthorn, *Returns to Corn and Soybean Tillage Practices*, Agricultural Economic Report No. 508 (Washington, D.C.: U.S. Economic Research Service, 1983).

32. Insecticide use fell from 73 million pounds in 1976 to 31 million in 1982; herbicide use rose from 84 million pounds to 97 million.

33. *Pesticide and Toxic Chemical News*, vol. 12, no. 17 (March 7, 1984), pp. 22-24.

34. *Norfolk Virginian-Pilot*, February 18, 1984.

35. *New York Times*, April 24, 1983; Joyce Egginton, "Temik Troubles Move South," *Audubon*, vol. 85, no. 4 (April 1983), pp. 34-37.

36. U.S. Geological Survey, *National Water Summary, 1983*, p. 111.

37. Veronica I. Pye, Ruth Patrick, and John R. Quarles, *Groundwater Contamination in the United States* (Philadelphia: University of Pennsylvania Press, 1983) p. 97.

38. *New York Times*, April 9, 1983.

39. *Atlanta Journal*, March 8, 1984.

40. *Low Herbicide Concentrations Found in Streamflow After a Grass Cover Is Killed*, U.S.D.A. Forest Service Research Note SE-108 (Asheville, N.C.: U.S. Department of Agriculture, Southeastern Forest Experiment Station, 1969).

41. James E. Kundell, Carl Vinson Institute of Government, University of Georgia, personal communication, June 1985.

42. Loris E. Asmussen, "Groundwater: An Emerging Issue in Agricultural Watershed Management," unpublished paper, Tifton, Ga., 1984, p. 9.

43. Quoted in *Raleigh News-Observer*, January 7, 1984.

44. *Jacksonville*, [Florida] *Times-Union*, February 16, 1984.

45. U.S. Fish and Wildlife Service and U.S. Bureau of the Census, *1980 National Survey of Fishing, Hunting and Wildlife-Associated Recreation* (Washington, D.C.: U.S. Government Printing Office, 1982).

46. Maureen H. McDonough and Larry D. Harris, "Perception and Use of Wildlife by North Central Florida People," *Proceedings of Annual Conference of Southeastern Association of Fish and Wildlife Agencies* (1977), pp. 204-11.

47. John D. Newsom, "History of Deer and Their Habitat in the South," in *White-Tailed Deer in the Southern Forest Habitat*, Proceedings of a sym-

posium at Nacogdoches, Tex., March 25-26, 1969 (New Orleans: U.S. Forest
Service, Southern Forest Experiment Station, 1969), p. 3.

48. Ibid., p. 3.

49. U.S. Fish and Wildlife Service, *A Summary of Selected Fish and Wildlife
Characteristics of the 50 States* (Washington, D.C.: U.S. Government Printing
Office, 1983), p. 27.

50. Richard Broach, "A Land Ethic—Is Arkansas Ready?" editorial in *Arkansas Game and Fish*, vol. 15, no. 2 (May/June 1984), p. 1.

51. For example, one southern wildlife expert writes, "Wildlife managers
know that the key idea in forest wildlife management is diversity in the habitat.
An abundance of research has shown this. Forest game and most other forest
wildlife thrive in situations where all their needs can be met within a short
distance." Dan W. Speake, "Even-Aged Forest Management and Wildlife
Habitat," in *Proceedings of the Annual Conference of Southeastern Association
of Game and Fish Commissioners* (1970), p. 3.

52. See, for example, J.J. Stransky, "Deer Habitat Quality of Major Forest
Types in the South," in *White-Tailed Deer in the Southern Forest Habitat*,
pp. 42-45.

53. *Assessment of the Weyerhaeuser Company's Forestry Operations in
Southwestern Arkansas and Southeastern Oklahoma*, report of the National
Wildlife Federation Blue-Ribbon Panel on Wildlife and Forestry, Washington,
D.C., October 1982.

54. Ibid., p. 61.

55. D.W. Speake, E.P. Hill, and V.E. Carter, "Aspects of Land Management
with Regard to Production of Wood and Wildlife in the Southeastern United
States," in *Proceeedings of the Fourth North American Forest Soils Conference*
(Quebec: Les Presses de l'Universite Laval, 1975), pp. 333-49.

56. U.S. National Academy of Sciences, *Impacts of Emerging Agricultural
Trends on Fish and Wildlife Habitat* (Washington, D.C.: National Academy
Press, 1982), p. 89.

57. Clark, Haverkamp, and Chapman, *Eroding Soils*, ch. 3.

58. Ibid., ch. 4.

59. Interview with Howard Clonts, Department of Agricultural Economics,
Auburn University, Auburn, Alabama, April 1984.

60. T.T. Leung, et al., "Paraquat Toxicity to Louisiana Crayfish (Procambarus clarkii)," *Bulletin of Environmental Contaminant Toxicology*, vol. 25,
no. 465 (1980), pp. 465-69, cited in Clark, Haverkamp, and Chapman, *Eroding Soils*, ch. 4.

61. Christopher J. Schmitt and Parley V. Winger, "Factors Controlling the
Fate of Pesticides in Rural Watersheds of the Lower Mississippi Alluvial Valley,"
*Transactions of the Forty-Fifth North American Wildlife and Natural
Resources Conference* (Washington, D.C.: Wildlife Management Institute,
1980), p. 372.

62. J.L. Landry and C.J. Killebrew, "Trends in Louisiana Pesticide Residues,
1977-1981," *Proceedings of Louisiana Water Pollution Control Association,
1983* (in press).

63. Interview with Joseph L. Landry, Louisiana Department of Environmental

Quality, Baton Rouge, La., May 1984.

64. Carol Polsgrove, "Conflict along the Carolina Coast," *Oceans* (May 1983), pp. 65-67.

65. Access has been less of a problem for anglers because most reservoirs are publicly owned and because highway crossings offer convenient access to many streams.

66. Roy A. Lassiter, presentation to 50th North American Wildlife Conference, Washington, D.C., March 1985.

67. Roy A. Lassiter, *Access to and Management of the Wildlife Resources on Large Private Timberland Holdings in the Southeastern United States* (Cookeville: Tennessee Technological University, 1985).

68. Jimmy Bonner, "Hunting Leases May Generate Income for Landowners," *The Stockman* (January 1983), p. 2.

69. U.S. Forest Service, *Forestland Grazing: A Guide to Service Foresters in the South* (Atlanta: U.S. Forest Service, State and Private Forestry, Southeastern Area, 1980), p. 29.

70. U.S. Fish and Wildlife Service and U.S. Bureau of the Census, *1980 National Survey of Fishing, Hunting, and Wildlife-Associated Recreation.*

71. U.S. Council on Environmental Quality, *Environmental Trends* (Washington, D.C.: U.S. Government Printing Office, 1981), p. 154.

72. *Endangered Species Technical Bulletin* (U.S. Fish and Wildlife Service), vol. 9, no. 3 (March 1984), p. 1.

73. *New York Times*, July 25, 1983.

74. Susan I. Mashburn and Bradley J. Hartman, "The Florida Panther: Hard Choices in Growth Management," *Florida Environmental and Urban Issues*, vol. 10, no. 4 (July 1983), pp. 3-7.

75. Additional snail darter populations have subsequently been discovered in other tributaries.

76. Milton N. Hopkins, Jr., *The Birdlife of Ben Hill County, Georgia and Adjacent Areas* (Georgia Ornithological Society, Occasional Publication No. 5, 1975), pp. 8-10.

77. U.S. Fish and Wildlife Service, "Endangered and Threatened Wildlife and Plants," 50 CFR 17.11 and 17.12 (July 27, 1983).

78. Robert Chipley, "The Red-Cockaded Woodpecker," *Nature Conservancy News* (September/October 1979), pp. 24-25.

79. *The Arkansas Natural Heritage Inventory Program* (Little Rock: Department of Arkansas Natural and Cultural Heritage and The Nature Conservancy, 1980), pp. 9-10.

80. George W. Folkerts, "The Gulf Coast Pitcher Plant Bogs," *American Scientist*, vol. 70, no. 3 (May-June 1982), pp. 260-67.

81. Ibid.

82. For a recent overview of wetlands conversion nationally, including some information about the South, see U.S. Office of Technology Assessment, *Wetlands: Their Use and Regulation* (Washington, D.C.: U.S. Government Printing Office, 1984), ch. 5.

83. See, generally, Charles H. Wharton, *Southern River Swamp* (Atlanta: Georgia State University, 1970), and John R. Clark and J. Benforado, *Wetlands*

of Bottomland Hardwood Forests (New York: Elsevier, 1981).

84. Purificacion O. MacDonald, Warren E. Frayer, and Jerome K. Clauser, *Documentation, Chronology and Future Projections of Bottomland Hardwood Habitat Loss in the Lower Mississippi Alluvial Plain* (Washington, D.C.: U.S. Fish and Wildlife Service, Division of Ecological Services, 1979).

85. See Trusten H. Holder, *Disappearing Wetlands in Eastern Arkansas* (Little Rock: Arkansas Planning Commission, 1970), p. 43.

86. S.G. Boyce and N.D. Cost, "Timber Potentials in the Wetland Hardwoods," in M.C. Blount, ed., *Water Resources, Utilization and Conservation in the Environment* (Reynolds, Ga.: Taylor Printing Co.), pp. 130-51, cited in Robert L. Johnson, "Timber Harvests from Wetlands," in *Wetland Functions and Values: The State of Our Understanding* (American Water Resources Association, 1978), p. 599.

87. See, generally, Curtis J. Richardson, ed., *Pocosin Wetlands* (Stroudsburg, Pa.: Hutchinson Ross, 1981).

88. There is some dispute over the rate at which pocosins in North Carolina have been cleared. Richardson, Ibid., shows an increasing rate of loss, but a more recent study indicates that pocosin clearing peaked in the decade 1962-74, then dropped off. See Philip S. McMullan, Jr., *Land Clearing Trends on the Albemarle-Pamlico Peninsula* (Durham, N.C.: McMullan Consulting, 1984). McMullan believes further clearing for cropland will be limited because, except on the Dare County mainland, most of the desirable agricultural soils have already been cleared.

89. The status of 19 percent was unknown. See Ibid., p. 100.

90. *Raleigh Times*, March 16, 1984.

91. R. Eugene Turner and Edward Maltby, "Louisiana Is the Wetland State," *The Geographical Magazine*, pp. 92-97.

92. Ibid.

93. *Notice of Study Findings: Initial Evaluation Study, Land Loss and Marsh Creation, Louisiana Coastal Area, Louisiana* (New Orleans: U.S. Army Corps of Engineers, New Orleans District, July 1984), p. 4.

94. "Fact Sheet: New Hope Rice Plantation on the Altamaha River," The Georgia Conservancy, Coastal Office, Savannah, Ga., March 1983.

95. Interview with Roger Banks, U.S. Fish and Wildlife Service, Charleston, S.C., June 1983.

96. J. Larry Landers and Dan W. Speake, "Management Needs of Sandhill Reptiles in Southern Georgia," *Proceedings of Annual Conference of Southeastern Association of Fish and Wildlife Agencies* (1980), pp. 515-28.

97. Interview with Robert Mount, Department of Zoology, Auburn University, Auburn, Alabama.

Chapter 7

Projecting Future Land Use

This chapter projects long-term allocation of land in the South among various economic uses. There are two reasons to do this. First, it is important to know which uses are expanding and the degree to which expansion of any one of the uses might reduce land available for other uses. Knowing this, one gains insight into future product supplies and can identify bottlenecks, localized areas of severe land-use competition, and needed areas for research in production technology. This information can help both private decision makers and those responsible for public policy. Second, knowing the future course of the economic uses of land helps in identifying impacts on the various unpriced values. For example, knowing future cropland demand can indicate future pressures on wetlands and other natural areas. This can also help one identify needed policies, including options for commodity production that avoid or minimize undesirable impacts.

Although the ability to look into the future generally declines as the time period considered becomes longer, it seems necessary to take a very long view of future land use. Partly this is because some aspects of land use inherently involve long time periods. For example, it takes approximately 30 years to grow a southern pine to sawtimber size, so decisions about reforestation must anticipate timber supply and demand well into the next century. A more important reason why a long view needs to be taken is our responsibility to our children.

On average, a child born in the South today can be expected to live for 75 years—a little less for males, a little more for females. Most likely, as medicine and other sciences advance, this figure will rise. It is quite sobering to consider that a 75-year life expectancy implies that half of the children born today will still be alive in the year 2060. Or, to put it another way, a child born today will spend more than half its lifetime in the world as it will be *after* the year 2020. Thus, a long view is necessary to protect the interests not of some hypothetical future generation but those of our own youngest generation.

Projecting an Uncertain Future

Projecting the long-term future of land-use in the South is not an easy task. There are some inherent difficulties in such an enterprise. They may be illustrated by assuming that we are fortunate enough to have a long-term land-use projection but wish to change a single variable affecting one of the uses. For example, suppose that world demand for paper is sharply higher than previously expected. Presumably this will affect not only the demand for southern timberland but also the availability of land for southern crop production and grazing.

The direction of the impact is clear—more paper demand means more southern land devoted to growing timber. But what is the magnitude? If we want to estimate it, we must know, among other things, how world paper users respond to higher prices, how competing paper producers in the western United States, Latin America, and Southeast Asia will react, and what the exchange rate of the dollar will be relative to foreign currencies. Even if we could derive exactly how much wood fiber will be demanded from the South, southern producers still have the choice of raising more wood on their existing land base or increasing the amount of acreage in forests. (Surely they would do both, but the mix is uncertain.)

If the "more timberland" option is chosen, supplies of land to crops, grazing, and even urban uses will be reduced. These uses adjust, partly by substituting other factors for land (for example, more fertilizer will be applied on pastureland), partly by raising prices to the consumer, which then reduces demand. The whole process can be described as a pebble thrown into a pool, raising rings of waves about the point of impact— or as a set of interlocked mathematical equations.

Actually, our example is still far too simple, for more than one force outside the system is changing at any given time, and the whole system is constantly adjusting to past perturbations. The best analogy, perhaps, is to a *handful* of pebbles thrown into a windwhipped pool!

Despite these difficulties, it still seems useful to make formal projections of the long-term future. Often we can anticipate magnitudes of changes, if not exact quantities, or directions of change, if not magnitudes. The mechanism of making projections also helps us systematically understand relationships. For instance, in the above example of the paper industry, the conscientious maker of projections is forced to consider quantitatively the role of foreign competition, a factor that might be overlooked or exaggerated in a more casual analysis. However imperfect the results, the making of projections tends to force the analyst to confront directly what is known and what is not.

Methods of Projection

There are a number of methods of making long-term projections of land use. This chapter discusses four of them: trend extrapolation, econometric modeling, linear programming, and potential cropland analysis. After briefly discussing how each technique works and outlining its strengths and limitations, I will show how each has been applied to projecting long-term change in southern land use.

Trend Extrapolation

One popular way of making projections is by trend extrapolation—for example, assuming that, if cropland area grew by 3 percent over the past decade, it will grow by the same amount in the succeeding one. Trend extrapolation is a more sophisticated technique than it appears; it relies on the not unreasonable belief that, when underlying processes are not well understood, their past behavior is a more reliable indicator of future patterns than the potentially false signals given by the forecaster's attempt to fully understand a complex process. One forecasting authority calls it "a position of intellectual modesty rather than blasé confidence."[1]

Table 7.1 presents the best available comprehensive data on land use in the South and changes over the period 1969-82. This period was chosen partly on the basis of availability of consistent data, partly because it is sufficiently long, yet sufficiently recent, to capture the working out of the principal forces whose influence on southern land use is likely to continue into the future. The table indicates that, during this recent period, the most significant land-use changes were in the cropland category, with acreage of cropland used for crops increasing rapidly, while acreage in idle cropland and cropland pasture fell. Land in grassland pasture and in forest also fell, while land classified as urban and built-up and as used for "wildlife and rural parks" went up very steeply.

The third column of table 7.1 shows what the distribution of land uses in the South would look like in the year 2012 if these recent trends were to continue unabated.[2] (The 30-year projection period is equal to one planting/harvesting cycle in growing pine trees). A look at the table reveals one internal inconsistency. If acreage in idle cropland were to continue to decline at its

Table 7.1

Land-Use Trends in the South

	1969	1982	Trend extra-polation 2012	Adjusted trend extra-polation 2012
Cropland				
Used for crops	41,476	52,414	77,655	74,255
Idle cropland	9,513	4,595	− 6,754	2,000
Pasture				
Cropland pasture	23,860	17,122	1,573	5,000
Grassland pasture				
and range	26,495	23,543	16,731	15,998
Forestland	188,538	183,108	170,577	163,109
Built-up land				
Urban land	7,470[1]	13,399[1]	27,081	27,081
Rural transportation areas	5,418	5,450	5,524	5,524
Farmsteads, farm roads				
and lanes	1,909	1,758	1,410	1,410
Wildlife and rural parks	5,022	8,452	16,367	16,367
Other land[2]	14,665	14,244	13,272	12,691
Total land area	324,366	324,085	323,436	323,436

Figures are for 11 southern states and do not include Texas or Oklahoma.

[1] Based on Census Bureau-defined urban area for 1970 and 1980 respectively.

[2] Other land is a residual and is not independently measured or projected.

Source: U.S. Department of Agriculture, *Major Uses of Land in the United States* 1969 and 1982 editions; U.S. Census Bureau, *1980 Census of Population*.

current rate, it would become zero by the mid-1990s, then become negative. Obviously, it is impossible for this quantity to be negative. In fact, idle cropland is unlikely to even approach zero, because this category includes land held idle for purely personal reasons or as part of a crop rotation cycle. Nor is cropland pasture likely to fall as low as the extrapolation indicates, because some of it is pastured in the course of a crop rotation or is an essential part of profitable dairy or horse-raising operations.

To eliminate these inconsistencies, one can assume that idle cropland will not fall below 2 million acres nor cropland pasture below 5 million, then reallocate the shortfall proportionately among all the other crop, pasture, and forest uses. This results in the "adjusted trend extrapolation" in the last column of table 7.1.

The trend extrapolation indicates some dramatic changes in land use in the South *if trends of the recent past continue.* The most obvious change would be a very large increase, almost 22 million acres, in cropland used for crops.[3] There would be an extremely large reduction of cropland pasture, presumably because most of this land would be converted to crops. Grassland pasture would also fall, giving an overall reduction in pasture acreage of almost 50 percent. Built-up land would rise by 65 percent, with all of the change due to increases in urban land rather than in land consumed by farmsteads or by rural transportation facilities. Forestland would fall by about 11 percent from its 1982 level, though, because cropland conversion is likely to affect the better forestland, one must suspect that potential forest productivity would be down by somewhat more than 11 percent.

A quite different result is reached if the extrapolation is based on a more recent period, 1978-82.[4] During that period, the rate of growth of cropland used for crops slowed, as did the rate of increase in parks and wildlife refuges. And there was a 17 percent increase in grassland pasture and range (although cropland pasture continued to decline). Extrapolating the 1978-82 experience results in a year 2012 cropland projection of 61 million acres (rather than 74 million), a slightly smaller drop in forestland (down 7 percent, to 170 million acres), a smaller projected increase for wildlife and rural parks, and a considerably smaller decline in total pasture and range (down 19 percent rather than 48 percent.) Although it can be argued that experience in recent periods may tell us relatively more about what the future holds, it is also true that considering a period of only four years, rather than one of more than a decade, tends to magnify the impact of measurement errors and random year-to-year fluctuations. Therefore, the extrapolation based on the 1978-82 period is not necessarily superior to the one based on 1969-82.

These scenarios, of course, are only extrapolations. They assume, therefore, that the next 30 years will be "like" the period 1969-82 or 1978-82. Implicitly, use of the 1969-82 period, for example, means another great boom in crop exports, such as occurred during the 1970s, relatively little growth in beef-cattle numbers, a high level of housing construction and other forms of development, continuation of a spread-out settlement pattern, and a very high level of interest in creating new parks and wilderness areas. Naturally, *exactly* the same things need not happen in the future, just forces similar in their overall impact.

An Econometric Model

Given a belief that the forces affecting land use in the future will be somewhat—or very—different from those of the recent past, one must step outside the assumptions of trend extrapolation. An alternative way of using what is known about the past to try to guess the future is econometric modeling. Although the techniques tend to be complex and mathematical, the idea of modeling is rather simple.

Modeling assumes that, although the forces causing future land-use change will not be the same as those in the past, certain relationships remain relatively stable. For example, the demand for new housing is closely related to the number of new households formed, and that, in turn, is related to the number of persons aged 20 to 30. Knowing the number of people likely to turn 20 in the year 1990 (an easy thing to do, because those people have already been born), one can venture a prediction about the demand for housing in 1990.

It is also known that the level of interest rates is very important in determining housing demand. So using what is known of the historical relation between housing and interest rates, the 1990 housing demand projection can be modified to account for either high or low assumptions about future interest rates.

Information about how quantities have varied from place to place (called "cross-sectional" data) can also help in making projections. For example, urban land consumption per capita is higher in Alabama (.63 acres per person) than in Kentucky (.31 acres per person). If some assumptions are made about future total population growth in the South, and how it might be distributed among the states, average land-consumption figures can be used to project the total amount of land that might be converted to urban use.

A number of researchers have used econometric techniques to project future land uses in the South. The most recent and comprehensive of these efforts has been by the U.S. Forest Service.

The Forest Service, concerned about how expansion of other land uses will affect the long-run availability of forestland in the South, used an econometric model to project the allocation of land among use categories for the period 1985-2040. The model makes the amount of land devoted to each use depend on the economic return in that use in comparison with returns for competing uses and considers as well such general influences as population and personal income.[5]

This procedure is at once the model's greatest strength and its greatest weakness. It is a strength because it accurately reflects how landowners make decisions—they use land for whatever seems most profitable in comparison with alternative uses. It is a weakness in that it requires knowledge about future crop, beef, and timber prices—no easy task.

The Forest Service analysis assumes that future crop and livestock prices will be no higher than those of today, that crop productivity will grow moderately, and that timber prices will increase quite rapidly. These assumptions are based on yet another set of models of product supply and demand for the nation as a whole.

The initial set of Forest Service projections tended to show future crop acreage *below* what it is today, as well as increases in urban area, and slight reductions in pasture and forest area. Subsequent, more judgmental, adjustments resulted in the projections in table 7.2. (These projections cover a geographic area slightly different from that of table 7.1—they include East Texas and eastern Oklahoma but not Kentucky—and thus are not comparable in absolute terms, though comparison of percentage distributions among uses is probably valid.) The projections show

Table 7.2

U.S. Forest Service Projection of Southern Land Use
(million acres)

	1985	2000	2020	2040
Crops	53.7	57.3	60.6	62.5
Pasture/Range	39.2	36.1	32.3	30.3
Urban/Other	50.4	56.1	60.5	62.7
Forest[1]	182.1	174.4	169.1	165.6
Farmer-owned	42.1	30.7	24.3	21.9
Industry-owned	39.6	40.5	41.2	41.7
Miscellaneous private	82.6	85.1	85.3	83.4
Public	17.8	18.1	18.3	18.6

Figures include East Texas and eastern Oklahoma and exclude Kentucky.

[1] Timberland only

Source: Unpublished projection, U.S. Forest Service.

major differences in the expected course of land use in the Southeast (the Atlantic coastal states) as compared with the rest of the South (Mid-South).

In the Southeast, cropland is projected to increase very little, even by the year 2040. Forestland and pasture are projected to decline very slightly, reflecting a rather modest increase in "urban and other" land. In the Mid-South, however, the projection points to a significant increase in crop acreage as well as in "urban and other." This is accompanied by a large fall in pasture and rangeland and a fairly large decline in forest acreage.

The Forest Service's projection indicates a relatively favorable environment for forestry in the South, based in great part on the assumption that returns to forestry will rise substantially faster than returns to crop or animal agriculture. Throughout the South, the timberland base would fall over 55 years from 182 million acres to 166 million, a level that, given expected increases in forest productivity, could sustain an amount of cut considerably higher than at present.

A particularly interesting feature of the Forest Service projection is that it indicates that the drop in forest acreage would be concentrated in farmer-owned forests, with a slight increase in industry forestland and little change in forestland owned by miscellaneous private owners. Given the relatively low productivity of farmer-owned forests, this shift tends to reduce somewhat the effects of a shrinking total forestland base.

A Linear Programming Model

Another way to project future land use is through linear programming. Although the name is imposing and the mathematics complex, the underlying principle is quite simple. The geographic area being investigated is divided into a number of subregions, each of which uses land to produce a mix of outputs—soybeans, cotton, beef cattle, softwood lumber. For an assumed national level of total output, a linear programming (LP) model distributes the production task among regions so as to minimize total production costs.

The applicability to the present projection problem is obvious. Optimistic or pessimistic assumptions can be made about future national and international demands for the various outputs produced by southern land, then an LP model run to see what the South produces (and at what cost) and what uses occupy the rest of the nation's land base.

A nationwide LP model for agriculture does exist, the result of two decades of effort at the Center for Agricultural and Rural Development (CARD) at Iowa State University. The model divides the United States into 105 "producing areas," of which 16 lie within the South.[6] Although the model provides extremely detailed information on crop agriculture, it entirely lacks forestry and pasture sectors. It thus can show how different assumptions affect the regional distribution of various crops but is unable to show how higher or lower crop production affects the availability of land for pasture or timber. However, one of an LP model's outputs is a set of so-called shadow prices, the amounts that various uses can afford to pay in rent for a piece of land. These can be used to see what return forestry or grazing would have to achieve to outbid crops for use of southern land.

Although the CARD model has been run for some 68 combinations of assumptions about domestic food demand, exports, and technological changes in the years 2000 and 2030, the results are of somewhat limited usefulness for the southern states, because the model's current version does not allow for the use of irrigation. (CARD has an irrigated production sector only for the western states.) CARD thus fails to take into account one of the South's major opportunities for expanding crop production. Also, some of the production cost data underlying the model are 10 or more years old, a factor of special importance to fast-changing southern agriculture. These factors may be remedied in future versions of the model.

Subject to these limitations, three of the available CARD outputs are of interest. First, one can look at what crop mix is expected to be produced in the South under high and low assumptions about future demand. Second, one can look at how much crops can pay in rental for land of various qualities, in various regions, thus getting an idea of how much grazing or forestry would have to pay to compete. Third, the CARD model allows a comparison of erosion rates for alternative levels of crop production.

In making these comparisons, I decided to look first at CARD's "Scenario #18," which projects what would happen in the year 2000 under a high-demand, high-export assumption. This is one of the most extreme of all the scenarios and would involve cultivating a large proportion of the idle cropland and cropland pasture that existed in the base year (1977), as well as bringing an additional 93 million acres nationally into crop use. It is best to look at this not as a projection of what will actually happen in the year 2000 but as an indication of what linear programming indicates would occur in the South under the assumption of very high national crop demand.

In this "high demand" scenario, the amount of cultivated cropland in the South would rise from 39.3 million acres to 58.6 million. This would not, interestingly enough, raise the South's share of national cropland, a finding that is difficult to reconcile with the Soil Conservation Service's (SCS's) contention that the South contains a disproportionate share of the nation's potential cropland. In this high projection, the South's corn acreage would be some 62 percent higher than in the base case, wheat acreage 25 percent higher, and soybean acreage 89 percent higher. Cotton acreage would decline, reflecting a projected decline in total national acreage, although the South would increase its share of national cotton acreage from 31 to 35 percent.

Increases in cultivated acreage would be particularly large (more than 50 percent over the base case) in a broad band of territory stretching over the Coastal Plain and Piedmont from the South Carolina-Georgia border to southern Louisiana. Major increases in acreage would also be expected in the White River basin in northern Arkansas and in the Tennessee and Cumberland River basins in Tennessee and Kentucky. For individual crops, the shifts could be particularly large. For example, in this high-demand case, the acreage planted in soybeans in the Lower Mississippi Delta area of Louisiana rises from 279,000 acres to 1.7 million.

The larger amount of land in crop production would—absent a change in conservation practices—result in a 54 percent increase in annual soil loss due to erosion.[7] A doubling of soil loss would occur in most of the area where the greatest crop expansion is expected to take place.[8]

The LP model also calculates the average net return to land (rent) after the cost of all other inputs has been paid. Even in the high-demand case, returns to land in the South are rather low, averaging about $14 per acre per year (in 1975 dollars). This is below the national average of $20 and suggests that, even under conditions of high demand, returns to southern cropland would be held down by the land's relatively low inherent fertility.

The land return data also shed some light on the possible competition between crops and timber. Consider land in SCS land capability class 4E—land that is not very productive of crops and that is subject to erosion. This land is relatively well suited to timber production, being capable of producing about 80 cubic feet of loblolly pine per acre annually.[9] The LP model indicates that, under the high-demand scenario, the average return to this land in crop use would in most of the South range between $0 and $22 per acre annually. This seems well within the bounds of what even moderately productive forestry could afford to pay for land, particularly under the conditions of rising timber prices projected by the Forest Service.

As an alternative to the high-demand scenario, I looked at a situation in which crop exports would grow very slowly and domestic demand moderately (CARD Scenario #9). Although in this case the amount of cropland cultivated nationally would be 310 million acres (against 287 million in the base case), the South would not have any expansion in cropland. In fact, acreage in some major crops would fall, particularly for soybeans (acreage down 18 percent). Certain subregions, such as the Tombigbee River basin in Alabama, would experience sharp declines in total acreage cultivated. However, erosion in the South would also fall, by about 4 percent.

Potential Cropland

Another way to look at the extent to which land uses in the South might come into competition is to consider the land identified by the Soil Conservation Service as "potential cropland." This is defined as land with a high or medium potential for conversion to crop use within the next 10 to 15 years, based on soil characteristics and on commodity prices, development costs, and production costs at their 1981 levels.[10] Analysis of potential cropland can be used to make projections in a manner analogous to linear programming (though without the mathematics). That is, one assumes that, as demand for crops grows, the land identified as having "high potential" for crop use will be converted first, then the land with medium potential.

Consider the possible conversion of the South's potential cropland under two scenarios. The first is an "all-out production" scenario, which would involve bringing under cultivation all of the nation's 153 million acres of "high and medium" potential cropland, including the 44 million acres in the South. This is roughly equivalent to the CARD model's "high demand" scenario. In a second scenario, only the 35 million acres of the nation's "high potential" cropland (10.8 million acres in the South) would be converted. This is about in line with the lower of the CARD scenarios, as well as with the Forest Service's projection that approximately 9 million acres of additional cropland will be needed in the South by the year 2040.

In the first ("high demand") scenario, an increase in land devoted to crops would have significant impact on other land uses. Conversion of the South's 44 million acres of high- and medium-potential cropland would remove 44 percent of the grazing land base and 14 percent of the forestland base. For some states, the impacts would be still larger; conversion of all this land would reduce North Carolina's forestland base by 31 percent, Alabama's grazing lands by 60 percent, and Georgia's grazing lands by 51 percent.

In this scenario, certain subregions within the South are particularly hard hit. Looking at the 27 "major land resource areas" (MLRAs) in the South, as defined by the Soil Conservation Service, there are 9 in which more than 50 percent of the grazing land base is converted to crops and 3 that would lose more than 20 percent of their forestland.[11] Although these losses could certainly prove damaging, it is perhaps remarkable that they are no higher, particularly for some forest areas. As measured by SCS, potential cropland is scattered throughout the South rather than concentrated in just a few major subregions. For example, contrary to my expectation, high- and medium-potential cropland makes up more of the current noncropland in the Piedmont (21 percent) than in the South Atlantic Coastal Plain (17 percent). And, despite the degree to which past cropland development has been concentrated in the Delta, that region contains only slightly more than its proportionate share of potential cropland (25 percent of current noncropland).

In the second scenario, only the South's high-potential land would be converted. Of the total of 10.8 million acres, 6.1 million are now used for pasture or range and 4.6 million are in forest. Relative to the noncrop land base, conversion of this land would have a much greater impact on grazing than on forestry—land with high conversion potential amounts to 14 percent of the grazing land base, only 3 percent of the forestland base. Looking at individual states, the impacts are somewhat larger, though they do not seem too serious. The largest percentage loss of pasture and range is Alabama's 21 percent; the largest loss of forest is North Carolina's 7 percent.

The overall implication of the potential cropland analysis, in both of the scenarios, is that, while a very high demand for southern agricultural products would have a severe impact on the grazing industry, forestry would not be hurt very seriously. This conclusion holds even when subregions within the South are considered. However, the subregions are still relatively large, so the analysis does not eliminate the possibility that particular mills might have to close for lack of fiber and some communities might be faced with high unemployment among woods and mill workers.

The conclusion that new cropland will be scattered around the South, rather than concentrated, particularly in the southern part of the Coastal Plain, is so much at variance with the rest of my analysis[12] that it leads me to question the validity of the SCS definition of potential cropland and how that measure was applied in the 1982 National Resources Inventory. In doing that survey, SCS asked its county-level employees (and a county review committee) to evaluate sample points in their county as suitable or unsuitable for conversion. I suspect that this procedure may have led the local classifiers to compare the sample points with other lands in their county rather than taking a view of the order in which various lands in the South as a whole would most likely be converted. This procedure may have caused each county to identify at least some land as suitable for conversion when, in actuality, land most likely to be converted may be highly concentrated in a few areas of the South. It may also have caused classifiers to downplay the possibility of large-scale drainage and irrigation projects in those counties where such projects have not already been initiated.

Says Norman A. Berg, former chief of the Soil Conservation Service, "The determination of potential cropland acreage is one of the weakest parts of the 1977 and 1982 NRIs. Potential cropland should have been identified by people with a national or regional viewpoint, rather than only by people in individual counties."[13]

This hypothesized flaw in the existing potential cropland data means that one cannot say with confidence that future cropland conversion will not take away important parts of the forest-industry land base in the Coastal Plain.

Evaluating the Alternative Projections

After considering the results of trying to project the land-use future of the South with four different techniques—trend extrapolation, econometric modeling, linear programming, and identification of potential cropland—one is led to several conclusions.

One conclusion is that each of the four projection methods has defects that limit its usefulness. Trend extrapolation suffers from its assumption that the course of the future will be very similar to the experience of the past. Econometric models and linear programming models are limited by the assumption that the relationships between variables will remain the same; they do not allow

Table 7.3

Projected Changes in Land Use over Next 30 Years
(in percent)

	1982 acreage[1] (million acres)	Adjusted trend extra-polation[2]		Econometric model[2]	Linear programming model		Potential cropland analysis	
		(A)	(B)	(C)	(D)	(E)	(F)	(G)
Cropland used for crops	52.4	+42	+16	+11	+49	0	+17	+71
Forestland	183.1	-11	-7	-6	na	na	-3	-14
Grazing land	40.7	-48	-19	-15	na	na	-14	-44
Urban and built-up land	20.6	+65	+54	} +18	na	na	na	na
Other land	14.7	-11	-16	}	na	na	-1	-2

[1] Figures are for 11 southern states and do not include Texas or Oklahoma. Because geographic area and/or land use definitions differ slightly from one projection to another, percentage changes are calculated relative to the base acreage used in each projection.

[2] Projected 30 years from base date.

A Based on 1969–82 trend.
B Based on 1978–82 trend.
C Based on observed land-use patterns, 1947–83.
D CARD scenario 18 ("high demand").
E CARD scenario 9 ("moderate demand").
F All high-potential land cropped.
G All high- and medium-potential land cropped.

Source: See text.

for the technological changes and interregional shifts in production costs that could prove very important if the South finds ways of taking advantage of its natural endowments of water and growing season. Potential cropland analysis suffers not only from this essentially static view of cropping systems but also from the fact that the only available estimates were built up county by county and do not fully reflect the great differences in agricultural prospects of various areas within the South.

With some effort, better models could be constructed. The most promising way to do this, I believe, is to combine already available information on southern soil types[14] with a more comprehensive view of possible productivity-raising options and thus to generate more sophisticated subregional supply functions. These could then become inputs into linear programming models that would generate costs and outputs for alternative assumed levels of demand.

Another conclusion is that existing models demonstrate great variation in projected long-run levels of demand on the South's land base. (Table 7.3 summarizes the results of the projections discussed above.) Much of the variation depends on alternative assumptions about the future level of a few key factors—the value of the dollar relative to other currencies, decisions by foreign governments about politically tolerable levels of food or fiber imports, water shortages or climate changes affecting competing production regions elsewhere in the United States or abroad, the degree of consumer preference for beef relative to other foods, the performance of the forestry sector in Canada and in Latin America. Probably the single most important assumption that must be made in any modeling effort is the level of export demand for U.S.-produced grain and soybeans, and most of the items just listed are determinants of what that demand will be. It is noteworthy that most of these determinants cannot be predicted with exactness and that they lie beyond the control of southern policy makers. Indeed, many of them cannot be entirely controlled even by policy at the federal level; some depend on decisions made outside the borders of the United States.

Under an assumption of moderate growth in agricultural exports and steady but not spectacular gains in U.S. farm productivity (scenarios B, C, E, and F in table 7.3), most of the models project little or no growth in southern cropland and hence little impact on competing land uses. As I noted in chapter 2, these

The International Factor

One of the most striking conclusions from my investigation of land use in the American South is the degree to which the future of the rural South is likely to be influenced by developments outside the United States. For example, the demand for southern cropland depends heavily on the inclination—and the ability—of foreign customers to purchase southern-grown soybeans. This, in turn, depends on economic growth and income levels abroad, on world weather patterns, on relative exchange rates of various currencies, and on the ability of other soybean exporting countries (notably Brazil) to increase production at reasonable prices.

Similarly, an increasing proportion of long-term demand growth for southern forest products, ranging from logs to lumber and paper, may depend on the expansion of foreign markets. Competition by foreign producers may occur for all these products, however, raising the prospect not only of increased competition for new export markets but also of possibly greater penetration of U.S. wood markets by foreign suppliers.

Agricultural specialty crops grown in the South, particularly citrus and vegetables, have already faced significant competition from Latin American suppliers, whose low labor costs offset the cost of transportation to U.S. markets. Yet the international market is growing for many other U.S.-grown food items, and southern farmers are well placed to compete vigorously.

Rural industrial plants in the South are also increasingly operating in the context of world markets. The longtime wage advantage that such plants enjoyed within the U.S. market has been eroded by competition from foreign manufacturers paying far lower wages. But southern firms are learning to export, and foreign companies setting up branch plants in the United States have looked very favorably on southern locations.

Whether as a promising source of marketing opportunity, or as a worrisome source of future competition, the international factor is something that an increasing number of southerners can ill-afford to ignore.

seem like the most reasonable assumptions under the conditions most experts think will prevail over the next few years. Although, under these low-demand conditions, the South would have an ample forest and grazing land base, it still would face problems in how that land was used. For example, the South would still face rising prices for pine timber, in great part because of low levels of pine reproduction on nonindustrial private forestlands. Its cattle industry would have a larger acreage of pastureland but would be under little pressure to improve either the quality of the animal stock or the management of the forage.

On the other hand, the possibility of rapid growth in exports and/or a fall-off in U.S. productivity cannot be dismissed. Indeed, these were the conditions prevailing for most of the 1970s, and, as recently as 1981, a large body of expert opinion indicated that they were likely to continue for decades to come.

The trend extrapolation analysis indicates the major increase in southern cropland that is implied by a continuation of 1970s conditions, as do the "high demand" projections of the CARD model. In the first case (scenario A), total cultivated cropland would be up 42 percent; in the second case (scenario D), 49 percent.

Even if U.S. grain exports do not increase greatly, there remains the possibility that the South will grow in total share of U.S. crop production. This could occur if the South somehow improved its competitive position, for example, by eliminating some insect pests or crop diseases, by greater use of double cropping, or by growing new kinds of crops. It could also occur if other regions lost some of their advantage, for example, by urbanization or erosion damage to farmland in the Corn Belt or loss of irrigation water in the West. Existing models give mixed signals about the possibility of the South's expanding its share of U.S. cropland. The potential cropland analysis (which is based on the observed behavior of landowners) suggests that the South will increase its relative position; the linear programming approach (which is based on relative production costs) suggests that it will not. Both approaches seem incomplete, as they are based on the current competitiveness of various regions and do not account for the changes that occur over time. Moreover, the CARD analysis does not even allow the South to expand what is probably its most dynamic agricultural sector, irrigated crop production.

In most scenarios involving major expansion of crop use of land in the South, the most pronounced impact is on acreage in pasture. Within some subregions, more than 50 percent of current pastureland could be converted to crops. The steady increase in urban and built-up land would compound this impact, because some of the land urbanized would come directly from pasture, while other pasture would have to be converted to cropland to replace cropland that would be urbanized. Although deprived of much of its land base, the South's cattle industry might still survive, partly on the basis of intensive, fertilized pasture, partly on rough, hilly lands not suitable for crops, partly through increased grazing of forestland.

The extension of urban and built-up areas in the South represents a significant but not overwhelming demand for land. I projected in chapter 5 that, as the U.S. population rises to 300 million, a prospect that may not occur until about 2030, the South could require between 8 and 21 million additional acres of urban and built-up land. The trend extrapolation and the U.S. Forest Service projection show, respectively, an increase of 13.4 million acres over a 30-year period and 12.3 million over a 55-year period. Although these quantities are small relative to the region's total land base—they amount to 3 to 7 percent of the South's total nonfederal, nonurban land—their impact could be somewhat magnified by the tendency of land of better than average quality to be urbanized and by management problems connected to the interspersing of built-up land and land devoted to agriculture and forestry production. In my judgment, however, urbanization is likely to raise major problems for food production in the South only if the high export scenario comes to pass.

The forest land base is likely to be much less affected than is grazing land by either additional crop acreage or further urbanization. This is partly because the cost of clearing discourages agricultural use, partly because of the sheer size of the forest land base relative to conversion pressures. To be sure, there could be a reduction in average forestland quality as a result of differential clearing and urbanization.

Anticipated land-use changes will have major impacts on the South's unpriced values. This will be particularly important if total cropland expands, but at least some impacts will occur in any case. For example, some wetlands and forests are likely to be converted to agricultural use, partly to replace agricultural land lost to urbanization, partly to replace economically marginal land taken out of crop production. Other impacts on unpriced values will occur as the use of certain production technologies expands—use of forest herbicides, for example, or expansion of irrigated crop production. These impacts are likely to occur even if total production does not expand, but an increased demand for farm or forest products would greatly accelerate their occurrence.

It is significant that the available projections of future land use have little or nothing to say about impacts on unpriced values.

The sole exception is the CARD model, which explictly considered
the impact of alternative levels of crop production on soil erosion and found that high levels of output could raise erosion rates
in the South by as much as 54 percent.

Taken as a whole, the above projections and the analysis in
the preceding chapters of this book tend to support the conclusion that the South is far from being an area where there is likely
to be a land shortage, in the sense that any given use of land cannot be expanded to meet additional demands. In crop production, in forestry, and in animal agriculture, there seem abundant
opportunities for major expansion of output, albeit usually at
somewhat higher prices. But the overall weight of the evidence
also suggests that the South, with its adaptable and relatively
unspecialized land base and its history of intraregional land-use
shifts, is likely to be characterized by continued competition
among various activities for the use of the same land. This is most
likely to have repercussions throughout the South only if there
is a continued increase in export demand for crops and only
moderate technological change raising output per acre.

But there seem to be abundant possibilities for more localized
competition for land: between soybeans and wildlife for the use

of forested bottomlands; among crops, beef cattle, and pine plantations for the use of high-quality land presently in timber; between crops and various urban and industrial uses.

A "Foresight and Insurance" Strategy

If one takes a long-term view of land use, it is easy to be discouraged by the many uncertainties that arise: uncertainties about future demands, particularly the difficult-to-forecast international demands; uncertainties about technologies; uncertainties about the application or effectiveness of current public policies that create or foreclose future land-use opportunities.

These uncertainties imply a need for flexibility in planning. There are so many variables affecting the long-term demands on southern land that even the most carefully laid quantitative plans would very likely be far wide of their intended mark. On the other hand, leaving land-use decisions solely to the market would probably result in foreclosing important long-term options because of short-term gains. Certainly it would result in neglect of many important unpriced values.

The best approach to land-use uncertainty, in my judgment, is to know enough about the economic and technological forces driving the use of land to get an early warning of changes when they occur—and to keep options open when this can be done at a relatively low cost.

This might best be termed a "foresight and insurance" strategy. The "foresight" consideration explains the effort I have put into analyzing in detail how various alternative uses place demands on land and what factors seem important in determining future land requirements. The "insurance" consideration provides the rationale for most of the policies outlined in the following chapter, which keep options open but which tend to be low in cost and not oriented toward meeting fixed quantitative output targets. The policies represent a moderate, but effective, program for helping the South take full advantage of its promising but often problematic land resource.

References

1. William Ascher, *Forecasting: An Appraisal for Policy-makers and Planners* (Baltimore: Johns Hopkins University Press, 1978), p. 41.

2. Extrapolating 1974-82 experience, rather than 1969-82 experience, makes very little difference to the cropland, pasture, and forest projections. A projection based on 1978-82 experience is discussed later in this section.

3. The magnitude of this increase raises the question of whether the South has enough land physically suited to crop use to make this level of cropping possible. Examination of the South's stock of "potential cropland" (discussed at greater length later in this chapter) indicates that even a 22-million-acre increase in cultivated cropland area would not exhaust the South's 44 million acres of land with high or medium potential for conversion to crop use.

4. As with the 1969-82 projection, the 1978-82 figures had to be adjusted to eliminate impossible or very unlikely results. This meant that cropland pasture was assumed to fall no lower than 5 million acres, and other land no lower than 12 million. It was assumed, moreover, that all of these adjustments would come out of the grassland pasture and range category, a use of land that is generally unable to compete when cropland is greatly expanding. Unadjusted, grassland pasture and range would have increased from 24 million acres in 1982 to 49 million in 2012; adjusted, it was projected to grow to 28 million.

5. The model was estimated on the basis of how acreage allocations by use among 51 southern Forest Survey units varied as relative returns to each use changed over the period 1947-83 (using multiple regression analysis of pooled time series data). Unpublished projections, prepared as part of ongoing research on southern timber supply, were obtained from U.S. Forest Service, Rocky Mountain Experiment Station, Ft. Collins, Colo. For details of the projection methodology, see Ralph J. Alig, *Forest Acreage Trends in the Southeast: Econometric Analysis and Policy Simulation*, unpublished doctoral dissertation, Oregon State University, School of Forestry, May 1984.

6. The correspondence with the South as I define it is not exact, as the CARD producing areas follow river basins, rather than state boundaries. Unpublished CARD computers runs were provided by Burton C. English, Iowa State University.

7. Interestingly, erosion in the South rises somewhat less than in the rest of the country, where increasing crop acreage would produce a 73 percent increase in soil loss.

8. Although the percentage increase in crop production is not particularly high, a great part of the *absolute* increase in soil loss would occur in the Mississippi Delta area of Tennessee, Mississippi, Arkansas, and Louisiana. The area now accounts for 60 percent of total southern soil loss and under the high-demand scenario would experience 43 percent of the South's additional soil loss.

9. U.S. Department of Agriculture, Office of Budget and Program Analysis, *Conversion of Southern Cropland to Southern Pine Tree Plantings* (Washington, D.C.: U.S. Department of Agriculture, 1983), appendix C.

10. Keith Schmude, National Resources Inventory Staff, Soil Conservation Service, telephone interview, June 1985. Other criteria are that the land not be held for another use (for example, land in young pine plantations) and, for "high potential" land, that similar land in the county had been converted to cropland during the past three years.

11. The Major Land Resource Areas (MLRAs) losing grazing land are: MLRA 129—Sand Mountain (-71 percent); MLRA 131—Mississippi Valley Alluvium (-63 percent); MLRA 138—North Central Florida Ridge (-60 percent); MLRA

153A—Atlantic Coast Flatwoods (-56 percent); MLRA 150A—Gulf Coast Prairies (-54 percent); MLRA 134—Southern Mississippi Valley Silty Uplands (-53 percent); MLRA 154—South Central Florida Ridge (-53 percent); MLRA 122—Highland Rim and Pennyroyal (-51 percent); and MLRA 133A—Southern Coastal Plain (-50 percent). Regions losing forestland are: MLRA 153B—Virginia-North Carolina Tidewater (-28 percent); MLRA 131—Mississippi Valley Alluvium (-23 percent); and MLRA 154—South Central Florida Ridge (-22 percent). The regions are defined and mapped in U.S. Soil Conservation Service, *Land Resource Regions and Major Land Resource Areas of the United States* (Washington, D.C.: U.S. Government Printing Office, 1981).

12. For example, the discussion of climate, double-cropping, and drainage in chapter 2.

13. Interview, Washington, D.C., June 1985. Berg notes, however, that the basic data needed to make the determination still must be collected locally.

14. See the discussion of the Soils 5 data base, in chapter 8.

Chapter 8

Land Policy for the South

Land-use policy is not a popular subject in the South, particularly in the rural South. Many rural southern counties still lack even the most rudimentary planning and zoning. Farmland preservation programs, which are spreading rapidly at the state and local levels in other parts of the United States, are extremely uncommon in the South. Except in Florida, parts of Virginia, and coastal North Carolina, the mid-1970s surge of activity in environmentally based land-use planning and greater state involvement in land-use control hardly touched the South.

"In my state," says a knowledgeable South Carolinian, "if you talk to people in rural areas about land-use planning, they think that you may be a socialist of some sort; if you talk to them about land-use regulation, they know you must be a communist."

Yet southern states have long had many policies, mostly at the state level, that quite directly affect land use. Most of these are not labeled "land-use policies" and often are not thought of as such. For example, virtually all of the southern states have active programs for the promotion of forestry, including in some cases state cost-sharing programs that subsidize forestry investments by private landowners. State game and fish commissions try to increase hunting and fishing opportunities, increasingly through the purchase or lease of habitat. States have a major role in agricultural research and in the dissemination of information to farmers about new cropping systems, irrigation, erosion control, and pest management. These activities have very real implications for land use.

Going beyond such traditional areas of policy, many southern governments have been innovators, both in traditional areas of activity and in entirely new ones. This chapter presents a wide

range of ideas for improving the use of land, nearly all of which
have precedent somewhere in the South: as proposed legislation,
as recommendations of state or local study commissions, or as
ongoing, successful programs. Despite the overall lack of land-
use policy in the South, these specific innovations are quite
numerous.

The chapter emphasizes the relationship between policies and
the South's specific land-use problems. "If it ain't broke," former
federal budget director Bert Lance is reputed to have said, "don't
fix it." The South does not need a land policy for land policy's
sake. Rather, its individual states and localities need sets of policies
that respond to their specific land problems. I offer a menu from
which to choose, suggesting specific ways in which present land
management can be improved, opportunities seized, and future
problems avoided.

The policies suggested by my research fall into three categories:
(1) further developing the South's agriculture and forestry by increasing production and efficiency; (2) conserving economically
valuable land and resources; and (3) protecting and enhancing
the natural and human environment.

Developing Southern Agriculture and Forestry

On the whole, the South has impressive opportunities to develop
its agriculture and forestry. Doing so will mostly require action
by private landowners and by industry, but public policy has a
role in providing leadership and removing obstacles. There are
two primary types of opportunities that might be pursued:
developing new production systems in crop agriculture, animal
agriculture, and forestry; and achieving better management of
what may be the South's greatest natural resource, its nonindustrial private forests.

Production Systems: The Research and Extension Role

In chapter 2, I noted the South's many advantages for expanded
crop production, which include suitable land, available water,
and a long growing season. I also observed that some of the
South's limitations, such as chronic pest problems and low average
yields, could be overcome by the development of new technologies or, in many cases, by simply narrowing the now substan-

tial gap between the performance of the better farmers and that of the average farmer.

The large amount of agricultural research now being done in the South, under both federal and state auspices, and the elaborate agricultural extension system that delivers the information to the farmer will be most useful if they take the South's advantages and limitations as their starting point.

Crop Agriculture. Although crop agriculture in the South has improved greatly since the 1930s, there is much scope for further development. Average yields of many major crops are quite low. For example, in 1981 southern farmers averaged 74 bushels of corn per acre, compared to 120 bushels per acre in the Corn Belt. For soybeans, the South's average was 23 bushels, against the Corn Belt's 35. If the South could raise its productivity in these crops to the present Corn Belt average—not an impossible task according to some agronomists—it could add nearly $3 billion to its gross agricultural receipts.

Although hampered by low native soil fertility and difficult pest problems, the South has production possibilities based on growing season and water availability that have barely been exploited. Among the most important areas for investigation appear to be: development of lower-cost irrigation systems; breeding crop varieties better adapted to southern conditions; double and triple cropping systems; use of crop rotation for pest control; and finding profitable cropping opportunities for part-time farmers.

It is true that most of today's research must necessarily go toward solving the immediate and often very specific problems of southern farmers. But the South will not be able to take full advantage of its cropping opportunities without a certain amount of broadly focused, even speculative, experimentation. The ultimate goal of such research, I believe, is to transcend the South's agricultural history (however rich and fascinating it has been) and traditional cropping practices and to "reinvent" southern agriculture.

The South's natural endowments are a good starting point for this research, not only because they offer unexploited economic possibilities but because they force the researcher to consider ecological constraints early on, not as an afterthought. As one research administrator has put it, "As scientists, we usually try to solve the problems associated with whatever crop the farmer decides to grow. Rarely do we ask what crop should be grown. . . . Choosing the right problem to solve, I submit, will always be more important than obtaining the right solution to the chosen problems."[1]

A "resource-based" approach to agricultural research would give major emphasis to developing multiple-cropping systems that take advantage of the South's long frost-free growing season, particularly in the Coastal Plain. The full range of possibilities, even for combinations of traditional crops, has barely been explored. Says one southern crop researcher, "Traditionally, agricultural research in the South has emphasized monocropping; only very recently have researchers even started to look at crop traits, such as timeliness of maturity, that would aid double-cropping. Increased attention by plant breeders to double-cropping will have a ripple effect through all the other agricultural disciplines and could lead to development of entirely new systems of farming for the South."[2]

I think there is a great need for research on additional crops for the Southeast. We need a real good winter legume for soil improvement, a winter grazing crop for cattle, and a crop to rotate with soybeans. We're in kind of a rut with soybeans. All the land not in corn or tobacco is in beans. You develop problems with pests and diseases when you grow soybeans continuously.

NED DARGAN, farmer, Mechanicsville, South Carolina

There is no reason to restrict research on cropping systems to the relatively small number of crops now widely grown in the South. There are dozens of possible new food crops, animal food sources, oil crops, and energy crops. Many originate in Asia and Latin America. Although some seem more suitable for the arid Southwest, others seem to require the sunlight, water, and warm temperatures found in the South. The South's long growing season may also give it an advantage if new perennial varieties can be developed for corn and other annual crops.

Most new crops that are studied will likely prove unsuitable for the South either from a biological or an economic standpoint. But the history of the soybean, which moved over a scant 50 years from an exotic forage crop to the South's agricultural staple, should serve as a potent reminder of the possibilities for adopting new crops.

The resource-based approach to research may be particularly valuable in trying to apply genetic engineering to southern agriculture, because genetic engineering offers the possibility of fitting the plant to the environment rather than modifying the environment (for example, through fertilization) to fit the requirements of existing plants. Precisely because environmental conditions in the South are far less favorable for present crops than are conditions in the Corn Belt, the South may have relatively more to gain as the application of biotechnology makes some of those constraints less important.

Although many new agricultural systems developed for the South will probably continue the long-standing trend toward larger farm size and greater capital intensity, there is nonetheless a real need to try to help the South's many small, limited-resource farmers. Many of them grow tobacco, a heavily subsidized crop with relatively poor prospects for market expansion. The various substitutes that have been suggested, such as vegetables and ornamental plants, are unlikely to fill the void, either in terms of number of acres required or amount of income generated. Finding a substitute crop, perhaps with the aid of biotechnology, should be a major assignment for agricultural research in the South.

One important reservation should be made concerning new cropping systems for the South. Many of the lands that seem to offer the best opportunities for new agricultural systems lie in the Coastal Plain. Their use to date has been limited by low-fertility or high water tables or both. Cropping of the low fertility lands would cut deeply into the Coastal Plain's timberland base, a particularly troublesome prospect because so many of the South's big paper mills are located there. New drainage techniques— controlled and reversible drainage, for example—could cause more cropping of lands now used by wildlife. Moreover, in large parts of the Coastal Plain, the sandy soils allow agrichemicals to leach into groundwater. Thus, while agricultural research offers major opportunities for greater prosperity in southern crop production, care must be taken so that prosperity is not purchased at a high environmental price.

Animal Agriculture. Among the opportunities for research and technology diffusion in animal agriculture, some of the most exciting are in aquaculture. Aquaculture offers the possibility of extremely efficient conversion of grain into high-quality, high-value animal protein. Demand for the product is growing and seems consistent with consumer preferences for lighter, more healthful foods. Aquaculture requires a relatively high labor input, particularly in harvesting and processing, but requires relatively little land. The raising of catfish, crawfish, shrimp, and other aquatic species may ultimately be as important to the South as is the broiler industry, one of the great agricultural success stories of the 20th century.

Another potentially important product is low-fat, grass-fed beef. There is considerable scope for better production methods in the South—improved pasture grasses, more elaborate systems for tracking herd health and nutrition, better breeds of cattle.

As with crops, a resource-based approach to grazing research would probably be the most rewarding. Much of the South's grazing is a casual, low-profit venture. Because of this, one might expect to find grazing concentrated on the South's poorest land. In fact, southern cattle grazing uses some good land and some poor land—its land base is distinguished mainly by the fact that it is land where no other use is planned *at the moment.* Thus, the grazing land base is inherently unstable; an increase in crop demand or increased interest in forestry could quickly reduce it. Resource-based research on grazing should recognize this by taking a two-fold approach: developing low-input systems for the land devoted casually or temporarily to grazing; developing permanent, higher-investment systems for lands identified as suitable for cattle production in the long run.

The greatest development opportunities for the South's cattle industry, however, may lie not in production but in marketing— gaining consumer acceptance of leaner cuts of grass-fed beef that are not graded "choice." Southern beef producers could take some direct action in this area by collectively sponsoring an advertising campaign, much as has been done by cotton and wool producers nationwide.

Forestry. The South's largest single land use, forestry, offers perhaps the greatest possibilities for increasing productivity. There is considerable scope for new advances in silviculture, particularly in developing genetically improved trees that grow faster and make more efficient use of light, water, and nutrients. Such "supertrees," however, are likely to be most profitable when raised in intensively managed plantations on land of higher than average quality.[3] Their use should further improve the economics of high-intensity forestry, which is increasingly practiced by the forest-products industry and by a minority of nonindustrial owners.

On the other hand, I have already noted some drawbacks of intensive plantation forestry, particularly its impacts on habitat diversity. Because of these problems, further development of intensive forestry—with or without supertrees—should not be considered as the sole answer to the South's wood-supply needs. A parallel research and extension effort should be made to develop and diffuse profitable methods of "soft silviculture."

Soft silviculture ought to have two characteristics. First, it should involve low initial investment, strengthening its appeal to nonindustrial private owners with limited capital and a short time horizon. Second, it should accommodate owners' nontimber objectives, including wildlife and esthetics. Soft silviculture represents a middle ground between the intensive plantation forestry practiced by timber companies and advocated by most state forestry agencies and the casual mismanagement characteristic of so many nonindustrial private owners. An increase in soft silviculture would result in more acres of southern timberland under active management but a lower average intensity of management.

It is not easy to say precisely what silvicultural methods might be employed. A central feature of the approach I recommend is that it be sensitive to variations from site to site and from owner to owner. There is likely to be considerable reliance on natural seeding, on aerial seeding, and on controlled fire (rather than mechanical cultivation or chemical spraying) to prepare sites for regeneration and to reduce competition by undesired species. There is also likely to be an emphasis on producing high-quality sawlogs, both softwood and hardwood. The quality aspect could become increasingly important in view of recent questions about the structural characteristics of lumber made from fast-grown pines produced under plantation conditions.

At present, most nonindustrial owners rely heavily on natural reforestation, which is practiced on 78 percent of total harvested acres, according to one recent study of the nonindustrial tracts in the South.[4] The potential for improvement lies in another finding of the same study. Owners of only 38 percent of nonindustrial acres harvested during the period 1971-81 were advised about regeneration by a government or private forester.[5] The initial decision to harvest was also made in two-thirds of the cases without a forester's help, despite the fact that careful harvest is crucial to the success of soft silviculture. In fact, on 35 percent of the acres harvested, the logger or timber buyer was allowed to determine what was to be cut.

The key to successfully practicing low-investment or soft silviculture is substituting information for capital. It involves knowing what to cut and how, when to use seed trees and patch clearcuts, and when controlled burning is indicated. It involves knowing when thinning a natural stand of timber or deadening the hardwoods is economically preferable to clearcutting and replanting. It also involves knowing when "soft" methods are inappropriate economically, despite the low investment, or when they would conflict with the owner's nontimber objectives. (For example, an owner may want to replant plantation-style so as to better accommodate cattle-grazing on the land.)

Government extension foresters in the South, as well as government-supported forestry research, should give equal prominence to "soft" and "hard" approaches to forestry. Too often at present, it is assumed that landowners are behaving irrationally when they fail to implement recommended forestry practices that would greatly increase output per acre, even if such practices are not economically attractive or interfere with recreational or other objectives. "The extension foresters," says a consulting forester in Mississippi, "would think it was wonderful if the small private owners would borrow themselves into the poorhouse to implement their recommendations." Rather than continuing to scold and cajole the owner of nonindustrial private forest, government agencies should give greater attention to the owner's own needs and motivations.

Whether the future of forest management in the South moves toward a mix of hard and soft silviculture, or simply continues the present pattern of either intensive management or no management at all, a major issue will be what to do with the region's enormous oversupply of low-quality hardwoods. Government and industry researchers can make a much greater effort than they have to date to develop new ways to use so-called junk hardwoods, both in papermaking and in solid wood products.[6] There is ample precedent for believing that new products can create markets for otherwise wasted resources—development of waferboard, which turned the Lake States' aspen trees from a nuisance to an asset, is a recent example.[7]

Finding new ways to substitute hardwoods for softwoods would have two important impacts on southern forests. First, it would reduce the immediate demand imbalance between softwood and hardwood trees, producing greater use of the hardwoods and taking some of the pressure off the softwoods. Second, it could provide a market for hardwood thinnings, making it possible to use this method more widely to upgrade the quality of existing hardwood and mixed stands.

Improving Forest Management

Beyond developing and promoting new silvicultural systems, what should public forestry agencies do to encourage wood production in the South? In my view, existing programs go about as far as desirable in subsidizing forest investments. In addition to forestry research, extension, and fire protection, these subsidies include favorable property taxes, capital gains treatment of timber income, an investment tax credit and rapid write-off of up to $10,000 yearly in reforestation expenses, and federal (and some state) cost-sharing aid.[8] Although it is clearly to the South's advantage to further develop its timber resource, it seems difficult to justify still further public subsidies in a time of general strain on government budgets, particularly when many of the landowning beneficiaries have higher than average income and wealth.

State Cost-Sharing Programs. Rather than transfer additional public monies to potential timber producers, it might be better

Land Data for Research and Action

I have suggested that research on southern production possibilities, whether for crops or beef cattle or trees, give more emphasis to exploiting the South's inherent resource potentials rather than concentrate on minor improvements to current crops and production systems. To identify these resource potentials requires large amounts of organized data for the South as a whole and for major land-use regions within the South.

Many of the required data now exist—in fact, with the 1984-85 release by the U.S. Department of Agriculture of the 1982 National Resources Inventory, there is more land-use information available than ever before in history. What is lacking still, at least at this writing, is the analysis that would make the data truly useful.

Consider a data set known by the Department of Agriculture as "Soils 5." It is a compilation, recently computerized, of most of what is known about each of the 14,000 types of soils found in the United States. It shows, for example, the productivity of a given soil (in bushels or bales per acre) for the principal crops that can be grown on it. It also shows how production changes if the soil type is irrigated as well as production if the soil is used for forage production or for trees.[1] It contains information on potential natural vegetation that is relevant to wildlife carrying capacity.

Combined with the new land-use data from the National Resources Inventory, Soils 5 could tell us where the South's best corn-producing land is located and how much of it is presently in corn production and how much in some other use. It could tell us how many acres of wetland might be physically suitable for soybeans,

where in the South those lands are located, and how productive they might be if drained. Using this information, one could get an overview of both long-term agricultural potentials and of the degree to which realizing those potentials would reduce forest output and damage habitat.

This analysis has not yet been done. The Soil Conservation Service, originator and keeper of these data, has thus far concentrated its analysis on erosion rather than on broader land-use questions. The data are so recently available that analyzing them is beyond the reach of my own study. However, I urge government and private researchers to mine this and other rich files of information on land-use aggregates. Efforts to do so will enable us to understand land-use opportunities and impacts as never before.

Regional data on land—available but unanalyzed—are important for research and policy. But for on-the-ground action, more information is needed that is not now being collected. Says Norman A. Berg, former Chief of the Soil Conservation Service, "We have a gap in land-use inventories between the very broad picture provided by the National Resources Inventory (NRI) and the very specific information offered to individual land users and local governments by about 8,000 soil conservationists operating at the local level. They need more information about land-use change in their own county, and much of it is not available."

The problem, of course, is cost. Therefore, new subregional data collection efforts should concentrate on geographic problem areas: rural-urban fringes, areas of wetland drainage, places with substantial development related to recreation, places where the structure of land-ownership is thought to be changing. Attention should also be paid to potential land-use "hot spots," places where future changes are likely to occur or where the various alternative uses of land are most likely to come into conflict. Because municipalities and counties rarely have the skilled personnel needed to collect and interpret these data, the task might best be assumed by state governments, which can obtain technical assistance from state universities and from state and regional offices of a number of federal agencies.

to redistribute resources within the timber sector so as to promote good forest management by a larger number of forest landowners. One possibility is state cost-sharing of expenses for reforestation and improvement of timber stands, paid for by a tax on harvested timber.

Currently, four southern states—South Carolina, Mississippi, North Carolina, and Virginia—offer forest owners some sort of state cost-sharing for reforestation expenses.[9] The state share varies between 50 and 75 percent, sometimes with a limit on the number of acres or cost per acre or both.[10] Most of the money comes from a severance tax on timber or a tax on forest products.

What is most attractive about such programs is that they link the harvest of timber, which generates cash for the owner, with reforestation, which commits cash to ensuring a future harvest. What is least attractive is that the recipients of the subsidy are not identical to those who pay the severance tax. The cost-sharing is done on a first-come, first-served basis, and demands for the funds generally far outrun supply. Moreover, this system tends to channel funds disproportionately to those counties that have aggressive state forest personnel and financially sophisticated owners (precisely the type of owner most likely to engage in forest management even without state aid).[11]

Although such programs are a step in the right direction, it would be even better to link tax and subsidy directly, perhaps through the state income tax (all southern states except Florida, Tennessee, and Texas levy such a tax). When timber is sold, a severance tax would be applied to the proceeds; reforestation expenditures could be applied as a partial credit against the tax due. This would not only better link harvest and regeneration but would significantly reduce costs of administration.

Because many desirable management practices do not involve commercial harvest, it might be useful to earmark part of the revenue from the timber severance tax (for example, revenues obtained from land that the owner intends to convert to another use and that is thus not replanted) for subsidizing such practices.

Some care must be taken to ensure that management subsidies do not promote investments, particularly "hard" or capital-intensive ones, that would have a low rate of return in the absence of the subsidy. Moreover, the severance tax cannot be very high, or it would in the short run severely reduce a state's current rate of timber harvest and thus injure its processing industries. The solution to both problems is a moderate severance tax used to fund cost-sharing that is widely dispersed among owners but is fairly low in absolute amount per owner. Rather than giving a minority of owners a 50 to 75 percent cost-share, it would seem better to offer all owners a 20 to 30 percent benefit, perhaps with a dollars-per-acre cap to encourage low-investment methods. The purpose of the "subsidy," in fact, should not be to encourage uneconomic investments but to motivate owners (through the severance tax/management credit mechanism) to devote more attention to profitable management opportunities.

Timber Development Districts. One of the South's greatest potential timber resources is its large amount of nonindustrial private land, principally in the Piedmont and Upper Coastal Plain, that is physically well suited for timber growing but is located in areas where the local market for stumpage is relatively poor. In addition to having the management problems associated with nonindustrial ownership generally, this land seems caught in a special sort of circularity that discourages timber management. Landowners in these areas are reluctant to put much money into forest improvement because current stumpage prices are so low. In large areas of the South, this is principally due to the fact that there are no nearby mills or such a small number that there is little competition in the stumpage market. From the processor's point of view, however, these areas are not promising as mill sites because so much of the land is unmanaged.

State policy can break this circle of low investment and low profitability. Promising but underproductive forest areas, probably several counties in extent, should be designated as timber develop-ment districts (TDD). Within a TDD, landowners could receive special incentives for forest management, including more access to forestry advice and greater cost-sharing for timber management. The additional costs would be financed by state revenue bonds, similar to those commonly used in financing industrial plants. At maturity, the bonds would be redeemed with the proceeds from an additional severance tax, levied only within the TDD.

On the strength of the expected, and relatively predictable, tree growth that would be induced within the TDD, the state could use its present industrial development agency (virtually all southern states have a very active one) to attract processing plants to the area. The availability of a guaranteed fiber base would be particularly appealing to paper mills, which because of their huge raw material requirements are running out of suitable locations in the South.

The TDD concept borrows two ideas from general economic development experience. One is the long-time practice in the South of attracting labor-intensive manufacturing firms by offering to provide appropriate training to a local labor force. In this case, the availability of raw material rather than of trained labor would be encouraged by the state. The second idea is "tax increment financing," the practice of financing public improvements that will increase an area's attractiveness to business by issuing bonds funded by the increased tax revenues that the new businesses would generate. This device has been widely and successfully used to finance urban infrastructure.

Other Forest Policies. There are four other important actions that would greatly aid the further development of the South's wood-production potential. The first is promoting exports of southern forest products.[12] As mentioned in chapter 3, both the South's natural endowments and the sophistication of its processing industry make it a potential world-class competitor. Yet most producers have little experience in selling abroad. The industry itself, through its regional and national trade associations, will have to do most of the job of export promotion. But state governments can make strategic grants for that purpose, can promote exports through conferences and publications, and can make forest products an important part of the foreign trade missions that public officials have increasingly undertaken.

A second important action is to make the stumpage market more competitive by providing landowners with timely and accurate information on prices for timber and for land. Some of this information can be obtained from commercial sources, notably *Timber Mart South*, a monthly compilation of stumpage and product prices that provides a subregional breakdown for 13 southern states.[13] Price data are also published by state forestry agencies in Louisiana and Mississippi (quarterly), Tennessee (bimonthly), and Kentucky (annually).[14] Several other southern states collect market information but do not publish it, although it may be used by forestry extension staff in dealing with landowners.

There are many nonresident owners of timberland who do not sell timber frequently and do not keep abreast of current market information. This deprives them of knowledge useful not only in getting a fair price for timber, but also in making decisions about harvest, stand improvement, or about buying or selling timberland.

At modest cost, a state forestry agency, a university, or a state forestry association could collect and publish regular data on representative land and stumpage sales and market trends, perhaps coupled with investment analyses of costs and returns to implementing management practices on a standard tract as affected by current costs and prices. This is very similar to what land-grant universities have long provided to farmers through market reporting services and "crop budgets."

A third action to aid development of the South's wood-production potential would be to overcome the limitations placed on timber management by small tract size. Roughly 20 percent of the South's forestland is in ownerships of fewer than 100 acres.[15] If one considers a management unit as a stand of more or less uniform age and species composition, the amount of land potentially affected by small tract size would be still higher. Moreover, there is some evidence that average tract size may be declining as forestlands are split into smaller parcels for investment or recreational purposes.[16]

Two approaches might be taken simultaneously to deal with this problem. First, state and local governments might make it more difficult to split parcels into sizes so small that productivity is reduced. One way to do this would be to withhold use-value assessment for forestry purposes (available in all southern states) on all newly created parcels below a certain size. Alternatively, new types of joint ownership for large parcels might allow several households to use land for recreation or investment without splitting it into small parcels.[17]

Second, ways should be found to aggregate the management of parcels that have already been split. Private forestry consulting firms sometimes do this on an ad hoc basis, arranging for simultaneous timber sales, planting, or thinning on the property of more than one customer at a time. More formal arrangements are also possible, such as the creation of timber cooperatives. A number of efforts have been made to form such cooperatives in the South, most of them unsuccessful. The timber industry has historically viewed them with suspicion, fearing that landowners might cooperate to force higher stumpage prices or to heighten competition between mills. Landowners, too, have been less than enthusiastic, because some have mature timber and others have little—thus, pooling their efforts results in unequal benefits.[18]

"Landowner objectives are just too diverse to get them involved in a true cooperative," says one forester familiar with the South, "but there are opportunities for more limited cooperation, such as aggregating half a dozen neighboring parcels for site preparation." Private consulting foresters might encourage more of this, if they can overcome many owners' fears that their services will be too costly and oriented to immediate harvest. As one forester put it, the consultants are "much better at forestry than at marketing their services." In recent years, industry, concerned about future fiber supply, has created what are, in effect, "captive" cooperatives by enrolling properties in landowner assistance programs. These programs raise timber productivity, but do not enhance competition and may overemphasize wood production at the expense of other values that owners desire.

Although both consultants and industry have an expanding role to play in the South, an additional source of management advice could be quite useful—namely, the creation of a "public interest consulting forestry firm," modeled after the New England Forestry Foundation (NEFF). The NEFF, founded in 1944, is a nonprofit corporation that provides a full range of forest management services, including planning and supervision of harvests, to owners of forestland in the New England states. A network of 20 field foresters serves 3,000 individual owners of over 1 million acres of land as well as 12,000 acres that the NEFF has acquired by donation. Field foresters charge market prices for their timber management services, but they offer owners advice attuned to both timber and nontimber values. "Most of our [clients] are just as interested in wildlife and the appearance of their property as in the income," says NEFF Executive Director John T. Hemenway. Nevertheless, under NEFF management many underproductive properties have been significantly upgraded over time as timber producers. A counterpart to NEFF in the South could serve as a model for soft silviculture and could encourage for-profit consulting foresters to broaden their repertory of recommended silvicultural approaches.

The fourth action to improve wood production would be to stimulate landowners to get in touch with professional foresters. One way to do this would be to require consultation with a forester as a condition of use-value taxation of timberland. Although all 13 southern states have use-value taxation laws (either preferential assessment or deferred taxation), most require the owners to do little or nothing to qualify for the benefit. About half the southern states require a minimum parcel size to qualify, but the minimums range only between 3 and 20 acres.[19] North Carolina requires preferentially taxed property to have a "sound management program," and Tennessee requires a "sound program of sustained yield management." However, there is no means of ensuring the owner's compliance.[20]

To ensure that the public actually gets good forest management in return for the tax break, preferential taxation should be conditioned on certification by a qualified forester that the land is "soundly managed consistent with the landowner's production objectives and with the long-term conservation of resources." The substance of the management requirement is so broad as to be easily met—the real purpose is to give landowners an occasion to periodically get in touch with a forester. The forester could be a state forestry employee, an extension forester, an industry landowner-assistance forester, or a private consultant.[21]

Conserving Productive Land and Resources

Although there are many opportunities for further developing the South's rural resources, not all of the available directions of development are sustainable over the long time periods for which the South must plan. Moreover, as I have indicated in previous chapters, some present uses of land in the South are permanently damaging the renewable resource base. There are three major problem areas: diversion of agricultural land and forestland to urban and built-up uses, soil erosion, and mismanagement of water resources.

In each case, policy should seek conservation rather than absolute preservation. If the South's population and industrial activity grows, surely some additional land will have to be urbanized. Similarly, it is unreasonable to try to hold erosion to zero or to fail to use some of the water that is available. The policy issue is to find the proper rate of resource consumption.

Urbanization of Productive Land

As was pointed out in chapter 6, two of the most persuasive reasons for limiting the urbanization of farm- and forestland in the South are the failure of the market to consider the unpriced values of open land (for example, esthetics, watershed, urban separation) and the problem of incompatibility between adjoining urban and nonurban uses. Both of these considerations appear to favor preserving agricultural land and forestland not in scattered parcels but in fairly large aggregations or "districts." Virginia, for example, adopted an agricultural districting law in 1977 that provides owners of farm- or forestland within districts with preferential property tax assessment, protection from special assessments for urban infrastructure, and protection from local laws that hinder agricultural activities. In return for these advantages, the landowner gives up, for the 4- to 8-year duration of the district, the right to develop or subdivide the land. (Provision is made for releasing land from the restriction on the death of an owner or in hardship cases.) A Virginia district must be at least 500 acres in size (with noncontiguous parcels allowed if they lie within a mile of the contiguous areas), and properties can only be included with the landowner's consent. As of mid-1984, Virginia had 107 agricultural districts in 19 of the state's 136 counties, including 468,000 acres.[22]

The large aggregation or "district" approach is also favored by the mechanics of preservation.[23] Designation of a critical mass of land devoted to either agriculture or forestry tends to support the various specialized markets and services without which agriculture or forestry could not thrive. Moreover, by excluding most or all urban-type uses, a district makes it less likely that the development of one parcel will set off a chain of speculative transactions affecting still other parcels. And, by concentrating land-retention efforts on properties within designated districts, government can better afford property tax abatements and other incentives than it could if such subsidies had to be universally available.

What characterizes an ideal district? It should be sufficiently large to provide the critical mass necessary for profitable farming or forestry. (In some cases, both uses might be encouraged within a single district.) It should contain land well suited to the use, both from the standpoint of fertility and operability and also with respect to social costs, such as soil erosion and pesticide runoff. The ideal district should also provide the public with esthetic enjoyment and more efficient settlement patterns. Naturally, in actual application, various compromises must be made. For example, in a given locality the most fertile soils may be so firmly in the path of development that the costs of retaining them would be unreasonable. Or a district might be created in conjunction with a proposed development or a rezoning so as to provide a wholesome mixture of developed and permanently undeveloped land.

Directing land-retention policy toward agricultural or forest districts by no means implies that there should be no other open land. The recommendation that land-retention efforts be concentrated in districts is simply a recognition that goals and mechanisms alike seem to favor preserving land aggregates rather than individual parcels.

More than one southern jurisdiction has already looked with favor on the district concept. Kentucky's agricultural district law, passed in 1982, is similar to Virginia's, with the added feature that land within districts is protected from annexation. In mid-1984, Kentucky had a total of 31 certified districts in 15 (out of 120) counties, with a total of nearly 38,000 acres within district boundaries.[24] An intergovernmental group in the fast-growing Raleigh-Durham-Chapel Hill area of North Carolina, the Triangle-J Council of Governments, has recently developed a variation on districting that would offer landowners tax assessments of 10 or 20 percent *below* use value in exchange for an 8- or 16-year commitment to the district.[25]

The Triangle-J proposal addresses what seems to be a major weakness of present districts—some of the benefits of joining a district, notably preferential assessment and exemption from regulation of nuisance-producing agricultural practices, are equally available to landowners outside the district.[26] Not all local governments, however, can afford to make still further tax concessions below use-value assessment. As an alternative, use-value assessment could be made available as a matter of right within a district but only by contract to properties outside a district. A contract, in this case, might require a commitment to agriculture for a specified period of time, with a particularly heavy financial penalty if the owner wishes to break the contract. It may be desirable to limit exemption from nuisance regulation ("right-to-farm" preference) to properties within the districts rather than allowing it for all scattered farm parcels.

The districting approach seems to be particularly suitable to the South because it is voluntary, because it concentrates on the better land, and because it addresses the issue of scale. Virginia economist J. Paxton Marshall, a close observer of the agricultural districts in his state, points out a further, long-term advantage. "The overriding merit of districting," says Marshall, "is that it requires landowners to cooperate to achieve a common goal."[27] By recognizing that an area is voluntarily earmarked for long-term agricultural or forest use, landowners and their local governments form common expectations that can guide future investment decisions, both in the private and the public sectors. Districts also become logical units for the promotion of forest productivity or for other public policies to aid agriculture.

In the absence of widespread adoption of agricultural districts, there are two other things that public authorities can do to protect farm- and forestland. First is simply to provide information about the location of a state's prime farmland and forestland. For several years, the local offices of the U.S. Soil Conservation Service have been releasing maps of prime and important farmlands in various counties, mostly using information from existing soil surveys. The maps are attractive and easy to understand. But, because of limited funding, the mapping job is far from complete. For example, maps are published or in progress for only 32 of Kentucky's 120 counties and 13 of Arkansas' 75.[28] Moreover, the maps do not identify prime forestland, either in terms of soil suitability or in terms of current forest cover. Expediting the publication of these maps, including information on forests, and distributing them widely may be the single most important thing the federal government could do to encourage the protection of rural productive lands in the South.[29]

A second interim step toward land protection is for state agencies to try, where technically possible and economically feasible, to avoid flooding, paving, installing sewers, or otherwise converting rural lands with important productive values. The federal government now has such a policy for its own projects. Some southern states, such as North Carolina, have state policies to that effect.[30] The object should not be to totally eliminate conversion of rural land to urban uses; rather, as with existing federal and state protection policies, there should simply be a requirement that government agencies consider impacts on productive lands and avoid adverse ones where there are reasonable alternatives.[31]

Controlling Soil Erosion

Another threat to agriculture, as well as a serious problem for water quality, is soil erosion. There is a large amount of literature on erosion policy in general.[32] Two ideas that have been extensively discussed at the national level appear to have particular relevance to the South.

One idea is "targeting"—that is, concentrating government erosion control efforts on the most erodible land rather than spreading them out evenly over all agricultural lands or making them available on a first-come, first-served basis. Targeting is particularly relevant to the South because of the drastic differences in erosion rates from one physiographic region to another.

For example, in the Piedmont, 41 percent of cropland is eroding at a rate greater than twice T-value (the "tolerable" rate of soil loss based on the rate at which new topsoil forms). In the Mississippi Valley Silty Uplands, 37 percent of cropland exceeds twice T-value. On the other hand, in the Mississippi Valley Alluvium and the Atlantic Coastal Flatwoods, only 3 percent of cropland has erosion of twice T-value or greater.[33]

In the [Virginia] coastal plain we know we need 4.3 million acres in pine to maintain the present industry and support limited expansion. We are losing 25,000 acres in the Coastal Plain and Piedmont—some to agriculture but most to urban use. We are never going to get the latter back. If the state had a real commitment to land-use planning, we could maintain that 4.3 million acres. What bothers me is that there is no broad policy toward land use.... It's not something even a governor can do. It's going to take a public groundswell over a long time.

JAMES GARNER, Virginia State Forester

Within subregions, erosion is also unevenly distributed, with some lands losing soil as much as 40 times as rapidly as it is formed. There are also differences from place to place in the sedimentation damage caused by a given rate of soil loss. Since 1981, a modest federal targeting effort has brought some concentration of resources in particularly erosion-prone sections of the country, including parts of Tennessee, Mississippi, and Alabama.[34] Thus far, the targeting has involved redirection of federal funds rather than a net increase, leading not unexpectedly to resistance from the areas losing support. Moreover, the number of "targeted" areas is threatening to balloon over time, again spreading out the funds.

Even if targeting is successful, it must be supplemented by a program to take certain of the most erodible and difficult to treat lands entirely out of crop production. Federal and state erosion control programs consist mainly of technical assistance to farmers and partial reimbursement of the cost of installing control measures. "It is not impossible to imagine," says one soil conservation writer, "that intensified educational, technical, and financial assistance in erosion-plagued West Tennessee. . .will not be enough to entice farmers into a conservation program."[35] Moreover, giving farmers in highly erodible areas additional funds for terracing or other structural methods of erosion control could represent a form of subsidy to farmers trying to cultivate land inherently unsuitable for crop production. It might be more cost-effective to simply pay the farmers to take the land out of crop use.

The federal government should help address this problem by denying participation in commodity price support programs to farmers who bring highly erodible land newly into production. And, as was done in the Soil Bank program in the 1950s and 1960s, there should be a program to retire to forest or pasture use existing croplands that cannot be cultivated without serious erosion damage or sediment production. The 1982 National Resources Inventory indicated that there are 5.0 million acres of cropland in the South where erosion currently exceeds twice T-value and where potential erodibility is so high that it could be reduced to a tolerable level only by conversion to grass or trees.[36]

Another study by the U.S. Department of Agriculture identified about 4 million acres of economically marginal cropland in the South that was in land capability classes averaging soil losses of 17.9 tons per acre per year (5 tons per acre is considered tolerable).[37] There are undoubtedly additional lands where crop production is more profitable but where the social costs of erosion exceed the private returns to continued crop production. Converting these lands to trees could help the South solve its softwood supply problem; devoting some of them to pasture would enable other, more suitable pasturelands to be used for crops without a loss in overall forage output. An encouraging note, as this book goes to press, is that Congress is giving serious consideration to including in the 1985 Farm Bill provisions that would penalize the draining of wetlands to increase crop production and that would encourage farmers to set aside their most erosion-prone land in a long-term "conservation reserve."

Managing Water Resources

As noted, the South has ample water for most uses, in most places, most of the time. The difficulties lie in periodic droughts and in the expected growth in industrial, irrigation, and household uses within particular watersheds or aquifer zones. The challenge for water policy is to manage these occasional conflicts without discouraging the use and development of what is otherwise a very abundant resource.

A first priority should be a better accounting of how water is currently used—by whom, for what purpose, and from what surface or underground source. A reporting requirement for large users (say, over 50,000 gallons per day) and a sample survey of other users would efficiently accomplish this and form the basis for identifying problem areas. Reporting requirements based on quantity used, not type of use, will ensure that agricultural irrigators and municipal water systems are treated the same as other users.

Surveys should also be conducted, where they are not now available, to determine the minimum stream-flow or reservoir-level requirements of the various "instream uses" of water—for navigation, fish and wildlife, recreation. Except in unusual circumstances, these uses should be given priority for the minimum amount of water needed to sustain them.[38] Adding instream requirements to the withdrawals of present users and subtracting both from available supplies will identify current problem areas; continued monitoring will help pinpoint areas of increasing demand.

After these diagnostic steps have been taken, state governments can move deliberately to set up a system that codifies the right to use water and specifies how the burden of drought will be apportioned among users. The best approach to take, in my judgment, is a system based primarily on freely transferable private property rights.[39] The initial allocation of rights should be based on currently established private rights (generally established under the riparian doctrine for surface water and the doctrine of reasonable use for groundwater) as limited by protection of the normal requirements of instream uses. In most places in the South, current users with riparian rights will not exhaust the available water supply, and users without riparian rights should be allowed to establish rights to water, again subject to reasonable use. Because groundwater and surface water are frequently physically interconnected, it may be advisable to set up the same system for managing both resources, or at least to coordinate management.

In most areas, a new source of demand for water, or expansion of an existing one, would be able to establish additional rights simply by putting water to a reasonable use.[40] If, as water demands increase, demand begins to outstrip normal supply, new users would have to purchase or lease rights from those who already have established them. For example, if municipal or industrial water demands rise in an area where irrigators already exhaust the water available in a normal year, the municipal or industrial users should pay the irrigators either to not irrigate, to shift to less water-intensive crops, or to install equipment (and several options are generally available) that would conserve water. It is probably best to let the market decide which of the economic uses of water should have precedence in a given area rather than trying to decide the matter politically.

Year to year droughts can be dealt with somewhat differently.[41] As water supplies fall below normal demand, each user ought to take a proportional cut in the amount that can be withdrawn from surface-water or groundwater sources. Instream uses should be guaranteed their normal amount, but a state committee, with

---

Lots of people who moved to Northwest Arkansas did so to get away from restrictions of society, to get out on their dirt road and do their own thing and not worry about anybody else. But now they have to get together with their neighbors to protect their water supply.

DONALD VOTH, rural sociologist, University of Arkansas

---

representation from wildlife, conservation, and recreation agencies, could be empowered to release part of the instream supply to other users provided findings are made that the damage of a lower water level to instream uses is outweighed by the economic value of the water to other users. (If that is the case, it might be best to auction part of the instream supply, with the proceeds put to some wildlife or recreational purpose.)

The economic users of water (agriculture, municipalities, industry) should be allowed to lease or trade their drought-restricted water allotments. In this way, those users who found a drought most intolerable would be able to bid water away from those users who find water useful but not essential. For example, a vegetable grower or an orchard owner might in a drought year bid water away from a farmer who irrigated wheat or corn.

In several parts of the South, important streams or aquifers cut across state boundaries and create potential interstate conflict.

To deal with present conflicts—and to anticipate the conflicts of the future—interstate compacts can be negotiated to determine how much water should be controlled by each state and under what circumstances. It is particularly important to protect in-stream uses in cases in which major Upland or Piedmont rivers provide water vital to wetland areas lying downstream in other states. The interstate agreement negotiated by Alabama, Georgia, Florida, and the U.S. Army Corps of Engineers in 1983 to guide water withdrawals and navigation development of the Apalachicola-Chattahoochee-Flint river system is a good example of both the problems of managing interstate water sources and of an attempt at a resolution that avoids lengthy and costly battles in administrative proceedings or in the federal courts.

Protecting the Natural and Human Environment

It would be a major achievement if the South were to enhance the economic value of its rural resources and practice enough stewardship to make a high level of productivity indefinitely sustainable. But that will not be enough. Many "unpriced values" would still be threatened, often in direct proportion to the success of economic development. There are a number of things that can be done, both publicly and privately, to see that the South's natural systems are protected, as well as the complex of cultural, historical, and recreational values that many call the "human environment."

Protection of Nature

A few of the steps needed to assure sustainable economic development also protect nature. For example, control of soil erosion not only conserves fertility but also keeps topsoil out of watercourses. The same water management system that assures equitable sharing of the burden of drought can, at least in theory, be modified so as to give a share to water-dependent wildlife. Generally, however, nature will not be protected unless specific measures are taken.

   Wetlands. Among the most valued—and most threatened—natural lands in the southern states are wetlands (see chapter 6). Since the early 1970s, most southern states have moved fairly aggressively to protect coastal (saltwater) wetlands, partly through specific state statutes, partly through more generalized coastal zone management or (in Florida) state land-use programs.[42] Alteration of coastal wetlands has also been regulated by Section 404 of the federal Clean Water Act of 1972, which set up a dredge and fill permit system administered by the U.S. Army Corps of Engineers.

Although there have been many specific lapses in both state and federal programs, the overall results in protecting coastal wetlands have been impressive. It is estimated that, in fiscal 1981, the combined application of federal and state permitting programs reduced the amount of conversion of vegetated saltwater wetlands in the Southeast and Gulf coasts by 70 to 85 percent of what was originally requested in permit applications.[43]

Inland or freshwater wetlands, however, are not adequately protected anywhere in the South.[44] Despite their significant values for wildlife, water purification, and flood control, freshwater

---

As other parts of the nation become more crowded and developed, it will not be jobs, growth, or energy availability that makes Alabama special. It will be Alabama's land—its forests, rivers, countryside, and wildlife—that truly makes our state special. And it will not be the potential to "develop" these resources that continues to attract attention, but rather their mere existence in such a natural and bountiful condition.

DOUG PHILLIPS, Board of Directors, The Alabama
Conservancy, remarks to Northern Alabama
Energy Seminar, Decatur, Alabama, June 1981

---

wetlands are subject to drainage or alteration for a wide variety of urban and agricultural uses. Of seven states nationally that have an explicit state act for the protection of such wetlands, none is in the South. Yet the South probably contains more freshwater wetlands than the rest of the coterminous United States combined.

A Georgia environmentalist, after praising his state's coastal wetland program, says flatly, "The State of Georgia does not have effective control over freshwater wetlands. Although the Corps [of Engineers] has some legal authority, it lacks manpower for oversight. In freshwater wetlands only big organizations even bother to apply for Corps permits." In South Carolina, a draft memorandum to the Governor's Council on Natural Resources and the Environment notes that in that state "there are no current state efforts to survey and protect freshwater wetlands."[45]

The extent of jurisdiction by the Corps of Engineers over the

South's freshwater wetlands is a matter of some dispute.[46] At present, the Corps does not claim authority over large areas believed by scientists to have wetland characteristics. The Corps also does not regulate a great deal of agricultural and forestry activity that involves drainage and removal of vegetation, without the deposit of fill material. In part, this limited jurisdiction is the result of the 1972 law, but it is also due to a tendency by the Corps to narrowly interpret its congressional mandate. In 1979, a Louisiana sportsmen's organization successfully sued the Corps to force it to require a permit for the clearing of bottomland hardwood forests for agricultural purposes.[47] However, the Corps has since maintained that the decision is binding only in the Western Judicial District of Louisiana and does not affect its Section 404 activities elsewhere in the South.

There are several things that might be done to better protect freshwater wetlands in the South. First, certain public subsidies that promote the draining and clearing of wetlands can be removed. These include the ability to write off a portion of clearing expenses against federal (and some state) income taxes. In addition, farmers who drain wetlands while enrolled in federal crop price-support or acreage set-aside programs could be penalized in proportion to the amount of wetland drained.

Second, there should be an accelerated federal program to monitor wetland status and trends. Although the Fish and Wildlife Service has recently added a great deal to knowledge of what is happening to the South's wetlands, these efforts are still incomplete. Moreover, they should be better integrated with the land-*use* surveys done by the Soil Conservation Service and the U.S. Forest Service, which might serve to connect trends in agricultural and forest production with trends in wetland area.

Third, the Corps of Engineers should be instructed by Congress to extend its 404 program to cover a wide range of wetland types and a larger number of the agricultural and forestry activities that are disturbing them. In theory, regulation of wetlands that do not directly affect navigable waterways might seem best left to the states rather than the Corps. But the Corps has now built up a significant body of expertise in wetland regulation—both developers and environmentalists are accustomed to dealing with it. Rather than immediately relying on the states, many of which lack the technical expertise, it seems better to give full respon-

sibility to the Corps initially, then let it slowly devolve some of
the implementation to the states. This has been done in some states
in coordinated state-federal regulation of coastal wetlands, apparently with some success.[48]

Natural Heritage Programs. When one considers protection
of the natural values of land, it quickly becomes apparent that
a systematic approach is needed. Limitations of funds, and the
legitimate demands of competing land uses, mean that not all
natural values can be preserved. But how can priorities be set?
As the director of preserve selection for the Nature Conservancy, a major land protection organization, put it:

> . . .it is difficult to evaluate and compare unlike entities—trees to snakes,
> oxbows to nesting areas. . . .We need a process that reduces natural
> phenomena to a common denominator so we can compare them.[49]

Starting in the early 1970s, the Nature Conservancy began to
develop a means of systematically inventorying those natural
features within a state that were most valuable and most threatened. The Conservancy's system, called a "natural heritage inventory," has three steps: (1) identify elements of natural
diversity—plant and animal species and communities—and rank
them according to rarity; (2) identify lands where the highest-
rated elements occur; (3) use the rankings, and information about
the sites' vulnerability, to set protection priorities.

Over the last decade, nearly all of the 13 southern states have
created state natural heritage programs based more or less on the
Nature Conservancy model.[50] There are several strong programs
that already have amassed large quantities of inventory data, a
couple of programs that are underfunded, and three very recent
programs that are just getting organized.

One of the most active state programs is the effort of the Arkansas Natural Heritage Commission, which began in 1978.[51] Its staff
of a dozen state employees tracks 500 species of plants and 200
species of animals. Data have been accumulated by surveying
scientific literature, by examining museum and university
specimen collections, by aerial survey, and by field inspections.
A computerized data bank, backed with maps, contains some
3,500 "element occurrences," consisting of places in Arkansas
where a species or vegetative community considered worthy of
preservation can be found. A landowner or a state agency plan-

ning a new development could, in theory, obtain information from this file about what natural systems might be affected.[52]

Because Arkansas does not have a state environmental impact statement (EIS) requirement, this potentially valuable feature is not automatically applied to all major projects, even those initiated

---

Even between rare communities it is possible to set priorities. If they cannot all be preserved or if some must be chosen to be preserved before others are given protection, then surely the rare communities that represent formerly widespread types of environments merit first attention.... The next generation of Arkansans likely will stand to gain less economic benefit from research on our uncommon native prickly-pear cactus than from understanding the hardwood forests that once covered most of the State and their relationships with the soils that supported them. It is sobering to note that not a single virgin hardwood forest has come to the attention of the staff that prepared this report.

STATE OF ARKANSAS, Arkansas Natural Area
Plan, 1974

---

by the state. However, the data file is used in reviews mandated by several specific state statutes as well as in reviews of federal or federally funded projects needing an EIS under the National Environmental Policy Act.

The Arkansas commission also tries to protect natural areas by acquisition. It has thus far acquired 28 tracts ranging in size from 13 to 1,200 acres. In some cases, the land has been bought outright; in others, only a conservation easement was sought. The state has also negotiated nearly 80 agreements with private landowners to have tracts listed in a state registry of natural areas, with a voluntary commitment to preserve important natural qualities.

A staff member emphasizes how the inventory helps to set protection priorities that are tailored to the particular needs of the state: "In Arkansas, we've been going after prairies, where several hundred thousand acres have been reduced to only a few thousand; high-quality bottomland timber areas; habitats of rare plants and animals; glades that have not been heavily grazed; upland forests, beech forests, cypress, and blackland prairies. We're trying to set aside areas as they were prior to settlement to serve as baseline cases."

The single greatest need of natural heritage programs across the South is more money, for speeding the rate of inventory (and in many cases making new biological surveys) and for protection programs. Says Robert Jenkins, vice-president for science of the Nature Conservancy:

> I'm tremendously proud of these programs in the South, but they need a federal partner to help with the funding. There are so many programs in state government that depend on the handing down of federal funds. But the Interior Department's Heritage Conservation and Recreation Service has been abolished and the Land and Water Conservation Fund cut severely. Now the federal funding [for land conservation] is just a trickle. If we had just $10 million yearly in federal funding, we could practically guarantee the continuance of these state programs and could keep them from the constant distraction of securing their futures instead of doing their job.

Land Protection. Although inventories are not very costly, actual land protection involves large sums of money. Both public and private agencies have important roles. On the public side, Florida has been a leader in natural area protection, earmarking large amounts of state funds for identifying and purchasing beaches, river corridors, and wetlands.

Private nonprofit organizations have also been increasingly active in land protection. The Nature Conservancy, which is a national organization based in Arlington, Virginia, has acquired tens of thousands of acres in the South, some of which it has retained, some of which have been resold to state or federal agencies. The organization has been particularly active along the South Atlantic Coast, where it has purchased important shoreline and barrier island properties, and in bottomland hardwood areas. In 1980, the Conservancy received a $15 million grant from the Richard King Mellon Foundation to acquire and protect bottomland hardwood forests along six important southern river systems. The Conservancy has over the years also received major donations of land from timber companies, much of it swampy or otherwise unsuitable for intensive silviculture.

At the regional and state levels, a number of nonprofit groups have also been active in land protection, particularly in educating landowners and encouraging them to donate easements that restrict development of scenic or environmentally sensitive lands. Among the more prominent southern groups are the Virginia Outdoors Foundation, the Georgia Conservancy, the Alabama Conservancy, the Southern Appalachian Highlands Conservancy (in Tennessee), and the Land and Nature Trust of the Bluegrass (in Kentucky).

Finally, one should not discount the land-protection actions of individual landowners, which are arguably more important than all the organized actions. In conversations with farmers and forest owners, one frequently hears of bottomlands and field margins left uncleared for wildlife, of large trees unfelled because the owner "just likes to have them around," and of small plantings of food crops for wildlife. Some of this activity is related to the owner's desire to improve hunting, but a great deal is motivated by a personal interest in wildlife or a sense of duty to the land. Timber companies, which own large tracts of land with environmental or recreational values, quite frequently protect these lands, either by setting aside tracts entirely or by modifying management to protect particular features such as den trees. Interest in land protection varies from company to company, but a few employ full-time wildlife biologists.

Wildlife Policies. Although the ideal way to protect the whole range of natural values associated with southern land is probably through systematic natural heritage programs, practicality dictates that protection efforts be closely allied with existing, usually species-specific, wildlife programs. Such programs include the traditional game management and game habitat programs of state fish and wildlife agencies as well as a recently burgeoning number of nongame programs. They also include the efforts of the federal Fish and Wildlife Service, which operates more than 90 national wildlife refuges in the South, and which takes a leading role in monitoring populations of endangered and threatened species and devising recovery plans for them.

Even when wildlife programs, whether game or nongame, are oriented solely to specific species, they often result in the protection of ecosystems with much broader natural values. For example, the Noxubee National Wildlife Refuge, in central Mississippi, was originally set up to aid migratory waterfowl; it is one of the southern refuges used most intensively for recreational hunting and fishing. But it also is home to one of the South's largest populations of endangered red-cockaded woodpeckers, individual trees of national-record size, many songbirds, and a number of special natural areas, including a pond with an array of unusual salamanders.[53]

Although there are countless such examples of the interaction of wildlife policies and natural-areas protection, the South could benefit greatly if the ties between the two were made more explicit. On one side, the relatively small group of scientists and environmentalists concerned with natural diversity could use the great political clout of the organized hunters and fishermen. On the other side, the game interests are finding increased pressure on both habitat and access and could use a new rationale for wildlife programs that are likely to be ever more costly in the years ahead. Both groups, moreover, could gain by tapping the substantial, but largely unorganized, public sympathy for the more glamorous nongame species.

Quite recently, state wildlife agencies all over the country, in-

cluding many in the South, have reached out to a broader con-
stituency by creating nongame wildlife programs supported by
state income tax "check-offs" (voluntary contributions on the tax
return). In the 1983 tax year, the states of Alabama, Arkansas,
Kentucky, Louisiana, North Carolina, Oklahoma, South Carolina,
and Virginia raised over $1.5 million through this device.[54]
Because these programs are so new and the amount of money
that will eventually be raised is so uncertain, many of the southern
states do not have firmly fixed ideas on what the scope of their
nongame program should be. Many anticipate educational activities, including work with the public schools; programs to
benefit endangered species; biological studies; and (if funds permit) habitat acquisition. Several programs have tried to capture
public attention by reintroducing species that have been extirpated
in all or part of their states—the osprey in Kentucky, the river
otter in Oklahoma, the bald eagle and peregrine falcon in North
Carolina, the Delmarva fox squirrel in Virginia.[55]

Nongame check-off programs offer a promising means of
broadening the view of state fish and wildlife agencies, which,
because of their traditional reliance on hunting and fishing license
fees, have understandably given most of their attention to the
relatively small number of game species. However, it would be
unfortunate if the single-species model so dominant in game management—and a concentration on a handful of desirable species—
is transferred into the nongame area. It is not encouraging that
several state nongame programs leave endangered plants under
the generally unenthusiastic purview of the state department of
agriculture and that Alabama's new nongame program excludes
not only plants but invertebrates.[56] Although the glamorous bird
and mammal species deserve attention and are useful in generating
public support, nongame programs offer a major opportunity for
moving wildlife management away from individual species and
toward the management of multi-species systems. Greater involvement of environmental groups in the nongame programs and
closer ties to state natural heritage programs may be one way to
ensure that this opportunity will not slip away.

Traditional wildlife managers and environmentalists should also
cooperate in addressing an increasingly serious question faced by
both. That is, how far should they push to commercialize or
"monetize" various unpriced wildlife values of rural land. As crop

production, forestry, and other marketed values increasingly compete for land, the unpriced values will be at an ever greater disadvantage. One way around this is to make marketable commodities out of some unpriced values—charging for hunting rights, for example, or giving landowners subsidies or tax breaks in return for protecting natural areas or allowing public recreation.

This option creates two generic problems. First, landowners may charge for doing things that they previously provided gratis. If leasing hunting rights spreads over the South, for example, timber companies will soon charge for hunting on land that heretofore was open to public use.[57] Or, if owners are subsidized to protect wetlands or natural areas, many of those who line up for the subsidy will be persons who would have protected the resource in any case.

Second, whatever values are commercialized become additional competing uses for land, and an economic incentive is created to produce more of them at the expense of those values that remain unpriced. For example, the increased commercialization of hunting would lead to more land managed to maximize production of game species, perhaps at the expense of nongame species.

Although the potential commercialization of unpriced values offers a promising answer to many of the South's land-use problems, it is not an unmixed blessing and its side effects must be carefully weighed.

Special Role of the Public Lands

Public lands occupy less than 10 percent of the South's land area.[58] But they have a special role because of the nature of their ownership and some of their physical characteristics. Particularly important are the 36 national forests in the South, plus a handful of other large federal landholdings, including the Everglades, Shenandoah, and Great Smoky Mountains national parks, and several large national wildlife refuges and national seashores. These lands are distinguished, first, by their size—the Ouachita National Forest in Arkansas and Oklahoma, for example, contains 1.6 million acres, and Everglades National Park has 1.4 million. Sixteen of the national forests in the South contain over 200,000 acres each.[59] The huge areas involved make public lands unusually important as wildlife habitats, particularly for such solitude-loving creatures as the black bear and the eastern cougar. They also allow opportunities for human solitude that are otherwise difficult to find in the densely settled eastern half of the United States. In the Everglades, for example, 1.3 million acres are in designated wilderness.

A second special characteristic of the South's public lands is that they contain so many areas of unusual scenic quality or natural rarity. Most of the highest mountain peaks in the Southern Appalachians are in state or federal hands, as are many of the remaining undisturbed barrier beaches and coastal wetlands. And public lands include literally hundreds of the South's minor beauty spots—places like Manatee Springs State Park in Florida or Shining Rock Wilderness in North Carolina's Pisgah National Forest or Chincoteague National Wildlife Refuge in coastal Virginia.

A third special quality of the public lands is that most are not managed to maximize revenues but to produce either unpriced values (such as wildlife or recreation) or for a mixture of market and nonmarket values (the "multiple use" national forests).

It is not my purpose here to give detailed policy recommendations for the public lands.[60] But the special qualities that I have just ascribed to the South's public lands strongly suggest an overarching principle to guide their management: the South's public lands should provide market and nonmarket goods that are not adequately produced on the region's private lands. This management principle suggests that public land managers should pay more attention to how nearby private lands are being managed. It also implies that some aspects of public land management should change over time as the uses of private lands change.

Timber management is a good example. During the 1930s and 1940s, when relatively few private lands in the South were managed for sustained-yield fiber production, it was quite appropriate for the national forests to provide large-scale demonstrations of reforestation and modern forest management. But now that industry lands are widely available as examples of intensive management, public forests should put relatively more emphasis on testing and demonstrating models of soft silviculture or wildlife management.

Public forests should also contribute to maintaining vegetative diversity, with consideration given to how these forests fit into the landscape mosaic of both private and public land. If, because of the current combination of land abandonment, natural succession, and timber cutting, private forestlands provide a diverse habitat, with many small openings and a great deal of land in relatively early stages of regeneration, then public forests might emphasize larger, more uniform areas of vegetation managed on long rotations. If vegetation on private lands is becoming more uniform and unbroken, then public lands should be managed for more frequent openings and greater habitat diversity.

More attention should also be paid to coordinating acquisition and management of lands among the many state and federal agencies that administer them. For example, it has been suggested that extensive state and federal lands running from the Okefenokee National Wildlife Refuge in southern Georgia to Florida's Waccassassa Bay State Preserve and other lands on the Gulf of Mexico could be linked by a series of protected riverine corridors that would allow free migration of wildlife.[61] This could greatly aid the recovery of large animals such as the Florida panther and the black bear.

The Distinctive Southern Landscape

The visual environment of the rural South may be even more in need of attention than is the natural environment. There are several obvious threats: urban sprawl, neglect of desirable features of the historic landscape, and lack of regional identity in new development. Although it is relatively easy to describe what one likes and doesn't like about the visual landscape, it is much more difficult to suggest relevant policies.

This is partly because the visual landscape is so much a matter of individual taste, an area in which coercive policies or even strong incentives tend to be as arbitrary as they are infeasible. It is partly a result of the fact that, even if there were general agreement on landscape tastes at any one point in time, the nature of landscapes is to evolve over time, responding to the changing economy and to changing tastes.

Despite these difficulties, there are positive things that can be done, not all of them by government. First, southerners need to become sensitized to the special qualities of their built environment, in much the same way that environmental education has made many aware of the special qualities of the natural environment. There is, of course, a general familiarity with a few of the features of colonial and antebellum architecture. Indeed, there is a lively tourist trade based on it, both in historic houses such as Shadows-on the-Teche (New Iberia, Louisiana) and Monticello (Charlottesville, Virginia) and in the many restored areas in southern towns and cities, including Charleston, South Carolina; Williamsburg, Virginia; St. Augustine, Florida; Winston-Salem, North Carolina; New Orleans, Louisiana; and Savannah, Georgia. But these places are so "special" that it is hard for people to make

---

Historically, the South has been a land-focused society. A farmer may not talk of a land ethic in the sense of Aldo Leopold, but there is a relationship with the land, a closer tie than you find in a large metropolitan area elsewhere in the country. We are a conservative, not very mobile people, and I think that is something that can be appealed to in getting people to protect wilderness. We may not have "crown jewels," but there is a feeling that we should protect the special places we have.

JIM PRICE, Southeastern States field representative, Sierra Club

---

the connection between the values they preserve and the more modest virtues of more typical examples of southern architecture.

There is also an increasing interest in "living historical farms," which combine the preservation of old farm structures with exhibits and demonstrations of how people lived and worked at various times in southern history.[62] State and local governments in the South have done at least as much as those anywhere in the country to mark historic sites, lay out scenic drives, and put old public buildings to new uses. And all over the South individual homeowners are restoring residential buildings, ranging from pillared plantation houses to Victorian cottages. But all of this activity has in most places not yet reached the "critical mass" necessary to reach the public as a whole.

A major public education and consciousness-raising effort is needed to get ordinary people across the South interested in their "built environment," both at the scale of individual buildings and at the scale of entire "landscapes." This effort should enlist state and local governments, the South's philanthropic organizations, schools and colleges, and museums. Environmental organizations, which have fixed most of their attention on the natural environment, should also participate. The effort could involve media presentations (films and television programs), museum exhibits, conferences and lectures, and identification of sites with suitable interpretative markers.[63] Just as decades of environmental interpretation and education preceded the sudden burgeoning of environmental policy in the early 1970s, a greater public appreciation of the man-made environment of the South is a necessary precondition to policies that would preserve and revivify it.

Getting people interested in the "built environment' and "human-influenced landscapes" is only the first step. Active preservation measures are needed, many of them rather similar to measures I have already described that protect the natural environment. Just as there is a need for more inventories of natural areas in the South, there should be more inventories of valued features of the man-made environment. Two good examples of what can be done on a scale that goes beyond individual structures are both the work of landscape architects: Meade Palmer's study of the Green Springs area of Louisa County, Virginia, and Allen Stovall's evaluation of the Sautee and Nacoochee valleys, historical rural areas in northern Georgia.[64] In a methodology closely paralleling that used in natural area protection, important historical, cultural, and landscape features were identified, as well as environmental constraints on development. The various constraints were then aggregated into composite maps that highlighted areas where absolute preservation was indicated and areas where some development could be absorbed.

Some of the new development should consist of restoring (and often moving to more suitable sites) some of the thousands of abandoned rural structures, many of them of great architectural merit. There is also a great deal of scope for creating a new southern architectural tradition that would borrow themes from the past in building new institutional, commercial, and residential structures. It happens that the architectural profession generally, influenced initially by a handful of "post-modernists," is turning to greater interest in historical borrowings, in decoration and in fitting new buildings into the context of neighboring structures. The South appears to offer a particularly fertile field for such endeavors.

Greater policy attention ought also to be paid to the pervasive visual clutter along southern roads and highways, which is among the worst in the nation. Says Charles Floyd, a University of Georgia professor who is president of the National Coalition for Scenic Beauty,

> We are pretty well junked up with billboards in the Southeast. We used to think that they were necessary for economic development. . .though attitudes are changing. But even now some states allow such practices as the cutting of trees on public property that obscure a clear view [from the roadway] of privately owned billboards.[65]

A recent report by the Federal Highway Administration seems to confirm his impressions. It ranked states on the basis of numbers of highway signs per mile. Of the 10 states with the highest sign density nationally, 6 (North Carolina, Louisiana, Mississippi, Arkansas, Florida, and Kentucky) were in the South.[66] Seven southern states were also among the top 10 nationally in density of unscreened roadside junkyards.[67] Visual blight is also very common along in-town commercial streets, particularly the "rollaway billboard," a portable marquee with flashing lights that lines southern commercial strips in enormous numbers.

A handful of efforts have been made to try to control billboard and commercial sign proliferation in the South. Virginia has limited billboards along interstate highways, replacing them with standardized informational signs near exits. There have also been some efforts by environmental organizations to limit visual blight. For example, the Sierra Club Legal Defense Fund has sued the southeastern regional administrator of the Federal Highway Administration to compel South Carolina to enforce the billboard controls of the 1965 federal Highway Beautification Act. The Sierra Club charged that South Carolina has violated the federal law by such practices as zoning huge stretches of roadside as commercial or industrial (which exempts them from federal sign control) and by failing to remove thousands of illegal billboards.[68] There are also some local organizations pressing for state or local sign control, including Vistas Unlimited, in Raleigh, North Carolina; Quality Forward, in Asheville, North Carolina; and Billboards Limited, in Houston. Some southern municipalities, both large ones such as Fayetteville (Arkansas), Raleigh, and Houston and small towns such as Garner, North Carolina, and Lake Wales, Florida, have acted on their own to limit commercial signs and billboards. In 1984, the city of New Orleans adopted new zoning provisions for commercial strips that not only tighten sign regulations (including a ban on flashing signs) but subject fast food restaurants and similar commercial developments to special land-scaping and setback requirements.

Protecting Drinking Water

The condition of the nation's drinking water has, in the last several years, become a major national issue. The 1974 Safe Drinking Water Act provides for testing public water supplies for a limited range of potential contaminants; there are a variety of federal and state programs limiting point-source discharges into both surface water and groundwater. Much of the pollution of drinking-water supplies in the South, as elsewhere, derives from industrial or municipal discharges or from improper disposal of toxic wastes, both of which are the subjects of many policies that cannot be addressed here.

However, there are two aspects of drinking-water policy that are particularly relevant to the land-use changes I have been analyzing. First is the need to protect important aquifer recharge areas from the impacts of unplanned human settlement. Florida, which faces intense development pressure atop several of the aquifers on which it depends for most of its drinking water, has tried at both the state and local level to zone sensitive lands for low densities.[69] But these activities are not systematic, either in Florida or in other southern states. Therefore, I suggest that, in those places where aquifer recharge areas are found, local governments be required to promulgate (under state supervision) development regulations sufficient to protect groundwater quality and quantity.

A second problem is the possible pollution of drinking water, either surface or subsurface, with farm and forest chemicals. The top priority in this case is better monitoring—looking in more places for a wider variety of substances. In 1984, Florida required public water suppliers to test for 127 chemicals in addition to those for which testing is required by federal law.[70] The new chemicals included the carcinogenic insecticide EDB as well as a number of other pesticides. But these are only a handful of the estimated 9,000 pesticides that have been used in Florida.[71] A state groundwater sampling program, budgeted at $2 million yearly, will greatly broaden Florida's monitoring of commonly used agricultural chemicals; EPA has recently begun a national testing program of its own.

Although agricultural chemicals are heavily used in the South, and many southern agricultural soils are highly permeable, there is a shocking lack of knowledge about how much of these substances are leaching into water sources. Monitoring programs should therefore be given high priority and be extended to all the principal agricultural areas of the South.

If pesticide contamination proves widespread, as many suspect, the existing regulatory system will have to be modified. Florida, for example, is a leader in aquifer classification and regulation of point sources of pollution that threaten aquifers. Yet the state lacks authority to regulate normal agricultural activities, such as pesticide application, that could cause nonpoint pollution of drinking water. Pesticides can be banned outright, but most government agencies do this with reluctance, given the economic importance of pesticides. One suggestion, made by an agricultural researcher at the big federal laboratory in Tifton, Georgia, responds to the fact that soil type is crucial to whether or not a given chemical will reach groundwater. He suggests that pesticides be registered for specific soils, much as they are now registered for specific crops. This would permit them to be used in agriculture but selectively banned for those soils where infiltration into groundwater is likely to occur.[72]

A Concluding Note

So distinctive have been the history and traditional culture of the South, so fascinating have been its human characters and its great social struggles, they have tended to obscure present-day conditions and the South's future possibilities. Outside of a narrow specialist audience, far more is known about slavery and the now-defunct sharecropping system than about the present behavior of soybean farmers or the structure and growth of the pine timber industry, two activities that in acreage occupied and in economic product rival cotton at its height.

After the wrenching agricultural changes of the 1930s, the post-World War Two growth of scientific forestry and of the cattle and poultry industries, and with the continuing changes in human settlement patterns, the South is a place very different from what it was only a few decades ago. I believe that future development will be even less dependent on its history, at least in the ordinary sense of social and cultural history. Yet future development in the South will be dependent on some other distinctive and fundamental qualities: its soils, its water resources, its sunlight and growing season, its location relative to national and regional markets. These factors, as I have pointed out in specific examples throughout this book, are vitally important to future opportunities—and limitations—in agriculture, in forestry, and in animal raising. In our mobile and amenity-seeking culture, the South's topography, its scenery, and its recreational opportunities will be increasingly important in determining how fast its population and even its industry will grow.

This book has tried to look comprehensively at the South's productive land base, tracing its recent history, analyzing its present use and conditions, and looking ahead to how it might face the uncertain demands of the future. Much as the South's future will be affected by soil, water, climate, and other such physical attributes, it will be, as in the colorful past, determined by what its people make of them.

References

1. Stephen L. Rawlins, unpublished paper delivered at Conference on Changing Agricultural Production Systems and the Fate of Agricultural Chemicals, sponsored by the Agricultural Research Institute, Washington, D.C., February 21, 1984.

2. Robert E. Sojka, Agricultural Research Service, Florence, S.C., telephone interview, April 1984.

3. One wonders whether if, like the improved strains of wheat and rice that launched world agriculture's "green revolution," the supertrees will be particularly responsive to fertilization and irrigation, increasing the incentive to use these techniques in forestry.

4. R.S. Fecso, et al., *Management Practices and Reforestation Decisions for Harvested Southern Pinelands* (Washington, D.C.: U.S. Department of Agriculture, Statistical Reporting Service, 1982) p. 60.

5. Ibid., p. 56.

6. This recommendation is echoed in a recent report on forestry by the Tennessee Valley Authority. "The key to improved forest management," says the report, "is to develop markets that will encourage the harvest of small, low-quality hardwoods now, and create the economic incentive to improve quality and productivity in the future." Tennessee Valley Authority, *Forestry in the Tennessee Valley: Looking Beyond the Year 2000* (Knoxville: Tennessee Valley Authority, 1984), p. iv.

7. Some specific suggestions on methods of hardwood utilization, as well as on new possibilities in hardwood silviculture, are contained in Thomas F. McLintock, *Research Priorities for Eastern Hardwoods* (Asheville, N.C.: Hardwood Research Council, 1979). A recent review of developments in wood products technology is contained in U.S. Office of Technology Assessment, *Wood Use,* Vol. II—Technical Report (Washington, D.C.: U.S. Government Printing Office, 1984).

8. In 1985, as part of a general tax revision, the Reagan administration proposed to eliminate capital gains treatment of timber profits and acccelerated amortization of reforestation expenses. At this writing, the proposals had not been acted on by Congress.

9. Since 1981, the Texas Forest Service has administered a 65 percent cost-sharing program funded entirely by the forest industry.

10. See Gordon Meeks, Jr., "State Incentives for Nonindustrial Private Forestry," *Journal of Forestry*, vol. 80, no. 1 (January 1982), pp. 18-22, and Southern Growth Policies Board, *Report on the Duke/SGPB Forest Policies Project* (Raleigh: Southern Growth Policies Board, 1982), appendixes C and D. Many southern states now levy a severance tax on timber to compensate for the fact that they do not apply ad valorem property taxes to standing timber. Any severance tax earmarked for forest management would have to be additional to the existing rate.

11. A recent study of North Carolina's state reforestation aid program found that most of the state funds were not going to those counties where the greatest timber harvesting was taking place. "This lack of correlation between the top

softwood producing counties and the counties receiving the most cost-sharing funds reflects poorly on the first-come, first-served system," said the study. Howard Muse and Bill Finger, "Small Woodlot Management: A New Challenge for Smokey," *North Carolina Insight* (June 1983), p. 36.

12. This is also recommended in the previously cited reports by the Southern Growth Policies Board and the Tennessee Valley Authority.

13. Priced at $175 per year and with a circulation of fewer than 1,000 copies monthly, the publication is intended for specialists.

14. Barry N. Rosen, "Price Reporting of Forest Products to Nonindustrial Private Forest Landowners," *Journal of Forestry*, vol. 82, no. 8 (August 1984), pp. 491-95. A Mississippi-based consulting forestry firm, James M. Vardaman and Company, publishes a quarterly newsletter for its customers with a region-wide index of land and sawtimber prices and with some analysis of trends and investment opportunities.

15. Thomas W. Birch, Douglas G. Lewis, and H. Fred Kaiser, *The Private Forest-Land Owners of the United States*, Bulletin WO-1, U.S. Forest Service (Washington, D.C.: U.S. Government Printing Office, 1982). The data are adjusted to account for government ownership.

16. See Robert G. Healy and James L. Short, *The Market for Rural Land: Trends, Issues, Policies* (Washington, D.C.: The Conservation Foundation, 1981).

17. This idea is explained at greater length in Ibid., p. 267-72.

18. See Perry R. Hagenstein, "Forestry and the Appalachian Regional Commission," Report to the Appalachian Regional Commission, May 1974.

19. Clifford A. Hickman, "Use-Valuation Eases Property Tax Burden," *Forest Farmer*, vol. 43, no. 2 (November-December 1983), pp. 16-17; telephone interview with Clifford A. Hickman, New Orleans, October 1984.

20. General Statutes of North Carolina Sec. 105-277.2; Tennessee Code Annotated Sec. 67-5-1001-1010. In Tennessee, county assessors have the option of seeking advice of the state forester before preferentially assessing forestland.

21. It is quite possible that some private consultants would offer such a service at very low cost or even gratis, because of the landowner contacts it would engender. I note that in 1983 the Alabama chapter of the Association of Consulting Foresters agreed to give up to one-half day of free service to members of the Alabama Forest Owners Association located within a reasonable distance (and generally with a 50-acre minimum-sized parcel).

22. Data from Virginia Department of Agriculture, August 1984.

23. U.S. National Agricultural Lands Study, *The Protection of Farmland: A Reference Guidebook for State and Local Governments* (Washington, D.C.: U.S. Government Printing Office, 1981), pp. 76-84.

24. Data from Kentucky Department of Natural Resources, June 1984.

25. Leon E. Danielson, *Public Policymaking: A Rural Land-Use Case Study of the Public Policy Process*, Economics Special Report No. 84 (Raleigh: North Carolina State University, Department of Economics and Business, 1984).

26. Virginia's districting law offers preferential assessment to properties in a district even if the county concerned does not offer such assessment to agri-

cultural properties generally. However, at present this incentive to join a district is relevant to only a single county.

27. Telephone interview, Blacksburg, Va., October 1984.

28. National Association of State Departments of Agriculture, "Current State Farmland Protection Activities," (Washington, D.C.: National Association of State Departments of Agriculture, Farmland Project, 1984).

29. The present SCS maps are derived rather mechanistically from soil survey information, and their usefulness in land-use planning has been questioned. See John Fraser Hart, "Cropland Change in the United States, 1944-78," in Julian L. Simon and Herman Kahn, *The Resourceful Earth* (New York: Basil Blackwell, 1984), pp. 244-46. In my view, the SCS maps are an extremely effective way to bring the issue of loss of prime lands to the attention of local officials and the public. Actual attempts at land retention, however, should be based on the underlying soil surveys, as well as relevant information on the local agricultural economy and local requirements for urban land.

30. The North Carolina policy is contained in a gubernatorial Executive Order and has not been endorsed by the legislature. The order applies only to agencies in state government where the governor appoints the head. Personal communication, Leon E. Danielson, North Carolina State University, Raleigh, June 1985.

31. The U.S. Department of Agriculture has devised a useful site analysis system, called LESA (Land Evaluation and Site Assessment), which enables agencies to weigh the agricultural and developmental values associated with alternative sites. Information on LESA is available at local offices of the Soil Conservation Service. For a critical analysis, see F. Steiner et al., *Adapting the Agricultural Land Evaluation and Site Assessment System (LESA) in the Pacific Northwest* (Corvallis: Oregon State University, Western Rural Development Center, 1984).

32. See Sandra S. Batie, *Soil Erosion: Crisis in America's Croplands?* (Washington, D.C.: The Conservation Foundation, 1983); Soil Conservation Society of America, *Soil Conservation Policies: An Assessment* (Ankeny, Iowa: Soil Conservation Society of America, 1979).

33. Unpublished data from 1982 National Resources Inventory, U.S. Soil Conservation Service.

34. There has also been since 1979 a joint agreement between the U.S. Department of Agriculture and the Tennessee Valley Authority to target erosion control efforts on 21 high-risk counties in West Tennessee.

35. Kenneth A. Cook, "Conservation Policy under a Tightening Belt," *Journal of Soil and Water Conservation*, vol. 36, no. 3 (May-June 1981), p. 151.

36. Unpublished data from 1982 National Resources Inventory. The southern states having the largest acreages of such land are Kentucky (1.1 million acres), Mississippi (906,000 acres), and Tennessee (894,000 acres).

37. U.S. Department of Agriculture, Office of Budget and Program Analysis, *Conversion of Southern Cropland to Southern Pine Tree Plantings* (Washington, D.C.: U.S. Department of Agriculture, 1983).

38. These uses should be given priority partly because of the likelihood that reduction below some minimum flow would cause long-term damage (for ex-

ample, to wildlife), partly because this class of user is less able to defend itself in times of drought. (For example, barge operators, unlike farmers or municipalities, cannot conserve water.)

39. Because there are real costs, both governmental and nongovernmental, in defining property rights, it may not be advisable to try to do so in places where water is so plentiful that there is little likelihood of future conflict. See William E. Cox and Leonard A. Shabman, "Interbasin-Interstate Transfer of Water in the South," in *Future Waves: Water Policy in the South* (Mississippi State, Miss.: Southern Rural Development Center, 1983), pp. 31-42.

40. Although the management system recommended here relies primarily on the establishment of private property rights to water, there would still have to be a governmental administrative body to set rules on what constitutes "reasonable use" and to develop procedures to settle conflicts among users over such issues as the quantity and quality of return flows.

41. It would be more economically efficient to use the price system in case of drought, as well as for long-term allocation of water among users, but the fact that allocation by price would make it appear that the agency selling the rights was "profiting from an emergency" probably makes such an approach politically dubious.

42. See Jon A. Kusler, *Strengthening State Wetland Regulations*, report to the U.S. Fish and Wildlife Service (Washington, D.C.: U.S. Government Printing Office, 1978).

43. U.S. Office of Technology Assessment, *Wetlands: Their Use and Regulation* (Washington, D.C.: U.S. Government Printing Office, 1984), p. 144.

44. A limited amount of protection is afforded to freshwater wetlands in Arkansas and Kentucky by state regulation of floodways and in North Carolina, Virginia, and Florida by procedures for designation of areas of critical environmental concern. The latter have been used very sparingly.

45. South Carolina Governor's Council on Natural Resources and the Environment, "Recognition and Protection of South Carolina's Outstanding Natural Resources" (draft report, 1984).

46. See U.S. Office of Technology Assessment, *Wetlands*, pp. 167-83.

47. *Avoyelles Sportsmen's League* v. *Alexander*, 473 F. Supp. 525 W.D. La., 1979.

48. See U.S. Office of Technology Assessment, *Wetlands*, p. 13.

49. Philip M. Hoose, *Building an Ark* (Covelo, Calif.: Island Press, 1981), p. 8.

50. Robert E. Jenkins, Jr., "Planning and Developing Natural Heritage Programs", paper prepared for Indo-U.S. Workshop on Biosphere Reserves and Conservation of Natural Diversity, Bangalore, India, March 1-14, 1982, and interview, October 1984. The states and the dates their respective programs began are South Carolina (1974), Mississippi (1974), Tennessee (1975), North Carolina (1976), Oklahoma (1977), Kentucky (1978), Arkansas (1978), Florida (1981), Alabama (1983), Texas (1983), and Louisiana (1984). Georgia pioneered state heritage programs in the South with its Georgia Heritage Trust (1972), which dealt with both natural and historic resources and antedated the Nature Conservancy model. Virginia has no official state program, but an active un-

official program of natural-area inventories is operated by Virginia Polytechnic Institute.

51. Based on State of Arkansas, *Executive Summary: The Arkansas Natural Heritage Inventory Program* (Little Rock: Arkansas Natural Heritage Commission, 1980) and interview with Kenneth Smith, Arkansas Natural Heritage Commission, April 1984.

52. A negative finding, however, does not mean that an important natural value is *not* present at the site.

53. Laura and William Riley, *Guide to the National Wildlife Refuges* (Garden City, N.Y.: Anchor/Doubleday, 1979), pp. 255-57.

54. Data from Carl N. Becker, secretary, Nongame Wildlife Association of North America. Figures for Louisiana and Oklahoma are for 1982 tax year.

55. *Nongame Newsletter* (Nongame Wildlife Association of North America), vol. 2, no. 3 (Spring 1983), and vol. 3, no. 1 (Fall 1983); telephone interview with Jack Donnelly, coordinator of North Carolina Nongame Wildlife Program, Raleigh, N.C., October 1984; "The First Year: Virginia's Non-Game Program," *Virginia Wildlife*, vol. 45, no. 1 (January 1984), pp. 23-24.

56. Telephone interview with Dale Jackson, Florida Natural Areas Inventory, Tallahassee, Fla., October 1984.

57. This assumes that there is sufficient public acceptance of leasing that the companies do not face unacceptably high levels of resentment—and even arson and vandalism—when they try to implement leasing on their properties.

58. There are 18.8 million acres of federal land in the South (11 states), of which about three-quarters is national forest; 3.2 million acres of commercial forestland owned by state and local governments; and 0.9 million acres of state parks.

59. Unfortunately, some federal holdings, particularly the national forests, have a great deal of interspersed private inholdings, which reduces the management opportunities otherwise afforded by their large size. See William E. Shands and Robert G. Healy, *The Lands Nobody Wanted: Policy for National Forests in the Eastern United States* (Washington, D.C.: The Conservation Foundation, 1977).

60. Other Conservation Foundation research has devoted considerable attention to this question. See Shands and Healy, *The Lands Nobody Wanted*; William E. Shands, *Federal Resource Lands and Their Neighbors* (Washington, D.C.: The Conservation Foundation, 1979); and *National Parks for a New Generation* (Washington, D.C.: The Conservation Foundation, 1985). A study of state park systems is now in progress.

61. Larry D. Harris, "Designing Landscape Mosaics for Integrated Agricultural and Conservation Planning in the Southeastern United States," in Office of Technology Assessment, *Technologies to Benefit Agriculture and Wildlife* (Washington, D.C.: U.S. Government Printing Office, 1985), pp. 102-11.

62. See G. Terry Sharrer, "Hitching History to the Plow," *Historic Preservation*, vol. 32, no. 6 (November-December 1980), pp. 42-49. Notable examples of living historical farms in the South are the Agrirama in Tifton, Georgia; Homeplace in Golden Pond, Kentucky; and George Washington Birthplace National Monument, near Oak Grove, Virginia.

63. For some excellent examples of how this can be done, see Thomas J. Schlereth, *Artifacts and the American Past* (Nashville: American Association for State and Local History, 1980).

64. Meade Palmer, *Green Springs, Louisa County, VA: A Land Use Study* (Warrenton, Va.: Meade, Palmer, 1973); and Allen D. Stovall, *The Sautee and Nacoochee Valleys: A Preservation Study* (Sautee-Nacoochee, Georgia: Sautee-Nacoochee Community Association, 1982).

65. Telephone interview, Athens, Ga., October 1984.

66. U.S. Federal Highway Administration, *Annual Statistical Progress Report, Highway Beautification Program, September 30, 1983* (Washington, D.C.: Federal Highway Administration, 1983), p. 7. South Carolina, Tennessee, and Virginia data were not reported.

67. Ibid., p. 15.

68. For discussion of the federal law and photographs of how some southern jurisdictions have tried to evade its intent, see Charles F. Floyd, "Requiem for the Highway Beautification Act," *Journal of the American Planning Association*, vol. 48, no. 4 (Autumn 1982), pp. 441-53.

69. For example, in 1974, 323,000 acres of recharge area in central Florida's Green Swamp were designated an "area of critical state concern," and state regulations were promulgated to govern its use. Dade County has tried to protect part of the recharge area for the Biscayne Aquifer by enacting five-acre minimum lot zoning. See James T. Tripp and A.B. Jaffe, "Preventing Ground Water Pollution: Towards a Coordinated Strategy to Protect Critical Recharge Zones," *Harvard Environmental Law Review*, vol. 3, no. 1 (1979), pp. 1-47. Other recharge areas around Miami, however, are still described as threatened by development. *Miami Herald*, March 19, 1984.

70. *Environment Reporter*, May 11, 1984, p. 52.

71. Telephone interview with Dr. Rodney DeHaan, Florida Department of Environmental Regulation, Tallahassee, October 1984.

72. Interview with Walt Kniesel, U.S. Agricultural Research Service, Tifton, Ga., April 1984.

Land Data for Research and Action

1. The information is based mainly on current or reasonably forseeable use, so it does not cover the full range of possible uses or combinations of uses.

Index

ABOUT THE AUTHOR

Dr. Robert G. Healy, a Senior Associate at The Conservation Foundation, is an economist specializing in the study of land and natural resources. He is author of *Land Use and the States* and coauthor or editor of several Foundation books, including *The Lands Nobody Wanted, The Market for Rural Land*, and *Protecting the Golden Shore*.

Photograph credits

Robert G. Healy, xxxiv, 70, 124, 167, 171, 174, 183, 240, 243, 250, 270, 304
Janet Mendelsohn, cover (log lifter), 76, 85
North Carolina Department of Transportation, 230
North Carolina Wildlife Resources Commission, cover (woodpecker), 158, 204, 274
James L. Short, 190
Thad Sparks, Duke University School of Forestry and Environmental Studies, 210
U.S. Department of Agriculture, 57 (top and bottom)
U.S. Department of Agriculture, Soil Conservation Service, cover (tractor, cattle grazing), 18, 23, 54, 62, 81, 102, 106, 111, 122, 129, 147, 152, 192, 216, 293, 316